Biological Anthropology:
Concepts and Connections

Biological Anthropology: Concepts and Connections

SECOND EDITION

Agustín Fuentes

University of Notre Dame

Published by McGraw-Hill, an imprint of The McGraw-Hill Companies, Inc., 1221 Avenue of the Americas, New York, NY 10020.

This book is printed on acid-free paper.

2 3 4 5 6 7 8 9 0 QVS / QVS 9 8 7 6 5 4

ISBN: 978-0-07-811700-8
MHID: 0-07-811700-3

Sponsoring Editor: *Gina Boedeker*
Marketing Manager: *Patrick Brown*
Developmental Editor: *Craig Leonard*
Production Editor: *Rachel J. Castillo*
Manuscript Editor: *Jan Fehler*
Design Manager: *Cassandra Chu*
Text Designer: *Jenny El-Shamy*
Cover Designer: *Linda Beaupré*
Photo Research Manager: *Brian Pecko*
Buyer: *Tandra Jorgensen*
Composition: *9/13 ITC Bookman Light, Aptara®, Inc.*
Printing: *45# New Era Matte Plus, Quad/Graphics*

Vice President Editorial: *Michael Ryan*
Editorial Director: *William R. Glass*
Director of Development: *Nancy Crochiere*

Cover: Adult footprint from the trail of fossilized hominid footprints discovered in volcanic ash at Laetoli, Tanzania in 1978: © John Reader/Photo Researchers, Inc.; Modern human walking on beach: Steve Mason/Getty Images.

Credits: The credits section for this book begins on page 363 and is considered an extension of the copyright page.

Library of Congress Cataloging-in-Publication Data

Fuentes, Agustín.
   Biological anthropology : concepts and connections / Agustin Fuentes.—2nd ed.
      p. cm.
   Rev. ed. of: / Core concepts in biological anthropology / Agustin Fuentes. c2007.
   Includes bibliographical references and index.
   ISBN-13: 978-0-07-811700-8 (alk. paper)
   ISBN-10: 0-07-811700-3 (alk. paper)
   1. Physical anthropology.   I. Fuentes, Agustin. Core concepts in biological anthropology.
II. Title.
   GN51.F83 2011
   599.9—dc22   2010045902

The Internet addresses listed in the text were accurate at the time of publication. The inclusion of a website does not indicate an endorsement by the authors or McGraw-Hill, and McGraw-Hill does not guarantee the accuracy of the information presented at these sites.

This book is dedicated to three amazing teachers: my parents, Victor Fuentes and Elizabeth Fuentes, and my graduate mentor, Phyllis Dolhinow. The book itself is the result of all the students who sat through my lectures, asked questions, and pushed me to really, really think about what we teach and how we teach it. Because of them, I also dedicate this book to all who love the quest for knowledge and ask their teachers and themselves for more.

Brief Contents

Contents

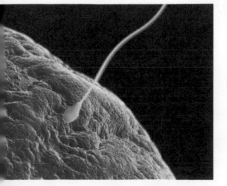

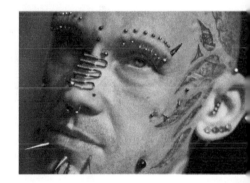

Preface

Do your students struggle with complex concepts like genetics and evolution? Do they have difficulty seeing the relevance of biological anthropology to their lives? If so, I have written this text for you.

How this book will help you . . .

I am a firm believer in the incredible importance of anthropology in our everyday lives. Yet, in speaking with colleagues around the country and reading McGraw-Hill's research, I've learned that instructors' greatest frustrations in teaching introductory biological anthropology are helping students understand certain key concepts (i.e., genetics, evolution) and—perhaps even more importantly—making them see the relevance of this course material to their lives.

. . . by helping your students

Biological anthropology classes are packed with information that is directly relevant to all of us and should be both interesting and exciting. Biological anthropologists are making exciting discoveries that change the way we view ourselves today, our understanding of our past, and our future as a species. Yet students often walk away from their textbooks with no understanding of how the information they have just read applies to their lives. That's why, in this book, I've introduced the theme of "Connections."

. . . connect the concepts to their lives

This text directly speaks to students and relates the concepts of biological anthropology to their lives. It does so in several ways:

Connections boxes

Several times in each Chapter, I include a "Connections" feature that directly shows students the relevance of the particular topic being discussed to them and their everyday lives. For example, in Chapter 5, we explore whether male aggression is an evolutionary trait; in Chapter 7, why bipedality made childbirth more difficult; and in Chapter 9, why humans feel a special connection to dogs.

Chapter-opening stories

In addition, each chapter begins with an example, taken from the headlines, of an important question biological anthropologists have asked or answered:

How do steroids affect athletes (Chapter 2)? What do discoveries about primate culture tell us about what makes humans unique (Chapter 8)? What is race and what is it not? (Chapter 10)?

Connecting students to related information

Callouts in the margin show students other places in the text a topic is covered, allowing the student either to review material that they have already studied or read more about a topic that interests them.

Understanding key concepts

By focusing on the key concepts and presenting them in a straightforward manner, this text encourages students to think about, assess, and use the information presented, not just memorize it and recite it back on a test. Several aspects of this text are designed to help students deal with challenging concepts:

- **The Introduction,** set up as a series of FAQs ("How old is the planet?" "Have humans changed over time?" "Where does modern science come from?") presents background information students need but do not always have access to.

- **Chapter 2: Basics of Human Biology** contains a review of human anatomy and biology, a chapter unique among introductory texts but extremely important to students' understanding of human evolution and variation.

- **Key terms,** defined in the margin where they are introduced, help students with new vocabulary and provide an easy review for exams.

The importance of critical thinking and the scientific process

To understand science, students must understand how scientists develop new knowledge, how new knowledge is determined to be valid, and what remains to be discovered. They need to understand how biological anthropologists "do" science. This is a key concern of this book.

- **Scientific Discovery.** The Introduction and early chapters focus on the process of discovery—not just what we know, but how we know it. I explore how scientific discovery builds on earlier knowledge. So, for example, I don't just tell the student about Darwin's theory of natural selection; I explain how Darwin built on earlier knowledge to form a unified and cohesive explanation for how life evolved.

- In addition, at the end of each chapter, students find a unique critical-thinking feature, **What We Know/Questions That Remain.** This feature summarizes key knowledge presented in the chapter and highlights the most important questions that remain to be answered. It will help students see that science is an ongoing process and that our current state of knowledge is subject to change. Most importantly, it demonstrates the exciting nature of ongoing research in biological anthropology.

- **Critical Thinking Questions** at the end of each chapter ask the student to analyze and synthesize material rather than just memorize it.

- **Focus on humanity's place in the natural world.** As a biological anthropologist and primatologist, I focus on humans as a part of the primate order. My goal is to give students a wide perspective on what it means to be human and to help them think critically about important issues that face all of humanity. Chapter 5 discusses human behavioral ecology in the context of primate behavior. Chapters 7 through 9 present an overview of human evolution in the context of the evolution of the entire primate order. Chapter 11 explains that humans are still evolving and speculates on what this means for global ecology.

How is this book organized?

This book is organized into an Introduction and 11 chapters.

- The Introduction, as described above, presents crucial background information set up as an engaging series of FAQs.

- Chapters 1 through 4 introduce students to the field of anthropology, the science of biological anthropology, Darwinian evolution, human biology, and the modern evolutionary synthesis.

- Chapter 5 is a uniquely fascinating introduction to primate behavioral ecology, written from the point of view of a working primatologist.

- Chapters 6 through 9 survey human evolution from the earliest mammals through *Homo sapiens.*

- Chapter 10 surveys human variation.

- Chapter 11 puts it all together by speculating on how humans are continuing to evolve.

Biological anthropology is a dynamic, fast-changing field, and its discoveries about genetics, human evolution, and human variation are vitally relevant to students' lives. I hope that students reading this book will come to understand the relevance of these concepts and become as excited to learn about biological anthropology as I am to teach it.

Supplements

For the instructor

The book's online learning center at www.mhhe.com/fuentes2e provides a multitude of password-protected instructor resources including an Instructor's Manual, Testbank, Computerized Testbank, and PowerPoint slides.

For the student

The Online Learning Center (www.mhhe.com/fuentes2e) also provides a wealth of study tools for the student, including chapter outlines, chapter summaries, and chapter quizzes with feedback and instructor reporting.

McGraw-Hill Higher Education and Blackboard have teamed up!

What does this mean for you?

1. **Your life simplified.** Now you and your students can access McGraw-Hill Connect™ and Create™ right from within your Blackboard course—all with one single sign-on. No more logging in to multiple applications.

2. **Deep integration of content and tools.** In addition to single sign-on, you get deep integration of McGraw-Hill content and content engines right in Blackboard. Whether you're choosing a book for your course or building Connect™ assignments, all the tools you need are right there: inside Blackboard.

3. **Seamless Gradebooks.** Tired of keeping multiple gradebooks and manually synchronizing grades into Blackboard? When a student completes an integrated Connect™ assignment, the grade for that assignment automatically (and instantly) feeds your Blackboard grade center.

4. **A solution for everyone.** Whether your institution is already using Blackboard or you just want to try it on your own, we have a solution for you. McGraw-Hill and Blackboard can now offer you easy access to industry-leading technology and content, whether your campus hosts it or we do. Be sure to ask your local McGraw-Hill representative for details.

Create

Craft your teaching resources to match the way you teach! With McGraw-Hill Create, www.mcgrawhillcreate.com, you can easily rearrange chapters, combine material from other content sources, and quickly upload content you have written, like your course syllabus or teaching notes. Find the content you need in Create by searching through thousands of leading McGraw-Hill textbooks. Arrange your book to fit your teaching style. Create even allows you to personalize your book's appearance by selecting the cover and adding your name, school, and course information. Order a Create book and you'll receive a complimentary print review copy in 3–5 business days or a complimentary electronic review copy (eComp) via email in about one hour. Go to www.mcgrawhillcreate.com today and register. Experience how McGraw-Hill Create empowers you to teach your students your way.

CourseSmart e-Textbook

This text is available as an eTextbook at www.CourseSmart.com. At CourseSmart your students can take advantage of significant savings off the cost of a print textbook, reduce their impact on the environment, and gain access to powerful web tools for learning. CourseSmart eTextbooks can be viewed online or downloaded to a computer. The eTextbooks allow students to do full text searches, add highlighting and notes, and share notes with classmates. CourseSmart has the largest selection of eTextbooks available anywhere. Visit www.CourseSmart.com to learn more and to try a sample chapter.

Tegrity

Tegrity Campus is a service that makes class time available all the time by automatically capturing every lecture in a searchable format for students to review when they study and complete assignments. With a simple one-click start and stop process, you capture all computer screens and corresponding audio. Students replay any part of any class with easy-to-use browser-based viewing on a PC or Mac. Educators know that the more students can see, hear, and experience class resources, the better they learn. With Tegrity Campus, students quickly recall key moments by using Tegrity Campus's unique search feature. This search helps students efficiently find what they need, when they need it, across an entire semester of class recordings. Help turn all your students' study time into learning moments immediately supported by your lecture.

Acknowledgments

Many reviewers provided useful feedback throughout the process of developing and producing this book. The following faculty members reviewed all or part of the manuscript; their comments were extremely helpful and are deeply appreciated:

Annalisa Alvrus, Mesa Community College

Eric Anderson, Yakima Valley Community College

Robert Anemone, Western Mich Univ—Kalamazoo

Diana Ayers-Darling, Mohawk Valley Community College

Dale Borders, Grand Valley State University

Ben Campbell, University of Wisconsin—Milwaukee

Judith Corr, Grand Valley State University

Fabian Crespo, Univ of Louisville—Louisville

Annlee Dolan, San Joaquin Delta Comm CLG

William Doonan, Sacramento City College

Arthur Durband, Texas Tech University

Phyllisa Eisentraut, Santa Barbara City College

Eva Garrett, Lehman College

Samantha Hens, CA State Univ Sacramento

Kathryn Hicks, Univ of Memphis

Madeleine Hinkes, San Diego Mesa College

Douglas Kemper, University of Cincinnati

Andrew Kramer, Univ of Tennessee—Knoxville

Kenneth Lewis, Michigan State University

Andrew J. Marshall, University of California

John McDermott, Fullerton College

Joan Miller, San Diego State University

Robert Paine, Texas Tech University

Bruce Pierini, Sacramento City College

Michael Pilakowski, Butte College

Aimee Preziosi, West Los Angeles College

Robert Quinlan, Washington State Univ—Pullman

Melissa Remis, Purdue University

Donna Ricca, South Puget Sound Community College

Kathleen Rizzo, Univ of Illinois—Chicago

Anne Titelbaum, Tulane University

Elizabeth Weiss, San Jose State University

Barbara Wheeler, Santa Rosa Junior College

James Stewart, Columbus State Comm Coll

Daniel Temple, Univ of Missouri—Columbia

William Whitehead, Ripon College

Many, many people at McGraw-Hill have made this book possible, but I only have space to thank a few of them. Developmental Editor Craig Leonard and Sponsoring Editor Gina Boedeker shepherded me through much of this project, and the book owes a substantial part of its inception to Janet Beatty and Michael Park. Rachel Castillo supervised production, and Robin Mouat produced the truly spectacular illustration program. Devi Snively provided a wide array of technical assistance and moral support throughout the process and Audrey the wonder dog provided unwavering support during the creative process.

About the Author

Agustín Fuentes completed a BA in Zoology and Anthropology and an MA and PhD in Anthropology at the University of California, Berkeley. He conducted his dissertation fieldwork in the remote Mentaiwai islands of Indonesia and has worked throughout Southeast Asia, North Africa, and the Southern Iberian Peninsula. Dr. Fuentes first taught Introduction to Biological Anthropology in the fall of 1995 at UC Berkeley. In 1996 he joined the department of Anthropology at Central Washington University (CWU), where he founded and directed the interdisciplinary undergraduate Primate Behavior and Ecology program. At CWU, Dr. Fuentes began working intensively with undergraduate students on original research, and between 1998 and 2002 he collaborated with Universitas Udayana in Bali, Indonesia, to run summer field projects involving over 80 undergraduates from 9 different countries.

Since 2002 Dr. Fuentes has been in the Department of Anthropology at the University of Notre Dame where he is a professor of Anthropology. His research and teaching interests include the evolution of cooperation and social complexity in humans, the evolution of social organization, conflict negotiation across primates, and reproductive behavior and ecology. His current research projects include human-monkey interactions in Asia and Gibraltar and assessing the roles of cooperation, social complexity, and patterns of peace in human evolution. He is also interested in issues of disease, inequity, and resilience. Dr. Fuentes is committed to an integrated holistic anthropological approach. He has published over 50 articles, 17 book chapters, 4 edited volumes, and 2 single-authored books.

Introduction

FAQs for biological anthropology

Because I teach biological anthropology, I know that students sometimes take this course without some useful background information about science. As a result, they have a lot of questions. Therefore, in this section, I'll answer the most common of these questions. You'll find this information, along with the illustrations in this section, useful throughout this course.

How Old Is the Planet and What Organisms Have Lived on It over That Time?

Before we begin discussion about human biological evolution, we need to provide a backdrop to give us context. Let's quickly run through the last 4.5 billion years of the planet's geological and biological history to give us a little perspective on the relative context of humankind. The history of this planet is divided into *eras*, which are divided into *periods*, which are further divided into *epochs* (Figure I.1). The majority of the earth's history is in the Proterozoic era. The Proterozoic began with the formation of the earth, approximately 4.5 billion years ago, and ended with the first major diversification of life-forms, approximately 600 million years ago. It is in this era that we find the first hints of life on this planet: tiny fossilized impressions suggesting clusters or chains of linked cells resembling today's blue-green algae and bacteria (*prokaryotic cells*, or cells that do not contain a nucleus). From about 3.5–1.5 billion years ago, these are the only kinds of fossils we find. So, prokaryotes were the only organisms on the planet for the first 2 billion years of life.

Starting around 1.2–1.5 billion years ago, life-forms became slightly more diverse. We begin to find evidence of *eukaryotic cells* (cells that have a nucleus, like those of all animals and plants). By 1 billion years ago, we find indirect evidence (fossilized burrowing tracks and fecal pellets) of multicellular organisms. Between 1 billion and 570 million years ago, we see a diversification of types of fossil organisms; however, all life is still very small and confined to limited habitats in the oceans.

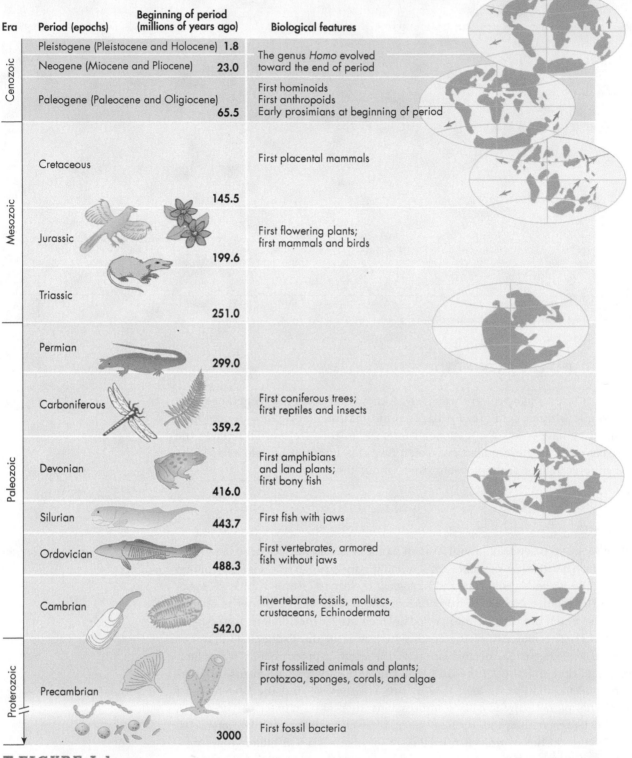

Era	Period (epochs)	Beginning of period (millions of years ago)	Biological features
Cenozoic	Pleistogene (Pleistocene and Holocene)	1.8	The genus *Homo* evolved toward the end of period
Cenozoic	Neogene (Miocene and Pliocene)	23.0	
Cenozoic	Paleogene (Paleocene and Oligiocene)	65.5	First hominoids; First anthropoids; Early prosimians at beginning of period
Mesozoic	Cretaceous	145.5	First placental mammals
Mesozoic	Jurassic	199.6	First flowering plants; first mammals and birds
Mesozoic	Triassic	251.0	
Paleozoic	Permian	299.0	
Paleozoic	Carboniferous	359.2	First coniferous trees; first reptiles and insects
Paleozoic	Devonian	416.0	First amphibians and land plants; first bony fish
Paleozoic	Silurian	443.7	First fish with jaws
Paleozoic	Ordovician	488.3	First vertebrates, armored fish without jaws
Paleozoic	Cambrian	542.0	Invertebrate fossils, molluscs, crustaceans, Echinodermata
Proterozoic	Precambrian	3000	First fossilized animals and plants; protozoa, sponges, corals, and algae; First fossil bacteria

■ **FIGURE I.1**

The geological time scale shows the sequence of appearance of the major forms of life on earth.

The next geologic era, the Paleozoic, began around 540 million years ago. The first period of the Paleozoic era, the Cambrian, shows the first major example of an **adaptive radiation** (expansion by a single group of organisms into a diverse array of forms) that we see in the fossil record. At the start of this period we see an explosion of forms moving into a wide array of new niches, or habitats and lifeways, in the oceans. From the basic structures of organisms in the late Precambrian, we see a multitude of variants arise as organisms exploit new oceanic environments and ways of making a living. By the end of the Cambrian period, we have the first precursors for many modern animal lineages.

Throughout the rest of the Paleozoic we see an array of new forms arising from existing varieties. In the Ordovician we see a great expansion in complex multicellular organisms, including the first fishes (jawless fishes). By the beginning of the Silurian we find fossils of jawed fishes, which suggests a radical change in the cycle of life (that is, the appearance of active chewing). These are the first active vertebrate predators. These earliest jawed fish have no bones, only cartilage, and at least one lineage of these early Silurian fish is ancestral to modern sharks and rays.

By the middle of the Silurian, bony fish show up in the fossil record and diversify into at least two main groups: the lobe-finned and the ray-finned fishes. The currently favored hypothesis is that one or more lineages of lobe-finned fishes gave rise to the first land vertebrates (the amphibians). The first fossils of land plants show up during this period. By the end of the Devonian, we have evidence of land animals (insects), complex land plant formations (like swamps), and a huge array of life-forms in the seas.

From the rest of the Paleozoic we find a growing number of fossils of land animals, especially in coastal areas, where the early amphibians (which looked very much like slightly modified lobe-finned fish) gradually changed into a wide array of amphibian forms and early reptiles. During the last period of the Paleozoic (the Permian), there was a broad radiation of reptilian forms, including a group called the therapsids, or mammal-like reptiles (the reptile group that mammals are hypothesized to be most closely related to).

The Mesozoic era began around 250 million years ago. By the early Mesozoic, reptiles had undergone a broad and dramatic adaptive radiation. Freed from the water by two crucial adaptations—self-contained eggs and skin that resists drying out—reptiles spread across the land environments and adapted to a broad spectrum of habitats. During this era the best-known reptile group, the dinosaurs, make up a large portion of the fossil remains. It is also during the Mesozoic that the first mammals show up (Figure I.2). These mostly small, probably nocturnal, insect-eating mammals are found throughout the era, but do not make their grand adaptive radiation until the Cenozoic.

The Mesozoic was the age of reptiles. The Cenozoic, which began around 65 million years ago, is the age of mammals and birds. After an enormous extinction event at the Mesozoic-Cenozoic boundary, mammals and birds began to diversify, filling many of the niches left vacant by the extinctions. The Cenozoic period is very important in the history of primates (and therefore humans) and is covered in detail in chapter 6.

■ FIGURE I.2
An artist's conception of an early mammal, *Hadrocodium wui*. Its skull was found in 195-million-year-old sediments in China; the paper clip is included to show the animal's size.

adaptive radiation
expansion by a single group of organisms into a diverse array of forms

Model of the earth's interior, showing the layers. This demonstrates the earth's crust "floating" on the liquid mantle.

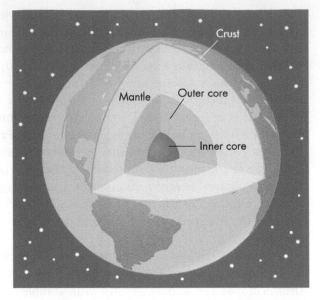

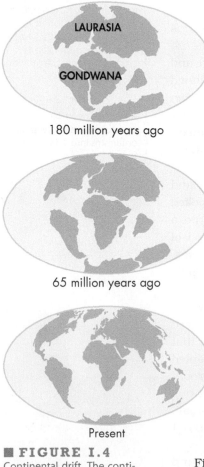

More than 200 million years ago

180 million years ago

65 million years ago

Present

■ **FIGURE I.4**
Continental drift. The continents took on their present relative positions only about 35 million years ago. The forces of plate tectonics continue to reshape the crust.

If Life on Our Planet Has Changed So Much Over Time, What About the Planet Itself?

During the time that life on earth has been changing, so has the surface of the planet. The process of **plate tectonics** drives the phenomenon of **continental drift**. Plate tectonics results from the continental plates floating on a layer of mantle (magma, or molten rock, like lava) (Figure I.3). Currents in the magma move the plates in a number of different ways. Sometimes magma pushes up between plates and solidifies, pushing them apart (spreading). When plates meet, one can overlap the other, driving it down into the magma (subduction). Plates can move against one another, pushing the earth up and creating mountain ranges (collision). If we look at the model of continental movement over just the last 200 million years, we can see that the earth's surface has changed dramatically over time (Figure I.4).

Understanding that the earth and life on it have changed over the last 4.5 billion years is an important basic concept. You will notice throughout this book that change over time is a recurring notion in biological anthropology.

Have Humans Changed?

Yes, absolutely, humans have changed. Change over time in humans is pretty much the core of biological anthropology. So, thinking about change on a slightly smaller scale than 4.5 billion years, let's turn to another basic set of information that we'll be expanding upon throughout this book—the history of humans and their immediate ancestors over the last 6 million years.

Figure I.5 is a time line of human history over the last 6 million years. This time line is just a brief outline to get you to start thinking about names, places, and dates in human evolution. We'll be discussing each of the names and types of human or humanlike organisms in detail in chapters 6 through 11. Notice, however, that during most of the time that our species has been evolving, more

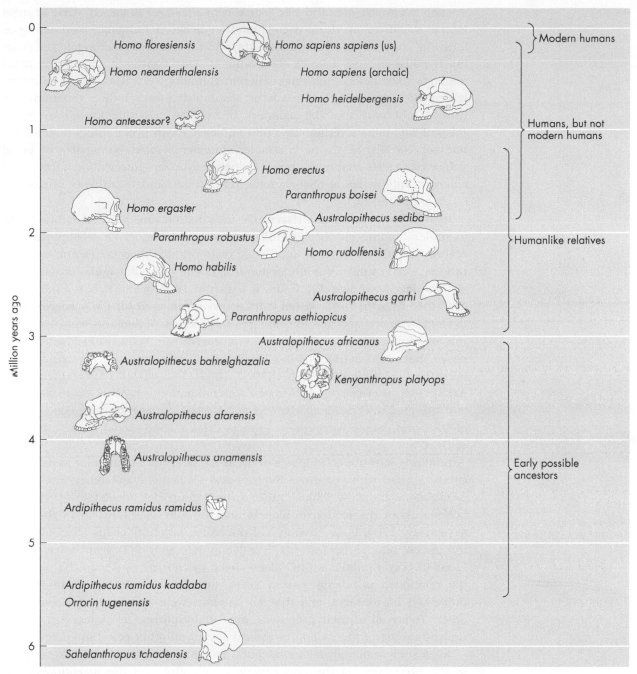

■ FIGURE I.5

An evolutionary time line of human history. In this book we will explain what these different organisms are and how they might be related to us.

than one humanlike species existed side by side. While trends and patterns are evident in the history of human evolution, there is not an inevitable trajectory. Knowing this may help you realize that our species is just one of many on this planet that evolved by filling (and modifying) a specific niche.

Where Did Modern Science Come From?

All of the information we've just reviewed and all that we will be introducing is primarily the product of a process we call *science.* What we call modern

plate tectonics
process by which the earth's crustal plates move independently of one another, resulting in continental drift

continental drift
theory that the present configuration of continents results from the movement of the earth's crust

science developed over the last 5 or 6 centuries and is largely what Francis Bacon called for in 1605: a collaboration between inductive methodologies (drawing conclusions from extant facts) and experimental methodologies (testing hypotheses and making observations). This contrasts with the *a priori* methods used before this time, wherein thinkers went from cause to effect, basing their reasoning on beliefs or assumptions rather than experience or testable observations. The hallmark of modern scientific knowledge is its *falsifiability,* not its verifiability; that is, science can prove things 100% false but not 100% true. To be falsifiable, statements must be capable of being subjected to tests that might result in their refutation. So scientific information emerges from series of observations, refutations, and hypotheses supported by rigorous testing.

In this book we focus on scientific information and processes that relate to understanding our bodies and our biological history. It is important to realize that all our current knowledge rests on past discoveries and collaborations. For example, our understanding of the cells that make up our bodies has developed over 350 years. It began in 1665, when Robert Hooke first described cells. In 1683, Anton van Leeuwenhoek used his early microscopes to examine blood and sperm cells. In 1883, August Weismann recognized the role of gametes (germ-cells, or egg and sperm). In 1902, Emil Fischer proposed that proteins (the building blocks of our cells) are made up of naturally occurring amino acids, and in 1926, J. Haldane described the complex internal structures of cells and their permeable membranes. All of these elements laid the groundwork for Erwin Chargaff's 1950 discovery of the composition of DNA and James Watson and Francis Crick's 1953 model of the structure of DNA.

Similarly, our understandings of the basic patterns in our solar system and galaxy started with Johannes Kepler's and Galileo Galilei's observations and proposals in the early 1600s. These in turn supported Nicolaus Copernicus's notions about the motion of planets and the sun as the center of the solar system. By 1704, Isaac Newton had published accounts of his ideas on gravity, optics, and particulate light; and approximately 200 years later, Albert Einstein began publishing his ideas about the energy source of the sun and the relationships among matter, mass, and light. In 1929, Edwin Hubble published his observations that all galaxies were moving away from each other. Today all of their proposals, plus many others, are integrated in our understanding of the motion of the earth and all other celestial bodies.

Even such seemingly minor scientific events as the discoveries that resulted in the production of the first electric refrigerator and the invention of the television tube (both in 1923) have had a great impact on our ability to conduct laboratory work and write it up. (Freezers and computers are now ubiquitous in laboratories worldwide.) Modern science comes from a specific set of methodologies and a continuous history of investigation, collaboration, and refutation. Understanding that our knowledge is based on prior knowledge, and is subject to change, is important for assessing the information presented in this text. In chapter 1, you will see how the theory of evolution developed out of investigations carried out over several centuries by numerous scientists in a number of different fields.

Where Is Uzbekistan?

A major piece of any college student's baseline education (regardless of your major) is a grasp of the geography of the planet. You are 1 of over 6 billion humans currently residing on earth; as a citizen of this planet you need to know where you and your neighbors live. Also, in this course you will be learning about discoveries that have taken place all over the world. Figure I.6 shows a current (as of the time this book was written) world map.

With these few basic bits of information under your belt, you are now ready to move on to the study of biological anthropology.

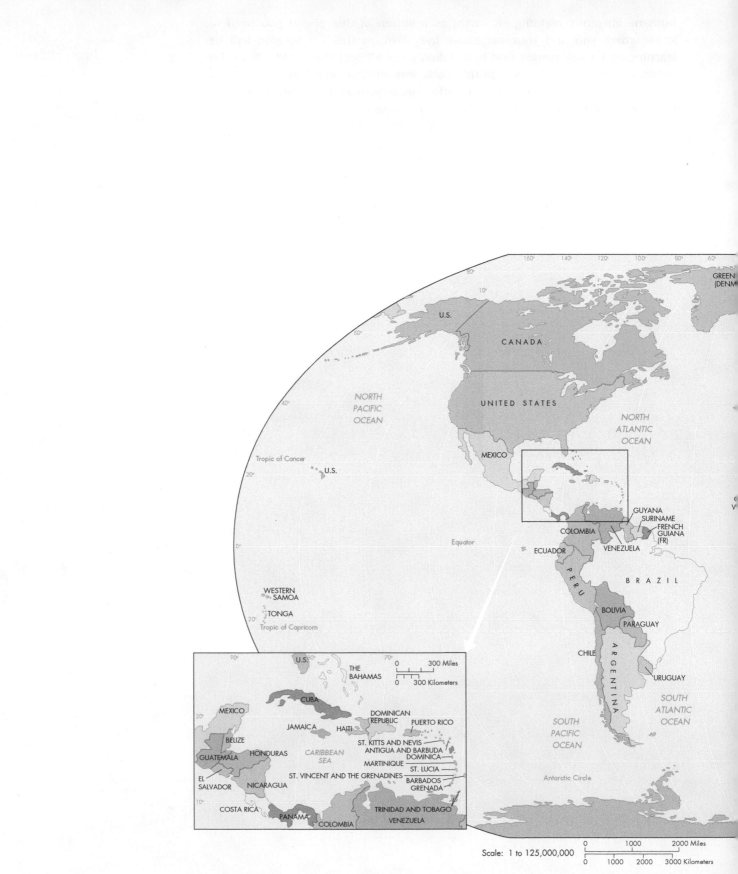

■ FIGURE I.6
The world today. Can you find Uzbekistan?

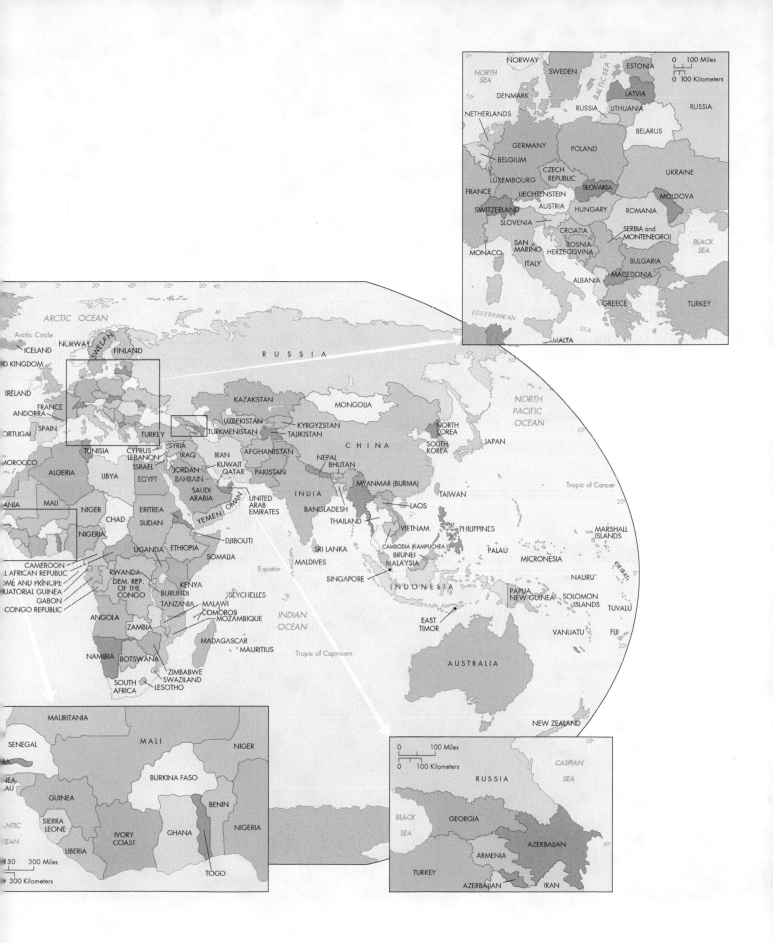

CHAPTER 1

Introduction to Evolutionary Fact and Theory

This chapter addresses these questions:

▲ What is anthropology, and what do its four subfields cover?

▲ What is science, and how does it work?

▲ Is evolution a fact or a theory? Where do our ideas about evolution come from?

▲ Why is the theory of evolution significant, and why is it so misunderstood?

In 1925 the theory of evolution went on trial in the United States. A Tennessee court case—the famous Scopes "Monkey Trial"—was the arena for a debate about whether evolution could be taught in the public schools. The case had all the elements of high drama, including great speakers, impassioned arguments, and a county courthouse packed with spectators and journalists in 100-degree heat (Figure 1.1). On trial was John T. Scopes, a 24-year-old science teacher who admitted teaching evolution in the local high school, in violation of state law. The American Civil Liberties Union wanted to test the constitutionality of that law, and Scopes agreed to be their test case.

Tennessee, like many states of that time, had passed a law against teaching evolution—specifically, against teaching "any theory that denies the story of divine creation of man as taught in the bible"—because it was viewed as a threat to the American way of life. The theory of evolution was popularly believed to suggest that humans were descended from monkeys, a notion considered both ridiculous and blasphemous. The prosecuting attorney, William Jennings Bryan, even called the case "a contest between evolution and Christianity" and portrayed the defense lawyer, Clarence Darrow, as "the greatest atheist . . . in the United States." Bryan had had a career in national politics, having served as secretary of state under Woodrow Wilson and having run for the presidency himself three times. In recent years he had joined the "tent revival" movement, touring the country as a fiery evangelical preacher. Darrow, the nation's most prominent defense attorney, wanted to challenge what he saw as

■ FIGURE 1.1

The Scopes trial. Clarence Darrow, the lead defense attorney, is leaning on the desk at the center of this photo; William Jennings Bryan is behind him (light jacket). The high-stakes nature of this trial is palpable.

provincial resistance to progress and scientific ideas. He also wanted to show that the theory of evolution did not inherently conflict with the teachings of Christianity.

Darrow had several experts lined up to explain evolution and show how it was compatible with biblical teachings, but the judge would not allow him to put them on the stand. Undeterred, Darrow asked Bryan himself to take the stand. Darrow then asked Bryan a series of questions aimed at exploring how a literal interpretation of the Bible could be reconciled with the laws of nature and with known facts about the earth and its peoples. Bryan started off gamely but soon became entangled in inconsistencies and absurdities; ultimately, he was revealed to be a man who had given little thought to any ideas that differed from what he had been taught as a child. The cause he represented was similarly tarnished.

The trial ended with Scopes being convicted of breaking the law against teaching evolution and fined $100. The verdict was overturned a year later, but only on a technicality, so the law remained on the books. The Tennessee law was finally repealed in 1967, and in 1968 the U.S. Supreme Court declared such state laws unconstitutional. The Scopes trial was dramatized (and partly fictionalized) in the mid-1950s in the play *Inherit the Wind,* by Jerome Lawrence and Robert E. Lee. Since then, the play has been performed innumerable times in countries around the world and has appeared as both a Hollywood film and a television movie.

With the Scopes trial more than 80 years in the past, the theory of evolution—an extremely well supported theory accepted by virtually all scientists in every country of the world—now enjoys a secure place in public school curricula, right? Wrong! In 2000, Kansas revised its statewide science standards to exclude all mention of evolution or any matters relating to the age of the earth or the universe, and in 2005 the Kansas board of education rewrote the definition of science. By 2007, state courts had overturned the board of education's revisions, but the battle continues in Kansas even today. In 2004, Ohio moved to label the discussion of evolution as only one theory among many in explaining life on this planet. As of 2010, some states continue to revise their standards to include topics related to biological and geological change over time without mentioning the word *evolution*. Still other states place disclaimer stickers on all science textbooks that deal with evolution, stating that evolution is a "controversial theory" presented by "some scientists." A recent study found that about one third of the states have science standards that, by omitting or distorting evolution, are shortchanging students and making it difficult for them to understand how science works (Lerner, 2000).

What is it about the theory of evolution that makes its detractors so angry and uncomfortable? Does it claim that people are descended from apes or monkeys? Does it try to disprove the Bible or make it impossible for people to hold religious beliefs? Is there an irreconcilable conflict between evolutionary perspectives and religious views and values?

As you will see in this chapter, the answer to these last three questions is no. Evolution is a core principal of the sciences and is at the heart of anthropology. It is also one of the most widely misunderstood sets of ideas in our culture today. This chapter will help you understand what the theory of evolution asserts, how it emerged from the thinking of many scientists over time, and what skills and methods are required in order to understand and investigate scientific issues.

Anthropology is the study of human and nonhuman primates

The word *anthropology* comes from two Greek roots: *anthropos*, meaning "human," and *logia*, meaning "study"—thus, "the study of humans." We can expand this definition by looking at the mission statement of the American Anthropological Association. The society's mission is to "advance anthropology as the discipline that studies humans and nonhuman primates in all their aspects, through archaeological, biological, ethnological and linguistic research, and to foster the use of anthropological knowledge in addressing human problems." From this mission statement we can see, then, that **anthropology** is the study of humans (us) and our closest biological relatives (other members of the order **Primates**—monkeys, apes, and prosimians).

Anthropology is divided into four subfields, or areas of investigation: archaeology, biological anthropology, cultural anthropology, and linguistic anthropology. Anthropologists in all these subfields are committed to ensuring that the knowledge they acquire is made available to nonanthropologists and is applied to issues facing humanity.

What areas of study are included in the four subfields of anthropology? **Archaeology** is the study of the material past of humans: what the people of the past made, how they lived, and how they modified their environment, as evidenced by the material clues they left behind. **Biological anthropology** (also called *physical anthropology*) focuses on the biological facets of the human species, past and present, along with those of our closest relatives, the nonhuman primates (monkeys, apes, and prosimians). **Cultural anthropology** is the study of that extremely complex entity we call human **culture**: the patterns of behavior we exhibit in our families, relationships, religions, laws, moral codes, songs, art, business, and everyday interactions. The main tools of the cultural anthropologist are **ethnography**—a study of a specific culture—and **ethnology**—the comparative study of cultures around the world. **Linguistic anthropology** is the study of language, its origins, construction, and uses.

Although we divide anthropological investigations into four subdisciplines, they are not actually separate lines of inquiry; in fact, they are all intertwined. Anthropologists take a **holistic approach** in their study of humans, considering evidence from all four subfields (Figure 1.2). It is only by investigating all

anthropology
the study of all aspects of the human experience

Primates
mammalian order to which humans belong

archaeology
the study of the patterns of behavior and the material record of humans who lived in the past

biological anthropology
the study of the biological and biocultural facets of humans and their relatives

cultural anthropology
the study of human culture in all of its complexity

culture
patterns of behavior human societies exhibit in their families, relationships, religions, laws, moral codes, songs, art, business, and everyday interactions

ethnography
the focused study of a culture or aspects of a culture

ethnology
the comparative study of many cultures

linguistic anthropology
the study of language, its structure, function, and evolution

holistic approach
the practice of drawing on all subdisciplines of anthropology, as well as other disciplines, to attempt to answer questions about humans

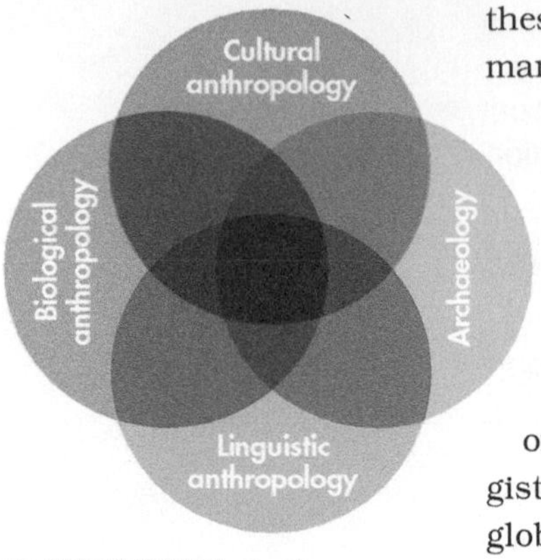

■ FIGURE 1.2
The four subfields of anthropology. They integrate to form the holistic approach.

these aspects that anthropologists have any hope of unraveling the complex, marvelous, and ongoing story of humankind.

Anthropologists also take a **comparative approach** in their work. They rely on specific studies to generate a large amount of information on one subject, and then they compare data and results across many studies, cultures, or populations. In this way they hope to understand, for example, the amazing array of similarities and differences we see in the human species and to determine which characteristics are universal to the human species and which are unique to particular groups or societies. Anthropologists work collaboratively with other anthropologists and researchers and try to tackle questions at both the local and the global levels.

Anthropologists also take a *historical approach*, keeping in mind the contributions and insights of previous scholars in their fields and applying them to their own work. And they are well aware that all people, themselves included, see the world through the lens of their own culture. They strive, if not for objectivity—an impossible goal—at least for vigilance against cultural and personal bias as they observe and study human beings of other times and places.

In this book we focus on biological anthropology, but you will see the other subfields in evidence throughout the discussions and examples. Biological anthropology itself can be divided into a number of subcategories. Probably the best known is **paleoanthropology,** the study of the **fossils** (the material evidence for past life) and fossil environments of past humans and nonhuman primates. Other biological anthropologists focus on the interconnections between human biological variation (such as differences in height, weight, and genetic makeup across different populations) and physiology, anatomy, disease, and demography. Still others look at the biological basis of behavior and how aspects of culture can be influenced by biology and **ecology** (the interrelationships between living organisms and their environments). Finally, there are those who focus their studies on nonhuman primate species; they use the comparative approach to understand what is common to all primates, what is common to some primates, and what may be unique to humans.

Anthropology is a scientific discipline

As a scientific discipline, anthropology shares certain characteristics with the other sciences. First, it requires that practitioners, students and professionals alike, use *critical thinking,* a certain way of approaching and thinking about information. Second, it makes use of the *scientific method,* a particular way of making observations, gathering data, and testing hypotheses. And finally, it operates through *collaboration,* a way of working together and building on the scientific work done by others. As you will see, critical thinking, the scientific method, and collaboration are recurring themes in anthropology, and they are three key themes in this book. We consider each of them in more detail in the next sections.

Critical Thinking Is the Systematic Assessment of Information

People today are bombarded with information via the media, the Internet, and even college classes; in fact, we may be said to suffer from information overload. As educated people living in a democratic society, we need to think about what we read and hear rather than accept everything at face value. In other words, we need to think critically.

comparative approach
the practice of comparing features across entities/cultures/organisms to elucidate similarities and differences

paleoanthropology
the study of fossil humans and human relatives

fossil
material evidence of past life on this planet

ecology
interrelationships between living organisms and their environments

Critical thinking means active participation in the learning process. It means taking control of the information presented to you and examining it. It means asking, Where did this information come from? What part of this information consists of **facts,** or verifiable, observable truths? What ideas and conclusions are being derived from those facts? What reasoning processes and assumptions were used to reach these conclusions; are they logical, or do they involve inconsistencies and false assumptions? In what form are the ideas and conclusions presented: Are they dogmatic assertions, or are they clear statements backed with logical arguments? Are nonfactual elements presented as facts? Does the person presenting the information have something to gain (or lose) by convincing you to accept a certain viewpoint? What are the implications of the conclusions for different groups of people or for society in general?

critical thinking
taking control of information presented to you and examining it

fact
a verifiable, observable truth

Let's take a current example of this critical thinking questioning process. Some researchers today believe that there are inherent (or biologically based) differences in intelligence between the groups we (in the United States) refer to as "Asian," "Black," and "White." What facts are provided to support this statement? Some standardized tests (such as the SAT) and some IQ tests show different average scores for these three groups. From these facts, these researchers conclude that there are inherent differences in intelligence among the three groups. What reasoning processes and assumptions lie behind these conclusions? The researchers make at least two assumptions: that the three groups are biologically distinct and that the tests actually measure innate cognitive abilities (intelligence). They then argue that the differences among the groups can best be explained as biologically based. Is this reasoning process logical, or are there inconsistencies and false assumptions?

CONNECTIONS

See chapter 10, pages 321–330, for further detail on "race" and racism.

The conclusions are based on false assumptions. For one thing, as we will see in chapter 10, the human species cannot currently be divided into large, biologically defined subunits (races or subspecies) labeled "Asian," "Black," and "White." For another, exactly what aspects of biology are measured by standardized tests is not clear (although something is definitely being measured, because people vary individually in their scores). Do the researchers' conclusions have any implications for the groups in question or for society in general? Yes: If differences in test scores are primarily biological in origin, then social, educational, or economically based programs will have minimal impact on improving the lower-end test scores. However, if these differences are not primarily biological, such programs may be effective. These two possibilities have significant economic, social, and political implications, and thus individuals making claims about this issue may have social, economic, and political motives.

To evaluate complex arguments and issues like this one, you need to use your critical thinking skills. You also need relevant information. In chapter 10 we deal in much more depth with issues related to race, behavior, and human biological variation. Throughout the book we provide a substantial amount of information that you can use to critically examine a number of "hotspot" issues related to human variation. Beyond what you read here, you have access to nearly limitless information at the library, in other classes, and on the Internet. If a particular topic intrigues you, by all means search beyond the introductory information given here and pursue it through the suggested readings and websites, recommendations from your instructor, and even field trips to natural history museums or archaeological sites. Part of the goal of this book is to help you hone your critical thinking skills and build up your knowledge base so you can more easily distinguish opinion from fact, wishful thinking from valid argument, and traditional belief from scientific practice.

The Scientific Method Is a Way of Testing Ideas about the World Around Us

Biological anthropology is an area of study that gathers information by a specific methodology: the scientific method. The scientific method is a way of asking questions about ourselves and the world around us, and all scientists use it.

In general the scientific method is very simple: You observe a fact (a verifiable, observable truth), construct a **hypothesis** (a testable explanation for the observed facts), and you then test that hypothesis. If your test demonstrates that your hypothesis is wrong (refutes it), you go back to the drawing board and try another hypothesis (and test it). If the test does not refute your hypothesis (in other words, supports it), you retest. If the tests you perform continue to support your hypothesis, then, as a serious scientist, you try to present or publish the results so that others will perform the same tests and/or examine your tests to confirm that the hypothesis is correct. If a set of hypotheses is supported again and again by multiple researchers, we call it a **theory**. This process is the scientific method, and this sequence of activities—observe → hypothesize → test → support or refute → retest—is the basic pattern of science (Figure 1.3).

Notice that when you use this methodology, you cannot prove yourself right; you can only prove yourself wrong. The test portion is designed as a refutation tool, not a "proving right" tool. This characteristic is what makes science different from all other modes of investigating human beings and the world around us (such as philosophical inquiries and religious doctrines). In fact, proving themselves wrong is exactly what scientists do. Every now and then they come up with a strongly supported hypothesis or even a really robust theory, one that consists of a set of supported hypotheses that all interconnect and act as a powerful tool for explaining natural phenomena. However, they do not produce "the truth." What scientists do is take an enormous array of possible truths and reduce them to a few probable truths.

This basic method is relatively straightforward, but in practice scientific inquiry does not usually begin with pure observation. Because there are already so many supported hypotheses out there explaining so many observations, much of scientific investigation is now driven primarily by hypothesis testing rather than observation gathering. That is, most scientists use the hypothetical-deductive approach: testing a hypothesis as a first step rather

hypothesis
a testable explanation for the observed facts

theory
a set of supported hypotheses

STOP & THINK

Is this what you think of when you hear the word "science"? If not, is that a problem?

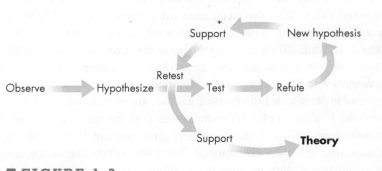

■ FIGURE 1.3
The scientific method. Note that the process is circular rather than linear.

That's a Fact, Jack . . . Or Is It?

People on television and the internet are always throwing around the word "fact," but those "facts" are not the same as science facts. A "fact" in a court case is a reasonably supported idea, observation, or statement. In everyday use, "fact" means something that someone believes is true or at least reliable. Wikipedia (many students' favorite source) defines a fact as "a pragmatic truth, a statement that can, at least in theory, be checked and confirmed." For scientists this is not enough. It does not matter what you believe in theory; it matters what is observable and verifiable. Scientific facts are verifiable truths, and there are very few of them. Facts can be readily observed and replicated again and again by anyone. For example, if I hold up a pen and let go of it in New York, Buenos Aires, Cairo, or Beijing it will drop. Anyone who repeats this will find the same result as long as they are standing on the surface (more or less) of the planet. Now, most of you would say that gravity is the fact behind the pen dropping. But gravity is not the fact; the fact is that the pen will drop, plain and simple. Gravity is a theory (a supported set of hypotheses) for why the fact (the pen drops) occurs. This is an important difference between scientific facts and popular facts. Popular facts are usually not scientific facts and therefore should not be given the same weight in thinking about the world. Popular facts are often ideas, opinions, or hypotheses and theories posing as facts. Think about this . . . what was the last thing you called a fact? Is it an observable, verifiable truth, or something else?

than making baseline observations and constructing hypotheses based on them. Their sequence is based on existing knowledge: They construct a hypothesis, test it, find it supported or refuted, and retest it. Still other scientists take theories and continue to test aspects or components of them (theory → hypothesize → test → support or refute aspects of theory → modify theory). In sum, researchers today are gathering baseline observations, creating hypotheses, testing new or existing hypotheses, and assessing and modifying theories. This is science at its core.

Although the scientific method has built-in mechanisms to ensure that it is as objective and bias free as possible, it does not exist in a vacuum. Humans are culturally complex beings, and science is always influenced by personal and cultural factors. Cultural factors and historical issues influence, among other things, the kinds of questions being asked and even how observations are conducted and reported. For example, before the 1970s most research on primates suggested that primate societies were male dominated and that males displayed most of the important behaviors; females appeared to play very minor roles in social interactions. Beginning in the 1970s, new studies began to appear that showed a great deal of complexity and variation in female behavior (Strier, 1984; Strum & Fedigan, 2000).

What had happened? Before the 1970s, most American and European **primatologists** (scientists who study primates) were men, but in the late 1960s and early 1970s, women began going into primatology (indeed, into all areas of academic and professional life). These female researchers—women like Phyllis Dolhinow, Linda Fedigan, and Jane Goodall, to name just a few—looked at primate society differently and asked different questions (Figure 1.4). With more women observing primate behavior and gathering data, a different picture of primate society began to emerge. In fact, a dramatic shift occurred in how female primates and primate societies were portrayed. The male

primatologist
researcher who studies primates

CONNECTIONS

See chapter 5, pages 137–151, for more details about primate lives.

■ FIGURE 1.4
The focus on female primates revealed a great deal of complexity in social networks and spot-lighted the social development of the young. Here we see two adult female long-tailed macaques (*Macaca fascicularis*) and their infants engaged in the sharing of close social space.

primatologists working in the field before the 1970s were not deliberately distorting their observations; they simply had certain prior ideas about what male and female roles *should* be, and they had been trained to ask questions primarily about male primates. Their research reflected their cultural back-ground and their training. They were practicing the scientific method, but the scope of behavior they observed and the types of hypotheses they pro-posed were limited by their experience and culture.

Different fields of science (and all fields in which knowledge is acquired and assessed) also have varying **paradigms,** or predominant ways of thinking about ideas. Because people are educated within these paradigms, their ques-tions and interpretations are influenced and directed by their training (as you are influenced by the way this book is written and the way your instructor delivers the information in the classroom). A main paradigm of biological anthropology is evolution by natural selection. For example, when biological anthropologists examine a given fossil, the questions they ask are usually related to how the patterns and processes of evolution have impacted the form and function of the fossil in question.

Technology and innovation alter the realm of possible investigations and influence what kinds of observations can be made and how they can be assessed. As an example, consider what could be investigated before and after the development of the telescope, the microscope, or even the computer. Despite these influences, the scientific method does provide the foundation for research and theory that we can accept with a reasonable degree of cer-tainty. The foundation provided by the scientific method has allowed for the enormous leaps in knowledge that have given us vaccines and antibiotics, long-lasting and safely preserved foods, air travel, personal computers, and a multitude of other scientific and technological innovations.

paradigm
predominant ways of thinking about ideas

A note of caution: Many people think of science as a belief system or a body of truth rather than a methodology. Why do television advertisements frequently proclaim "9 out of 10 doctors prefer" a given product? Because doctors are considered men and women of science and therefore thought to possess "expert" opinions on any subject that might be thought of as having a scientific basis (like pain relievers or toothpaste). If we think of science as a body of truth or a belief system—the truth as validated by experts—then whatever the experts prefer or like the most is important. But if by science we mean a methodology, the preference of scientists is irrelevant; the only information that matters is the outcome of tests and experiments and the assessment of hypotheses and observations. Because science is a methodology, not a belief system, it doesn't matter what "doctors" or "scientists" think or like about a product. As students and active learners, you need to remember that science is a methodology and not a system of expert validation. Scientists frequently disagree, and this disagreement is a good thing. Researchers with differing backgrounds and orientations are going to look at data in different ways and ask different types of questions giving various types of answers. These variations are beneficial to the practice of science because the more questions asked, the more observations made, and the more tests conducted, the more knowledge we gain and the better directed our investigations are. Resolving disagreements by observing, hypothesizing, testing, and retesting is science; resolving disagreements by "expert" opinion is not.

STOP & **THINK**

Should we care what "experts" think? Who decides who an "expert" is?

Science is a unique and valuable way to ask questions about ourselves and the world around us. It differs from other systems in two important ways: First, it is self-correcting; second, it does not provide ultimate "truths." If your question is a moral, ethical, religious, spiritual, or otherwise philosophical one, such as Why are we here? Is there a supreme being? or Why does evil exist? do not look to the scientific method for an answer. Rather, turn to your family, friends, counselor, clergyperson, or spiritual advisor. Such questions are better debated, discussed, and answered in these contexts than in the realm of science.

Scientific Investigation Is a Collaborative Process

Collaboration, or working together, is central to scientific inquiry. Scientists collaborate by performing experiments and observations together and by using the published results of other scientists' work. Collaboration allows scientists to maximize the quality of tests and data and, importantly, to get multiple views on every issue. Working collaboratively has special significance today, when we have such a huge amount of information about the living and non-living forms on our planet. For example, consider the study of human ancestry. To ask relevant and effective scientific questions about human fossils, we need people capable of working in the fields of anatomy, anthropology, biology, chemistry, climatology, ecology, geology, paleontology, and zoology, among others. If we want to get into further depth, we will also need people competent in the fields of evolutionary biology and physics. Nor can we forget that to conduct research we need money and permits from federal and local governments; so we also need individuals who speak different languages and who understand communication, economics, and political science. In short, it is impossible for a single individual to do extensive and effective research today; too much knowledge is required to answer even one simple question.

Scientists have always collaborated on scientific investigations. Remember that humans do not really live that long and research can take enormous amounts of time and effort. Many scientists have conducted research that was not used in their lifetimes but was vital to the work of future generations. Gregor Mendel, for example, spent his life conducting experiments on plants to reveal the mechanisms of inheritance. In his lifetime, his work was relatively unknown. After his death, his findings provided the basis for the modern study of genetics. Thus, when we talk about scientific collaboration, we do not always mean that the collaborators worked directly with one another; rather, scientists used previous findings in their own research or thinking. This is why publishing and presenting information is so important. Data are useless if no one sees them; hypotheses are useless if no one hears or reads them. Today, most academic scientists present their work at professional meetings and publish their research in journals. Every piece of information adds to the overall knowledge base, and everyone's work contributes something at one point or another.

Probably the most important example of scientific collaboration discussed in this book is that which resulted in Charles Darwin's publication of *On the Origin of Species*. As you will see later in this chapter, Darwin's ideas did not originate solely with him; rather he was able to formulate them because of the body of knowledge that existed at the time he lived combined with his own life experiences. This collaborative experience primed him to synthesize an enormous amount of information into a comprehensive theory of evolution, one that has held up to this day.

Evolutionary theory is the cornerstone of anthropology

Evolution Is Both Fact and Theory

Evolution is biological change across generations. It is a fact—that is, it is an observable, verifiable truth—that life on this planet has changed over time. By examining fossils, by doing biochemical analyses of humans and other organisms, and by studying the geology of the planet, we can see that change has occurred over time. That is the *fact* of evolution. The *theory* of evolution is a set of hypotheses that explain *how* the change occurs. This theory is an explanation, a proposed mechanism, for change, and it is testable and thus

CONNECTIONS

Making a Monkey Out of You?

We do not come from monkeys. This is one of the most common misconceptions of evolutionary ideas and, if you think about it, is really silly. Monkeys and humans are both around today . . . one cannot come from the other. Monkeys, you, and I share a common ancestor (about 35 million years ago or so; see chapter 6) that was neither a human nor a monkey. Life has changed a lot throughout the history of this planet and many forms gave rise to many others, but those forms that exist now cannot be the ancestors to other forms that also exist now. Evolutionary relationships between ancestors and descendant species are like a tree. Consider whatever is alive now to be like the very tips of all the twigs extending from the branches of the tree. The ancestors are the places along the branches leading back to the trunk, the trunk itself, and even the roots. Some twigs are close to each other, and thus share the "ancestors" of the branch they both come off of (like humans and chimpanzees), others are more distant and only share the trunk of the tree in common (like humans and mushrooms). So monkeys cannot be our ancestors, but they can be close branches on the tree of life.

scientific. Currently, the theory of evolution is well supported by repeated testing. Evolution, then, is both a fact and a theory. The fact is that the earth and things on it have changed over time, and the theory is an explanation for how those changes have occurred.

We know that life has changed and continues to change. Biological anthropology studies the mechanisms of that change and how we have come to understand them at the beginning of the 21st century. To see how we arrived at our current theoretical understandings, we need to look back at the ideas and innovations that gave rise to our current concepts, as well as the cultural context in which they arose.

STOP & **THINK**

When most people talk or think about evolution, are they using evolution the *fact* or evolution the *theory?*

Early Explanations of Life Were Both Philosophical and Religious

All human societies classify the components of the world around them and have explanations for how things came to be and how they work on a day-to-day level. All have origin stories—myths about how the world was created. The Judeo Christian Islamic creation stories, in combination with ancient Greek and Roman philosophies, have greatly influenced the European natural sciences from which we derive our current ideas about evolution.

The Greek and Roman Legacy

An important idea in Greek and Roman philosophy was the *Scalae Natura*, or Great Chain of Being. This idea dates back to classical Greece and the philosopher Aristotle (~384–322 BCE) or even earlier, and until the 18th or 19th century, it represented the established order of life for most Western cultures. In essence, this notion is that all forms of life on the planet can be ranked in order from the most important to the least important (Figure 1.5). Early forms of this idea place gods and demigods at the top; human males next; then elephants, dolphins, and human females; and then the entire panoply of life on earth (usually ending with the earthworm at or near the bottom). By the 18th century this concept was commonly held by Europeans with only slight modification: God at the top, angels below God, humans next, and then all the beasts of land, sea, and air. Although this notion may seem simplistic to us today, it influenced how people saw the world for centuries. Such a linear ranking of organisms supports the beliefs that higher ranked forms are better than lower ranked forms and that humans are superior to other life-forms.

The Greek and Roman philosophers also embedded the idea of *essentialism*—the notion of ideal types—in our philosophical heritage. This concept dictates that each organism has a true, ideal form and that all living representatives of that organism are slight deviations from the ideal type. This notion is important because it provides an explanation for the slight variations we see in different forms, even among members of the same species.

Within this belief system, then, you would not ask scientific questions about why an ape, a human, and a monkey all have five fingers and a prehensile thumb, for example; or why a dog and wolf are almost identical in

■ FIGURE 1.5
The Scalae Natura, or Great Chain of Being, from a 1579 engraving. What species are seen as high ranking? Low ranking?

CONNECTIONS

See chapter 3, pages 82–87, and 4, pages 96–114, for examples and discussions of why essentialism was wrong.

every way; or why an ostrich has wings and cannot fly while an eagle has wings and can. In this belief system the answers are self-evident: Apes and monkeys are degenerate humans or mistakes in human form; wolves are the evil twins of dogs; and ostriches rank lower than eagles so they are clumsy and ugly and cannot fly.

Combining the Great Chain of Being with essentialist perspectives provided a perfect explanation for the diversity of life on earth. Everything is ranked in a specific order (with humans near the top), and things never really change much from their essential form. Variants might arise, but they are just poor versions of the ideal type. These concepts were used to explain variation not only in animals but also in human beings.

Judeo-Christian-Islamic Contributions

The Judeo-Christian-Islamic tradition contributes origin stories to these Greek and Roman conceptualizations. Two versions of an origin story appear in the Bible in the book of Genesis. Version one (Genesis 1:1-2:3) begins with "In the beginning when God created the heavens and the earth" and goes on to outline God's next 7 days. Over the course of 6 days, God first creates light, then day and night, then the sky, separating the "waters from the waters." He then separates the dry land from the waters and creates vegetation and trees. Next, God creates the sun, moon, stars, and seasons, followed by the living creatures of the sky and sea (birds, sea monsters, and fish). Following this, God creates the living things of the earth—cattle, creeping things, wild animals, and lastly, humans, male and female, created together in God's image. On the 7th day God finishes and rests; he also blesses the male and female and tells them to be fruitful and multiply.

Version two (Genesis 2:4-25) begins, "In that day the Lord God made earth and the heavens." God then creates a man from the dust of the ground (*Adamah*, Hebrew for "ground" or "earth") and plants a garden, in Eden, and puts man there. There is a tree of life and a tree of knowledge in the garden, and man is forbidden to eat from the tree of knowledge. God then creates every animal and bird to be man's helpers, and the man names them all but does not find a suitable partner among them. God then takes a rib from man and makes a woman.

STOP & THINK

Did you know about the two versions of creation? Do you think many people form opinions about religious beliefs without knowing much about the religions?

What does this have to do with evolution? These origin stories (either one) clearly explain the origin and diversity of life on earth; all the many and diverse creatures were created by God in the beginning, roughly at the same time. In version two, Adam (the man) names all forms and thereby confers upon them their essence. The vast majority of people in 18th- and 19th-century Europe (where we will be tracking our history of evolution) were embedded in a culture and belief system that embraced a literal interpretation of these ideas. Challenging these beliefs was neither easy nor socially acceptable, and the general thought at the time was that there wasn't any need to challenge them. Laid out in Genesis were not only the Great Chain of Being but also an explanation for all the variation in the world: Everything that exists was created exactly as it is now. Not only was this done flawlessly, but it was also done in a fixed time—6 days, or longer if the Bible is not interpreted literally.

The Bible also contains possible explanations for other natural phenomena. Fossils, for example, had long been recognized as a problem, because many fossil remains that were discovered clearly represented life-forms that no longer existed in Europe (such as dinosaurs and woolly mammoths). Furthermore, fossils of recognized animals (such as shellfish) were occasionally found in places where they currently did not occur (such as high in the Alps in northern Italy). However, the story of the great flood and Noah's ark offers an explanation for these occurrences: Extinct forms did not make it onto the ark, and fossils of sea animals could be found on mountaintops because they were deposited there during the flood.

In 1650 the archbishop of Ireland, James Ussher, using aspects of books of the Bible, calculated the actual date of creation: 4004 BCE, making the earth about 6000 years old. Seventeen years later the vice-chancellor of Cambridge University, John Lightfoot, narrowed it down even further: 9:00 a.m., Sunday, October 23, 4004 BCE. Interestingly, this was also the date and time—October 23 at 9:00 a.m.—when Cambridge began its fall term.

The Scientific Revolution Opened the Door to Systematic Study of the World

While Ussher, Lightfoot, and others were debating theology, some thinkers were attempting to explore the natural world in new ways. A significant change in the cultural climate came with the introduction of *heliocentric theory*, the idea that the earth revolves around the sun. Until this theory gained prominence, the general belief was that the sun and stars rotated around the earth, a concept that placed humans and their home planet at the center of the universe. Nicolaus Copernicus (1473–1543) was among the first to propose the robust (and ultimately supported) hypothesis that the earth revolves around the sun. The Christian church denounced Copernicus, and his ideas were aggressively suppressed as heresy.

The inventor Galileo Galilei (1564–1642) was also a strong proponent of Copernicus's heliocentric theory and added to it by testing and supporting some of its hypotheses in the early 1600s. When Galileo published these results, he was quickly arrested and charged not only with publishing support for heliocentrism but also with proposing a strong atomic theory, and he was condemned to burn at the stake. The atomic theory, which states that all matter consists of small, unchangeable atomic particles, was looked upon as even more dangerous to the order of the day than heliocentrism. Luckily, Galileo was able, through influence and connections, to plead guilty to promoting heliocentrism and was "allowed" to retract his support for the atomic theory (which we now know to be accurate). His sentence was commuted to house arrest, and he spent the rest of his life continuing his studies at his villa near Florence. Although Galileo was forced to deny his belief in the Copernican model of the solar system, his emphasis on observation, sensory evidence, measurement, and mathematical proof helped open the door to further naturalistic observations.

The English philosopher Francis Bacon (1561–1626), a contemporary of Galileo, introduced the precursor to the modern scientific method when he developed systematic rules for observation and the collection of data. Bacon encouraged scientists to gain knowledge through the observation of nature rather than through the application of pure theory. He also emphasized the importance of experimentation in the quest for information.

The methodologies of Bacon and of others who added to them opened the floodgates for a series of discoveries in the physical sciences. Isaac Newton (1642–1727), through observation, hypothesis building, and experimentation, proposed a series of mechanistic patterns in the natural world. His theory of universal gravity and his hypotheses for the laws of motion and optics are valuable scientific concepts even today. Interestingly, Newton (and others at the time) also hinted that the earth had to be older than 6000 years.

By the late 17th and early 18th centuries, the cultural climate in Europe was conducive to scientific investigation of the natural world. The concepts of heliocentrism, gravity, and atomic theory were gaining acceptance, and the scientific method with its systematic gathering of information carried grave implications for the status quo. Although most scientists were religious, they were also keen observers of the natural world; they observed discrepancies and inconsistencies between the world around them and biblical explanations. They began to raise questions: How old is the earth, really? How can the diversity of life-forms be accounted for? What are the meanings and implications of fossils and extinct organisms? Through questioning and examining the prevailing paradigm, people realized that all was not as simple as it seemed. They were also collaborating, working with each other's ideas, publications, and experiments. The earth was beginning to look dynamic; the grip of existing philosophical and religious ideas on the thinking of the time was starting to loosen.

Evolutionary Thought Emerged from Scientific Collaboration

Many individuals made significant contributions to what we consider modern evolutionary thought, and we discuss a few of the primary ones in this section. Unfortunately, by discussing only a few, we really can't do justice to the many critical thinkers and scientists who paved the way for our current understanding of evolution. Here we will focus on the naturalists who laid the groundwork for the emergence of Charles Darwin and his remarkable synthesis.

At the end of the 17th century, four scientists stood out for their contributions to the evolutionary story. John Ray (1628–1705), an English naturalist, classified plants and animals on the basis of similarities and differences; he laid the foundation for the work of Linnaeus (see the next section). The Englishman Edward Tyson (1650–1708) could be considered one of the first primatologists for his work in comparative anatomy of a young chimpanzee (although he mistakenly referred to it as an orangutan), which paved the way for investigations into relationships among the primates. The English natural philosopher Robert Hooke (1635–1703) believed that fossils represented extinct organisms and proposed that extinctions occurred because of changes in the earth. The Danish naturalist Nicolas Steno (1638–1686) founded the science of **stratigraphy,** the study of the rock and soil layers of the earth. He proposed that the **strata** of the earth represented a chronological history of a constantly changing planet. Because fossils of different life-forms were found across the different layers, indicating that they existed at different times, it was becoming evident that change in life-forms occurred on the planet. Both Hooke and Steno adhered to the biblical chronology and therefore had to explain how all of the change they saw could have occurred in just 6000 years. To resolve this problem, they proposed that great disasters regularly befell the earth, causing massive change in very short periods of time. This explanation for change is called **catastrophism** (Figure 1.6).

Linnaeus: The Classifier

Carl von Linne, better known as Carolus Linnaeus (1707–1778), was a Swedish naturalist and the "father" of **taxonomy**—the system of naming and classifying organisms that we still use today with modifications. The son of a

stratigraphy
the study of the layering of the earth's sediments

strata
layers of the earth

catastrophism
the belief that great catastrophes regularly wipe out much of life on earth

taxonomy
naming and classification of organisms based on morphological similarities and differences

■ FIGURE 1.6
One explanation for change is catastrophism. The crater created by a meteor impact (top) is an example of catastrophism. The Grand Canyon, created by eons of erosion by rivers and wind (bottom), is an example of gradualism.

country pastor and an avid gardener, Linnaeus was a calm, affable man and a pious Christian (Figure 1.7). From an early age he showed a great interest in nature, especially the variety and diversity of living organisms. Despite his scientific approach, Linnaeus's goal was to understand God's wisdom by studying his creation (the natural world).

Linnaeus developed his system of classification by grouping together organisms with similar anatomical structures. He used *binomial nomenclature*—a two-name system—to identify and group different forms. He grouped clusters of organisms that were most similar to one another into categories called *species* and then grouped species into higher categories called *genera* (singular, *genus*). Genera could then be grouped into even higher categories, such as *family, order,* and *phylum* (Figure 1.8). In this system, we humans are *Homo sapiens* (genus *Homo,* and species *sapiens*).

While Linnaeus believed in a fixity of nature (no new species could arise from others, nor could substantial change occur in living forms), he did, indirectly, challenge the prevailing notions of a Great Chain of Being. His way of grouping had the remarkable effect of destroying the linear ranking of organisms and placing all species, essentially, at the same level. Although Linnaeus believed that nature had been constructed "in the hand of God," his recognition

■ FIGURE 1.7
Carolus Linnaeus (1707–1778).
The father of modern
taxonomy.

and cataloging of anatomical similarities across organisms laid the basis for later evolutionary approaches to the natural world.

Buffon: A Hint That Species Could Change

George-Louis Leclerc, Comte du Buffon (1707–1788), could be considered an arch-critic and rival of Linnaeus. Buffon, born into a French noble family, was a writer, philosopher, and natural historian (Figure 1.9). Buffon thought there was a dynamic relationship between organisms and their environment. Unlike Linnaeus, Buffon retained a belief in a form of the Great Chain of Being. However, he believed that life-forms were the outcome of active processes and that biblical creation "started the ball rolling" and led to a proliferation of forms. Although he did not quite believe that one species could change into another, he did believe that many forms degrade into lower forms. Buffon also believed that the earth was older than 6000 years—he suggested that it could be more than 160,000 years old—and that active forces played roles in the organization of nature. Buffon's famous volume, *Natural History* (1749), was one of the first works to address the origin and age of the earth from a nonbiblical perspective. In it he even proposed that the solar system arose after creation as a product of celestial dynamics (he was forced to take this idea out, but he sneaked it back in a later version). Buffon strongly argued against a perfect, static creation, pointing out that not all structures have a function (hind toes on pigs and large dogs, nipples on men,

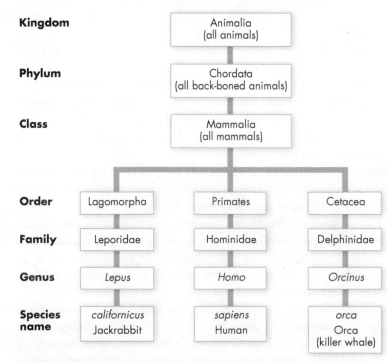

■ FIGURE 1.8
Three examples of the Linnaean classification system. We know them as a rabbit, a human, and a killer whale.

for example). This point was critical, because it diverged from the observations of Linnaeus, who held that all forms were functional and resulted from divine creation.

Erasmus Darwin: Early Modern Ideas about Evolution

It was still the 1700s when the first, and lesser known, Darwin made his appearance. Erasmus Darwin (1731–1802), grandfather of Charles Darwin, was a respected physician, poet, philosopher, and naturalist (Figure 1.10). He proposed one of the first structured theories of evolution in his book *Zoonomia, or, The Laws of Organic Life* (1796). He believed that life had arisen from an original filament (God) and that the process of speciation—gradual change of one species into another—had produced the diversity of forms we see on the planet. This notion is best (and prophetically) captured in verse in Darwin's 1802 posthumously published poem *The Temple of Nature*:

> *Organic life beneath the shoreless waves*
> *Was born and nurs'd in ocean's pearly caves;*
> *First forms minute, unseen by spheric glass,*
> *Move on the mud, or pierce the watery mass;*
> *These, as successive generations bloom,*
> *New powers acquire and larger limbs assume;*
> *Whence countless groups of vegetations spring,*
> *And breathing realms of fin and feet and wing.*

Erasmus Darwin took an integrated approach to examining the natural world: He combined observations of domestic animals, wildlife, fossils, and comparative anatomy to arrive at his conclusions. In fact, his views were sufficiently well constructed that these ideas about evolution were already referred to as "Darwinism," even before his grandson was born. In many ways it is no wonder that Charles Darwin came up with the ideas that he did.

Lamarck: Environmental Challenges and the Inheritance of Acquired Characteristics

While Erasmus Darwin may have been the first to put forward formal ideas about evolution, it is Jean Baptiste Pierre Antoine de Monet, Chevalier de Lamarck (1744–1829), who first clearly laid out a theory of evolution (Figure 1.11). The youngest of 11 children, Lamarck spent his youth in a Jesuit seminary and then in the French army. By the 1770s he had seriously undertaken the study of botany and in 1793 was appointed a professor at the French National Museum of Natural History. Lamarck counted Buffon as a friend and benefactor, but the older man never agreed fully with Lamarck's theories.

Lamarck believed in dramatic and significant change both in species and individual organisms. Where Buffon left off, Lamarck began: He believed that species could change. He believed that organic forms are constantly changing. In fact, he correctly recognized that the relationship between an organism and its environment was a dynamic one and that the environment, far from being arranged so as to minister to life, actually established the constantly changing conditions to which organisms must adapt if they are to survive.

Lamarck proposed a process of evolution with three major components: the will to change, the inheritance of acquired characteristics, and the law of use and disuse. All of these components are based on the notion that the environment challenges organisms. According to Lamarck, when an organism

■ **FIGURE 1.9**
The Comte de Buffon (1707–1788). He contributed to early ideas of organic change.

■ **FIGURE 1.10**
Erasmus Darwin (1731–1802). Charles Darwin's grandfather and early evolutionist.

STOP & THINK

Lamarck's ideas are closer to what many people today think evolution is. Why is that?

■ **FIGURE 1.11**
Jean-Baptiste Lamarck (1744–1829). He proposed the first full hypothesis for evolutionary change.

CONNECTIONS

See chapter 4, pages 96–105, for ways in which we can see Lamarck's ideas still at work in some senses.

adaptation
change in response to environmental challenges

encounters an environmental challenge, the organism could will fluids and forces into action. As a result, appropriate organs would appear and develop via constant and vigorous use. In other words, the organism would change its form to meet the environmental challenge. Once an organism acquired a new organ or set of characteristics, it could pass them on to its offspring (Figure 1.12). If the new organs fell into disuse, they could be reabsorbed or modified into another form. All of this, Lamarck believed, could occur within the lifetime of a single organism. Although Lamarck correctly identified the environment as a challenge to organisms and **adaptation** as the result of changing to meet environmental challenges, his mechanism (the will to change), his inheritance patterns (inheritance of acquired characteristics), and his time frame (within a generation) were largely incorrect.

Today we recognize Lamarck's enormously significant contribution, but during his lifetime his work achieved little popularity. In fact, he was actively discredited by rivals and faced a constant battle with poverty. When he died, he received a poor man's funeral and was buried in a rented grave, which was dug up after 5 years; today no one knows the location of his remains.

Cuvier: Catastrophes Change the Planet

Rival to Lamarck and staunch antievolutionist, Georges Cuvier (1769–1832) was also a professor at the National Museum of Natural History. Cuvier was a student of Buffon's and a highly proficient comparative anatomist. Although he did not believe that species could change over time, he did recognize that many forms of life on the planet no longer exist. To explain extinction, he (like Hooke and Steno before him) espoused a theory of catastrophism, which explained how bones of forms that no longer exist (giant mammals, for example) could have existed in the past and how new forms could have been created after catastrophic events (the biblical flood, for example).

Hutton and Lyell: Uniform Geological Processes

Cuvier's catastrophism was countered by the ideas of Scotsmen and geologists James Hutton (1726–1797) and Charles Lyell (1797–1875). In Hutton's *Theory of the Earth* (1795) and Lyell's *Principles of Geology* (1830), the modern

■ **FIGURE 1.12**
Lamarckian evolution. An organism wills itself to change in order to meet an environmental challenge. It then passes its acquired characteristics on to its offspring. What is wrong with this theory?

geological concept of **uniformitarianism** and the recognition that the planet is very old are both laid out. These scientists suggested that geological processes (erosion, mountain formation, and so on) observed in the present are the same as those that were functioning in the past; thus, processes at work on the planet are and have been uniform over time. Observing the height of mountain ranges, the depth of canyons and river valleys, and the erosion of seaside cliffs, Hutton and Lyell realized that an enormous amount of change has occurred on this planet. They also realized that, given the slow pace of geological processes, the earth must be very old! They proposed the concept of *deep time*, meaning that the earth must be older than 6000 years for the uniform processes of geological change to have had sufficient time to result in such geological features as the Alps.

By the mid-1800s the time was ripe for an active, critical thinker to pull together all these threads of information: The age of the earth seemed to be much greater than previously thought, and the strata of the earth suggested that many types of organisms had lived and become extinct, implying that change is ongoing. Lamarck and Erasmus Darwin pushed the role of the environment into the forefront, and Linnaeus and Cuvier demonstrated the importance of similarities in anatomical form. Buffon, Erasmus Darwin, and Lamarck proposed that organisms change and had even suggested ideas for how change might occur. The stage was set for a new theory of evolution.

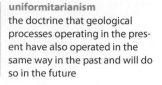

uniformitarianism
the doctrine that geological processes operating in the present have also operated in the same way in the past and will do so in the future

STOP & THINK

When most people think of evolution only Charles Darwin comes to mind. Why are all of these other folks ignored?

Charles Darwin Proposed Natural Selection as the Mechanism of Evolution

Into the world of scientific engagement and study constructed by these and many other researchers during the 17th, 18th, and 19th centuries stepped Charles Darwin (1809–1882) who, along with Alfred Russel Wallace (1823–1913), formulated the currently accepted theory of evolution (Figure 1.13). Their ideas permanently changed our conceptualization of life on earth.

■ **FIGURE 1.13**
Charles Darwin (left) and Alfred Russel Wallace (right). Each independently discovered the idea of natural selection, based on observations of a variety of animal species.

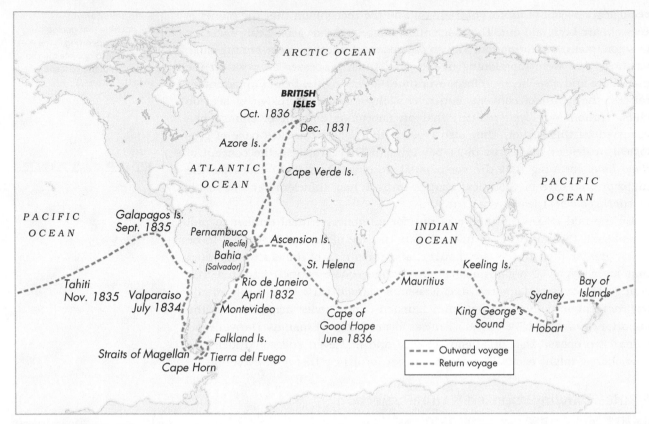

■ FIGURE 1.14
Voyage of the *Beagle* (1831–1836). Darwin observed an enormous variety of plants and animals in various parts of the world. Later, these observations formed the basis of his theory of evolution by natural selection.

Darwin's Life and Experiences

Charles Darwin was born into a fairly affluent English family. Although he never attained exceptional marks in school, he always displayed a keen interest in animals and natural history. Originally planning to enter the clergy, he could not resist his native inclination and took up the study of natural history. In 1831, at the age of 22, he received the position of naturalist aboard the HMS *Beagle* on a 5-year scientific journey bound for South America and other parts of the world (Figure 1.14). Darwin took a number of books with him and received books via mail along the way. Thus, he was able to constantly review and examine the current state of knowledge in natural history, geology, and other scientific realms during his voyage. In this context, freshly out of school, surrounded by ideas about change (those of Lamarck, Buffon, Lyell, Hutton) and about structure and form (those of Linnaeus, Cuvier, and others), he was exposed to something that few other scientists of his time were: natural diversity across a wide range of habitats, geographical locations, and geological formations.

Upon returning to England in 1836, he married, settled down, and began to write up copious research reports from the voyage. At the same time, he began to formulate a proposal for how living forms change over time. By 1844 he had a working version of his theory of evolution, which he eventually called "descent with modification via natural selection." While Darwin was somewhat concerned about how his ideas would be received by his fellow scientists and the public at large, he did not, as has often been said, hold off on publication because of such fears. Rather, Darwin was a diligent and devoted scientist.

For the 20 years after his voyage on the HMS *Beagle*, he was compiling a great body of evidence for his ideas about evolution and at the same time extremely busy publishing books and research articles on things as diverse as geology, barnacles, birds, flowers, and domestic animals. He was finally persuaded to publish after he began receiving letters in 1856 from Wallace, who had come up with very similar ideas about biological change based on experiences similar to Darwin's—travel, observations of natural diversity, and exposure to current ideas about evolution. Born into a modest social class, Wallace developed a zest for adventure and the natural world. He found he could pay his way to distant lands and continue his studies if he worked as a collector for museums and other scientific organizations. Through many years of such travel, he came up with a set of ideas similar to Darwin's, which he called "the tendency of varieties to depart from the original type." These are the ideas Wallace described to Darwin in his letters of 1856.

In 1858, Darwin and Wallace had a joint paper read before the Linnaean Society of London by Charles Lyell. The theme was a new theory of evolution: descent with modification via natural selection. In 1859, Darwin published his book, *On the Origin of Species By Means of Natural Selection or the Preservation of Favoured Races in the Struggle for Life.*

Darwin's Theory: Evolution via Natural Selection

Darwin synthesized his observations of natural history with his knowledge of animal breeding in the context of the ongoing scientific dialogue of the day about environments, time, and change. During his 5-year journey he saw a huge array of diverse forms of life. Especially in the Galapagos Islands off the coast of Ecuador, his observations led him to realize the fine fit of many organisms to their specific environments. He saw that within a species no two individuals were exactly alike. Members of a species are all highly similar in form, but they vary in specific traits, such as beak form, leg length, or feather colors. What others had seen as divine creation, Darwin saw as an interaction between organisms and their environment. Darwin had also had extensive experience with animal husbandry. He knew that a farmer could selectively breed individuals to get certain results (although he did not know the mechanism for this process); in fact, Darwin himself raised and bred show pigeons.

reproductive success
a measure of the number of surviving off-spring an organism has

Darwin had also read Lyell and Hutton and realized how old the planet actually was. He knew of Lamarck's ideas about adaptation and the role of the environment. By at least 1837 (although probably earlier), Darwin had also read *The Essay on the Principle of Population*, by Thomas Robert Malthus. Malthus, a clergyman and political economist, proposed that populations grow exponentially and food production grows arithmetically (Figure 1.15). Thus, if all organisms that are born survive, all populations should outgrow their food supply. But this does not happen. In fact, most born do not survive. Darwin cites this book as giving him the final clue to the puzzle.

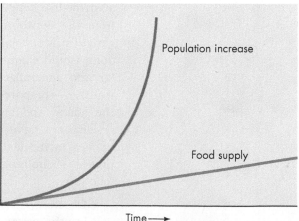

Time ⟶

■ FIGURE 1.15
The population–food supply curve. Malthus observed the relationship between food supply and population growth.

Darwin realized that all organisms that are born do not survive because the environment challenges them. Acquiring food and reproducing are difficult, and not all organisms in a species do so equally well. There is a competition for survival, or more specifically for **reproductive success** (how many

There is variation in forms of traits in a population.

The traits that do best are termed "fit" in a given environment. If these traits are heritable (can be passed to offspring), over time those individuals with the fit traits produce a higher average number of offspring per generation.

These fit traits become increasingly represented in subsequent generations of the population as a result of this differential reproductive success (they become *adaptations*). Over time more and more individuals in the population display the fit traits.

■ FIGURE 1.16
The process of natural selection. Natural selection occurs as a result of variation within a population.

fit
having the set of heritable traits that are best suited to existing and reproducing in a given environment

heritable
capable of being passed to offspring biologically (through reproduction)

natural selection
process by which the better fit variants in a population become over-represented over time

surviving offspring an organism has). If some individuals have traits that better enable them to compete, they may acquire more food, do better in a given environment, and in turn leave more offspring. Organisms whose traits best adapt them for their environment are said to have the best **fit** with that environment. If these traits are **heritable** (can be passed to off-spring), the offspring inherit the traits and benefit from them. Over time, more and more individuals in the population will have those fit variants. Notice how this explanation differs from Lamarck's ideas. Darwin realized that variation does not arise from a will to change but is actually found in the existing traits of individuals in a population and is passed to offspring. Darwin called this mechanism of change **natural selection.** His basic idea was that changes come about in populations of organisms due to differences in the reproductive success of individuals based on their fit to a given environment (Figure 1.16).

How Natural Selection Works: Darwin's Finches
One way to demonstrate Darwin's ideas is an example from animals he collected: the Galapagos finches. When the HMS *Beagle* visited the Galapagos Islands, Darwin collected many specimens, including 13 varieties of finch (a sparrow-like songbird). He also collected specimens of the same type of bird from the South American mainland, but there he found only one or two varieties. Much later, upon returning to England, he had the ornithologist John Gould examine the specimens. The mainland finches were fairly similar and generalized—that is, they did not appear to have any specialized features—compared to the island varieties, which showed great variation in the shape and size of their beaks (Figure 1.17). Although a number of researchers have collaborated on the final assessments of the Galapagos finches in the last 150 years, we can envision a summary of the scientific process examining Darwin's finches in the context of natural selection as follows:

- *Observations:* There was a great deal of variation in the Galapagos finches, but the general similarities between the island forms and the mainland form suggest that the island finches are descended from mainland forms that arrived on the Galapagos (because they share nearly all anatomical traits in common). The main differences between the finch species of the Galapagos Islands are in the shape and structure of their beaks. What changed when the mainland finches came to the Galapagos? The environment.

Large seed-eating ground finch

Cactus ground finch

Insectivorous tree finch

Small seed-eating ground finch

Vegetarian tree finch

Woodpecker finch

■ **FIGURE 1.17**
Darwin's finches. Note the diverse beak structures.

Visiting the Galapagos Islands, you can see that each island has a few different environments, and each different environment has a finch with a slightly different kind of beak. What are these beaks used for? Acquiring food. The varieties with heavy beaks exploit seeds and leaves; those with long, stout beaks eat insects from inside trees (like a woodpecker); and those with long, thin beaks catch the insects on the fly or off the ground or leaves.

- *Problem:* There are only 1 or 2 types of mainland finch, but there are 13 types of Galapagos finch. Could the ancestral finch have evolved into so many different species? If so, how?

- *Hypothesis:* There would have to be some sort of challenge to the finches to result in such a change in their forms (beaks). If beak structure and form were variable in the ancestral population, and if that variation was heritable, then those with certain variations would do better in certain environments, by acquiring more food more effectively, and thus have a better chance at leaving more offspring. Over time there would be "selection" for those that had the beak form that allowed them to do slightly better (acquire food and leave more offspring) in their **niche** (specific environment). Gradually (over many, many generations), the different specialists would begin to look quite different from one another; by the time Darwin collected them, they had differentiated so much that they were separate species.

> **niche**
> habitat or ecological role filled by an organism; the way in which an organism "makes a living"

- *Test:* Collecting finch species by environment type and carefully measuring and comparing their beaks show that beak form closely matches the type of environment and the primary foods within that environment. They also show that there were few finches with beak types suited for one environment living in another type of environment. These measurements and comparisons supported the hypothesis.

- *Retest:* Darwin spent many years looking at species and their diversity in relation to the environments in which they were found. He also studied in great depth the breeding and selection processes in domestic animals. Since that time many, many researchers have also followed the same trajectory of testing and retesting the pattern of certain traits being passed more frequently to subsequent generations. The result is the theory of evolution via natural selection.

CONNECTIONS

See chapter 4, pages 95–114, for an expanded account of how we view evolution today and how much more we know than Darwin did.

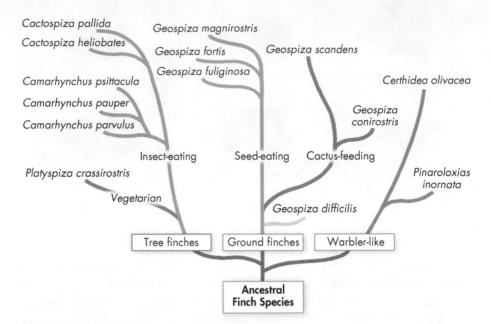

■ FIGURE 1.18

A family tree of finches. Descent of Galapagan finches from the original parent species.

In this case a group of organisms (a species) that already contained individuals with some variation in beak form moved into a new set of environments (on the different islands). On each island there were environmental challenges that differed somewhat from those on the mainland. Over time, the descendants of the original colonizing finches with beak shapes that helped them do a little better in the new environment left more offspring. Because beak shape is heritable, over time, the better fit variants came to make up the majority of the population (Figure 1.18).

Additional support for this hypothesis comes from evaluating possible explanations for variation. Most of the anatomical traits of the finches are very similar. This similarity could be explained in two ways: (1) The same set of traits could have evolved independently in each species, or (2) the species could have a common ancestry. Which is more likely, a complex set of traits evolving 13 times or evolving once? Here we apply the concept of **parsimony**. In the context of science, parsimony, or extreme economy or frugality, means that we generally assume that the least complex explanation is the most likely. Just as water flows around rocks, organic development also tends to follow the path of least resistance (or take the fewest number of complex steps).

We could also ask, Is there variation in the beaks in each species today? The answer is yes. Are beak shapes directly related to feeding strategies, which in turn are directly related to reproductive success? Yes. Our tests and observations today continue to support the hypothesis.

In Darwin's and Wallace's view, organisms fit into their environment not because they were created that way but because generations of interaction between the traits of those organisms and the challenges of the environment resulted in descent with modification, or evolution via natural selection.

Reaction to Darwin's Ideas

Although other hypotheses about evolution had been proposed, most of them posited some internal force or mystical driving element behind the process.

parsimony
economy in explanation; the least complex path

■ FIGURE 1.19

Darwin as a monkey. Nineteenth-century caricatures of Darwin showing the popular misunderstanding of his ideas.

Darwin's idea of evolution was based simply on the interaction between organisms and their environments; there was no internal drive or will to change in the organism itself. This view was essentially nonreligious or nonspiritual and thus unwelcome in Darwin's time.

Darwin was a meticulous scientist and was constantly gathering data and refining his ideas so they would be as clear and well supported as possible. Thus, Darwin may have intentionally prepared such a comprehensive case because he anticipated both indignation from the public and intense scrutiny of his work from other scientists.

After the publication of *On the Origin of Species*, many people developed misconceptions about natural selection and evolution, and these misconceptions continue in the minds of many people today. Darwin's ideas were, and still are, misrepresented as suggesting that humans are descended from monkeys, that acceptance of natural selection means that one cannot believe in God, and that humans are no different from earthworms (Figure 1.19). Although Darwin's book was published during a time when scientists and scholars were debating the nature of the planet and life-forms, the general public still held to the prevailing religious and philosophical beliefs of the time. Most believed that the pattern and structure of nature was preordained, not the result of environmental change and adaptation to it. Many were not prepared to hear "radical" ideas like Darwin's.

Yet another part of the problem stemmed from the general public's lack of familiarity with the scientific method and its pattern of distinction among fact, hypothesis, and theory. Many people did not understand that Darwin gathered data, that the data supported his hypothesis, and that the testing of hypotheses is core to scientific inquiry. Because they did not understand this scientific process, they considered Darwin's ideas purely philosophical and thus fully debatable, just as any other philosophy is. There has been, and continues to be, an intense and sometimes violent debate over the meaning and

STOP & THINK

Have reactions to evolutionary ideas changed that much since Darwin's time?

implications of evolution. It is important to understand, however, that the debate over evolution is not about whether change over time occurs but rather *how* it occurs.

Even those who supported Darwin's ideas frequently misconstrued them. For example, many of Darwin's contemporaries mistook natural selection for a goal-directed process. They then misapplied it to human political, social, and economic realities of their day. These ideas came to be called "Social Darwinism"; they implied that those who did better in society (as measured by wealth and power) did so on the basis of some biological superiority. Many proclaimed that society was ruled by "survival of the fittest" (a phrase Darwin did not use until the 2nd edition of *On the Origin of Species*) and people became prominent or wealthy due to their innate abilities, not because of socioeconomic, political, or historical processes. Many of Darwin's colleagues thought that evolution via natural selection was best seen as progress leading to increasing complexity. They felt that human cultures that had more complex technologies and were more "civilized" were "further along" on the evolutionary ladder. Embedded in these thoughts is, once again, the idea of the Great Chain of Being. When applied to human socioeconomic and political stratification and cross-cultural technological differences, the concept of natural selection provides a false, or at least incomplete, explanation for the great diversity we see in technologies and social stratification across human societies.

In fact, evolution via natural selection is neutral, not goal directed. There are no "higher" or "lower" forms; everything that is currently in existence is equally "evolved"; that is, it has arrived at its current form as a result of long periods of interaction by its ancestors with specific environments. An earthworm is adept at what it does, as are humans, but neither would survive very long in the other's environment. Evolution does not plan for the future and therefore does not represent "progress." Darwin emphasized that descent with modification via natural selection leads only to increasing adaptation between organisms and their own environment, not to an abstract notion of progress as defined by structural complexity or increasing heterogeneity. Misinterpretation of the theory of natural selection was borne out in many ways, as social theorists, politicians, and other scientists misrepresented Darwin's work for social, economic, and political ends.

There has also been, and unfortunately continues to be, a misconception about the relationship between the theory of evolution and the beliefs and doctrines of the Judeo-Christian-Islamic religions. Religion and Darwinian evolutionary theory need not be at odds. Only if one believes that the earth is static and organic change has not occurred is there a conflict between evolutionary fact and theory and religious belief. Most of the mainstream representatives of world religions (Buddhism, Christianity, Confucianism, Hinduism, Islam, Judaism, Shinto, Taoism, and others) accept the fact of evolution (change over time) and agree that Darwin's (and others') contributions have furthered human understanding of the natural world. We can debate the role of the soul and its relationship to the organic self and the uniqueness of the human spirit, but, as pointed out earlier, this is not the realm of science. Here, we keep the discussions of organic change limited to the physical realm and leave the spiritual matters to others, as Darwin himself did. Darwin was a man of strong personal faith; he ends his book *On the Origin of Species* with a testimonial to his awe of nature:

> *It is interesting to contemplate a tangled bank, clothed with many*
> *plants of many kinds, with birds singing on the bushes, with various*

CONNECTIONS

Can You Understand Evolution and Be Religious?

Of course you can, with a few exceptions. Countless people, from scientists, to poets, to priests, have no problem holding both sets of ideas. Understanding evolution simply means that you are aware of the fact that life has changed over time on the planet and that we have some robust notions about how those changes occur. This understanding says nothing about the soul and the spiritual beliefs of humanity. However, there is one catch: If you understand evolution, then you realize that the earth was not created in a short time span and that humans did not appear fully formed overnight on the planet. This means that certain beliefs that some people have of how humans came to be do not fit with the reality of the fossil record and geological record (which are facts). However, if we consider that origin stories are not literal but moral and philosophical comments on who we are and why we do what we do, then there is no problem. The fact that life has changed on this planet does not force us to take one philosophical position on how humans came to be, but it does make us aware of certain histories of the planet and life on it. What do you believe? Do you see any problems melding faith and the facts that the earth is old and life has changed over time?

insects flitting about, and with worms crawling through the damp earth, and to reflect that these elaborately constructed forms, so different from each other, and dependent upon each other in so complex a manner, have all been produced by the laws acting around us. These laws, taken in the largest sense, being growth with reproduction; inheritance which is almost implied by reproduction; variability from the indirect and direct action of the external conditions of life, and from use and disuse: a ratio of increase so high as to lead to a struggle for life, and as a consequence to natural selection, entailing the divergence of character and the extinction of less-improved forms. Thus, from the war of nature, from famine and death, the most exalted object which we are capable of conceiving, namely the production of higher animals, directly follows. There is a grandeur in this view of life, with its several powers, having been originally breathed into a few forms or into one; and that, whilst this planet has gone cycling on according to the fixed law of gravity, from so simple a beginning endless forms most beautiful and most wonderful have been, and are being evolved.

By the middle of the 20th century, Darwin's ideas had become a core part of our science and our culture. What we refer to as Darwin's ideas, however, was really the culmination of centuries of collaborative investigation and brilliant critical thinking by many individuals. These endeavors went on in spite of societal scorn and a strong cultural paradigm of a predetermined, unchanging world. Today, we have a much broader base of knowledge than did Darwin—as the result of scientific collaboration over the past 150 years—and we have greatly expanded the ways in which we hypothesize about how evolution works. As you will see in chapters 2, 3, and 4, our knowledge of genetics, anatomy, and populations has expanded our understanding of the mechanisms of evolution and given us even better explanations of change than

What We Know

The scientific method is a highly effective way to gain reliable knowledge about the world. It is a self-correcting mode of asking questions about ourselves and the world around us. It is not the only method of acquiring knowledge, but its reliance on refutation and its emphasis on testing make it very effective for these endeavors.

What We Know

Organisms vary and some of that variation is heritable. In certain environments some variants do better and leave more offspring per generation than other variants. Over time the population in that environment looks more and more like the variants with the better fit. If the environment changes, a new variant may be favored (or selected).

What We Know

Evolution is a fact: Things have changed over the history of this planet.

Questions That Remain

Questions about ultimate matters, especially spiritual, moral, and philosophical matters, will never be answered by science. They are all not testable and thus not within its realm. Science does, however, give us much information to consider when debating/discussing social and philosophical matters.

Questions That Remain

How does variation arise? Are there other forces that affect survival and reproduction? What about nonheritable variation? Is natural selection affecting humans today? (These are questions we tackle throughout the subsequent chapters in this book.)

Questions That Remain

We may not know all the mechanisms of change. We have a number of strongly supported hypotheses (theories) for how things change, and we continue to test and retest them. Darwin's and Wallace's ideas about natural selection have withstood more than a century of testing and are considered to be a very robust theory. Current and ongoing collaboration (especially at the level of molecular genetics) continues to fine-tune our understanding of evolutionary change, and new ideas and concepts continue to emerge.

were offered by Darwin's original ideas. Nevertheless, Darwin's and Wallace's basic ideas—that heritable variation occurs in nature, that the environment poses a challenge to organisms, and that some variants do better and leave more offspring in certain environments and therefore become better represented in subsequent generations—remain invaluable gems in our quest for understanding of the natural world.

SUMMARY

▲ Anthropology is a scientific discipline that studies humans and non-human primates in all their aspects. It is generally divided into the four subdisciplines of archaeology, biological anthropology, cultural anthropology, and linguistic anthropology.

▲ Critical thinking is the careful, active analysis and evaluation of information.

▲ The scientific method consists of observation, hypothesis formulation, testing, and retesting. Observable, verifiable truths are facts, testable explanations for them are hypotheses, and well-supported hypotheses are theories.

▲ Science is a collaborative process.

▲ Evolution is a fact: Life-forms have changed over the history of this planet. While there is debate about the exact mechanisms of change, there is no doubt that change has occurred.

▲ The last 500 years has seen a shift in explanations of the natural world from exclusively philosophical and religious explanations to a broader, science-based set of explanations. Many individuals have contributed to this change in orientation and new set of understandings.

▲ Evolutionary theory is the product of a collaborative effort, with many scientists contributing pieces to our current understanding. The theory of natural selection was proposed jointly by Charles Darwin and Alfred Wallace. Darwin's 1859 publication and his subsequent works have laid the foundation for modern evolutionary perspectives.

▲ Natural selection is the result of existing, heritable variation in organisms and the interaction of these organisms with their environment. Over time, some variants become more common in the population due to differential reproductive success because of a better fit with that environment than other variants.

▲ Many people misunderstood the concepts of evolution and natural selection in the past and continue to do so today.

CRITICAL THINKING

1. In what ways does an explanation for existing organic variation like natural selection differ from an explanation like the origin stories in Genesis? Are the two types of explanations always mutually exclusive?

2. Why do you think Darwin's explanation for evolution received such a strong public response when it was published? Why do you think it still does in some areas of the United States today?

3. Was Lamarck's hypothesis that there were "internal fluids" that moved about the body when an organism "willed itself" to change a reasonable scientific conclusion at the time? Why or why not? What basic knowledge do you have that he did not have? Did 18th-century technology and Lamarck's knowledge base limit his ability to construct hypotheses? How?

4. What did you think about evolution before reading this chapter? Had you heard about natural selection? What information presented here is new to you, and why had you not encountered it before? What information is just slightly different from what you already have, and in what ways is it different? What information presented here did you already know, and where did you learn it? Do you think your experience with information about evolution and natural selection is similar to that of your peers? Why or why not?

5. Peoples around the world were able to gain technological information and displayed all sorts of innovation without explicitly using the scientific method for hundreds of thousands of years; how did they do this? What are some methodologies other than science for asking questions about the natural world, and what kind of information can they give us?

RESOURCES

DARWIN'S AND WALLACE'S IDEAS

The Complete Work of Charles Darwin Online: www.darwin-online.org.uk
This site, maintained by Dr. John van Wyhe, is the best site to access Darwin's writings and nearly all available historical records about his life and the development of his ideas.

Darwin, C. *Journal of a naturalist* (originally published 1836); *On the origin of species by means of natural selection* (1859); *The descent of man and selection in relation to sex* (1871).
Any republications of these classics will do. Reading what Darwin had to say and also the manner in which he said it will give you a valuable perspective on his ideas.

Gould, S. J. (1977). *Ever since Darwin: Reflections in natural history.* New York: Norton. This collection of essays on Darwin, Darwin's ideas, and selected issues in evolution is by one of the best science writers of our time.

Gould, S. J. (1987, January). Darwinism defined: The difference between fact and theory. *Discover Magazine.*
This is a concise overview of just what the title indicates.

Grant, P. R. (1999). *The ecology and evolution of Darwin's finches.* Princeton U. Press. Best overview of the full story of Darwin's finches on the Galapagos.

Quammen, D. (1996). *The song of the dodo: Island biogeography in an age of extinctions.* New York: Simon 8 Schuster.
In spite of its daunting subtitle, this book is a fascinating description of current work on natural selection and one of the best accounts of Wallace's contributions.

Weiner, J. (1995). *The beak of the finch: A story of evolution in our time.* New York: Random House.
This is a highly readable account of ongoing research into the evolution of the Galapagos finches.

HISTORY OF DARWINIAN THOUGHT

Greene, J. C. (1959). *The Death of Adam.* Ames, IA: Iowa State University Press. This book gives an overview of the thinkers and events that precipitated Darwin's publications. A must-read for those interested in how our concepts of evolution came to be what they are.

FRAUDS, MYTHS, AND MYSTERIES

Feder, K. L. (2001). *Frauds, myths, and mysteries: Science and psuedoscience in archeology.* New York: McGraw-Hill/Mayfield.

This book provides excellent information on critical thinking and the scientific method. It offers several real-life examples and a highly readable text.

REFERENCES

Lerner, L. S. (2000). Good science, bad science: Teaching evolution in the states. The Thomas B. Fordham Foundation. Retrieved from www.edexcellence.net/library/lerner/gsbsteits.html.

Strier, K. (1984). The myth of the typical primate. *Yearbook of Physical Anthropology, 37,* 233–271.

Strum, S. C., & Fedigan, M. L. (Eds.). (2000). *Primate encounters: Models of science, gender and society.* Chicago: University of Chicago Press.

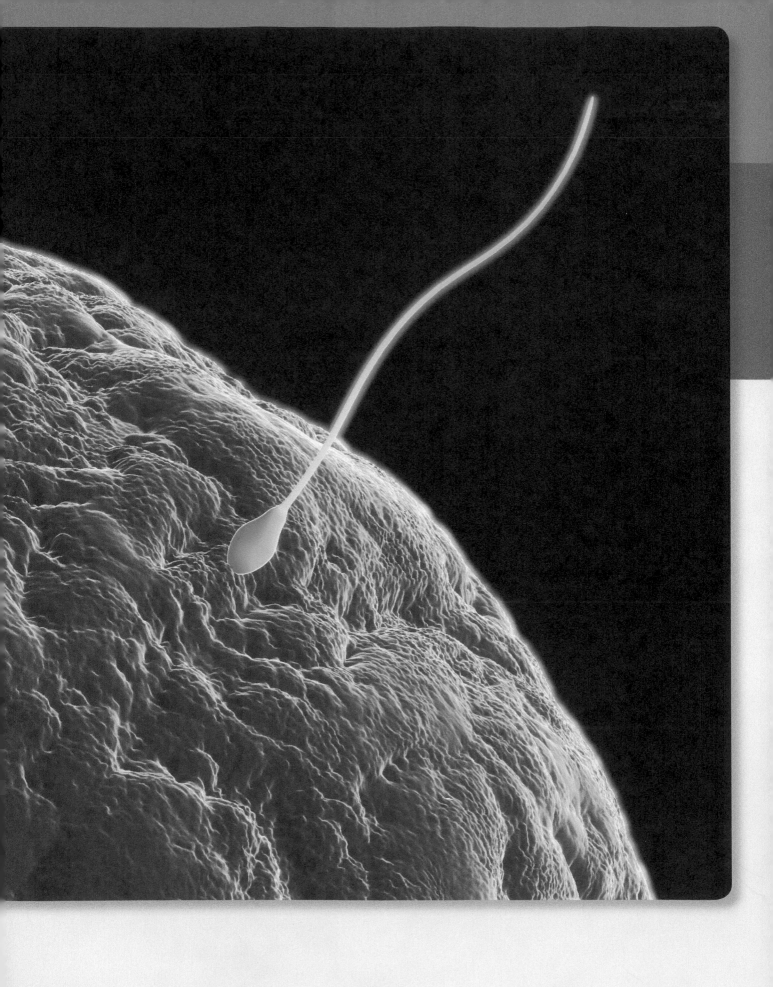

CHAPTER 2

Basics of Human Biology

This chapter addresses the following questions:

▲ How do humans fit within the classification of living things?

▲ What are the basic characteristics of human morphology?

▲ What are the basic physiological systems in the human body?

I n 1999, 56-year-old American sprinter Kathy Jager ran 100 meters in 13.55 seconds and 200 meters in 28.34 seconds at an international masters athletes meet in England, leaving her nearest competitors in the dust (Figure 2.1). But after she won, she was asked to submit to a drug test, and subsequently she was informed that she had tested positive for anabolic steroids, performance-enhancing substances that are banned in track and field. Her times were expunged from the records, her awards were canceled, and she was suspended from competition for 2 years.

Jager, a grandmother of four from Phoenix, Arizona, was not taking anabolic steroids, but she was taking Estratest, a hormone-replacement drug, for menopause-related hot flashes. Estratest contains a small amount of synthetic testosterone, which is what had shown up in the drug test. Despite appeals, Jager was not able to get the decision reversed, but after the suspension period ended, she resumed her competitive running career and began winning medals again.

Why would both athletes and grandmothers be taking anabolic steroids? These substances are a group of synthetic derivatives of testosterone, a primary sex hormone. They cause a rapid gain in muscle size and increased strength, speed, and power. They can help athletes use muscle and bone more efficiently, exert themselves with less effort, and become both more positive, or euphoric, and more aggressive in whatever physical activity they do. Because these substances are seen as conferring an unfair advantage, they are banned in many sports.

■ **FIGURE 2.1**
Kathy Jager. This grandmother races competively.

Testosterone belongs to a group of hormones called androgens, which are produced in the testes in men and in the adrenal glands in both men and women. When menopause begins, women experience a drop in hormone levels that can cause unpleasant symptoms like hot flashes as well as more serious physical problems. Some women, like Jager, take hormone replacement therapy to relieve these symptoms and improve their general sense of well-being.

Despite their benefits, steroids can also have a substantial negative impact on the body. In males, overuse of steroids can lead to reduced ability to produce sperm and engage in sexual behavior, as well as inflammation of the prostate gland. In females, overuse can have a masculinizing effect on the body and a deleterious impact on the menstrual cycle. For both females and males, the use of anabolic steroids can cause fluid retention, liver damage, heart disease, high blood pressure, mood swings, depression, and addiction to the steroids themselves, among other effects.

In short, this single substance, synthetic testosterone, can have a huge range of effects, extending to nearly every system of the body. Taking steroids invokes actions, reactions, and interactions involving the digestive system, the endocrine system, the circulatory system, the skeletal and musculature systems, and the nervous system, among others. The human body is much more than just the sum of its parts, whether we think of those parts as genes, cells, hormones, organs, or internal systems. It is a complex, integrated whole that functions to make us what we are: living organisms. Even a miniscule amount of a substance—especially a substance as powerful as a major hormone—can have unexpectedly broad-ranging effects.

In chapter 1 we covered the history of evolutionary thought and ended with a focus on the theory of evolution via natural selection. We saw that it was the variation in traits, the makeup of the body, that are core to understanding evolutionary processes. From Lamarck to Darwin, evolutionary thinkers realized that the form of the body, the way the body works, and the body's interface with the environment were core parts of the evolutionary process.

In this chapter we focus on the human **phenotype**—the basic systems and traits of the human body—looking especially at morphology (form and structure) and physiology (the functioning of our bodily systems). Because we share many of these systems and traits with other life-forms on the planet, examining them and comparing them with the systems of other forms can help us see evolutionary relationships and better understand how humans came to look and behave as we currently do. In upcoming chapters we will be focusing on bones and other biological facts about ourselves, our ancestors, and our near and distant relatives. A grounding in basic human biology will provide the foundation for a fuller appreciation of all the core concepts in biological anthropology.

The place of human beings in nature

Where Do Humans Fit In?

In order to understand the human form, we must consider ourselves in the context of other living forms, especially the other animals. The placement of humans in the great assemblage of life enables us to see how we share a great deal with some animals and less with others. It gives us a basic starting point to talk about the human body in an evolutionary context.

Because we are mobile, multicellular organisms composed of tissues that derive energy from the consumption of other organisms, we are classified as part of the kingdom **Animalia**. Because we are animals with central nerve cords and backbones, we belong to the phylum Chordata, subphylum Vertebrata; and because we have fur or hair and nurse our young, we are members of the class of vertebrates called **Mammalia**. Our grasping hands, bony, enclosed eye sockets, and relatively large brains place us in the order Primates, infraorder **Simiiformes** (anthropoids). Our ability to swing our arms in a circle, our flat, broad chests, and our lack of a tail place us in the family Hominidae. Finally, our specific anatomy for bipedal walking, our facial

phenotype
observable, measurable characteristics of an organism

Animalia
a class of living things that includes all organisms that are heterotrophs (they eat other organisms to obtain energy)

Mammalia
an order of animals characterized by traits that include, among others, effective internal temperature generation and regulation (including the presence of hair for warmth) and mammary glands (which provide milk to suckle young)

Simiiformes
the infraorder of primates to which humans belong (also called anthropoid primates)

Homo sapiens
the genus and species names for modern humans

CONNECTIONS

Why Do Monkeys Look Like Little People and Our Dogs Understand Us?

Humans are animals; of the animals we are of a type called mammals; and within that group we are in a subgroup called primates. We share a lot of our biology with other living forms and especially with those forms that are also mammals and primates. When you are mad, your dog can sense it because you and your dog share a mammalian limbic system; the biological system that is involved in emotion. When your dog is sad, you can recognize it because you identify the mammalian patterns of behavior and expression that equate to "sad." You are not a dog, but you are a mammal and that allows us to sense the world in some similar ways. With primates there are even more similarities. We think monkeys look like little people because their hands, upper bodies, and faces are very similar to ours. But they do not look like us, they look like primates; and we are primates too. The hands, face, and upper body of monkeys, apes, and people are very similar due to common ancestry. Being humans we anthropomorphize (describe animals in human terms) a lot, but when we do that we make the error of thinking that something is humanlike when actually it turns out that we humans are mammal-like or primate-like because we are mammals and primates.

TABLE 2.1   Taxonomic Classification of Four Animals

Category	Human	Gorilla	Squirrel	Katydid
Kingdom	Animalia	Animalia	Animalia	Animalia
Phylum	Chordata	Chordata	Chordata	Anthropoda
Class	Mammalia	Mammalia	Mammalia	Insecta
Order	Primates	Primates	Rodentia	Orthoptera
Family	Hominidae	Hominidae	Sciuridae	Tettigoniidae
Genus	*Homo*	*Gorilla*	*Sciurus*	*Scudderia*
Species	*sapiens*	*gorilla*	*carolinensis*	*turcata*

Source: *Biology* (6th ed.), by P. Raven and G. Johnson, 2002, New York: McGraw-Hill.

structure, and our large brains place us in the genus *Homo*, species *sapiens*. This is where we fit into the diversity of life on earth (Table 2.1).

How Are Relationships Among Organisms Determined?

How do we know our place in the panoply of life? How do we look at all the organisms on this planet and know how to classify them? How do we try to understand how they relate to one another? The answer to these questions is that, basically, we look at organisms and examine their **morphology** (their inner and outer form and structure) and **phylogeny** (their evolutionary relationships), using a system developed nearly 250 years ago.

As described in chapter 1, the anatomist Carl von Linne (better known by his Latin name, Carolus Linnaeus) developed a method for classifying life on earth back in the 1700s. His system arranged organisms into groups, or taxa, based on similarities in their body structure, or morphology. That is, by comparing the bones of a large number of organisms, he was able to sort the organisms into groups sharing similar shapes and structure. This basic system of classification, combining and segregating organisms according to similarities in morphology, creates a nested hierarchy with seven basic levels: kingdoms, phyla, classes, orders, families, genera, and species. The Linnaean classification method is still the most common system in use today, and it helps us organize the diverse forms of life on this planet.

Linnaeus also developed the system we use to name organisms, as described in chapter 1. Recall that this system is a binomial nomenclature, or two-name naming system. Those organisms that are generally similar in form are grouped into a genus (plural, genera); the genus is the first of the two names in the Linnaean system. For example, dogs, wolves, coyotes, and jackals, very similar animals, all belong to the genus *Canis*. Organisms that share more specific features are grouped into a species, the second of the two names in the Linnaean system: Gray wolves are classified as *Canis lupus*, coyotes as *Canis latrans*, red wolves as *Canis rufus*.

Using the methods established by Linnaeus, scientists can produce a structural classification (called a taxonomy) of all living forms on earth. However, a traditional taxonomy, based on similarities in morphology, provides no information about evolutionary relationships. The dimension of time, the ancestor-descendant relationship, is absent. Taxonomies thus are useful for classification but are not necessarily the best representation of evolutionary relationships. To describe these evolutionary relationships, we use phylogenies.

morphology
the internal and external form and structure of an organism

phylogeny
the evolutionary history of a group of organisms

STOP & THINK

Does this mean that we are not "better" than a squirrel or a katydid?

Phylogenies are constructed using multiple lines of evidence, including both morphology and molecular data (that is, the genetic and biochemical components of the organisms). If we want to establish evolutionary relationships between species based on structural traits, such as facial structures or dental patterns, we examine both modern and fossil forms. Traits or structures shared by all or most species in a group are called **ancestral**. Ancestral features are widespread in a related group of organisms because they were inherited from a common ancestral species. A good example of an ancestral characteristic in mammals is hair.

Characteristics that are unique to a species are called **derived**; they are traits that evolved after the two or more species being compared last shared a common ancestor. An example of a derived characteristic is the pronounced chin in modern humans—it is found in modern humans but not other closely related species. Those features common to some species but not others are called **shared derived** traits. These traits evolved after all the species being compared shared a common ancestor but before some more recent speciation events. An example of a shared derived trait is the larger brains of humans and great apes relative to the brains of the smaller apes (gibbons) and monkeys and are reflective of the closer evolutionary connection between humans and great apes than either has to gibbons or monkeys. Distinguishing among traits that are ancestral, derived, or shared derived allows scientists to establish the evolutionary history of a group of species and consequently their evolutionary relationships (Figure 2.2).

Examining molecular data is a complementary technique used to establish evolutionary relationships and determine the validity of a species or subspecies designation. In this technique, scientists compare the sequences of DNA (discussed in chapter 3) and the mutations, or changes, in those sequences in order to determine ancestral, derived, and shared derived molecular patterns. This approach provides a method independent of morphological comparison for testing hypotheses about the taxonomic status and evolutionary histories of different species.

Morphologies and phylogenies are useful for investigating relationships among organisms across time. If we wish to examine behavior in a similar way, we are limited to living forms for direct comparisons. Behavior and morphology are parts of an animal's phenotype (its observable, measurable traits). When we study the living animals, we realize that certain anatomical structures are associated with specific behavior patterns. For example, the shape of leg and arm bones can tell us whether an animal leaped from one limb to another, swung by the arms, or walked on all four limbs.

With this in mind, following is a review of the human body, in both form and function, to lay a foundation for the subsequent chapters in this book. As we attempt to answer questions about human evolution and biology, we will need to constantly draw on basic understandings of our phenotype and physiological systems.

Human morphology: the body's form and structure

Tissues Cover Us and Bind Us Together

Tissues are what bind the different components of the body together. Two types of **epithelial tissue** cover the surface of our bodies. The stratified epithelium

ancestral trait
characteristic found in an ancestor and all (or most) of its descendants

derived trait
characteristic found only in one descendant branch and not in the ancestral form

shared derived trait
characteristic found in more than one, but not all, descendant forms and not in the common ancestor

epithelial tissue
tissues that cover the surfaces of our bodies

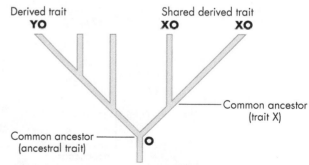

■ FIGURE 2.2
A phylogeny showing three traits. Distinguishing among an ancestral trait (O), a shared derived trait (X), and a derived trait belonging to only one branch of descendants (Y) allows scientists to establish evolutionary relationships.

tissues make up the outer layers of our skin and mouth lining and act as a protective coating for our bodies. The simple epithelium tissues line our blood vessels, glands, stomach, and intestines and act both as a membrane cover and as a permeable transport organ.

Connective tissues create much of the internal cohesion of our bodies. Loose connective tissue is found between organs and under the skin. It acts as insulation and support and even helps keep the skin nourished. Dense connective tissue covers the muscles, organs such as the kidney and liver, and inner layers of the skin. These tissues hold things in place and provide a degree of flexibility. Other connective tissues include cartilage, which provides shock absorption and flexible support in the joints and other places in the body; blood, which forms the basis of the circulatory system and provides nutritional and immune system connections; and bone, which provides rigid support for the muscles and organs.

Muscle tissues are the motors of the body; they are found throughout the organism. There are three types of muscle tissues: smooth muscle, located on the walls of the blood vessels, stomach, and intestines; skeletal muscle, which connects to the skeleton and is responsible for most movement; and cardiac muscle, which powers the contractions of the heart. The last tissue type, nerve tissue, consists of cells called neurons and neuroglia; they make up the main portions of our brain and nervous system. These tissues are very important in understanding the makeup of bodies, but as you will see in chapters 6–9, when studying human evolution we almost never have fossil preservation of tissues. Rather, what we do get is bone.

connective tissue
tissues responsible for the internal cohesion of the body

cranium
set of bones encircling the brain and making up the skull, exclusive of the jaw

■ **FIGURE 2.3**

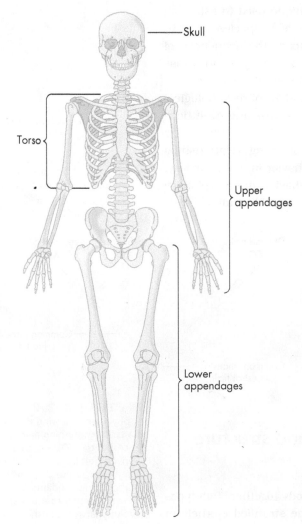

The skeleton: our basic form

From the perspective of understanding human form, function, and evolution, bones are of particular importance. Along with teeth, bones are often the only tissues that fossilize and are thus a primary source of insight into the nature and appearance of organisms that are no longer living. Bones form the stable core to which other tissues attach. The inner framework of bones that supports and gives rigid structure to our bodies is the skeleton. Bones can tell us how an organism walked, what kind of growth patterns it had, what its muscle development looked like, and where it fits in relation to other living forms. In short, the study of bones is one of the central core concepts and skills in biological anthropology.

The human skeleton can be divided into four main regions: the skull, the torso, the upper appendages (arms and hands), and the lower appendages (legs and feet) (Figure 2.3). Because bones are so important in studying human evolution, we look at each group in some detail.

The Skull Is Made Up of Multiple Bones
The skull can be divided into two major regions: the **cranium** (the skull without the jaw) and the mandible (the lower jaw). Many of the bones in the skull have a left-side version and a right-side version.

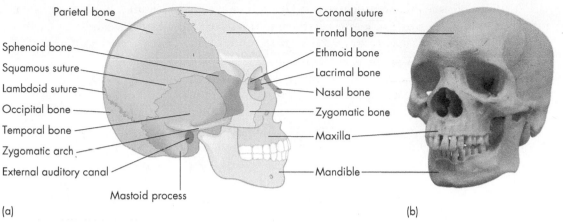

■ FIGURE 2.4
The human skull. The bones of the skull (a) and a modern human skull (b).

The cranium itself is made up of a set of major bones. The frontal bone makes up the forehead, and the two parietal bones create the sides and top of the cranium. Two temporal bones make up the sides of the head around the ears, and the occipital bone creates the back and the base of the skull. The maxillae make up the upper jaw and central face, and the zygomatics (cheekbones) create the sides of the face. The areas where these major bones meet are called sutures; different sutures fuse shut as the bones grow together at different times over the life span. There is also a series of bones that make up the inner portion of the mouth, nose, eye sockets, and ears. The mandible is really two segments that fuse into one bone during the first year of life. On the bottom of the skull is an opening, called the **foramen magnum**, through which the spinal cord passes. The placement of this opening, as we will see in upcoming chapters, is related to the degree to which an animal walks on four legs or two. These basic structures will be very important when we review the human fossil record in chapters 6, 7, 8 & 9. Much of what we have to work with, especially from our earliest ancestors, are primarily small pieces of cranial and mandibular bones. The basic structures of the skull and many of its features are illustrated in Figure 2.4.

Within the mouth are four types of teeth: the incisors, the canines, the premolars, and the molars. If we consider just one quarter of the mouth, from the centerline of the mouth back toward the throat on the top or the bottom, we get a sequence of the total dentition called the **dental formula**. The human dental formula is 2 incisors, 1 canine, 2 premolars, and 3 molars, written 2:1:2:3. Today, many humans have their third molar removed, and in some people it never grows in at all. This molar, sometimes called the "wisdom tooth," is the last tooth to grow in. As a result of changes in the shape of our cranium and mandible, there is less and less room for this tooth. (Possible reasons for such changes in the human cranium and mandible are discussed in chapter 9.) The dentition of adult humans is illustrated in Figure 2.5. Teeth can tell us about diets and the ways in which organisms obtained their food. The relative size of molars, the sharpness and size of the canine, and even the patterns of wear on the incisors will all play roles in helping us determine how our ancestors lived and what key changes occurred throughout our dietary history.

CONNECTIONS

See chapter 6, pages 168–182, chapter 7, pages 189–206, chapter 8, pages 217–245, and chapter 9, pages 259–266, and 272–277, to see how knowledge of basic bone structure helps us to identify our fossil ancestors.

foramen magnum
opening on the bottom of the skull through which the spinal cord passes

dental formula
one quarter of the full complement of teeth, counted from the centerline of the mouth back toward the throat

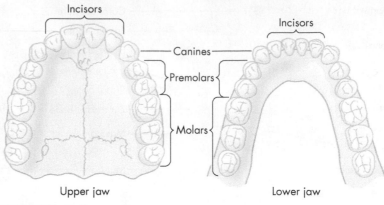

■ FIGURE 2.5

Human dentition. Note that there are four different kinds of teeth.

The Torso Centers Around the Vertebral Column

The central portion of the body is supported by the **vertebral column,** or backbone. In the hollow center of this series of bones sits the spinal cord, which facilitates much of our movement, tactile sensation, and general bodily activity. The vertebral column is made up of a series of 24 individual vertebrae, which are grouped into three types. The cervical vertebrae are the first 7 vertebrae under the cranium, making up the neck. The thoracic vertebrae are the most numerous (12) and run from the base of the neck through to the lower curve of the back. The ribs are attached to the thoracic vertebrae. Finally, the 5 lumbar vertebrae make up the lower curve of the back and attach to the pelvic girdle. In addition to the vertebrae, the vertebral column is also composed of cartilage rings, other connective and nerve tissues, and a series of blood vessels.

There is one other bone in the neck besides the cervical vertebrae, the hyoid. The hyoid bone acts as an attachment for various muscles and ligaments (strong connective tissues) and has the unique characteristic of being the only major bone in the human body that does not attach directly to another bone (Figure 2.6). It has also been implicated in the human ability to produce the complex sounds required for language.

Attached to the thoracic vertebrae is the thorax, or rib cage. The thorax is composed of 12 sets of ribs and a sternum, or breastbone (the bone in the center of the chest). Ribs 1–7 attach both to the thoracic vertebrae in the back and directly to the sternum in the front. Ribs 8–10 are also attached in both front and back, but their attachment to the sternum is via a cartilage bridge and thus indirect. The last two pairs of ribs come out of the lower thoracic verte-brae but do not attach to the sternum and are frequently called "floating" ribs. The rib cage, a "basket" created by bony and cartilaginous tissues, provides strong protection for the internal organs and allows flexibility for breathing.

The shoulder girdle consists of a clavicle (the collar bone) and a scapula, or shoulder

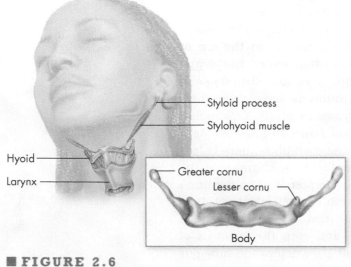

■ FIGURE 2.6

The hyoid bone. This bone is located in our neck.

blade, on each side of the body. These sets of bones attach to approximately 16 muscles and facilitate a wide array of shoulder and arm movements.

The pelvic girdle consists of two mirror-image **os coxae,** or pelvic bones, joined together in the front of the pelvic region; a central sacrum bone that joins the os coxae in the rear; and a coccyx, or tail bone, that makes up the hindmost portion of the sacrum. Both os coxae and the sacrum are really multiple bones fused together (Figure 2.7).

Each os coxae consists of three bones, the ilium, the ischium, and the pubis, that fully fuse together by early adolescence. The large round hollow that makes up the socket of the hip joint is called the acetabulum. Both os coxae fuse in the front at the pubis and in the back to the sacrum, completing the bowl shape of the pelvic girdle. The sacrum is actually four to six sacral vertebrae that fuse into an immobile bone early in life. The coccyx consists of three to five fused segments and is quite variable in size and shape; it is the vestigial tail in humans. It serves as an anchor for some pelvic muscles and ligaments. The pelvic girdle can tell us a good deal not only about how an organism moved but also, for humans, what sex the bones come from. In chapter 10, we will see that important morphological differences between male and female humans can be found in the pelvic girdle.

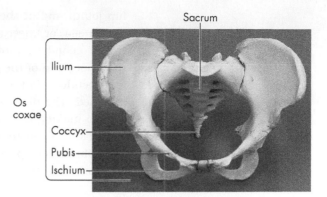

■ FIGURE 2.7
The pelvis. These bones connect the lower and upper body.

os coxae
two sets of three bones each that are fused to the sacrum and make up the pelvic girdle

The Arms and Hands Make Up the Upper Limbs

The upper limbs, or arms, consist of three main bones, the humerus, the radius, and the ulna. The humerus is the bone of the upper arm; it sits with one end in the socket created by the clavicle and scapula (shoulder), and at the other end (elbow), it joins with the ulna and radius. The upper end of the ulna has a U-shaped notch that fits into the lower hollow on the humerus to create an elbow joint that has limited directionality of movement. The ulna loosely connects with a set of bones at the wrist to provide a wider range of flexibility for the hand. The radius is the shortest of the arm bones; it is so named because it moves around the ulna and facilitates a range of twisting or rotating movement in the lower arm. The shape and structure of arm bones help us understand whether organisms used their arm as part of moving around or not, a major difference between humans and other primates.

The hand is a very complex structure consisting of three groups of bones, the carpals, the metacarpals, and the phalanges. There are 27 separate bones in the hand and wrist and a number of very small minor bones inside ligaments in the hand (called sesamoid bones). The carpals are the 8 bones that make up the base of the hand and the wrist. The 5 metacarpals make up the main body of the hand and the base of the fingers, and the 14 phalanges make up the middle and terminal portions of the fingers and thumb. The way the hand bones fit together and the length of the phalanges allow us to figure out what kind of grip an organism had and therefore whether or not it could make tools, a feature that plays a key role in human evolution.

The Legs and Feet Make Up the Lower Limbs

Almost exactly as in the upper limbs, the legs consist of three main bones, the femur (comparable to the humerus), the tibia (comparable to the ulna), and the fibula (comparable to the radius). The femur is the longest single bone in the body. At one end it inserts into the acetabulum of the os coxae (the hip joint), and at the other end it joins the tibia and a separate bone called the patella, or kneecap, to make up the knee joint. The lower end of the femur has two condyles (projecting knobs) that sit on two complementary grooves at the upper end of the tibia. The patella sits in front of this juncture embedded in a tendon that helps keep the two bones (femur and tibia) stable and attached. The tibia bears the majority of the weight in the lower leg. In addition to making up the lower portion of the knee, it combines with the lower end of the fibula to make up the upper portion of the ankle. The small and thin fibula acts primarily as an attachment for ligaments and as a major component in the outside portion of the ankle.

The foot, like the hand, consists of three groups of bones, numbering 26 in all. They are called the tarsals, the metatarsals, and the phalanges. As in the hand, there are also several smaller sesamoid bones in the ligaments of the foot. The 7 tarsals make up the heel, ankle, and first third of the foot. The 5 metatarsals, just like the metacarpals of the hand, make up the central body of the foot and the base of the toes. Finally, the 14 phalanges (also just as in the hand) make up the toes themselves. The major bones of the human skeleton are illustrated in Figure 2.8. Just as with the upper limbs, the legs and feet are critical to our understanding of how we move and how our ancestors moved. As you will see in later chapters, the point at which our ancestors

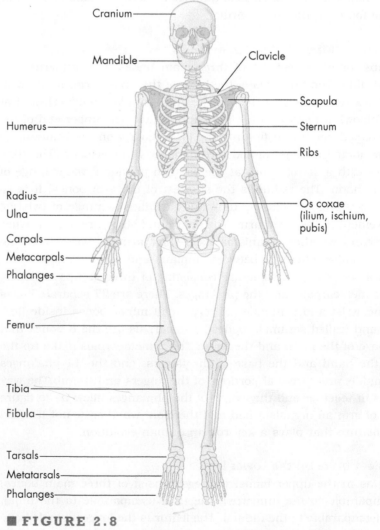

■ FIGURE 2.8
Major bones of the human skeleton. A more detailed look at our anatomy.

My Bones Ache...

Sometimes it feels that way, but do they really? The bones themselves have little in the way of nerve tissues so they can't really ache, but they are part of a very complicated system that is constantly changing, growing, and responding to your lifestyle. Most people tend to think of the skeleton as fixed in growth and shape by adulthood, but this is not true. The bones are alive (as is every other part of you), and their shape changes over their lifetime depending on what you do, what you eat, and how you live your life. Far from being just the internal support for your body, the bones, muscles, tendons, and ligaments are all constantly pushing and pulling on each other, changing shape and density as the patterns and pressures on them change. Playing football, dancing ballet, or sitting in front of the television will cause your bones to change in very different ways. True, your bones stop getting longer by early adulthood, but some bones in your skull continue to change shape and fuse together up through your 80s. The muscles on your neck, arms, and legs pull at and shape the bones they attach to throughout your life. The foods you eat affect the strength and resiliency of your bones, so that if your bones break, they can grow back together and re-shape themselves to work as they are supposed to. Your bones don't ache, but they are dynamic and changing all the time.

shifted from primarily moving on all four limbs to primarily moving on the legs and feet is a major event in human evolutionary history.

The Musculature Interacts with the Skeleton

Nearly all the bones of the skeleton are attached to one or more muscles. These muscles are the primary agents responsible for the movement of the body and its parts. Muscles are generally attached to bones by tendons, and they cause movement by contracting (getting shorter). These contractions can cause both flexion (bending) and extension (straightening). For example, in the human leg, the main flexors (the hamstring muscles) are attached to both the os coxae and femur and to the tibia; when they contract (flex), they pull the leg back. The extensors (the quadriceps) are attached to the femur and patella; when they contract, they straighten (extend) the leg. The knee joint gives pivoting capability to this flexor-extensor set (Figure 2.9). In the leg, most skeletal movement is accomplished by the coordination of multiple muscles attached to bones, which are in turn attached to one another via joints. When biological anthropologists study bones, they are often looking for structural clues to how muscles were attached. As you will see in later chapters, these clues in turn help us figure out how the entire skeleton was constructed and thus how the animal moved.

All Mammals Share Common Skeletal Structures

Although we have focused on the human body to illustrate the basic structure of the skeleton, the same bones are found in all mammals. For example, the bones in our forearm (the radius and ulna, along with the metacarpals, carpals, and phalanges) can be found in all

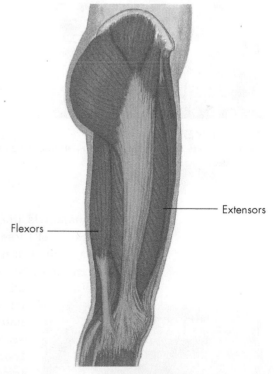

Extensors

Flexors

■ FIGURE 2.9
Flexors and extensors of the thigh.

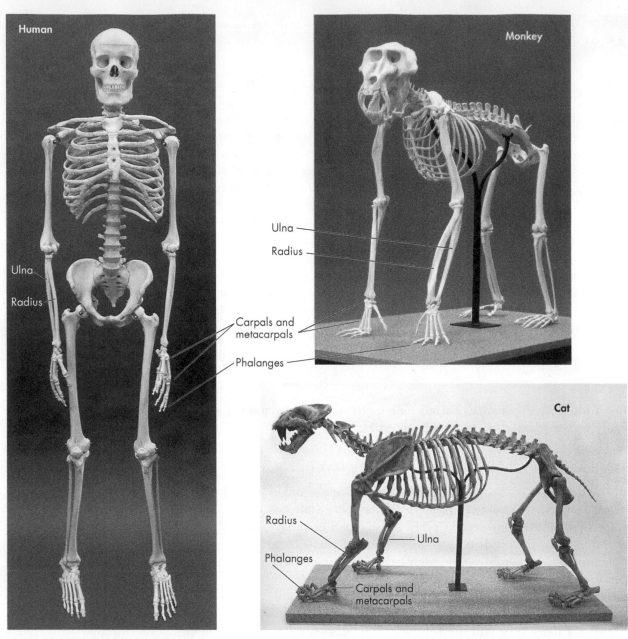

■ FIGURE 2.10

Mammals share the same bones. Compare the skeletons of a human, a monkey, and a cat. What are the major differences and similarities?

mammals (they are ancestral traits), but with modifications (derived traits). Some of these commonalities are illustrated in Figure 2.10. Here we see that a human, a monkey, and a cat all have the same bones, just in slightly different shapes and orientations. The reason for this structural similarity is that all mammals share a common ancestry. Variations in this basic form (the ancestral mammalian skeleton) are the material on which natural selection has acted, producing the wide variety of forms seen in modern mammals. Throughout this book, in the process of trying to understand the selective pressures that have had an impact on our evolutionary history, we will often refer to these basic skeletal structures and the changes that have occurred in them over the millennia.

CONNECTIONS

See chapter 6, pages 165–183, for examples of structural similarities across animals.

Human physiology: the systems of the body

In addition to the structures that provide support and facilitate movement, the body also has a number of systems that keep it functioning. Like bones and muscles, these biological systems are common to all mammals, but variations are seen in different living forms. The major systems that keep our bodies going are the circulatory and respiratory systems, the nervous system and brain, the endocrine system, the digestive system, and the reproductive system.

The Circulatory and Respiratory Systems Transport Nutrients and More

Our bodies require nutrients and oxygen to function. They also need to remove waste products and to defend against infection. The circulatory and respiratory systems work together to meet these needs.

The circulatory system includes the blood, the blood vessels (arteries, capillaries, and veins), and the heart. The blood provides the means of transport for the elements required by the body's tissues for survival (Figure 2.11). It consists of plasma (the fluid of blood); **red blood cells (erythrocytes)**, which assist in respiration; **white blood cells (leukocytes)**, which protect the body from invading elements; and platelets, which help clot the blood when a tear or rupture occurs in the vessels. Humans vary in some of the structures and patterns in red and white blood cells. This variation in what we call blood

red blood cells (erythrocytes) a major component of blood, functioning primarily to transport oxygen

white blood cells (leukocytes) a major component of blood, functioning primarily as part of the immune system

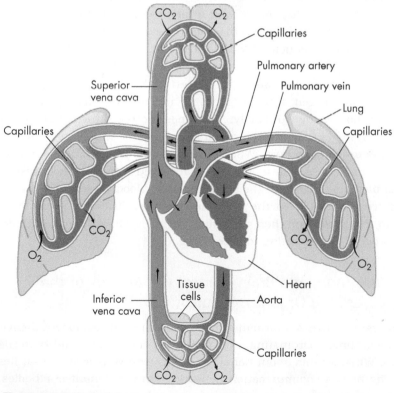

■ FIGURE 2.11
Diagram of the human circulatory and respiratory systems. Blood is pumped from the heart to the lungs. In the lungs, carbon dioxide is eliminated and oxygen is taken in. Oxygenated blood is then carried throughout the body tissues via the arteries. The body cells use the oxygen and give off carbon dioxide, which is carried back to the lungs in the blood.

groups is an important tool in our understanding of human biological variation that we will review in depth in chapter 10. The blood vessels and heart are the structural components of the transport system. The circulatory system has three main functions: transportation, regulation, and protection.

The circulatory system transports oxygen from the lungs throughout the body via the red blood cells and returns carbon dioxide to the lungs from other parts of the body, thus facilitating respiration. The blood vessels also transport the nutrients (resulting from digestion) to the organs and other tissues and cells of the body. The final transport role of the circulatory system is to pick up some of the waste materials from the cells and tissues and take them to the kidneys, where they are filtered out and excreted through the urine.

The circulatory system also assists in regulating hormone function and body temperature. Hormones are taken from the **endocrine glands,** where they are produced, and carried to target tissues in the blood. The circulatory system helps regulate temperature by controlling the flow of blood in the vessels nearest the surface of the skin. When external temperatures are well below body temperature, blood flow is restricted in the vessels closest to the surface so that heat will not diffuse across the skin and leave the body. When external temperatures are high, the vessels nearest the surface of the skin dilate to allow extensive blood flow, thus encouraging heat loss via dissipation through the skin. In this way the circulatory system and the skin work in concert to help humans cope with the stresses of extreme environments.

The final function of the circulatory system, protection, is undertaken mainly by the white blood cells and platelets. There are six types of white blood cells, all of which function to attack foreign elements in the body, such as disease-causing bacteria. They are transported in the blood to sites of infection, where they examine, mark, and attack the invading elements. The white blood cells are the front line of the immune system. The platelets assist in protection by rapidly reducing blood loss via clotting when blood vessels are damaged.

The respiratory system also works in concert with the circulatory system to provide cells with oxygen, a requirement for life, and to remove the waste product carbon dioxide from the body. The lungs are the principal organs of the respiratory system. They are composed of millions of alveoli, small structures where gas exchange occurs. When we inhale, we take a large volume of air into our lungs. The oxygen in the air is absorbed into the blood system across a thin membrane between the alveoli and the blood vessels and carried away by the red blood cells. At the same time, carbon dioxide is excreted by the blood into the alveoli and then pushed out of the system when we exhale. This is the process of respiration, or breathing.

The Nervous System and Brain Control the Actions of the Body and Assess the Organism's Surroundings

The nervous system gathers information about our internal and external environments, integrating, coordinating, and regulating the actions and patterns of our bodies. When we talk about behavior, it is the nervous system that lies at its root. The brain's communication network runs throughout our bodies, enabling humans to engage in a wide range of behavior. As we will see in chapters 6–9, it is the greater size and complexity of human brains that sets us apart from many other organisms on the planet. The nervous system consists of a set of specialized cells called **neurons** and their support cells, called neuroglia. These cells communicate with each other and with other cells and

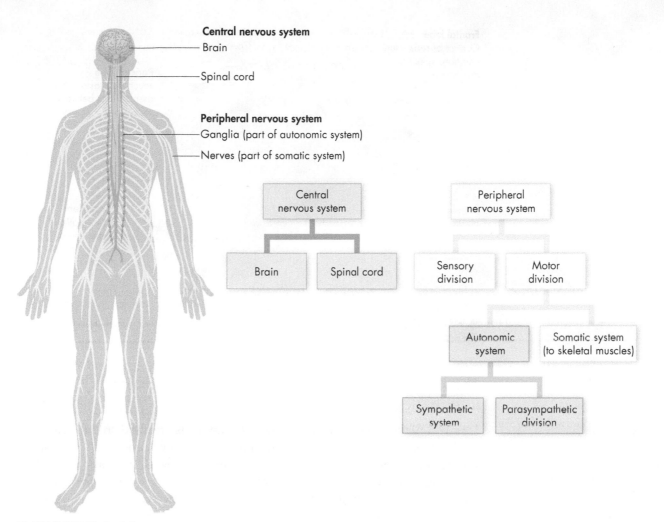

Central nervous system
— Brain

— Spinal cord

Peripheral nervous system
— Ganglia (part of autonomic system)

— Nerves (part of somatic system)

```
Central                    Peripheral
nervous system             nervous system
    |                          |
 ___|___              _____|_____
|       |            |                 |
Brain  Spinal cord   Sensory          Motor
                     division         division
                                         |
                                 _____|_____
                                |                 |
                           Autonomic        Somatic system
                           system           (to skeletal muscles)
                               |
                        _____|_____
                       |               |
                  Sympathetic      Parasympathetic
                  system           division
```

■ **FIGURE 2.12**
The human nervous system. This diagram shows the different subdivisions.

tissues of the body via chemical and electrical signals. The nervous system has two main parts, the central nervous system and the peripheral nervous system (Figure 2.12).

The central nervous system consists of the brain and the spinal cord. The brain is divided into regions, which are further subdivided into multiple areas (Figure 2.13). Each of these areas has specialized tasks and works with other areas for generalized tasks; all act together to control the conscious and unconscious actions of the body. The brain acts as the integration station for everything the body does, from basic automatic functions, to the processing of sensory input, to executive decision making. The spinal cord is the main conduit for connecting the brain with the rest of the nerve cells throughout the body.

The peripheral nervous system consists of millions of neurons and their associated cells, distributed throughout the body, that are responsible for both sensation (sensory neurons) and movement (motor neurons). The motor system is further divided into somatic and autonomic parts. The somatic system includes the neurons that react to conscious control (as when you decide to walk or grasp a pencil); the autonomic system includes the neurons that work without your direct conscious control (as when your heart beats and your lungs breathe, or when you are scared or surprised).

STOP & THINK

What might the relationship between our brain and our mind be? Are they the same thing?

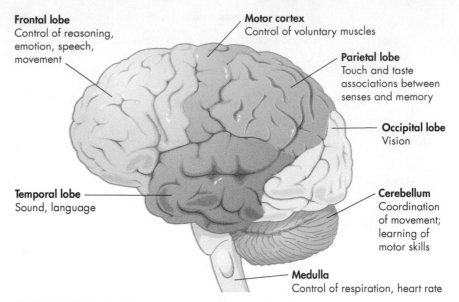

Frontal lobe
Control of reasoning,
emotion, speech,
movement

Motor cortex
Control of voluntary muscles

Parietal lobe
Touch and taste
associations between
senses and memory

Occipital lobe
Vision

Temporal lobe
Sound, language

Cerebellum
Coordination
of movement;
learning of
motor skills

Medulla
Control of respiration, heart rate

■ **FIGURE 2.13**
The human brain. Here you see the seven major areas of the brain.

The Endocrine System Regulates and Communicates Hormonal Information Throughout the Body

Like the nervous system, the endocrine system is involved in the regulation of the organs and functions of the body, primarily through the actions of **hormones.** These chemical agents are secreted by the glands (specialized secreting tissues) and then transported to target tissues and organs to regulate their function (Figure 2.14). Hormones are involved in a wide array of regulatory processes, including stress responses, water absorption and conservation in the kidneys, the development of adult sexual characteristics, preparations for pregnancy, sperm production, the control of calcium levels in bone, and many, many more. The endocrine system is also very much interconnected with the expression and function of behaviors. Our external environment, age, life experiences, and health status all affect the patterns and functions of the endocrine system.

Hormones can be divided into two general categories: steroid hormones and amino acid–derived hormones (amino acids are the naturally occurring building blocks of most structures in the body, as discussed in chapter 3). Steroid hormones are derived from cholesterol and are produced by the testes, ovaries, and adrenal glands. Common steroid hormones are cortisol, progesterone, and testosterone. Some well-known amino acid–derived hormones are insulin, epinephrine (also called adrenaline), and follicle-stimulating hormone (FSH). Some hormones regulate cell and tissue actions by entering the target cells and affecting internal cell functions; others function by binding to the outside of cells and affecting their function by causing chemical changes in the cell. When athletes take steroid hormones, as described at the beginning of this chapter, they are taking extra amounts of hormones already in their system. The extra dose increases the impact of these chemicals and triggers their dangerous side effects.

The endocrine system works together with the nervous system and circulatory system in producing and distributing hormones around the body as we interact with our physical and social environments. For example, in the flight-or-fight response, the hormones testosterone and cortisol work together to

hormones
chemical agents produced in the endocrine glands that cause specific effects on target cells

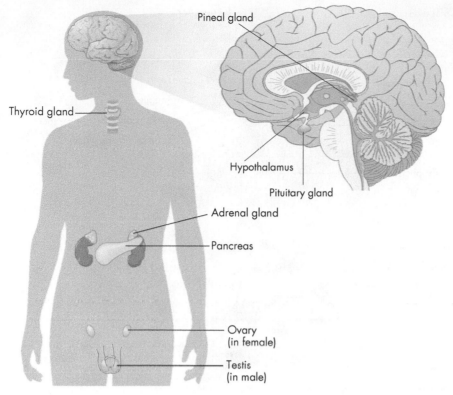

Pineal gland

Thyroid gland

Hypothalamus

Pituitary gland

Adrenal gland

Pancreas

Ovary
(in female)

Testis
(in male)

■ **FIGURE 2.14**

The glands of the human endocrine system. These are responsible for much of the production of hormones.

enable our bodies to react in ways that help us survive. When extreme stress occurs, such as someone attacking us, testosterone floods the circulatory system which helps our muscles and respiratory systems work more efficiently and powerfully. After the immediate threat passes, cortisol levels go up throughout the body which brings the testosterone levels back down. This is important because long-term high levels of testosterone can be damaging to various systems in the body.

The Digestive System Processes Nutrients

Humans obtain energy by consuming other organisms, and the patterns of human diet are a very important component in our attempts to understand human evolution and modern human biological variation. The human digestive system allows us to consume, process, and digest plant and animal matter; the nutrients making up the plants and animals then become available for our use as energy to power our cellular and tissue functions. The human digestive system centers around a processing system that starts at the mouth and ends at the anus (Figure 2.15). The mouth, esophagus, and stomach are the primary processing tools of the digestive system. The salivary secretions (saliva) and the teeth take care of the preliminary processing of food in the mouth. Once the particle size is relatively small, the food is transported through the esophagus to the stomach, where gastric juices (acids secreted by the glands lining the stomach) break it down into even smaller particles that are more readily digestible by the body. The resulting mixture of gastric juices and partially digested food is called *chyme.*

The chyme moves from the stomach into the small intestine, where a suite of chemical and tissue agents break it down further and move the usable

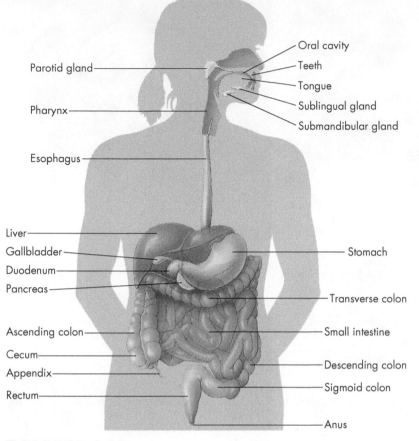

Parotid gland

Pharynx

Esophagus

Liver
Gallbladder
Duodenum
Pancreas

Ascending colon

Cecum

Appendix

Rectum

Oral cavity
Teeth
Tongue
Sublingual gland
Submandibular gland

Stomach

Transverse colon

Small intestine

Descending colon

Sigmoid colon

Anus

■ **FIGURE 2.15**

The human digestive system. All of these parts play a role in the extraction of nutrients from food.

placentals
mammals that have a placenta (the organ that links the circulatory systems of the fetus and mother in the uterus during gestation)

nutrients across the tissue boundaries of the intestine into the bloodstream for transport to the rest of the body. The small intestine is also where the majority of fluids are absorbed into the body. After passing through the small intestine, whatever is left of the chyme moves into the large intestine, where a small amount of fluid absorption takes place but no further digestion occurs. A few minerals and vitamins are absorbed in the large intestine, but the main function of this organ is to store and concentrate the nondigestible material in the food consumed, with the help of numerous bacteria. This compacted, nonusable waste is called feces and is eventually excreted through the rectum and anus.

The Reproductive System Enables Us to Produce Offspring

Reproduction is a critical element in the process of evolutionary change, as we saw in chapter 1 in the discussion of Darwin's and Wallace's ideas about how evolution occurs. As sexually reproducing organisms, human beings have sets of organs specially designed to create gametes (sperm and eggs) and ensure that those gametes come into contact with one another so that fertilization can occur. In mammals, reproduction is internal: The embryo develops and is carried internally by the female of the species. Humans are part of a group of mammals called **placentals**; the placenta is an organ that links the circulatory systems of the fetus and mother in the uterus during gestation, allowing nutrients in the mother's blood to be passed to the fetus and acting as an active endocrine and filtering organ for the developing fetus.

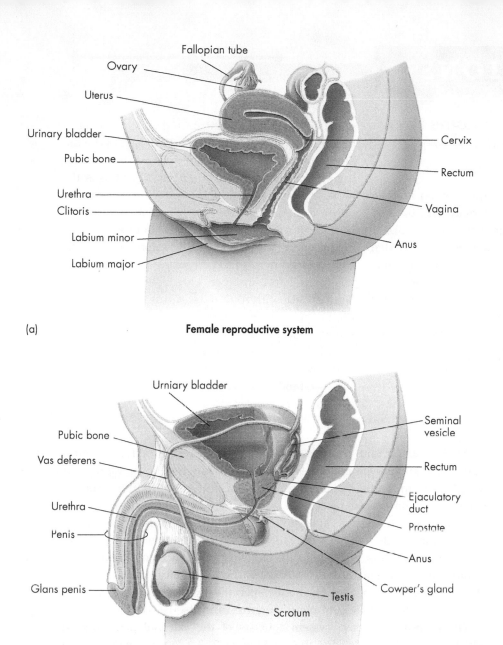

(a)   **Female reproductive system**

(b)   **Male reproductive system**

■ **FIGURE 2.16**
The human female (a) and male (b) reproductive systems. Humans, as do all mammals, have complementary genitalia.

Both female and male reproductive tracts are generated from the same tissue masses early in development (starting at about 6 weeks after fertilization), so they share many structural similarities, although their functions are divergent. The female reproductive system includes the external vagina and clitoris and the internal uterus, ovaries, and fallopian tubes (Figure 2.16). The ovaries are important both for the storage of egg cells (female gametes) and for the production of a wide array of hormones, such as estradiol and progesterone. Eggs are transported to the uterus via the fallopian tubes, which are also the site of fertilization if sperm cells are present. On reaching the uterus, an egg that has been fertilized will be implanted in the uterine wall and begin development. The uterus changes its internal tissue morphology on a regular cycle (usually referred to as the menstrual cycle), which is tied to the timing of egg release and potential fertilization.

Whoa, Where Did That Come From? The Fascinating Development of Human Genitals

Most people think that men and women are two completely different types of person, and that, as a sign of this, male and female genitals are about as different as can be. But this is not correct: Men and women (humans) are all made of the same stuff, even our genitals. We are just different variants on common themes. Until about 6 weeks of age the human fetus has a set of relatively undifferentiated (not male and not female) tissue where the genitals will eventually be. At the 6-week mark, depending on whether the fetus has XX or XY chromosomes, a series of hormone and other chemical signals are distributed to these tissues and they begin to differentiate. One part of the tissues begins to form the clitoris or penis (depending on the chemical cues) and another forms the labia or scrotum. Another area begins to form into either the testes or the ovaries. This means that physiologically, male and female genitals are made of the same stuff and work in more or less the same ways. For example, in sexual response physiology the clitoris and penis are basically the same. Did you know that? Far from our genitals being the badge of difference between men and women, it turns out that they are just another sign that we are all human beings and that while we vary in many ways, we are a lot more alike at the core than we tend to think (see chapter 10).

mammary glands
glands in female mammals that produce a high-fat nutrient, milk, for the offspring

Another important component of the female reproductive system are the **mammary glands.** In mammals, the female can provide a highly nutritious supplement to the newborn infant in the form of milk produced and dispersed via these glands. Most mammals have six or more mammary glands, but in most primates (monkeys, apes, and humans), the number has been reduced to two. Another difference is that the amount of fatty tissue around the glands is larger in humans (resulting in breasts) than in most mammals. The development of breasts at puberty is one of the secondary sexual characteristics that are regulated by hormones secreted by the ovaries. (Human female and male secondary sexual characteristics are discussed in chapter 10.)

The male reproductive system consists of the external penis and scrotum, which contains the testes and the epididymus. The internal vas deferens connects the testes to the seminal vesicles, and the Cowper's and prostate glands are involved in the production and ejaculation of sperm (male gametes). Sperm are produced in the testes, transported across the accessory sex organs, and eventually ejaculated via the penis (see Figure 2.16). Unlike the eggs, sperm are motile (they can move on their own), and once deposited in the vagina they attempt to move up into the female tract and contact an egg. As in females, the male testes (counterpart to the female ovaries) are important in the production of hormones, such as testosterone. Interestingly but not surprisingly, the development and function of the male reproductive tract is heavily regulated by the same hormones that regulate much of the female reproductive function, including follicle-stimulating hormone (FSH) and luteinizing hormone (LH).

CONNECTIONS

See chapter 6, pages 165–166, for more details on the differences between mammals and reptiles that result from lactation.

All of These Systems (and More) Are Interconnected

It should be apparent that all of the systems of the body are integrally related and function together, even though we have discussed them separately in this chapter. In fact, any in-depth understanding of the evolution and function of these systems in humans can come only from an understanding of how they interconnect. For example, when assessing how we derive energy from food by eating, we must examine the following: the structure of the teeth and the muscles of the mouth and jaw; the musculature and chemistry of the throat, stomach, and intestine; the manner in which the circulatory system absorbs the nutrients from the intestine and distributes them throughout the body; and the manner in which the cells in the body then use the energy and return waste products to the circulatory system, which then uses organs to help excrete the waste.

We cannot explore fully such a complex topic in this brief overview; in fact we have not been able to cover many other systems that also play critical roles in the functioning of the body. What you should take away from this discussion is a general idea of the major components in these systems and how they function. With this basic understanding, you will be better able to understand the discussions later in this book of the fossil record, the evolution and patterns of behavior, and even the ways in which modern humans vary biologically.

What We Know
Questions That Remain

What We Know
Humans are animals and share a set of biological characteristics in common with other animals as a result of our evolutionary relationships. We can see our common heritage in the bones and other morphological structures found in all the mammals.

Questions That Remain
Although we know a great deal about our evolutionary history, questions about human traits remain unresolved. We know which of our morphological traits are ancestral, derived, and shared derived, but we know less about the evolution of our behavioral phenotype. Questions remain about what patterns of human behavior are unique to humans (derived), what patterns are common to just humans and apes (shared derived), and what patterns are found across all primates or even mammals (ancestral). Throughout this book we will be examining the data relevant to these questions.

What We Know
The masses of specialized tissues and physiological systems that bind us together interact and interconnect in complex ways to make up the human body.

Questions That Remain
Although we understand the function and makeup of tissues, it is not always clear how the developmental process works, enabling us to develop from a simple fertilized egg to a complex set of tissues and systems. Researchers continue to make significant breakthroughs in our attempts to understand the epigenetic (outside of the DNA) systems that facilitate the healthy growth and functioning of human beings.

What We Know
All of our physiological systems are integrated to provide support, nutrition, regulation, and coordination for our every movement, breath, and behavior.

Questions That Remain
We don't know how advancing medical technologies will help, hinder, or change the ways our physiological systems work. For example, when the use of such pharmaceutical products as steroids or painkillers is long term, we don't know what their impact on our bodies will be. Questions like these, once the stuff of science fiction, are becoming more and more relevant to our daily lives.

SUMMARY

▲ Humans are members of the kingdom Animalia, the phylum Chordata, the class Mammalia, the order Primates, the family Hominidae, the genus *Homo*, and the species *sapiens*.

▲ Constructing phylogenies by comparing morphology and molecular data helps us understand the evolutionary relationships among organisms.

▲ As living organisms, humans are made up of cells and tissues. Epithelial tissue covers the surface of the body, and connective tissue creates internal cohesion.

▲ The skeleton is the basic support structure for the body and acts as the anchor for the muscles and other organs.

▲ The circulatory and respiratory systems ensure that oxygen, nutrients, and immune system agents are able to move around the body and function effectively.

▲ The nervous system and the brain are composed of neurons and neuroglia that act to gather information and coordinate and regulate the actions and patterns of the body.

▲ The endocrine system consists of glands and hormone products that use the circulatory system to reach their target organs and tissues. This system helps regulate the functions of the body.

▲ The digestive system allows us to process and absorb nutrients required by cells for functioning.

▲ The functions of the reproductive system include the production of gametes, the provision of triggers for the appearance of secondary sexual characteristics, and the propagation of life.

▲ All of these systems are interconnected and integrated in the functioning human being.

CRITICAL THINKING

1. What is the benefit of a binomial naming system? How does our understanding of the relationships among organisms in the natural world benefit from using the Linnaean system? Why do all mammals share similar skeletal structures?

2. How might the kind of food we eat affect how our digestive system functions? Can the foods we eat affect our circulatory and endocrine systems as well? How might the processing/treatment of foods or food animals affect our physiologies?

3. If steroids improve athletic performance and they occur naturally in our bodies, why is taking them any different from taking vitamin pills or other nutritional supplements? Consider the different roles that nutrients and hormones have in the human body and the systems they travel through.

4. If both male and female reproductive tracts come from the same tissue, are males and females as different as is generally portrayed in our culture? Biologically, what are the differences between males and females? Are they the same as cultural differences?

RESOURCES

THE HUMAN BODY

Kapit, W., & Elson, L. M. (2001). *The anatomy coloring book* (3rd ed.). San Francisco: Benjamin/Cummings; Kapit, W., Macey, R., & Meisami, E. (2000). *The physiology coloring book* (2nd ed.). San Francisco: Benjamin/Cummings; Zihlman, A. (2001). *The human evolution coloring book* (2nd ed.). New York: Harper Resource.
All three of these books are informative and enjoyable overviews of human biology. Although they are called coloring books, they are written for adults and clearly illustrate the basics of human biological systems.

White, T. D., & Folkens, P. A. (2000). *Human osteology* (2nd ed.). New York: Academic Press.
This offers a thorough discussion of our bone structure.

THE HUMAN BODY ON THE WEB

www.csuchico.edu/anth/Module/skull.html This site has an overview of the human skull and its component bones. You can see each individual bone in a 360-degree rotation as well as how the bones fit together in the skull.

www.med.harvard.edu/AANLIB/home.html This site, entitled the Whole Brain Atlas, has excellent imagery and information from Harvard and MIT researchers on the structure and function of the human brain.

www.palaeos.com/Systematics/systematics.htm This site has an excellent overview of systematics, links to evolutionary history and application sites, and a very coherent review and discussion of taxonomy.

www.ptcentral.com/muscles This site has an excellent text overview of all the human muscles and how and where they attach to bones.

www.ptcentral.com/radiology This site has a series of radiographs (X-rays) of parts of the human skeleton and examples of common pathologies (problems/injuries).

CHAPTER 3

Introduction to Genetics and Genomics

This chapter addresses these questions:

▲ What is heredity, and how is information passed from generation to generation?

▲ What is the structure of DNA, and what are its functions?

▲ How did Mendel's studies explain heredity? How have we improved on Mendel's original understandings?

▲ What is the relationship between genes and behavior?

▲ What is a gene pool, and why do we look at the genetics of populations to understand evolution?

Imagine having a really tasty meal with perfect flavors. You'd like to have one like it again in the future, right? What if the beef industry, or any animal food industry, could guarantee that same taste with each bite, even from different animals? Is this possible? On April 22, 2002, scientists at the University of Georgia and researchers from the biotech company Prolina announced the birth of a calf that had been cloned from a side of beef. Actually, the calf was "made" from a kidney cell taken 48 hours after the animal was slaughtered. The DNA in the kidney cell was manipulated to make the cell begin developing as if it were a fertilized egg; the cell was then implanted in a cow, which subsequently gave birth to the calf.

Can we really raise the dead by cloning? Not quite. The clones don't usually turn out exactly like the original, and multiple cloning of mammals (repeated cloning of the same line) usually fails. In this case, the plan was to use the cloned calf as a breeder in an attempt to produce cattle similar to itself, but none of the animals was expected to be an exact replica of the original. Today it is possible to take cells from an organism, even a recently deceased organism, and manipulate the process of cell reproduction and cell growth such that we get an embryo that develops—some of the time—into a healthy organism.

In 1996 Dolly the sheep became famous as the first successfully cloned mammal, and since then, a diverse array of mammals, including monkeys, has been cloned. Today there are many cloned animals on farms around the United States, although their meat and milk products are not yet available to consumers. There are even a few research firms (outside the United States) that are reportedly engaged in the cloning of human beings. In fact, in January 2003, one such company, Clonaid, reported the birth of at least one cloned baby girl (although to this date there is no concrete evidence they succeeded). The discussion and controversy surrounding cloning research have become explosive. Recently, the U.S. Congress and the Parliament of the European Union have initiated bans on human cloning in their respective jurisdictions.

In addition to the cloning research, experimentation with embryonic stem cells (cells that are not yet "earmarked" to become specialized parts of your body) has led to significant changes in the way we see the biology of development, cell function, and growth. All of these developments are possible because of our greatly increased knowledge of the inner workings of the cells—more specifically, the processes and patterns associated with DNA. We call this field of knowledge genetics and genomics. The term **genetics** is traditionally used to refer to the basic structure and processes of the DNA and its related machinery; the term **genomics** refers to the emerging study of the increasingly complex interactions that characterize the function and behavior of DNA and all of its associated molecules and chemical patterns.

The **human genome** is the name for the myriad DNA sequences that make up all the DNA common to our species. The Human Genome Project (HGP), a multinational collaboration, recently finished mapping the general sequence of human DNA. We already have full maps of the DNA of many other animals, including mosquitoes, and plants, including rice. It has been just over 50 years since the shape and structure of DNA were determined and only about a century since the term *gene* was introduced. Today we have a vast, yet still incomplete, body of knowledge about the interactions of the DNA, cells, and organisms. We know that DNA is found in nearly all forms of life and that it works in the same manner in each of them. We know that DNA contains information crucial to life and that it plays a prominent role in heredity. We also know that most clones that are produced do not survive, but we are not sure why. No two clones are exactly alike as adults, even though their DNA is identical. Despite our knowledge about genetic systems, there is still a great frontier to explore.

In chapter 1 we discussed the history of evolutionary thought and the concept of natural selection, or Darwinian evolution. In this chapter we discuss the mechanism of evolution, information that Darwin and Wallace did not have—information that changes some of our ideas about evolution and allows us to have much greater insight into how organisms function. From chapter 1 we understand that organisms change over great periods of time by adapting to environmental pressures. In chapter 2 we reviewed the anatomy and major physiological systems of the human body. We know that the human organism is characterized by a complex set of biological systems that are all fairly consistent from one individual to the next and from one generation to the next. Finally, we know that we can create copies of an individual by cloning its cells. These understandings present us with two very important questions: First, exactly how do biological organisms undergo change over time? And second, how do they remain relatively constant from one generation to the next?

These two seemingly contradictory questions can be answered, at least partially, by reference to the same thing: the genetic/genomic system. We focus on the first question a bit in this chapter but delve into it more deeply in chapter 4. Most of this chapter is devoted to answering the second question and to gaining a small understanding of one of the most wondrous systems on the planet.

Heredity is the passing of genetic information from generation to generation

Humans have long been able to see that from generation to generation organisms remain relatively the same. That is, babies tend to grow up looking more or less like their parents, or at least like others in their population. Throughout history people have come up with many explanations for how this process

---

genetics
study of the basic structure and processes of DNA

genomics
study of DNA including all associated molecules, chemicals, and evolutionary patterns

human genome
all the DNA in the human species

■ FIGURE 3.1

Heredity explains why the members of this family resemble each other. Can you tell which people are the offspring of the elderly man and woman?

works. Most of the explanations revolve around the notion of **heredity** (the passing of biological information from generation to generation), the idea that organisms pass on some factor(s) to their offspring such that the offspring resemble the parents in many ways (see Figure 3.1). People assumed that these factors, or units, contained some sort of instructions or preformed matter that would unfold, in utero, into a fetus, then develop into a baby and proceed to grow after birth into an adult.

By the late 1800s and early 1900s, many different terms were being used to describe these units of heredity. Charles Darwin hypothesized about units

heredity
the passing of biological information from generation to generation

CONNECTIONS

"Gene"—What Is in a Word?

We tend to think that if something is genetic (gene-based) then it is a core part of our nature; the blueprints for our being. The word "gene" has come to reflect the most basic biological aspect of human nature, but really it is merely a term describing a stretch of DNA that does something. Originally called "pangens" and later shortened to "genes", the word really just indicates a unit of heredity. Researchers in the late 1800s and early 1900s knew that some sort of unit passed from generation to generation, but it

was not until the 1950s that DNA and genes were truly visualized for the first time. Today we know that the DNA is amazingly complicated and that heredity and what makes us human is much more than pieces of DNA. So, why is this word so powerful? Popular science reporting and popular ideas frequently associate genes with very specific effects and powers (a gene for cancer or alcoholism), thus giving us the impression that a gene can directly produce massive effects. Reality is much more complex (as you will see in this chapter). We are much more than a collection of genes.

called "gemmules"; zoologist August Weismann called them "determinants"; biologist Hugo de Vries called them "pangens"; and a little-known Augustinian monk named Gregor Mendel (whose work we will discuss in more detail later in the chapter) called them "alellomorphs." These units were assumed to be in the gametes, or sex cells, and to combine in some manner to form the zygote. In 1906, Wilhelm Johannsen coined the term *gene*, which he described as "nothing but a very applicable little word, easily combined with others, and hence, it may be useful as an expression for the 'unit factors,' 'elements,' or 'allelomorphs' in the gametes." Johannsen meant this term as a placeholder or marker that would be used as a common term for the discussion of heredity (Fox-Keller, 2000). How did the word *gene* change from a placeholder to the powerful term in use today? To understand what a gene is and what it is not, we need to look first at the molecules of inheritance, the DNA.

DNA is the molecule of heredity

deoxyribonucleic acid (DNA) the chemical compound, found in most living organisms, that contains basic information for the structure of life

The vast majority of organisms on this planet have **deoxyribonucleic acid (DNA)** as a core part of their biological system. DNA plays a critical role in the structure and function of nearly everything that happens inside an organism and is especially important in heredity. In biological anthropology we are interested in the human organism from biological and cultural perspectives. So to understand any aspect of this field, we need to have an idea of how the DNA works in us and in any other living organism.

CONNECTIONS

See chapter 7, pages 191–194, and 9, pages 284–290, for how this structure lets us compare relative evolutionary relationships among us, chimpanzees, and Neanderthals.

DNA is Found in Cells

All animals are made up of one or more cells. Complex vertebrate mammals are made up of millions of cells of many different kinds that all interact at different levels to produce the living, breathing organism. Although there are many cell types, most cells found in animals have a similar structure. A membrane surrounds the cell

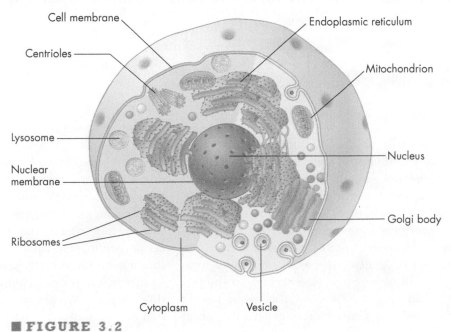

■ FIGURE 3.2
An animal cell. This basic structure is found in all animals.

and separates its inner contents from the other cells and elements around it. This membrane is very permeable, and many cell functions consist of molecules and gasses moving back and forth across the cell membrane boundary. Within the cell is a group of structures called organelles (the machinery of the cell), which sit in a semiliquid matrix called the cytoplasm. Of special importance is the nucleus of the cell, which contains all of the organism's DNA. Figure 3.2 shows a cross-section of an animal cell with many of its structures identified.

DNA Has a Specific Structure

A significant part of what DNA does is related to its physical and chemical structure. James Watson and Francis Crick successfully described the structure of DNA in 1953. We know that in its most basic form, the DNA molecule is a double helix. Figure 3.3 shows a DNA molecule and its double helix structure, in both its "twisted" and its "untwisted" (ladderlike) form. The double helix structure allows the DNA molecule to be easily opened and closed.

Chemically, DNA is composed of three major units: **nucleotide bases,** sugars, and phosphates. A series of sugars and phosphates make up the backbone of the "ladder," and two nucleotide bases make up each rung. Like the double helix structure, this chemical structure facilitates the opening and closing of the DNA molecule. The chemical bonds between the sugars and phosphates are fairly rigid, but the hydrogen bonds between the nucleotide bases (making up the rungs) are easier to open. Once the bonds are opened, however, the two nucleotides seek each other out to rebond. This is because of the complementary nature of the nucleotides. There are four nucleotide bases—adenine (A), cytosine (C), guanine (G), and thymine (T)—and each has a specific affinity to one of the other bases. That is, adenine (A) and thymine (T) seek each other out chemically, as do cytosine (C) and guanine (G). The rungs of the ladder of DNA are always composed of an A-T or C-G pair. The chemical bond between the two parts of each rung can be opened and closed many times.

Although we talk about DNA as ladderlike, it almost never actually appears in this easily observed (and discussed) uncoiled form. Most of the time, DNA is tightly bound up by a group of proteins and condensed into **chromosomes,** supercoiled masses of DNA found in the nucleus of your cells. The multiple levels of coiling and condensation by which DNA is wound onto chromosomes are shown in Figure 3.4. Human DNA is grouped onto 46 chromosomes, represented as 23 pairs of chromosomes (see Figure 3.5). A cell with the 23 pairs (46 chromosomes) is called a **diploid** cell. Each person has two copies of chromosomes 1 through 22, and one from the mother and one from the father. Chromosomes 1 through 22 are called *autosomes,* and each pair has the same structure. Chromosome 23 is the pair of sex chromosomes and comes in two forms: an X and a Y. If you receive an X from your mother and an X from your father, your sex is female. If you have an X from your mother and a Y from your father, your sex is male. We will review sex differences and similarities in greater detail in chapter 10.

In our bodies there are two different types of DNA. As we have just noted, the DNA discussed here, and that we will focus on in this chapter, is found in the nucleus of the cells in the body. Additionally, all humans have mitochondria in their cells (small energy-producing organelles). Each mitochondrion has a set

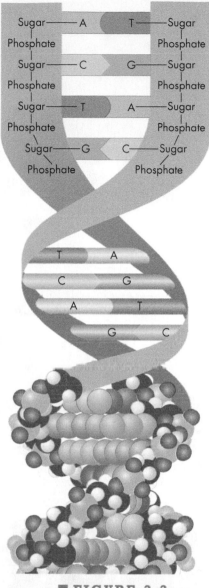

■ FIGURE 3.3
The DNA molecule. This figure shows the molecule with its sugar-phosphate backbone (bottom), as a double helix (center), and uncoiled, showing its paired bases (top).

nucleotide bases
the four chemical bases that make up the core portion of DNA (adenine, cytosine, guanine, and thymine)

chromosomes
complex structures that house the supercoiled DNA in the nucleus

diploid
having 46 chromosomes, arranged in 23 pairs

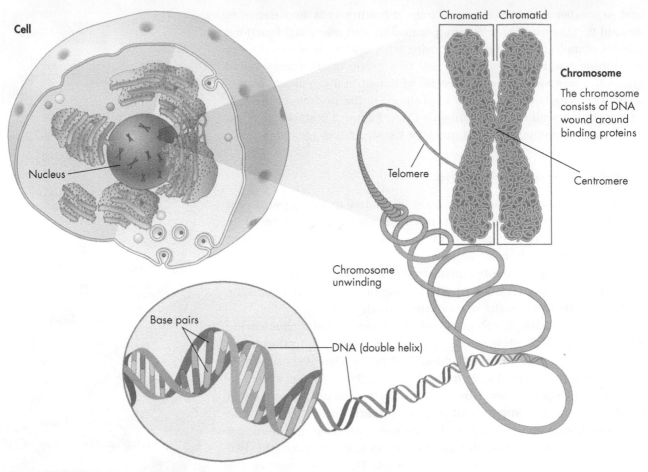

Cell

Chromatid   Chromatid

Chromosome

The chromosome consists of DNA wound around binding proteins

Nucleus

Telomere

Centromere

Chromosome unwinding

Base pairs

DNA (double helix)

■ **FIGURE 3.4**

The human chromosome. Chromosomes are supercoiled masses of DNA found in the nuclei of cells.

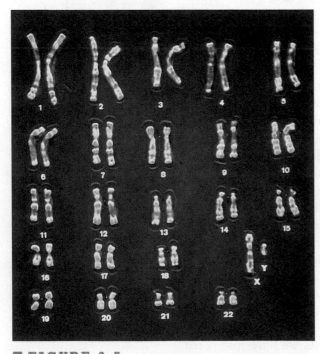

■ **FIGURE 3.5**

Image of the 23 pairs of chromosomes found in human cells. This set of chromosomes comes from a man. Note the different sizes of the X and Y chromosomes.

of DNA as well. We call this mtDNA. This mtDNA is much shorter than nuclear DNA and is inherited solely from the mother, because mitochondria are found in the egg cell and not in the sperm. So in the human body we have two sets of DNA, one in the nucleus that is a combination of both parents' nuclear DNA, and another in the mitochondria that is exclusively inherited from the mother.

DNA Has Three Main Functions

DNA is a core component in the activity of cells. We typically talk about DNA "doing" a few very important things; however, it never does anything by itself. To function, DNA requires the presence of a number of enzymes, structural proteins, and other chemical actors. All of this equipment is found inside the nucleus and throughout the cell. Even at the very first stages of life, when an egg and sperm combine to produce a zygote, all of this machinery is already in place, provided by the maternal contribution (the egg).

DNA has three main functions: *replication* (making copies of itself), *protein synthesis* (helping in the creation of the molecules that make up organisms), and *regulation* (regulating itself in the first two functions).

Replication

The ability of DNA to copy itself, known as **replication**, is based on its physical and chemical structure. The physical structure, the double helix, allows it to unwind into the ladderlike shape. Then, because the bonds between the nucleotide bases are more easily broken than the sugar-phosphate back-bone, the ladder can be made to open. The sequence of DNA replication is shown in Figure 3.6. The unwinding is accomplished with the assistance of a variety of nuclear enzymes that respond to specific chemical cues. These enzymes, mainly a group called ˙DNA helicases, provide the chemical and structural elements to begin and maintain the unwinding process.

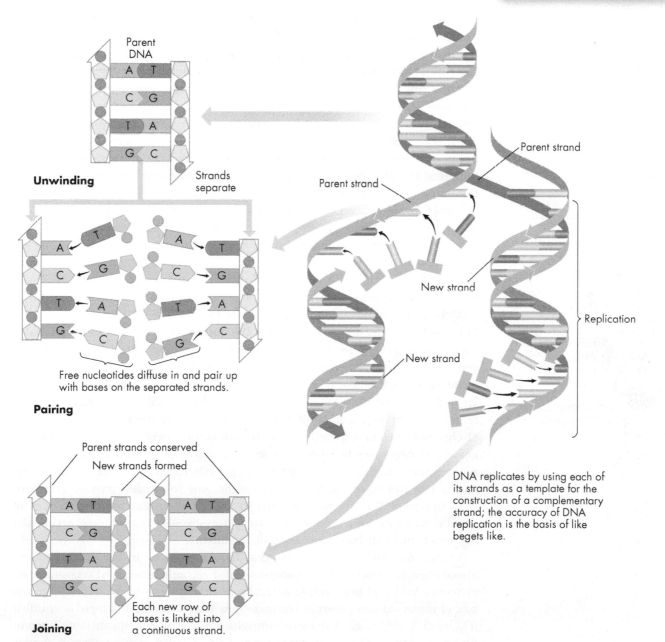

DNA replicates by using each of its strands as a template for the construction of a complementary strand; the accuracy of DNA replication is the basis of like begets like.

■ **FIGURE 3.6**

Replication of the DNA molecule. The strands unwind, and each base pairs up with its complement. Finally, each new row of bases is linked into a continuous strand.

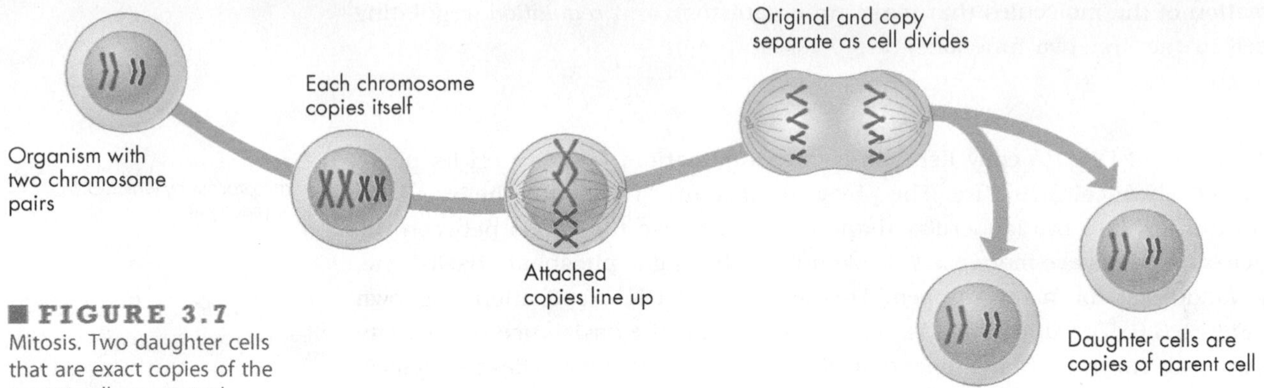

■ FIGURE 3.7
Mitosis. Two daughter cells that are exact copies of the parent cell are created.

Organism with two chromosome pairs

Each chromosome copies itself

Attached copies line up

Original and copy separate as cell divides

Daughter cells are copies of parent cell

mitosis
the process of cell division and replication

meiosis
the production of gametes (haploid cells)

haploid
having 23 single chromosomes, half the genetic complement; found in gametes

recombination
shuffling of maternal and paternal chromosomes during meiosis

Also present in the nucleus are unattached nucleotide bases and sugar and phosphate molecules. Once the ladder is opened, the chemical signature of the bases proves to be a strong allure for complementary bases. That is, if a thymine is exposed, an adenine is drawn to it. Along with the adenine come a sugar and a phosphate (see Figure 3.6). The process of pairing bases is repeated along the entire length of both sides of the opened ladder with the assistance of a specific set of enzymes. These enzymes, primarily DNA ligase, polymerase, and primase, facilitate the connection between the nucleotide bases and the sugar and phosphate groups by pulling them together and initiating the chemical bonds between them. Once this process is complete, the entire length of DNA has been copied.

This copying of the DNA is required for two major functions of cells: mitosis and meiosis. **Mitosis** is the creation of two cells from one cell (Figure 3.7). This is the process by which our bodies grow and heal themselves and by which a single cell becomes an organism consisting of billions of cells. Every day you lose a number of cells to cell death, injury, and other causes. Those cells need to be replaced constantly; mitosis allows replacement to occur.

Meiosis is similar to mitosis but occurs in only one set of specialized cells. These cells are the ones that produce the gametes (sperm and eggs). In males this process goes on for most of the life span. In females the entire process is complete before birth (that is, all of the egg cells have been prepared and set aside for storage before a female baby leaves the womb). The process is similar to mitosis but includes some extra steps (Figure 3.8). These extra steps are required to produce a **haploid** cell (a cell with half of the normal complement of chromosomes and therefore half the full complement of DNA). The haploid gamete is necessary because in a sexually reproducing species, each parent must contribute one copy of her or his genetic material so the resulting offspring has two copies of each chromosome, one from each parent. This process underlies the diversity we see in the combination and expression of genetic elements and explains the fact that sexually reproducing organisms are much more diverse than asexual organisms.

During meiosis, structural changes frequently occur in the chromosomes. These changes, produced by processes called recombination and crossing over, introduce variation into each individual's genetic system. In **recombination**, the mix of maternal and paternal chromosomes that occur in a gamete is shuffled (Figure 3.9). Although it does not introduce any new genetic variants, recombination ensures that each gamete will have a novel combination of genetic material from its parents. This happens because even though homologous chromosomes (the same chromosomes; that is, chromosome 1 from the mother and

Chromosomes copy
themselves and line up
as in mitosis

Pairs
segregate

Each sex cell has half
the normal number of
chromosomes

■ **FIGURE 3.8**
Meiosis. Four daughter cells,
each with half the normal
number of chromosomes, are
created.

chromosome 1 from the father) have the same kind of genetic information, they each are slightly different in certain details. These details, when shuffled and put together in new ways, give us unique sequences of existing genetic information. Recombination helps to explain why every offspring from the same parents is different and why every human being is unique. **Crossing over** occurs when homologous chromosomes exchange segments as a result of their extreme structural and chemical similarity (see Figure 3.8). By actually mixing the

crossing over
homologous, or sister, chromosomes exchange segments

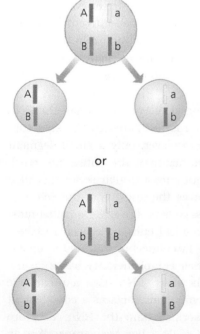

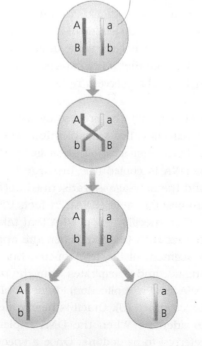

■ **FIGURE 3.9**
Recombination and crossing over. In recombination, the chromosomes can pair up in two different ways, resulting in four possible combinations of alleles. In crossing over, genes located on the same chromosome are inherited as a unit.

or

Recombination: Here offspring
can get four different combinations
of maternal and paternal chromosomes

Crossing over: Here you can see
the chromosome a–b has changed to
have the new genetic combination of a–B.

sequences of genetic material on chromosomes, crossing over shuffles DNA segments in new ways (switching segments of maternal and paternal DNA), thus increasing the existing genetic variation on the chromosomes. This shuffling of DNA segments is quite important in how the genetic units of heredity and their resulting traits are related, as we will see later in this chapter.

Protein Synthesis

proteins
building blocks of organic life

protein synthesis
the process by which the nucle-otide "message" is taken from a gene, transcribed, and trans-lated into a protein

amino acids
building blocks of proteins

polypeptide
a string of amino acids that folds in on itself and becomes a protein

triplet
three-nucleotide sequence in which the DNA's code is written

transcription
copying the DNA message to RNA

ribonucleic acid (RNA)
a molecule similar to DNA that is responsible for taking the mes-sage from the DNA in the nu-cleus of a cell to the ribosome in the cytoplasm and facilitating translation into a protein

messenger RNA (mRNA)
the form of RNA that takes the transcribed DNA message to the ribosome

codon
a three-nucleotide sequence in which the DNA's triplet code is written onto the mRNA

Proteins are the building blocks for the organic structures that make up your body, and **protein synthesis** is the process by which they are produced. As we saw in chapter 2, these structures range from bones to skin to organ systems to endocrine hormones. Proteins are the main pieces that make up all of our body's systems. There are structural proteins, catalytic proteins, transport proteins, and many other types. A protein is a folded string of naturally occurring compounds called **amino acids**. The string of amino acids by itself is called a **polypeptide**. To become a protein, the polypeptide under-goes a series of folding and shape changes (depending on the specific amino acids that make it up) and subsequently acquires a specific chemical signa-ture. DNA contains the "code" for the sequence of amino acids that form the polypeptide that serves as the basis for a protein. The process of protein synthesis has many steps, and we can use the metaphor of language to explain it. First, the code is copied ("transcribed") inside the nucleus. Then, the transcribed code is carried from the nucleus to the cytoplasm and trans-lated into a string of amino acids. Finally, the string of amino acids (the polypep-tide) undergoes folding and becomes a protein.

The Code The portion of DNA that contains a code, or basic assembly instruc-tions, for proteins is written in a specific language. This language consists of words that are three nucleotide bases long, called **triplets**. Table 3.1 shows the DNA triplet/amino acid dictionary. The three base sequences are read by machinery in the cytoplasm of the cell as meaning a certain amino acid. As you can see from the DNA dictionary in Table 3.1, many triplets are translated as the same amino acid. Because there are 64 possible three-letter combinations of the four nucleotides (4^3) but only 20 amino acids, several different combina-tions represent the same amino acid. Thus, redundancy is built into the genetic code. Note that a few triplets (ATT, ATC, ACT) do not translate as an amino acid; instead, they serve a regulatory, start-and-stop function during transcription.

Transcription The process by which the meaning of the message from the DNA is read is called **transcription**. The transcription is facilitated by the structure of DNA, just as replication is. In this process, however, only a small segment of DNA is copied (the message for a protein rather than the entire molecule), and the message is transcribed not onto DNA but onto a similar molecule called **ribonucleic acid (RNA)**. In fact, DNA never leaves the nucleus of the cell.

The specific type of RNA that takes the message from the DNA is called **mes-senger RNA (mRNA)**. When the appropriate chemical cues have been received, a segment of the DNA opens. Enzymes assist in connecting nucleotide bases, sugars, and phosphates from the nucleus to their complementary bases on the DNA (as in replication). Instead of thymine, however, RNA uses a nucleotide called uracil (U). Uracil is nearly identical to thymine and acts as a complement to adenine. When the DNA triplets are transcribed onto the RNA, they are referred to as **codons**. Once a specific segment of DNA has been transcribed to the mRNA (via the nucleotide complementary matching process), the mRNA seg-ment is clipped off and leaves the nucleus of the cell. When the mRNA leaves,

TABLE 3.1

Amino Acid	DNA Triplets	RNA Codons
Alanine	CGA, CGG, CGT, CGC	GCU, GCC, GCA, GCG
Arginine	GCA, GCG, GCT, GCC, TCT, TCC	CGU, CGC, CGA, CGG, AGA, AGG
Asparagine	TTA, TTG	AAU, AAC
Aspartic acid	CTA, CTG	GAU, GAC
Cysteine	ACA, ACG	UGU, UGC
Glutamic acid	CTT, CTC	GAA, GAG
Glutamine	GTT, GTC	CAA, CAG
Glycine	CCA, CCG, CCT, CCC	GGU, GGC, GGA, GGG
Histidine	GTA, GTG	CAU, CAC
Isoleucine	TAA, TAG, TAT	AUU, AUC, AUA
Leucine	AAC, GAA, GAG, GAT, GAC, AAT	UUG, CUU, CUC, CUA, CUG, UUA
Lysine	TTT, TTC	AAA, AAG
Methionine	TAC	AUG
Phenylalanine	AAA, AAG	UUU, UUC
Proline	GGA, GGG, GGT, GGC	CCU, CCC, CCA, CCG
Serine	AGA, AGG, AGT, AGC, TCA, TCG	UCU, UCC, UCA, UCG, AGU, AGC
Threonine	TGA, TGG, TGT, TGC	ACU, ACC, ACA, ACG
Tryptophan	ACC	UGG
Tyrosine	ATA, ATG	UAU, UAC
Valine	CAA, CAG, CAT, CAC	GUU, GUC, GUA, GUG
Terminating triplets	ATT, ATC, ACT	UAA, UAG, UGA

the segment of DNA that has just been transcribed is closed. Figure 3.10 shows the process of transcription from the creation of the RNA copy to its exit from the nucleus. Now the sequence of codons containing the message for a protein is transported out of the nucleus and into the cytoplasm as a segment of mRNA.

Translation and Folding Once the mRNA segment bearing the sequence of codons that code for a string of amino acids clears the nuclear membrane, a series of chemical signals initiate the process of **translation**. Two molecules come together with the mRNA to form a **ribosome**. Once this structure is formed, the mRNA begins to move through it approximately one codon (three nucleotide bases) at a time. Stimulated by the ribosome and allied enzymes, a group of **transfer RNA (tRNA)** segments (found in the cell's cytoplasm outside the nucleus) cluster around the ribosome/mRNA combination. Transfer RNA segments are small molecules that contain a specific three-nucleotide base sequence and carry an attached amino acid. The specific three-nucleotide base sequence of the tRNA is called an **anticodon** because it contains the complement for the codon word for a particular amino acid. As each codon of mRNA moves through the ribosome, the complementary tRNA anticodon matches up with it (remember the strong attraction between complementary bases). Figure 3.11 shows this process of translation, the mRNA and ribosome interacting with the tRNA.

As multiple codon-anticodon matches are made, a set of auxiliary enzymes modifies the resulting ribosome/mRNA/tRNA/amino acid complex by breaking

translation
converting the mRNA message into a protein

ribosome
site of protein synthesis

transfer RNA (tRNA)
form of RNA that brings amino acids to the ribosome

anticodon
three-nucleotide sequence on a tRNA molecule that helps match the appropriate amino acid with a specific mRNA codon

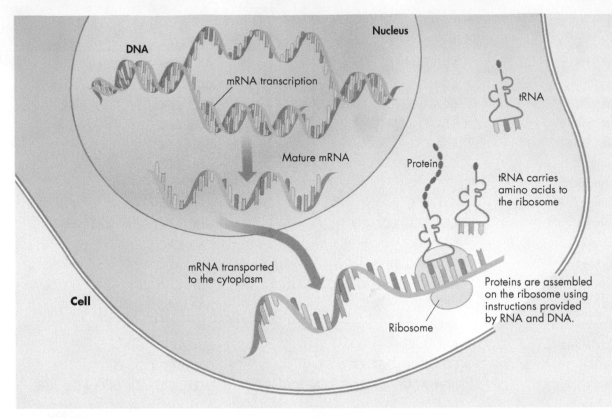

■ FIGURE 3.10

Overview of protein synthesis. Transcription takes place in the nucleus. The newly created messenger RNA is transported to the cytoplasm. In the final step, translation, proteins are assembled on the ribosome using the instructions coded in the mRNA.

Messenger RNA travels to the ribosomes, the site of protein synthesis. As ribosomes move along mRNA, tRNA picks up amino acids and lines up according to the base complements. Each tRNA molecule transfers its amino acid to the next active tRNA as it leaves, resulting in a chain of amino acids.

This chain of amino acids forms a protein.

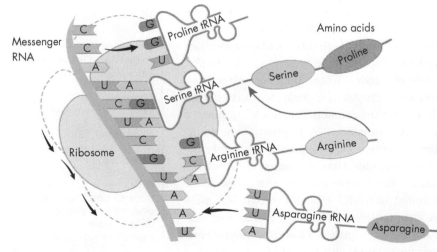

■ FIGURE 3.11

Translation. In the ribosome, transfer RNA picks up the correct amino acid and adds it to the growing chain, forming a protein.

the bonds between the nucleotide bases and the sugars and phosphates (in the mRNA and tRNA) and creating bonds between the amino acids. The result is a growing string of amino acids as the mRNA moves through the ribosome (see Figure 3.11). Once the mRNA message is finished, the ribosome and remaining RNAs are dismantled, leaving a string of amino acids, a polypeptide. This polypeptide then undergoes primary, secondary, and possibly tertiary folding and becomes a protein (Figure 3.12).

In reality, protein synthesis is much more complex than can be described in this very basic overview. For example, the process of transcription includes steps in which the initially transcribed segment of mRNA is chemically modified before leaving the nucleus such that specific noncoding sequences called *introns* are removed, and the remaining sequences, called *exons,* are actually the segments that contain the correct codons for the production of the protein. As another example, sometimes the message for a protein is in many pieces at different locations on the DNA and the pieces have to be put together before connecting with the ribosome and undergoing translation. Nevertheless, this overview should provide you with a basic understanding of how protein synthesis works.

This basic understanding of protein synthesis provides sufficient information for our first definition of a gene. We know that DNA and the maternal cellular elements are transmitted across generations. Therefore, parents pass on the information for the construction of polypeptides/proteins (as DNA segments) and the regulatory mechanisms in the female gamete (egg) to their offspring. The segments of DNA that contain the messages for a protein are one type of unit of heredity. We can say, in a simplistic sense, that a **gene** can be defined as a segment of DNA that contains the sequence for a protein.

Regulation

The third main function of DNA is regulation. We have already mentioned that some of the codons do not contain a code for a protein; instead they have a three-nucleotide sequence that causes the enzymes to stop or start a specific activity. This signaling is how the enzymes that facilitate replication and transcription "know" when to turn on and off. Additionally, DNA has an elaborate series of self-examination and repair mechanisms. Because DNA is copying itself and being transcribed onto mRNA constantly throughout an organism's life, there is bound to be a multitude of small errors (estimates put this error rate at around 1 in every 100 bases during replication). Even though the attraction between A and T and between G and C is very strong, the overall similarity of all the nucleotides and the nature of the enzymatic process by which they are joined together allows for occasional G-T, C-A, G-A, or C-T pairings.

If we look at the final products of replication, however, the error rate is only about 1 in 10 billion! This remarkable accuracy rate is established through four repair mechanisms (Fox-Keller, 2000). First, a monitoring system aligns the appropriate enzymes and nucleotide bases. Second, a proofreading system examines nucleotides as they are joined, searching for incorrect pairings. If too many errors have accumulated in a stretch of replicated DNA, a third mechanism attempts to repair the segment. If that is not possible, the whole replicated segment is scrapped and the process starts anew. Finally, a fourth repair mechanism works on damage to the DNA that results from external causes (for example, radiation). These mechanisms cut out damaged segments and facilitate the creation of new segments to replace them. So, in part, an answer to our earlier question Why do things remain relatively constant? is that the DNA displays a high degree of stability, not only as a result

Unfolded polypeptide

Protein

■ **FIGURE 3.12**
Folding. An unfolded polypeptide folds into a protein.

gene
segment of DNA that contains the sequence for a protein

Why Is It Important to Understand What DNA Does?

Knowing that genes mainly help create proteins which make up the basic building blocks of our bodies is really important. This knowledge arms you with a greater understanding of what genes are and what they are not. Now when you are told that a new gene for breast cancer or alcoholism has been found, you can be skeptical. You might ask "So are you telling me that this gene codes for a protein that causes cancer?" If the answer is "yes," then you can ask how the protein works and what does it do. But in reality the answer is almost never yes. More likely the answer will be "Well, no, what we see is that 56% of the patients with this type of cancer also have this form of the gene," so you will understand that the gene is not the cause of the cancer but rather might be part of a complex system that potentially results in cancer. As we noted in the previous box, there is a tendency to misuse the word *gene*—but armed with the basic knowledge of genetics you will have a better understanding of what is really going on.

STOP & THINK

Is this what most people imagine when they think about genetics?

of its chemical and morphological structure, but also because of its regulation and repair mechanisms. This means that the proteins the DNA codes for and their subsequent functions are also highly stable across generations.

DNA is not a passive holder of the blueprints for an organism, nor is it the single force of heredity. Rather, DNA is part of a complex set of cellular machinery responsible for protein synthesis, cellular function, and a major part of heredity. There are limits to the stability of DNA however. Mistakes are made, and changes in the sequences of nucleotide bases do occur. These changes are called mutations, and they play a vital role in the process of evolution (as we will see in chapter 4).

Mendel's basic model of inheritance

Although we now have a strong understanding of the molecular and chemical components of heredity as they relate to proteins, we are still learning much about the patterns and processes by which whole traits are passed from generation to generation. Much of our basic understanding of the inheritance of traits comes from the pioneering work of an Augustinian monk named Gregor Mendel. In the 1860s and 1870s, Mendel worked with a variety of plants, trying to understand how external, easily perceived traits are passed from generation to generation. His work with the common garden pea plant shed light on the simplest forms of inheritance. Unfortunately, during his lifetime very few individuals knew of his work (he was a contemporary of Darwin). It was not until the early 1900s that Mendel's work, along with the work of others reporting similar findings, became widely known.

Traits Are Passed from Generation to Generation

Mendel created a model for the transmission of traits across generations based on a simple set of assumptions. The main assumption is that a specific unit of heredity (called the allelomorph, or **allele**) causes a specific observable trait in an organism. In Mendel's model, each parent contributes one allele per trait, meaning that the offspring has a representative allele from each parent

allele
a variant sequence of nucleotides in a gene; a form of a gene

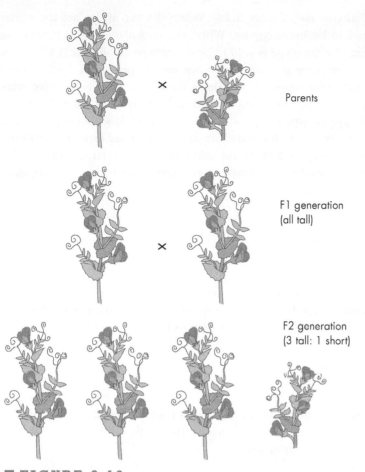

■ FIGURE 3.13
Mendel's first experiment. Because tallness is a pure dominant trait, all
the offspring in the F1 generation were tall. In the F2 generation, three
quarters were tall and one quarter was dwarf.

(a process called *segregation* of alleles). The offspring has two alleles for its
genotype (the genetic component) and one resultant **phenotype** (the final
product, the observable trait). The offspring's appearance, or observable trait,
is determined largely by the relationship between the two parental alleles.

The example that is most often cited from Mendel's work is
height in pea plants. Mendel successfully cultivated pure-breeding
short pea plants and pure-breeding tall pea plants. *Pure-breeding*
means that combining short parent plants always produces short
offspring plants, and combining tall parent plants always produces tall offspring plants. Mendel's deduction was that the short
plants had only the allele that determined the trait "short," and
the tall plants had the allele for "tall." He then cross-pollinated
the short and tall plants. One hundred percent of the resulting
offspring (called the F1 generation) were tall. What happened to
the allele for short? To answer this question, Mendel crossed the
F1 generation with itself. The resulting offspring were tall and
short in a 3-to-1 ratio (Figures 3.13 and 3.14). Using these and
other experiments, Mendel came up with a set of explanations
that still form a general basis for understanding heredity.

Using the model for the pea plant, we see that each plant has two alleles per
trait, one contributed by each parent (remember the process of segregation of
alleles). A pure-breeding tall plant has two "T" alleles and a pure-breeding

genotype
the genetic representation; the
alleles in an organism's DNA

phenotype
an organism's observable, measurable traits

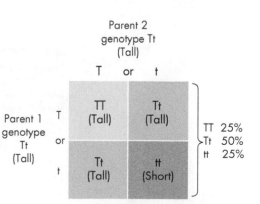

■ FIGURE 3.14
Punnett square showing inheritance of height in pea plants.
This shows the result of crossing two heterozygotes (*Tt*).
Both genotype and phenotype
are shown.

short has two "t" alleles (see Figure 3.14). When the two alleles are the same, the genotype is said to be **homozygous.** When the two alleles are different, as in the F1 generation, the genotype is said to be **heterozygous.** Figure 3.13 shows that although there are three possible genotypes for the pea plant height, there are only two possible phenotypes. These alleles have a dominant-recessive relationship, meaning that when they are paired in a heterozygous state, the dominant allele's phenotype is expressed and the recessive allele's phenotype is not. Being dominant does not imply that the allele functions better or is more robust; it simply means that there is a chemical relationship between the two alleles such that the recessive allele's phenotype is not produced in the heterozygous state.

Mendel's work continues to inform current knowledge

Today we have a much better understanding of the structure of the units of heredity (alleles) and the molecule of heredity (DNA), and we can graft Mendel's observations onto our current knowledge. For example, we can now place an allele at a location on a specific chromosome; this location is called a **locus** (plural *loci*). Because we inherit one set of chromosomes from each parent (half of the full set of DNA), we can see that each parent contributes one allele at the same locus to its offspring, resulting in two alleles per individual per locus (Figure 3.15). The alleles at all the loci in an individual make up her or his total genotype. Therefore, we can see the individual, from a genetic perspective, as a constellation of alleles.

Earlier we defined a DNA "gene" as a segment of DNA that contains the sequence for a protein. Combining this with our ideas derived from Mendel's work, we can say that an allele is the sequence of DNA that contains the code for a protein. Different alleles contain slightly different sets of triplets (codes), which result in different proteins, which in turn have different end effects (phenotypes). Thus, alleles are best seen as variant forms of a gene, and a gene is the segment of DNA at a specific locus (Figure 3.16). For example, in Mendel's pea plants we can see a "gene" for height that has two different forms (alleles T and t), resulting in different phenotypes.

homozygous
the state of having the same allele at both loci for the same gene

heterozygous
the state of having different alleles at both loci for the same gene

locus
the place on a chromosome where a specific gene occurs

Maternal chromosome

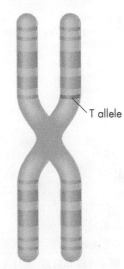

T allele

Paternal chromosome

T allele

■ FIGURE 3.15
Loci for the gene for height in pea plants. This example shows a T allele at the locus on both the maternal and paternal homologous chromosomes.

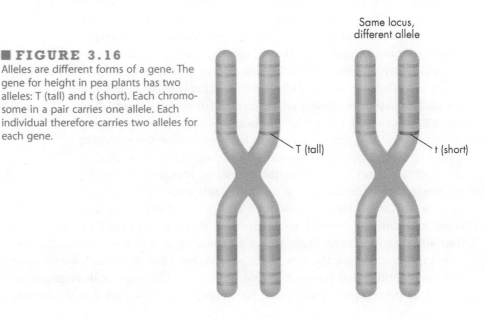

Same locus, different allele

T (tall)

t (short)

■ FIGURE 3.16
Alleles are different forms of a gene. The gene for height in pea plants has two alleles: T (tall) and t (short). Each chromosome in a pair carries one allele. Each individual therefore carries two alleles for each gene.

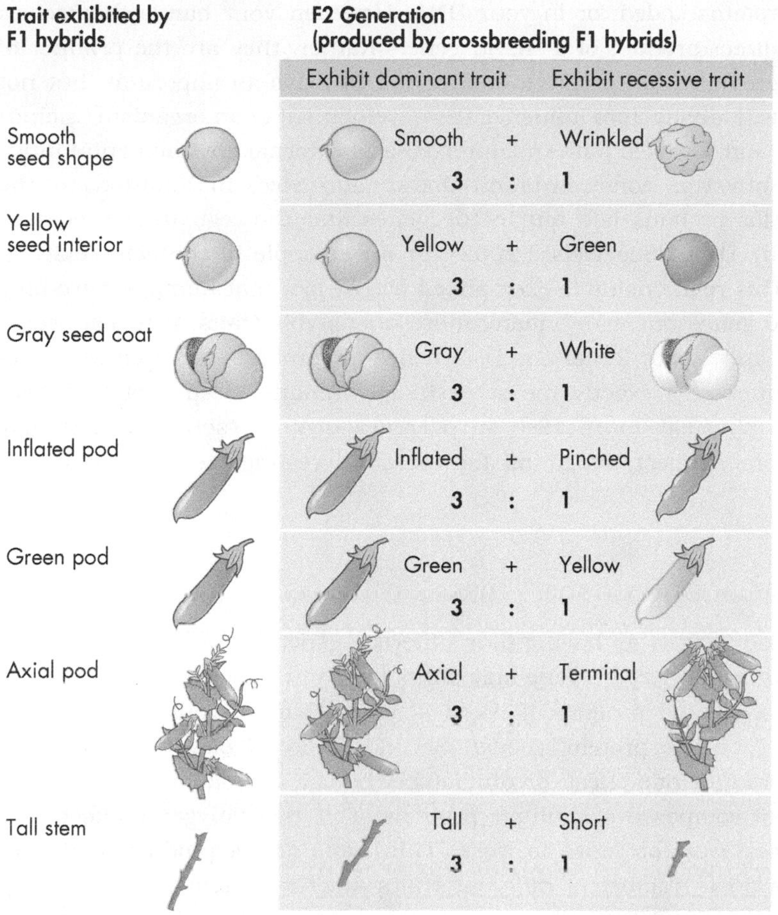
Trait exhibited by F1 hybrids
F2 Generation (produced by crossbreeding F1 hybrids)
Exhibit dominant trait
Exhibit recessive trait
Smooth seed shape
Smooth + Wrinkled
3 : 1
Yellow seed interior
Yellow + Green
3 : 1
Gray seed coat
Gray + White
3 : 1
Inflated pod
Inflated + Pinched
3 : 1
Green pod
Green + Yellow
3 : 1
Axial pod
Axial + Terminal
3 : 1
Tall stem
Tall + Short
3 : 1

Offspring exhibit dominant or recessive traits in ratio of 3:1.

■ **FIGURE 3.17**
Mendel's experiments with pea plants. Dominant traits are shown on the left.

Another interesting set of observations by Mendel related to the relationships between traits. When he tracked different traits, such as height and seed color, across generations of pea plants, Mendel could see that they did not cluster together. He referred to this pattern as **independent assortment.** Because alleles are not linked together and are not inherited as fixed clusters, individuals have a mix of traits. Today, however, we know that independent assortment is not always the case. If two loci are very close together on the same chromosome, they appear to be linked, that is, they almost always appear together. This appearance of being "linked" is due to their proximity on the DNA, not to any specific functional bond between them. The seven traits that Mendel studied are shown in Figure 3.17.

independent assortment
the observation that each locus sorts independently (in general)

The relationship between genes and traits is complex

Although we can say that alleles contain the codes for proteins, the relationship between genes and traits is actually extremely complex. A multitude of complex chemical interactions take place within the cell, within the nucleus, between cells, and throughout organisms that make most one-allele-to-one-trait analogies pretty unrealistic. For example, your hands are composed of

STOP & THINK

How can we have fewer genes than a "less complex" animal like a fruit fly?

numerous proteins coded for in your DNA. However, your hands themselves are not the direct product of a "hand gene." Rather, they are the product of a complex developmental program in which DNA plays an important, but not exclusive, role. Many factors influence the development of an organism, including chemical and physical patterns, internal and external environmental influences, and physical constraints on shape and size, in addition to the instructions for proteins laid out in the genes and the regulatory processes carried out by DNA. (See Weiss, 2002, for an example of the complexity of final form.) This relationship is exemplified by the fact that humans have only about 25,000 genes but many, many more phenotypic traits. It is also worth nothing that only about 2% of our DNA codes for proteins and that 99.9% of our DNA sequence is exactly the same in all humans in spite of our great variation in physical form. (See http://www.ornl.gov/sci/techresources/Human_Genome/project/info.shtml for these interesting pieces of data and many more.)

Four Ways Genes Produce Traits

We can envision genes as having four different general types of causal relationships with traits. First, a gene may simply contain the code for one protein (or one set of related proteins if there is more than one allele). This is a simple "one gene–one protein" model. Second, a group of genes may work together to produce one effect, or phenotype, be it a complex protein or even a specific trait composed of multiple proteins. This is a **polygenic** effect, and it is a common way for genes to work. Third, one gene's product may have many effects on a number of different traits and/or systems. This effect is called **pleiotropic,** and it is also quite widespread. Finally, it is common for a given gene to have both polygenic and pleiotropic effects at the same time within an organism (Figure 3.18).

By now it should be clear why clones are not all identical. Even when the same segments of DNA are involved, there are still many complexities in the ways that genes are expressed and that the DNA is interconnected with other

polygenic
the situation wherein many genes combine to have one effect

pleiotropic
the situation wherein one gene has many effects

■ FIGURE 3.18
Relationships between genes and biological effects. Most genes have very complex polygenic and pleiotropic effects.

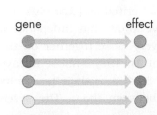
Each gene has a distinct biological effect.

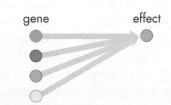
Polygenic trait: Many genes contribute to a single effect.

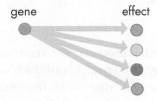
Pleiotropy: A gene has multiple effects.

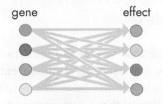
Polygenic traits and pleiotropy

organismal functions. The sheer number of variables that go into the expression of genes and the development of organisms ensures that no two individuals, even genetic copies, will have the same phenotype.

Are There Specific Genes for Certain Diseases?

You have probably heard references on TV and in the news to the gene for certain diseases. In this case the media are usually oversimplifying a biological relationship. When a news story refers to a gene for cancer, for example, it probably means that a correlation has been found between the frequency of certain alleles and the occurrence of certain types of cancerous growth, or, in other words, that a certain allele or set of alleles is more commonly associated with a type of cancerous growth than are other alleles in that population. Situations like this almost never mean there is a one-to-one causal relationship between an allele and cancer. Occasionally, we are lucky and do find relatively straightforward relationships between specific alleles or mutations and diseases, but usually it is not that simple. We will review some of the direct gene-disease cases in chapter 10.

Most DNA Doesn't Appear to Do Anything!

Another complication in understanding genetic function is that the vast majority of our DNA appears not to be "active," that is, it does not appear to code for any particular protein. Recent estimates suggest that as much as 98% of our DNA is not "doing" anything that we can currently detect! This includes the introns mentioned earlier, the noncoding pieces of RNA that are cut out of genes before the genes are transcribed, and the vast stretches of the human genome that do not appear to have any active genes in them. Thus, not only does most of our DNA not have any active genes, but much of the genetic material within a gene (the sequence of DNA at a locus) may not code for anything as well. However, some biologists suggest that this vast array of "inactive" DNA might be important as a reservoir of genetic variation; or it may even be linked to the concept of **evolvability**—the idea that the genome (our genetic complement) can be an active participant in evolution even to the point of having systems for generating variations upon which natural selection can act. Think, for example, of all the extra DNA in our genome. Is it simply junk, or might it be a reservoir of potentially useful information? The Human Genome Project and other research endeavors show us that a good deal of our DNA reflects ancient replication and insertion events (our DNA made copies of itself and put them into the genome multiple times). This repetitive DNA might also be remnants from viruses that were able to insert their genetic material into our own. What if this is an important part of the biological variation that was core to Darwin's ideas about how things change (remember natural selection from chapter 1)? What if some of this noncoding DNA is a hedge against future selection? It is not clear if this is the case, but if it is, it might give our species an extra degree of flexibility in dealing with complex and changing environmental challenges. Another possibility is that this "inactive" DNA may play a role in regulating or otherwise participating in the turning on and off of genetic sequences (coding regions).

Our framework and technology for understanding the structure and function of DNA has significantly improved over the last few years, and the work of the Human Genome Project has changed the way we can investigate our DNA. The ongoing projects in genomic research involve attempts to isolate

evolvability
the notion that much DNA may act as reserve variation for future selective pressures

genes and gene function, to better understand the inner workings of the DNA and its associated molecules, and to harness this knowledge in various biomedical formats.

Does DNA cause certain behaviors?

Just as you often hear about genes for certain diseases in the media, you may also hear about genes for certain behaviors, tendencies, or abilities. At this point in the chapter, however, you may be wondering how genes, with their extremely complex and specific functions, could possibly cause or even influence behavior.

As mentioned, very few of our alleles function in a simple Mendelian manner (although some do), and there is little evidence to support any one-to-one relationship between a single set of alleles and any behavior. However, since we are biological organisms, our DNA influences our structure, and since behavior is exhibited via our structures (brain, eyes, mouth, hands, and so on), all behavior has some genetic component. For example, you are reading this page using your eyes (optical tissue, muscles, nerves) and maybe your hands (muscle, bones, tendons) to scan the letters and words on the page. You are also using your brain (a set of neurons, vascular tissues, and various hormones that connects all the organs in your body and mediates among them) to process the meaning. Obviously, all of these elements have a genetic component. However, you are *reading* the words, a behavior that must be taught to you, and you are reading them in *English*, something else that must be taught to you. Do reading and using the English language have a genetic component? Yes, the neurons, eyes, muscles, and other parts of the body used in reading are composed of proteins initially coded for by DNA. Are there genes for reading in English? No, the particular language that any human reads is a cultural factor, as languages are cultural systems. Can aspects of our genetic complement impact our ability to acquire specific reading skills? Possibly: Structural differences in the eyes, motor connectivity, and even hormone pathways in the brain might impact the pace and pattern of reading acquisition. These differences could be the result of allelic variation or other genetic patterns.

CONNECTIONS

My Genes Made Me Do It!

Do men commit rape because of the genes? Do women naturally have the urge to be mothers because of their genes? Are humans always going to engage in wars because it is in our genes? At this point in the chapter you know enough about genetics to realize these statements are gross oversimplifications. Of course, much of what we do is strongly influenced by our biology, but complex cultural actions like those listed above are not basal urges coded in the DNA; instead, they are complicated outcomes of biological, social, historical, and situational factors. Whenever you hear someone resort to arguing that it is in our genetic nature to do something you need to ask how this could be possible. Are the things they blame on genes really simple traits that can be related to proteins and basic biological structures? Are the things they are talking about even comparable? Do they involve behavior, biology, experience, and culture? You know that the individuals making those assertions are making too many assumptions and have shaky understandings of what genes really do. In the next chapter, as we talk in more detail about evolution, you will see how such deterministic statements about complex behaviors being outlined in our genes make little sense.

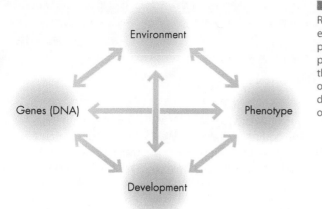

Relationships among genes, environment, development, and phenotype. There is a very complex set of relationships among the phenotype, or end product, on the one hand, and DNA, development, and environment on the other.

Clearly, then, we encounter complexities when talking about the genetics of behavior. We know there are genetic components to all aspects of life, but how specific alleles affect complex behavior patterns (or if they do at all) is far from obvious. If a particular behavior functions to improve an organism's chances to reproduce in a given environment, Darwin's ideas about natural selection would predict that that behavior will be passed on to the next generation—but only if it has some basal relationship to the organism's DNA (that is, if it is biologically heritable).

If you do hear an assertion about a relationship between genes and behavior, you need to think critically and ask a few basic questions: Where is the locus or gene? How many alleles are there? What protein or proteins are coded for? How do these proteins affect the organism such that a specific behavior is performed? As our technological abilities advance, we may be able to dissect the mechanism of DNA function as it relates to behavior, because we know it must. But for the present we need to acknowledge the limits of our current understanding and carefully assess any such claims (Ehrlich & Feldman, 2002). As it stands we do not even know what nearly 50% of the genes that the Human Genome Project identified actually do.

Everything we have covered in this chapter suggests that there is a very complex set of relationships between the phenotype, or end product, on the one hand, and DNA, development, and environment on the other (Figure 3.19). This relationship is not linear, nor can it be easily described as a simple equation. The DNA is too interconnected and interactive with the cell to allow us to use simple models or labels such as "blueprints," "building blocks," or "code of life." Rather, the DNA is an integral component of life itself, and understanding the units of heredity and the function of genetic material is critical to understanding evolution and organismal functioning. But an understanding of genetics is by no means the complete picture. By combining our understanding of genotype and phenotype, we can then move on to explain how the processes of evolution work to change organisms over time (as we will do in chapter 4).

Population genetics helps us understand evolution

When we talk about genetics in an evolutionary sense, we are interested primarily in population genetics—that is, the distribution of alleles within a population. Remember, evolution is change over time; biological evolution can

What We Know / Questions That Remain

What We Know

DNA plays a core role in structure and function for the vast majority of life-forms on this planet and carries much of the hereditary material in living organisms.

Questions That Remain

We don't understand why only about 2% of human DNA contains coding sequences. We don't fully understand what the other 98% does, although it may be a reservoir of variation for future adaptation through natural selection.

What We Know

DNA replicates itself, carries the "code" for the creation of polypeptides (the basis for proteins), and acts to regulate itself during both replication and protein synthesis.

Questions That Remain

Protein synthesis is actually only part of the process. We have much to learn about the interactions between the DNA, the protein products, and the mechanisms that result in a final phenotype. Current work investigating genome function is moving toward a more comprehensive view of the role and interactive functions of DNA.

What We Know

One allele per locus is inherited from each parent, and all the alleles in our body make up our genotype. Some alleles act in a simple dominant-recessive relationship, but most do not.

Questions That Remain

How alleles interact to create complex phenotypes is still rather unclear. Again, the recent sequencing of the human genome and the investigations into genomic function should begin to help us unravel the mechanisms that tie the genetic sequences to complex developmental patterns and events.

What We Know

All humans share the same loci, but individually they vary in the alleles at most of those loci. Understanding the variation of allele frequencies across populations helps us to examine evolutionary processes.

Questions That Remain

Although we know many causes for allelic variation in humans and other organisms, there remain multitudes of changes that occur in development and throughout the life of individuals. It remains very difficult to connect specific variations in allelic frequencies with significant, or functional, phenotypic changes.

What We Know

Every part of the human organism has some genetic component.

Questions That Remain

We don't know how our genotype affects our behavior. Our current knowledge does not allow us to make any substantive assertions regarding the relationship between specific genetic components and any human behaviors.

---

be measured as changes in the frequencies of alleles in a population from generation to generation. When Darwin noted the variation in the beaks of the finches on the Galapagos Islands, he was describing variation in phenotype. But underlying that phenotypic variation there must be genetic variation. Otherwise, the phenotypic elements are not heritable, and natural selection cannot affect their distribution into subsequent generations. **Population genetics** is the study of the distribution of the genetic variation within and between populations. It is an evolutionary approach to looking at how our genetic makeup changes over time. In the next chapter we will look, in details at how this happens.

population genetics
study of the distribution of the genetic variation within and between populations

SUMMARY

▲ DNA (deoxyribonucleic acid) is found in most forms of life on this planet. DNA plays a critical role in the structure and function of nearly everything in a living organism and is especially important as a major factor in heredity. DNA is found on chromosomes in the nucleus of the cell.

▲ Humans have 46 chromosomes (23 pairs)—22 pairs of autosomes and one pair of sex chromosomes.

▲ DNA is made up of four nucleotide bases (adenine, cytosine, guanine, and thymine) and sugar and phosphate groups.

▲ Replication is a prime function of DNA. DNA replicates itself during cell division (mitosis) and gamete production (meiosis).

▲ Novel arrangements of genetic variation can occur during meiosis via recombination and crossing over.

▲ Protein synthesis is a second function of DNA. DNA carries the core information for the construction of a polypeptide (chain of amino acids), which in turn becomes a protein.

▲ The main information in the DNA is carried in the sequence of nucleotide bases. Segments of three bases are called triplets. Each triplet codes for an amino acid or gives a start-or-stop signal during translation.

▲ The DNA code is transcribed onto mRNA for translation into a protein. The transcribed triplets are called codons on the RNA.

▲ A segment of DNA that contains the code for a protein is called a gene. A gene is transcribed from the DNA to a strand of mRNA (messenger RNA), which then moves into the cytoplasm and, with the help of ribosomes and tRNA (transfer RNA), is translated into a polypeptide. The polypeptide then folds in on itself to become a protein.

▲ Genes can have single effects, pleiotropic effects, polygenic effects, and effects that are a mix of all three.

▲ Regulation is a third function of DNA. DNA regulates itself via self-correction mechanisms and interactions with enzymes.

▲ Different sequences of nucleotides at the same place on the DNA (a locus) are called alleles. Alleles are variant forms of a gene.

▲ Gametes (sex cells) carry the genetic information from one generation to the next. Each gamete has one half of the full genetic complement. Therefore, each gamete has one allele per gene.

▲ As much as 98% of the human DNA does not appear to have active genes on it. It is currently unclear what the function of this "noncoding" DNA is.

▲ There is a complex nonlinear relationship between genes and behavior.

▲ All of the alleles in a population make up its gene pool. This gene pool represents the total genetic variation available to that population and, thus, the pool of variation upon which evolution can act.

CRITICAL THINKING

1. What are the evolutionary implications of the fact that most living forms use DNA and the same code to form the basis of their structures? What are possible explanations for this fact?

2. If only about 2% of the DNA has active genes, why do we have the other 98%? With this in mind, what does it mean to say that humans and chimpanzees share 98% of our DNA sequences? Are humans and chimpanzees 98% identical?

3. What happens when DNA self-correction breaks down? How might that be beneficial in some cases?

4. How could natural selection act on DNA?

5. With advancing technology we are able to insert genes into organisms. Given this chapter's information on how genes work, what are some of the potential repercussions of this research?

6. How is cloning different from sexual reproduction at the level of DNA and genes? Why is it that cloning the same individual would not produce two identical adults? Why would you expect these adult clones to behave differently from one another?

RESOURCES

GENES

www.ncbi.nlm.nih.gov This site provides a great deal of information on Mendelian inheritance patterns in humans (including examples).

www.ornl.gov/sci/techresources/Human_Genome/Project/about.shtml This site provides a basic introduction to the Human Genome Project.

www.sciencegenomics.org The *Science* magazine genomics site has an array of education links and a number of articles dealing with issues of genomics and genetic research.

Comfort, N. C. (2001, June). Are genes real? *Natural History*, 28–37.
This essay offers a concise summary of the use of *gene* over the last century, with a conclusion somewhat different from Fox-Keller's.

Fox-Keller, E. (2000). *The century of the gene*. Cambridge, MA: Harvard University Press.
This is a readable and well-constructed overview of the history and current knowledge of the gene and genomics.

GENETIC COMPLEXITY

Ehrlich, P., & Feldman, M. (2002). Genes and culture: What creates our behavioral phenomena? *Current Anthropology, 44*(1), 87–107.
Ehrlich and Feldman offer a strong viewpoint on the difficulty of assessing the genetic contribution to, and the evolution of, human behavior. Taking some specific paradigms in current human behavioral studies to task, the authors propose some potential alternative paths of inquiry. The article is accompanied by commentary from scientists who agree, disagree, and offer differing viewpoints.

Marks, J. (2003) 98% Chimpanzee and 38% Daffodil: The human genome in evolutionary and cultural context. In *Genetic nature/culture: Anthropology and science beyond the two-culture divide*. Edited by A. H. Goodman, D. Heath, and M. S. Lindee. University of California Press Berkely. Pp. 133–152.
This essay is a well-structured and highly engaging review of the complexities, pitfalls, and potentials for applying the human genome information to understanding humankind.

Lewontin, R. (1995). *Human diversity*. New York: Freeman, Scientific American Library. The section on genetics is well written, and the overviews of genetic variation in humans are informative and accessible to college students.

Weiss, K. (2002). Good vibrations: The silent symphony of life. *Evolutionary Anthropology, 11,*176–182.
This essay offers a look at the similarities between the development of biological form and musical waves. Weiss is a genetic anthropologist and presents the information in a congenial, reader-friendly style.

REFERENCES

Ehrlich, P., & Feldman, M. (2002). Genes and culture: What creates our behavioral phenomena? *Current Anthropology, 44* (1), 87–107.

Fox-Keller, E. (2000). *The century of the gene.* Cambridge, MA: Harvard University Press.

Lewontin, R. (1995). *Human diversity.* New York: Freeman, Scientific American Library.

Weiss, K. (2002). Good vibrations: The silent symphony of life. *Evolutionary Anthropology, 11,* 176–182.

CHAPTER 4

Modern Evolutionary Theory

This chapter addresses the following questions:

▲ How does evolutionary change occur in populations?

▲ What is speciation and how does it occur?

▲ Why should we care about biological variation?

Microbes, or bacteria as we commonly call them, are everywhere, and some of them are dangerous to human beings. Over the past 50 years we have become adept at creating drugs, called antibiotics, that kill the dangerous strains of these microbes. In many cases we have even come close to wiping out these microbial diseases. But lately, something sinister has emerged—the microbes are fighting back.

Each year in the United States, more than 14,000 people become sick and die as a result of infections caused by antibiotic-resistant microbes they picked up in hospitals. As many as 25% of dangerous streptococcus ("strep") bacteria are now resistant to penicillin, and perhaps as much as 48% are resistant to erythromycin, two of the most common antibiotics. The incidence of antibiotic-resistant staphylococcus ("staph") bacteria has increased as much as 25 fold since 1974, and more than 10% of the tuberculosis cases spreading through China and Russia are resistant to the two most powerful medicines against it. And in 2001 the British medical journal *The Lancet* reported that the first novel antibiotic introduced in almost 30 years is already running up against microbes that resist its brand-new kind of biochemical attack.

The Centers for Disease Control (CDC) estimates that a third of the 150 million antibiotic prescriptions written each year may be inappropriate; frequently, antibiotics are prescribed for infections caused by viruses (for which they do no good) rather than bacteria. Every day, millions of Americans reach for antibacterial hand soap, even though the American Medical Association (AMA) has repeatedly recommended ordinary soap and water over those products and stated that there is no scientific support that the antibacterial soaps actually clean more effectively. The World Health Organization (WHO) reports that almost all major microbial infectious diseases are becoming antibiotic resistant. In 2001 the awareness of the problem became so widespread that members of the U.S. Congress introduced a bill (HR 1711) called the Antibiotic Resistance Act!

What is going on? Are alien strains of microbes invading the earth? Are the bacteria of the planet finally wising up to our attempts to destroy them? No, microbes are simply doing what Charles Darwin and Alfred Russel Wallace said everything in nature does: They are evolving. The microbes are responding to new environments, ones we are creating by rampant overuse of antibiotics. Human-induced change causes natural selection, resulting in very "fit" bacteria. By putting enormous amounts of antibiotics into and on ourselves, into the meat we eat (nearly half of all antibiotics are given to livestock and fish to prevent disease), and into the environment, we are setting a natural process in action. As we discussed in chapter 1, when the environment challenges organisms, certain variants do better than others. Those genetically based variants that do better—in this case, those that survive the onslaught of antibiotics—leave more offspring, so the resulting population looks more like them. In other words, by wiping out the bacteria that cannot survive treatment by antibiotics, we increase the numbers of those that can.

Remember, evolutionary change happens across many, many generations. For humans, evolutionary change is slow, but for bacteria, which can go through multiple generations in a few days, change is very, very quick. You might want to think about this evolutionary process the next time you reach for the antibacterial soap.

Antibiotic resistance in bacteria clearly demonstrates that evolutionary processes, biological changes over time, are real, that they are ongoing, and that they are affecting humans right now. Why do we cover evolutionary theory a number of times in this text? Why is this entire chapter about the ways in which genetic patterns and organisms change over time? The reason is that everything is evolving. To understand the world around you and to grasp the basic elements of our own biological history and the biological components of our environment, you need to fully understand the basic processes of evolution.

In the nearly 150 years since Darwin published his first edition of *On the Origin of Species,* we have learned a great deal about the relationship between genetics and evolution. During the 1930s, 1940s, and 1950s, a growing understanding of inheritance patterns, coupled with an emphasis on statistical modeling of change and on studying populations, allowed researchers to gain insights unavailable to Darwin and the earlier evolutionary thinkers. The expanded description of evolution put forward by these scientists is referred to as the *new synthesis.* Since the 1970s we have made additional leaps in our understanding of the processes and patterns of evolution.

In chapter 3 we discussed genes and alleles, and we are now ready to put those concepts into the larger context of a population. Although we tend to use individualistic, simplified examples when we talk about evolution, remember that evolution can be measured only within populations and across generations. That is, individuals do not evolve within their own lifetimes; evolution occurs from generation to generation as a result of numerous factors, which are the topic of this chapter.

Evolutionary change occurs in populations in four ways

population
cluster of individuals of the same species who share a common geographical area and find their mates more often in their own cluster than in others

A **population** is a cluster of individuals of the same species who share a common geographical area and find their mates more often in their own cluster than in others. Large populations can be further subdivided into smaller clusters that interbreed most often among themselves. (These smaller clusters can also be referred to as *breeding populations.*) It is within a population that we can observe changes in allele frequency over time (the genetic definition of evolution). Later in this chapter we will see that a larger cluster of closely related populations is also an important evolutionary assemblage, the one we call a species.

All of the genetic variation (all the alleles for each locus) in a population is called a **gene pool**. The gene pool represents the total genetic variation available to that population and, thus, the pool of variation upon which evolution can act. As populations become less diverse—there are fewer alleles per locus and everyone in the population has the same alleles at any given locus—the potential for genetic adaptations (responses to environmental pressures) diminishes.

gene pool
all the alleles within a population

If we examine all individuals in a population and then add up all the alleles they have at any given locus (two alleles per individual), we can represent the distribution of the alleles as a frequency or even a percentage representation in the population. For example, let's consider the human blood system. In one simple form, our blood system has one locus with three alleles (A, B, and O). Sampling humans across the planet, we find that, globally, approximately 63% of all alleles are O, 22% are A, and only about 16% are B. This pattern is the average distribution of these alleles across our species. If we look at any given population, however, we will see some variation on that distribution. For instance, the frequency of the allele A is more than 50% in rural southern England, but less than 25% in Scotland and parts of Ireland. Similarly, the frequency of the A allele is generally greater than 30% in southern and eastern Korea, but it drops below 24% in eastern Japan, especially on the island of Hokkaido (Lewontin, 1995). The gene pool for the species contains three alleles at the ABO locus, but the distribution of those alleles in any given population will vary from the species average. Note that all humans have the same genes (at the same loci), but individuals may have different alleles at those loci.

When Darwin was describing the changes in finches' beaks over time, he assumed that there must be some form of genetic variation underlying those traits such that, from generation to generation, selection would favor the genetic representations of the better "fit" beaks. From our brief overview, however, we can see that there are probably no single genes for beak shape and size. Rather, what we see is selection (and other processes of evolution) acting on the resultant phenotype, which then feeds back (via differential reproductive success) to the entire genotype and thus affects the gene pool. The result of this selection and feedback via reproduction is change in the distribution of alleles from generation to generation—which is biological evolution.

In chapter 1 we introduced the Darwinian notion of descent with modification via natural selection. However, this is only one of four basic ways in which evolutionary change can occur. The four core processes of evolution are mutation, gene flow, genetic drift, and natural selection. The last three processes all require that genetic variations exist within a population in order to have an effect. In other words, gene flow, genetic drift, and natural selection only move variation around (*variation* meaning allele frequencies); they do not create new genetic sequences. Novel genetic complexes arise only via mutation. In addition to these four core processes there are also other patterns that help us understand how evolution occurs. We will cover some of these later in the chapter.

One of the core concepts in evolutionary theory is the ability to document that evolution, or change in allele frequency, is occurring within a population. In 1908, two researchers (the physician Wilhelm Weinberg and the mathematician Geoffrey Hardy) published papers showing how basic notions of Darwin's and Wallace's concept of natural selection could be melded with Mendel's

TABLE 4.1

| | | Number of Alleles | | |
Genotype	Number of Plants	Total	T alleles	t alleles
TT	40	80	80	0
Tt	36	72	36	36
tt	24	48	0	48
Total	*100*	*200*	*116*	*84*

TABLE 4.1   Computing Allele Frequency

STOP & THINK

When most people talk about evolution they are actually thinking about natural selection. Why are mutation, genetic drift, and gene flow ignored?

descriptions of alleles and genetic inheritance. Their insights became the foundation for the integration of the study of population-level genetics and evolutionary processes. Hardy and Weinberg noted that alleles have frequencies in populations. A *frequency* is the percentage of the individuals in the population with a given allele. For example, in a population of pea plants having the alleles T and t at a locus, the combination of the two alleles' frequencies must add up to 1 (as those are the only two possibilities at the locus). Table 4.1 illustrates this for a population of 100 individuals, with a total of 200 alleles at this locus. Using these data, we can calculate the relative frequency of each allele by dividing the total number of that allele by the number of individuals. In this population, the frequency of the T allele is 0.58, and the frequency of the t allele is 0.42.

Hardy and Weinberg created a simple but elegant equation that predicts the pattern of allelic representation over generational time. From their equation we learn that in a large population, if there are no extraneous forces (evolutionary pressures) and mating is random, allele frequencies reach an equilibrium and do not change from generation to generation (Figure 4.1). Therefore, by calculating the Hardy-Weinberg equilibrium for any given locus, we can produce a benchmark against which to test whether evolutionary forces are acting on the alleles at that locus. If we measure frequencies of alleles and find that they have changed, we can say that evolutionary processes are affecting that locus. This equation and its use expanded the ability of scientists to examine evolution at a population level. Prior to this equation many researchers could only look at simple mating predictions (from a Punnett square as in Mendel's work, chapter 2), and they also thought that dominant alleles would increase from generation to generation. The Hardy-Weinberg equation shows that both dominant and recessive alleles can increase or decrease over time and allows us to predict allele frequencies across entire populations rather than just predicting the genetic makeup of offspring. The next step is to attempt to determine which of the four processes (mutation, gene flow, genetic drift, and natural selection) are affecting the locus. To determine which, or how many, of these processes are affecting a population, we first need to clarify what they are.

Mutations Are Changes in the DNA

We learned in chapter 3 that alleles are forms of a gene, or more precisely, slight chemical variants at the same locus on a chromosome. Changes in the nucleotide base sequence in the DNA can (and do) occur regularly and are usually repaired. These changes to the nucleotide sequence are called **mutations.** Sometimes, however, changes are not repaired, and new combinations of nucleotides create codes for different proteins or act in new regulatory ways.

mutation
changes to the nucleotide sequence in the DNA

For alleles to be in equilibrium, the following assumptions must be met:	The Hardy-Weinberg Equation in Mendel's Pea Plants from Chapter 3

For alleles to be in equilibrium, the following assumptions must be met:

1. Mutation is not occurring.

2. Natural selection is not occurring.

3. The population is infinitely large.

4. All members of the population breed.

5. All mating is totally random.

6. Everyone produces the same number of offspring.

7. There is no migration in or out of the population.

The Hardy-Weinberg Equation in Mendel's Pea Plants from Chapter 3

$$p^2 + 2pq + q^2 = 1$$

where

p = the frequency of the dominant allele (such as T in Mendel's pea plants)

q = the frequency of the recessive allele (such as t in Mendel's pea plants)

Note that p^2 is the predicted frequency of homozygous dominant individuals, $2pq$ is the frequency of heterozygous individuals, and q^2 is the frequency of homozygous recessive individuals.

If you know the values of p and q, you can use the equation to predict the frequencies of all three genotypes in the population.

The next step is to compare genotype frequencies from one generation to the next. If the values deviate from the expected values predicted by the equation, you know that one of the assumptions has been broken and evolution may be occurring in the population. This allows you to determine whether evolution is occurring, and in what direction for the selected loci. However, the Hardy-Weinberg equation *cannot* tell you which possible cause of evolution is responsible for the change.

■ **FIGURE 4.1**

The Hardy-Weinberg assumptions (left). Are these assumptions ever met in a real population? The Hardy-Weinberg equation (right) allows researchers to model whether evolution is occurring in a population.

In addition, whole segments of DNA sometimes switch locations on the chromosomes. Usually this is harmful or neutral (meaning it has no effect on the function of the gene or is not in an area of DNA that is transcribed—see chapter 3). But sometimes the resulting new arrangement of DNA is beneficial to the organism. That is, the DNA change results in a change in some aspect of the organism's phenotype that gives it a benefit in its environment. The bottom line is that mutation produces variation in the DNA. Mutation is the necessary fuel for evolutionary change. Without variation at the genetic level, change from generation to generation is unlikely. If there is no variation in the DNA sequences within organisms in a population, then each generation can have only the same alleles in the same frequencies as its parental generation.

There are some exceptions to this rule at the level of the phenotype. Current cloning research has shown us that two organisms with the same DNA makeup can have somewhat different phenotypes. Later in this chapter we will introduce a few ideas about why these differences occur in spite of identical genetic makeup and what this might mean for our ideas about evolutionary change.

Gene Flow Is the Movement of Alleles Within and Between Populations

In sexually reproducing organisms, each individual in a new generation receives a set of alleles (half the full DNA complement) from each of two parents. How and where individuals mate is therefore key to the distribution of alleles and thus the change in allele frequencies across generations. Gene flow—the movement of alleles within and between populations—occurs in two main ways:

gene flow
movement of alleles within and between populations

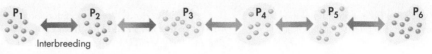

Interbreeding

■ FIGURE 4.2

Gene flow between populations. P_1 through P_6 represent local populations of the same species. All are linked through gene flow, even though members of all populations do not interbreed with members of all other populations.

migration (movement between populations, or where mating happens) and nonrandom mating (who mates with whom).

Migration

The movement of individuals in and out of populations can affect allele frequencies. Since each individual has a slightly unique assemblage of alleles, and different populations can have different allele frequencies, the interchange of individuals across populations can alter the allele frequencies of all populations involved (Figure 4.2). Populations that are geographically very distant from each other are unlikely to experience much gene flow. As we might expect, the less gene flow between populations, the greater the likelihood that those populations will have differing allele frequencies and be different in some aspects of their phenotype (appearance, physiology, etc.—see chapter 2). Conversely, the more gene flow between populations, the higher the chances that they will share allele frequencies and be similar. A modern example of gene flow can be seen in the movement of humans into the United States. This has resulted in enormous genetic variability in the U.S. population and a great deal of phenotypic variation among the people of the United States.

Nonrandom Mating

Very few, if any, organisms mate randomly. There are a multitude of mating patterns, but they can be grouped in two general categories: inbreeding and assortative mating. **Inbreeding** occurs when individuals within a small subunit of a population mate more with each other than with individuals from any other subunit. This has a homogenizing effect—it reduces the amount of genetic variation in the cluster of individuals breeding. There are many misconceptions in popular opinion about what inbreeding means. In fact, most human cultures practice some form of culturally sanctioned inbreeding, usually resulting from marriages between second cousins or other cultural sanctions on who can marry whom. **Assortative mating** occurs when individuals seek mates with traits similar to their own (positive assortative mating) or different from their own (negative assortative mating). Positive assortative mating has the same general effect as inbreeding in that it reduces variation, whereas negative assortative mating increases variation.

Generally, most organisms appear to practice limited outbreeding via migration. That is, most organisms mate within the population subunit in which they live, but in many species, one or both sexes leave the specific groups into which they were born to find a mate. They end up in the same population but in a different group or subpopulation.

Genetic Drift Is a Change in Allele Frequency Across Generations Due to Random Factors

Genetic drift is a difficult process to conceptualize, yet it is the simplest mechanism of change. Basically, **genetic drift** occurs when a random event

---

CONNECTIONS

See chapter 8, pages 237–252, chapter 9, pages 274–277, and chapter 10, pages 320–321, for a discussion of how important migration is in understanding human evolution and modern human diversity.

migration
movement of alleles in and out of populations

nonrandom mating
pattern of mating in which individuals mate preferentially with certain others

inbreeding
mating among close genetic relatives

assortative mating
mate selection based on similarity (positive assortative) or differences (negative assortative) in traits

genetic drift
random changes in allele frequencies across generations

alters the allele frequencies in a population such that subsequent generations have allele frequencies different from their parental generations.

The process is most easily observed in small populations, because random events are more likely to have an impact on a small population than a large one. A simple example will illustrate this concept. If you flip a quarter 10 times, it is highly unlikely that you will always come up with five heads and five tails. However, if you flip that quarter 1 million times, you will come closer to a 50-50 distribution. Each time you flip the coin, there is theoretically a 50-50 chance of heads or tails, but many random factors (hand size, flipping speed, perspiration, wear on the coin, and so on) actually influence the coin's trajectory. The more times you flip the coin, the greater the likelihood that random factors will influence the results in both directions, eventually giving you a near-even distribution.

If you substitute random genetic changes for the coin flip, you have an example of drift. Chance events that alter allele frequencies occur continuously, but in large populations they occur so frequently in each direction that they cancel each other out and are nearly invisible. Thus, they are hard to observe and measure. In a small population their impact is greater and therefore easier to observe and measure.

An example of drift in a human population is that of the Tristan da Cunha islanders. In 1816 a small group of British settlers left South Africa to settle this island in the Atlantic Ocean. There was little or no migration to the island after the initial colonization, and the population had very little interaction with the outside world. By 1961 the population had grown to 294 individuals. In that same year a storm threatened to wipe out the island, and the British government evacuated the islanders. Upon their arrival in Britain, all of the islanders were given routine physical examinations. It was discovered that the group had an extraordinarily high frequency of the alleles for a recessive disease called retinitus pigmentosa. Alleles that occur at extremely low levels in the broader British population were found at very high levels in the Tristan da Cunha islanders. Why? A few members of the original founding population (back in 1816) carried single copies of the allele for the disease. High inbreeding, coupled with little gene flow, resulted in the relatively frequent distribution of the alleles for the disease in the population.

The fact that the founders had a higher frequency of the alleles than the general population was due to chance; there were no environmental or cultural reasons for it. They didn't even know it—it was just a case of bad luck. This type of genetic drift is called a **founder effect**. A founder effect is frequently the result of a dramatic reduction in population numbers, also known as a **bottleneck**. Following the bottleneck there is an increase in population such that the resulting large population has only the limited variation from the founding population that made it through the bottleneck (Figure 4.3).

Current Concepts of Natural Selection Involve an Understanding of Genetics

We currently understand that a population is an assemblage of individuals who share the same DNA (genes) but have slightly different allelic combinations. If some individuals in part because of factors related to their specific combination of alleles, are better able to produce offspring than others, over time these more successful (or fit) genetic variants will become more represented in subsequent generations of the population. In short, adding what we learned in chapter 3 to what we learned in chapter 1, natural selection is the

founder effect
evolutionary process in which a small group of individuals account for all of the genetic variation in a large population

bottleneck
dramatic reduction in the size of a population such that the genetic diversity in the population is substantially curtailed

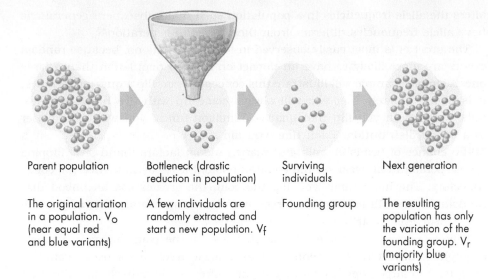

Parent population

Bottleneck (drastic reduction in population)

Surviving individuals

Next generation

The original variation in a population. V_o (near equal red and blue variants)

A few individuals are randomly extracted and start a new population. V_f

Founding group

The resulting population has only the variation of the founding group. V_r (majority blue variants)

■ FIGURE 4.3
The bottleneck effect. Note that the original population differs from the resulting variation in the distribution of phenotypes, represented by the color of the marbles.

process whereby individuals with genetic variants that do best in a given environment have more offspring than individuals with other genetic variants. The simple example of natural selection involving bacteria and antibiotics from the introduction to this chapter is illustrated in Figure 4.4.

As suggested in chapter 1, natural selection can be thought of as a giant filter system (Figure 4.5). On top of the filter we see a population with a large amount of variation. The filter in the middle is the current environment in

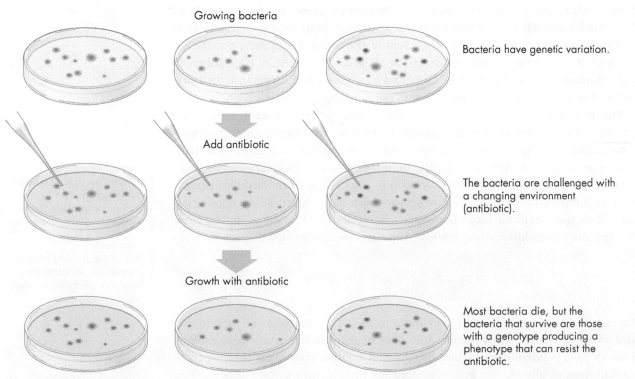

Growing bacteria

Bacteria have genetic variation.

Add antibiotic

The bacteria are challenged with a changing environment (antibiotic).

Growth with antibiotic

Most bacteria die, but the bacteria that survive are those with a genotype producing a phenotype that can resist the antibiotic.

■ FIGURE 4.4
The development of antibiotic resistance in bacteria. The bacteria vary in their resistance to antibiotics. When challenged with an antibiotic, those that are resistant are more likely to survive and reproduce. Succeeding generations will therefore include a larger proportion of resistant bacteria than the original population.

which that population lives. On the bottom is the population of subsequent generations who have lived in that same environment for a long time. The environment has served as a filter selecting certain genetic variants that do best and hindering those that do not. We sometimes hear the phrase "force of evolution" used to describe natural selection. Natural selection is not really an active force or "invisible hand" picking and choosing which organisms survive and which do not. It is a process by which, over many, many generations, the interactions between organisms and their environment result in a set of genetic shifts within a population. A phenotype (and its underlying genotype variant) that is favored in a given environment today may be selected against in the future if the environment changes.

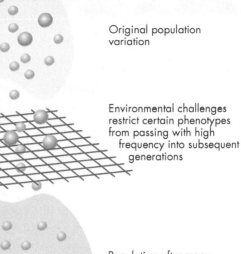

Original population variation

Environmental challenges restrict certain phenotypes from passing with high frequency into subsequent generations

Population after many years of environmental "filter"

■ **FIGURE 4.5**
Natural selection as filtration system. Natural selection works as a filter, allowing only certain variations to flourish.

Alleles Do Not Generally Interact Directly with the Environment

As noted in chapter 3, DNA does not generally interact directly with the environment. It is primarily the phenotype that interacts with the environment. The phenotype must pass through the environmental filter successfully (that is, effectively reproduce) and leave copies of its genotype in the next generation. This means that only those phenotypic traits that are somehow linked to genetic information are subject to natural selection. Keep in mind too that phenotypes are packages (consisting of collections of traits in novel combinations), and it is the entire package that interacts with the environment. Certain aspects of the phenotypic package (traits) might vary across individuals within a population, and that variation sets up differential reproductive success among individuals in that population.

Thus, natural selection is the result of phenotype–environment interactions in which some phenotypes do better, on average, than others in a given environment. The genetic basis for these phenotypes is then increasingly represented in subsequent generations of the population. Remember that "success" in an evolutionary sense means leaving more successful offspring, on average, per generation. Natural selection is not a life-or-death battle between individuals in a population in every generation; rather, it is a long-drawn-out series of interactions in which a slight reproductive advantage changes the genetic makeup (allele frequencies) in a population in the long run.

The more successful phenotypes in a given environment are said to be best adapted to that specific environment. Specific traits (components of the phenotype) that do best in a given environment are called *adaptations*. Although we discussed adaptation in chapter 1, we can more accurately describe it here as the result of a genetic change in response to selection (that is, phenotype-environment interaction). When we consider the giraffes discussed in chapter 1, we can see that their long necks are an adaptation to a specific environment, arising from a pool of variation relating to neck length (among other things).

We do have to be careful, however, not to assume that all characteristics of an organism are adaptations (Lewontin, 1978; Ho, Saunders, & Fox, 1986). Many traits may arise as sets or by default because of structural or physical

Survival of the Fittest? Not Really

Darwin did not originally like the term "survival of the fittest" (remember chapter 1). Darwin's ideas and our current understanding of evolution clearly demonstrate that bigger, faster, meaner are not equal to evolutionarily "best." Survival of the fittest does not mean that the stronger survive. Being evolutionarily fit means having a set of traits that enable you to do well (better than most) in a given environment. Being "fit" does not mean necessarily being able to win a fight. In fact, evolution is not about individual survival at all, it is about genetic lineages and certain traits becoming more common over many, many generations. The biggest lion is not necessarily the most fit. The bully at school may not be fit at all. There is

a long history of what has been mistakenly called "Social Darwinism," which is not Darwinism at all but rather the application of a poor understanding of what "fit" is to human situations. In human societies we see that some groups dominate and exploit others and that some people are rich and others are poor. This is due to social, political, and economic relationships, but not genes and evolution. However, many people, scientists and evolutionary theorists among them, wanted to have a natural (or biological) explanation for oppression and suffering that validated their views. This is where we get the misapplication of survival of the fittest. The way that most people talk about evolution is actually a misuse of the term and a misunderstanding of what natural selection really is.

laws (see the discussion of the human chin in chapter 7). Others are vestigial or have lost any current function (the human appendix is nearly, but not completely, without function). In fact, some traits are the result of adaptation but are currently co-opted to function in a different way. These co-opted traits are called **exaptations** (Gould & Vrba, 1982). An example of an exaptation would be flight feathers. Reliable evidence suggests that feathers arose well before flight and functioned to help early birds (which were still dinosaurs at that time) maintain their warm body temperatures. Over time, certain feathers (on the arms and later, wings) became co-opted by natural selection to serve in a flight function (Figure 4.6).

exaptation
trait that is currently serving a function other than that for which it originally arose

We can describe our current understanding of natural selection as a set of basic requirements that are necessary if selection is to effect evolutionary change in a population. First, there must be both genetic variation in a population *and* phenotypic variation tied to this genetic variation. Second, the traits (the phenotypic variants) that do best in a given environment must be heritable (have a genetic basis). Third, over time the traits that contribute to organisms' leaving, on average, more offspring per generation must become increasingly represented in the population as a result of this differential reproductive success (that is, the traits become adaptations).

By envisioning natural selection in this manner, we can see that it results from individuals' interacting with their environments, but because it results in differential reproductive success, it is observable only at the level of the population over generations. Natural selection acts on phenotypes, but the resulting evolution results in changes in allele frequencies in subsequent populations. Finally, it is very important to remember that natural selection can act only on existing traits; it cannot introduce new variation.

STOP & THINK

Can you think of any possible human exaptations?

Natural Selection Can Affect the Distribution of Traits in Several Ways

There are several ways in which natural selection can affect the way a trait is distributed within a population: Selection can be stabilizing, directional, or

■ **FIGURE 4.6**

Exaptations. Feathers originally evolved as insulation. Over many generations, the wing feathers of an eagle took on another function—flight. Similarly, the feathers on a male peacock's tail took on the function of sexual display.

disruptive (Figure 4.7). *Stabilizing selection* favors the variation on a trait that occurs in the middle of the distribution, such as medium height in a plant. This selection mode actually reduces variation in the trait over time. *Directional selection* favors one of the extreme ends of a trait's variation, resulting, for example, in very short or very tall plants. Finally, *disruptive selection* is bimodal; that is, it favors more than one form of the trait's variation, usually those at opposite ends of the spectrum. The result would be *both* very short and very tall plants, with medium-height plants being selected against. Remember, selection can affect different traits in different ways, but it is the whole package (the individual organism's phenotype) that actually interacts with the environment, not disembodied traits.

The Four Core Processes Do Not Explain All Change

All the processes of evolution (mutation, gene flow, genetic drift, and natural selection) are always occurring in any given population of organisms. At different times in a population's history, one or another of the processes may

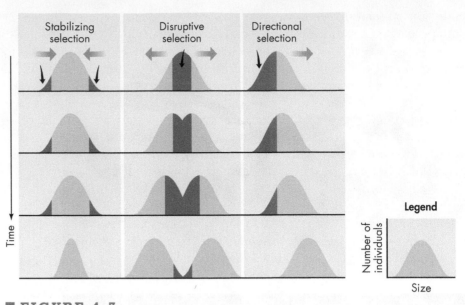

■ FIGURE 4.7
The different types of natural selection. Each of these can change populations in different ways.

play a particularly significant role, but all are always occurring. These processes do not explain all the variation and change we see, however, as mentioned earlier in this chapter. For example, identical twins and even clones do not always have identical phenotypes. These differences are due to a range of developmental factors, including epigenetic (outside the DNA) effects.

Modern evolutionary theorists have developed new understandings of the complex evolutionary patterns beyond the core evolutionary mechanisms we have just reviewed (natural selection, genetic drift, gene flow, and mutation). It is especially important to note that for humans, both behavior and culture can affect evolutionary processes, and therefore both can become involved in shaping biological processes in important ways. Let's briefly examine a few of these new understandings in evolutionary theory to round out our assessment of the core concepts in evolutionary processes.

Four Systems of Inheritance

The biologists Eva Jablonka and Marion Lamb point out that most examinations of human evolution focus on only one system of inheritance—the genetic system (see chapter 3)—which relies on explanations at the level of the genes (that is, evolution is seen as change in allele frequencies over time). However, what if evolution has four systems of inheritance to work from? Jablonka and Lamb suggest that in addition to the genetic system, there are the epigenetic, the behavioral, and the symbolic inheritance systems.

The **epigenetic system** includes all the biological factors in the body that work in combination with the genes and their protein product (those highlighted in chapter 2). These include the machinery of the cells, the chemical interactions between cells and between types of tissues, organs, and systems of the body. The epigenetic system helps the information in the DNA (the genes) actually get expressed; therefore, it impacts genes as well as the whole body. The **behavioral inheritance system** refers to the types of behavior that parents and adults pass on to young members of their group by way of their learning and imitation. For example, most birds need to learn from their parents which foods to eat and which to avoid; there are no "genes" for this. In humans we all are capable of learning a language, but the specific one we do learn from our parents and peers then helps shape the way we see and interact with the world. This is an

---

epigenetic system
the factors in the body that work in combination with the genes and proteins to affect phenotypes

behavioral inheritance system
the system of imitation and learning by which behavior passes from generation to generation

important mechanism for passing on behavior, but again, it is not located in any specific genetic sequences. Finally symbolic inheritance, the passing down of knowledge based on symbol and language is a system unique to humans. You can think of all that you have learned in school or how you see your flag and realize it represents a nation. Think of how often we as humans rely on symbolic cues to decide who to mate with, where to migrate to, and so on and you can see how it might affect biological evolution. Again, none of it is coded in the genes. These additional types of inheritance demonstrate that there is more to inheritance than genes and that important change can result from epigenetic, behavioral, and symbolic systems as well as natural selection.

symbolic inheritance
the passing down of knowledge via symbols and language

Developmental Systems Theory (DST)
an approach that includes the development of biological and behavioral systems as a core part of evolutionary processes

Niche Construction Theory
the modification of niches by organisms and the mutual interactions between organisms and environments

Developmental Systems Theory

Another major change in the way we think of evolutionary theory came with the introduction of **Developmental Systems Theory (DST)** (Oyama et al. 2001). This approach focuses on the development of biological and behavioral systems (phenotypes) over time, rather than focusing only on the genes (genotypes) as the core of evolutionary processes. Development is the growth and interaction of systems such as genes and cells, muscles and bone, brain and nervous system, over the lifetimes of individuals (again remember the systems reviewed in chapter 2). By taking this approach we realize that evolution is not a matter of organisms or populations just being shaped by their environments (as in basic natural selection theory) but of many, many developmental systems changing over time. This theory views evolutionary change as much more than genotype change occurring through phenotype–environment interaction. Instead, DST proposes a complex organism–environment system in which organisms can influence their ecologies and thus the selection pressures on themselves. This view leads to the final new understanding about the ways that evolution works.

Niche Construction Theory

The final addition to our theories of evolution is the concept of niche construction. A niche is the relationship between an organism and its ecology, the way an organism makes a living within a particular environment. **Niche construction**, then, is the building and destroying of niches by organisms and the mutual interactions between organisms and environments. F. John Odling-Smee, Kevin Laland, and Marcus Feldman (2003) describe this as the process by which living creatures, through their metabolism, their activities, and their behavior, partly create and partly destroy their own niches, on scales ranging from the local to the global. Think about earthworms in the soil. If you introduce earthworms to a patch of soil where there have never been earthworms, that first generation begins to consume and defecate the soil, changing its chemical properties. This changes the whole soil area so that the next generations of earthworms are born into a soil that is more conducive to their ways of living (they better "fit" with the niche) and they keep maintaining that ecology by their actions. (As a by-product, what is good for the worms is also great for plants; this is why gardeners put worms into their gardens to do a bit of niche construction.) On a broader human level, agriculture changes our diets, our bodies, and the climates where we live (see chapters 9 and 11 for further discussion on this topic). Niche construction creates a kind of ecological inheritance (such as in the worm and soil example above). As both DST and the ideas of Jablonka and Lamb assert, organisms inherit more than genes (such as behavior and symbol); in this same vein, the idea behind niche construction is that organisms inherit the ecologies they are born into. So if we change ecologies (say, by building cities), children born into those environments inherit the kinds of ecological challenges that come with cities. Finally, the theory goes, niche construction, along with natural selection, contributes to changes in organisms' relations with their environments.

These emerging dynamic views are of growing interest, especially in light of the dramatic changes that we humans are causing for ourselves. Consider the example of antibacterial soap at the beginning of this chapter. We create and use antibiotics to modify our environment, our food, and our bodies. We don't yet know how such environmental modifications (or niche construction) may affect us biologically as we develop from fertilized eggs into billion-celled adults—*after* we have already inherited our genotypes.

Speciation is the process by which new species arise

So far we have discussed the processes by which variation arises and is shuffled around within populations and the various ways that evolutionary change might occur. What happens when genetic variation and phenotypic change within a population become so extensive that one group within the population becomes substantially different from others? Sometimes groups become different enough to be termed separate species.

Speciation is the process by which new species arise. Speciation, the logical extension of Darwin's ideas about descent with modification, is the part of evolutionary theory that many people strongly reacted against, as described in chapter 1. New forms of life on this planet arise from previously existing forms; they are not created anew. This notion remains one of the most misunderstood components of evolutionary theory. To understand the process of speciation, we first need to define the term *species*.

Species Can Be Defined in Many Ways

In chapter 1 we saw that Linnaeus created a system for naming species and that Darwin and Wallace explained why there were so many different species on the planet. Although most people can readily name some different species if asked (dog, human, dolphin, and so on), they are usually hard pressed to say exactly what a species is. The most common definition is "a group of interbreeding natural populations that are reproductively isolated from other such groups." This definition, based on the **biological species** concept, describes a species as a set of populations that can, under natural conditions, mate with one another. This is fine for distantly related organisms like a dog and a dolphin, but what about a dog and a wolf (Figure 4.8)? A domestic dog (*Canis familiaris*) and a wolf (*Canis lupus*) can mate and will do so if the conditions arise. (The coyote, *Canis latrans*, can also mate with both the dog and wolf.) Does this mean that they are not "real" species?

The commonality of genetic elements (DNA) across all organisms and the biological similarities shared by members of the same order (Mammalia, for example) dictate that closely related forms (those sharing a recent common ancestor) will be very similar and thus may have compatible mating physiology. As emphasized throughout this chapter, our world is dynamic, not static, and all organisms are undergoing change. Therefore, many groups of organisms that we think of as separate species could be in the process of speciation and not yet effectively distinct. Large-scale evolutionary change in complex organisms (like mammals), even rapid evolutionary change, may take hundreds or thousands of generations to occur. Thus, organisms like dogs and

speciation
the process by which new species arise

biological species
a group of interbreeding natural populations that are reproductively isolated from other such groups

CONNECTIONS

See chapter 7, pages 191–205, chapter 8, pages 237–245, and chapter 9, page 264, for examples of species definition problems in our own evolutionary history.

Species, Schmeecies . . . I Know One When I See It and So Do They

Ok, so we just told you that there are a number of ways to define a species, but in practice you can tell most of them apart. The key point is that our inability to perfectly define species shows that evolution is ongoing. The fact that some species are able to reproduce with one another just shows that they have recent common ancestry, and they are not that different. Problems in differentiating species in the past arose from the question of how much difference there must be between organisms for them to be classified as different types of creatures. But if we realize that evolution is an ongoing process over enormous amounts of time, then this is really not a problem. Species come and go as populations change over time. Any particular slice of time will give us one view of what species are out there, but a slice a million years later will show dramatic change and probably a whole new set of species in the same place. However, if we had the ability to watch the populations in a location continuously over that same million-year time period we would see the derivation of new forms and types as a continuous process, not necessarily one that can be divided into clearly differentiated species at every stage. Remember, as long as members of a species recognize each other and can mate, then they really don't care what we call them.

dolphins, which may have had a common ancestor some 40 million years ago, are easy to define as distinct species. Organisms like dogs and wolves, which may have diverged as recently as 15,000 years ago, are not.

The study of speciation is a complex and fascinating endeavor, especially when we attempt to describe and catalogue species that are now extinct (as we do in later chapters). For practical purposes we will use two species concepts here, the biological species concept, as described earlier, and the **paleospecies** concept, referring to species that are now extinct. Since paleospecies are not around for us to observe their mating patterns, we use morphological, temporal, geographic, and inferred ecological similarities when attempting to decide whether two fossils belong to the same or different species. Using these two

paleospecies
species defined on the basis of fossil evidence

(a)   (b)   (c)

■ FIGURE 4.8
The canids. Three closely related species—a dog (a), a wolf (b), and a coyote (c).

concepts of species will give us a well-defined set of working tools; however, we are necessarily ignoring a multitude of other ways to define species.

Subspecies Are Divisions Within a Species

Biologists, zoologists, and anthropologists frequently use the term *subspecies* when discussing a subunit of a species. A subspecies is generally defined as a population within a species that is somehow biologically distinct from other populations of that species and engages in little to no gene flow with other populations. Usually this distinctness can be measured by genetic differences or some other factors that indicate a different evolutionary trajectory in the subspecies compared with other populations in the species. It is possible that subspecies are a precursor to speciation. However, there is a great deal of variation in the naming and classifying of subspecies. Conservation biologists, anthropologists, entomologists, botanists, and paleontologists all use varying definitions of subspecies because of the variety of organisms they work with and the differences in the specific research questions they ask. For the rest of this book we will use the definition of subspecies summarized by Templeton (1999): a population that is geographically circumscribed and genetically differentiated and that represents a distinct evolutionary lineage within a species.

Allopatric Speciation Results from Separation and Isolation

allopatric speciation
mode of speciation that involves a separation and isolation of populations of the parent species

The primary model of speciation, known as **allopatric speciation,** involves a separation and isolation of populations of the parent species (Figure 4.9). Once these populations are truly isolated from one another—once there is no gene

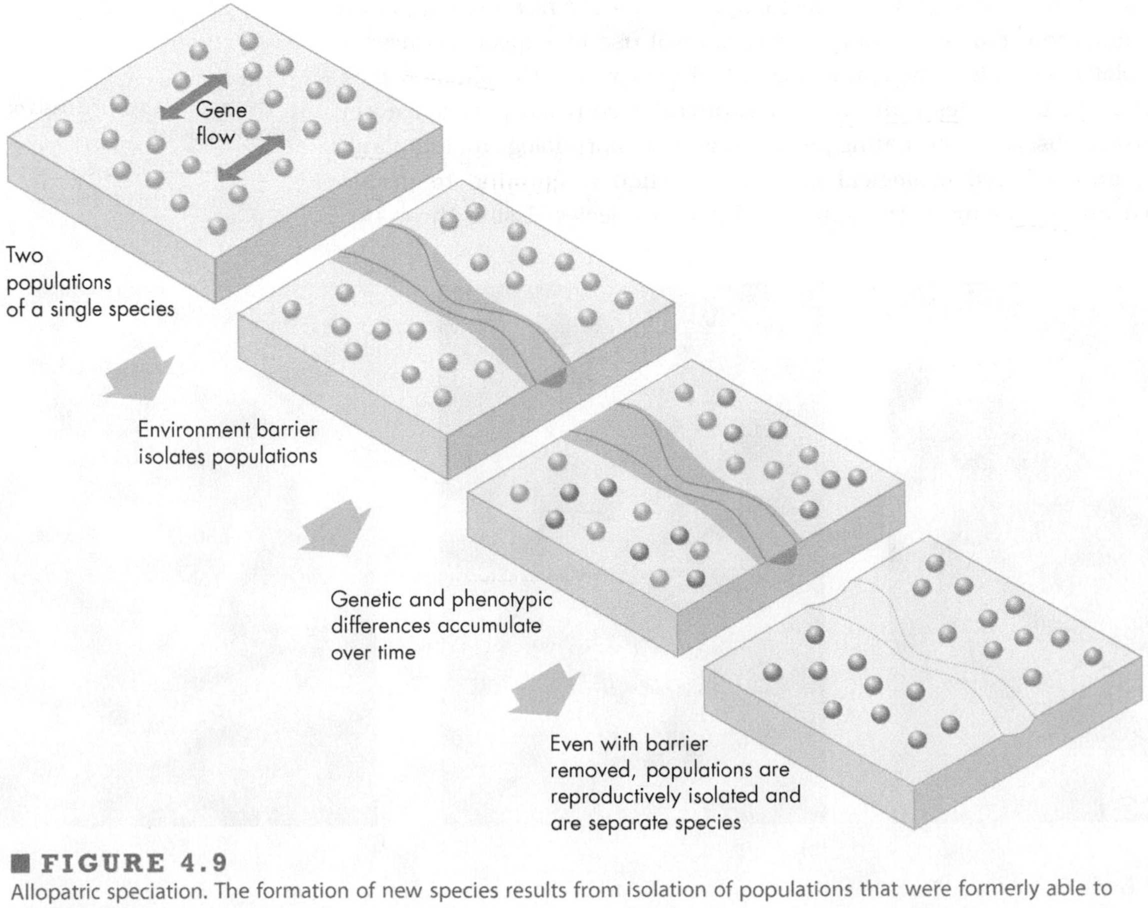

Two populations of a single species

Gene flow

Environment barrier isolates populations

Genetic and phenotypic differences accumulate over time

Even with barrier removed, populations are reproductively isolated and are separate species

■ **FIGURE 4.9**
Allopatric speciation. The formation of new species results from isolation of populations that were formerly able to interbreed.

flow between them—they may encounter differing environments. Even though they have extremely similar genetic makeups, over time their responses to different environmental pressures (via natural selection and other patterns of evolutionary change) can result in new allele frequencies that lead to new phenotypes. If these daughter species' phenotypes become distinct enough from the phenotypes of the original parental species, neither of them may recognize each other as potential mates, and they would therefore be reproductively isolated. This level of isolation would indicate that speciation has occurred (according to the biological species concept).

In this type of speciation, we would expect that species recently diverged from a common ancestor would share many similarities in both genotype and phenotype, as we see in the dog, the wolf, and the coyote. Species that share a more distant common ancestor may have less resemblance to one another, as in the dog and the dolphin.

Phyletic gradualism and punctuated equilibrium: different paces of change

We know that speciation is the result of changes within populations, but currently there are different ideas about the pace of that evolutionary change. Traditional Darwinian evolution, as we have been discussing it here, consists of small changes over dramatically long periods of time, slowly adding up to significant change and potentially, speciation. This pattern is called **phyletic gradualism.** Gould and Eldredge (1977) proposed that evolutionary change could also occur at a different, faster rate and that rapid changes to one or a few populations could result in a speciation event. This event is followed by a long period of relatively minor change, or equilibrium, in the species. They called this pattern **punctuated equilibrium.** Contentious debate continues over the pace of evolutionary change, with both of these modes of evolution supported by evidence from different lineages. It is possible that over the course of history on this planet, both gradual and rapid evolutionary changes have occurred (Figure 4.10).

phyletic gradualism
slow accumulation of small changes in populations such that over time enough change has occurred to result in a speciation event

punctuated equilibrium
rapid biological changes in organisms followed by long, relatively static periods during which little biological change occurs

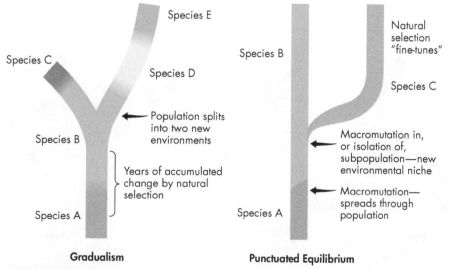

■ **FIGURE 4.10**

Gradualism and punctuated equilibrium. Two different paces of evolutionary change have been proposed.

Similarities can result from either parallel or convergent evolution

parallel evolution
type of evolutionary process whereby species come to share phenotypic characteristics due to recent common ancestry

convergent evolution
type of evolutionary process whereby species come to share phenotypic characteristics due to similar environmental pressures

Although phenotypic similarity often indicates recent common ancestry, this is not always the case. For example, an eagle and a bat are more similar in the way they move than an eagle and an ostrich are, and even a bee has more effective wings than an ostrich. Nevertheless, the eagle and the ostrich share more recent common ancestry than do the eagle and the bat or the eagle and the bee. Given what we know about natural selection and speciation, we can envision two separate ways in which organisms could come to resemble one another. These two modes are termed parallel evolution and convergent evolution.

So far we have focused on **parallel evolution**, the case when species share phenotypic characteristics due to recent common ancestry. You and I look a lot more like a chimpanzee or a monkey than we do a cow or a camel, but all of us, as mammals, are more similar to each other than any of us is to a fish. If you look at any primate species (monkeys, apes, lemurs, or humans), you will notice that they have eyes that are close together on the front of the skull and hands and feet with five digits. These similarities result from our shared ancestry (compared with a cow, for example, which has eyes on the sides of its skull and fewer digits on its feet). If you look at a human, a dog, a bird, and a whale, you can see that their front limbs are morphologically nearly identical, even though the animals use those limbs in different ways (Figure 4.11). Again, the parallels result from common ancestry.

Alternatively, **convergent evolution** is seen when two distantly related forms exhibit similar phenotypes. A bird, a butterfly, and a bat all have functionally similar structures called wings. However, the wings are derived from very different tissues and facilitate flight in very different ways (see Figure 4.12). They are the result of similar natural selection pressures acting on different phenotypes, genotypes, and developmental systems. Wings are an adaptation for flight, but each species arrived at that adaptation in a very different way. We can say that each of these types of animal converged at a similar morphology.

In sum, parallel evolution has occurred when similarities in traits are due to close common ancestry; convergent evolution has occurred when similarities in traits are due to similar adaptations, not to a close evolutionary relationship.

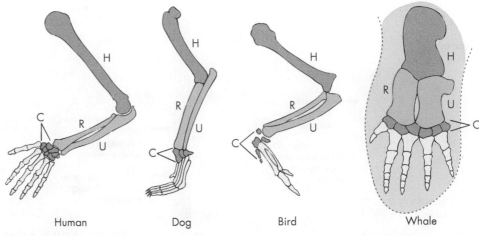

■ FIGURE 4.11

Parallelism. The bone structure of the human, dog, bird, and whale is very similar, resulting from a common evolutionary heritage. The bones shown are the humerus (H), radius (R), ulna (U), and carpals (C).

Biodiversity in evolution: why we should care about biological variation

Given that most life-forms on our planet use the same genetic molecules (DNA), are subject to the same evolutionary processes, and undergo similar patterns of speciation, we should expect to see a great deal of similarity among them. If we look around the planet, however, it becomes obvious that there are millions of life-forms that are in fact quite different from one another. Diversity in organisms occurs because of the complexity of environments on this planet and because environments themselves change over time. The combination of changing environments over time and the tendency of organisms to change in response to mutation, gene flow, genetic drift, natural selection, multiple systems of inheritance, developmental variation, and niche construction produces the amazing diversity of life that we see on our planet today (Figure 4.13).

The value of biological variation, at least at the level of the population, should be clear from our discussion of evolutionary processes. Without variation in the genotype and associated variation at the level of the phenotype, adaptation to changing environmental conditions cannot occur. Why is this important to you?

First, our species (*Homo sapiens*) is very numerous, widespread, and variable in many biological traits. From a biological perspective, this variation is a storehouse for a wide array of potential adaptive change and is extremely beneficial for our species. An understanding of the positive benefits of variation contributes to tolerance as our world becomes increasingly globalized and each of us comes into contact with more and more other humans from around the planet. Although biological differences are an important and evolutionarily significant aspect of the human species, when these phenotypic differences are mixed with cultural preconceptions, historical misunderstandings, stereotypes, and linguistic barriers, they can translate into substantial problems between people. In chapter 10 we examine more closely the benefits of biological variation, how it is distributed in our species today, how and why we classify that variation, and what it means for us as a species and as individuals.

The second reason that we should care about biological variation is that our species is part of a large and dynamic global ecosystem, functioning through the interactions of climate, soils, microorganisms, plants, and animals. We rely on this system for our continued existence. Unfortunately, we are currently in the midst of one of the largest and most dramatic extinction events in the history of our planet, caused in large part by us. Countless species and whole ecosystems are disappearing from our planet at an alarming rate. These species represent biological variation that humans need both directly and indirectly, for several reasons. We rely on soil systems and water reservoirs to provide us with our food and water, and these systems depend

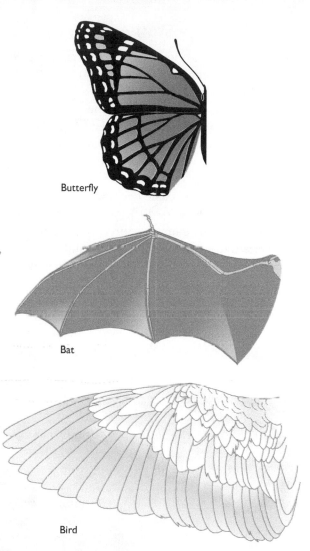

■ FIGURE 4.12

Convergence. The wings of the butterfly, bat, and bird serve the same function, but they evolved independently.

STOP & THINK

All three of these animals have wings and fly, but do they fly in the same ways?

Why Conserve Stuff Anyway?

Why recycle? Who cares if we use most of a given type of tree or fish? As humans we use stuff (a lot of stuff) that we extract from the world around us (think of our discussion of niche construction, and see chapters 7–9 and chapter 11). In fact, we modify and manage many of the major ecosystems on the planet. We could probably keep up this pace for another century or so before we start truly running out of basic necessities. So one good reason to conserve is so that our descendants have some of the same resources we do. Another reason is that we do not yet understand how many ecosystems really work. Take global warming, as an example. We now know that human actions are changing the climate patterns around the planet. How will that affect all of the diverse types of ecosystems that we rely on? Will a small change in temperature in Alaska affect the salmon fisheries worldwide? Will a shift in rainfall patterns across the Midwest change the rate at which our soils can serve to grow corn (which we use in almost everything now)? We have some ideas, but we really do not know. So ignorance of our impact is another reason to be cautious in how fast we use things up. If a major part of human evolutionary success involves our ability to niche construct, then we also have a major responsibility to ensure that this alteration of the environment is sustainable for our descendants and other organisms sharing the spaces and places we occupy.

■ FIGURE 4.13
The diversity of life on earth. Here we see diverse forms of life that have arisen and diversified via evolutionary forces.

What We Know

Questions That Remain

What We Know

Evolution can be seen only at the level of the population across generations. Allele frequencies change over time largely because of mutation and the effects of gene flow, genetic drift, natural selection, and niche construction.

Questions That Remain

We do not yet fully understand how developmental, epigenetic, and other inheritance systems affect evolutionary processes.

What We Know

Natural selection is not an active force; rather, it is the result of interactions between an organism's phenotype and its environment, which lead to adaptations.

Questions That Remain

We do not know what percentage of traits are adaptations and what percentage are exaptations or the result of physical linkage between structures or other processes.

What We Know

Species are clusters of very closely related populations in which individuals are more evolutionarily similar to one another than to individuals from other species.

Questions That Remain

We do not know how some of the paleospecies are related to one another, particularly those in the human lineage. Consistent and accurate identification of species in the fossil record is difficult.

What We Know

Biological change (evolution) has taken place continuously over the history of this planet and continues to do so today.

Questions That Remain

It is not clear whether the pace of evolutionary change is slow and gradual, rapid and sharp, or a mix of the two.

What We Know

Biological variation is important not only to the health of our own species but to the health of the planet as well.

Questions That Remain

We cannot yet see what the overall effects of the current extinction event will be, either for our species or for our planet.

on plants and microorganisms for their maintenance. We need a diverse biota (set of living things) around us so that the resources we use remain available and resilient. Biological diversity also represents a potential reservoir of medicines and nutritional components that we have yet to discover; countless plant and animal species contain elements that are useful to humans. Finally, only those biological communities that maintain diversity are resilient enough to sustain environmental challenges without disappearing.

Therefore, it is imperative that we think about how we are affecting the planet; we need to minimize the destructive aspects of our behavior and maximize practices that are oriented toward sustainable use. An understanding of the vital role played by biological variation in evolution can also help us appreciate the marvelous diversity of life on earth.

SUMMARY

▲ A population is a cluster of individuals of the same species who share a common geographical area and find their mates more often in their own cluster than in others. It is in populations that we can observe and measure the changes in allele frequencies over time (evolution).

▲ Allele frequencies change over time because of mutation, gene flow, genetic drift, and natural selection. However, phenotypic changes can arise due to epigenetic, behavioral, developmental, and niche construction processes in addition to the four core processes of evolution.

▲ The genotype does not generally interact directly with the environment. The phenotype interacts with the environment, and the genotype is affected by the phenotype's success.

▲ Mutation is the only way novel genetic combinations are introduced.

▲ Gene flow is the process by which allele frequencies are changed, largely through migration and nonrandom mating.

▲ Genetic drift is the process by which random events affect the frequencies of alleles from generation to generation. Founder effects are frequent cases of genetic drift. Drift is most noticeable in small populations.

▲ Natural selection can be seen as the filtering of phenotypes (and their genotypes) by the environment, resulting in an overrepresentation of better fit phenotypes (and their associated genotypes) within a population in a given environment over time. The better fit phenotypic variants are considered to be best adapted to the environment. The traits they carry that help them do well in the environment are called adaptations.

▲ Speciation is the process by which new species arise. There are several different definitions for *species*, but most see the species as a viable evolutionary unit.

▲ A subspecies is a population that is geographically circumscribed and genetically differentiated and that represents a distinct evolutionary lineage within a species.

▲ Epigenetic, behavioral, and symbolic inheritance can also affect evolution.

▲ Complex developmental systems and the process of niche construction play roles in the patterns and processes of the evolution of populations.

▲ Two paces of change have been proposed for speciation events: phyletic gradualism and punctuated equilibrium. The fossil record shows some support for both hypotheses.

▲ Organisms can have similar characteristics as a result of either common ancestry (parallel evolution) or similar environmental pressures (convergent evolution).

▲ We are part of a large and dynamic global ecosystem, and we rely on the functioning of this system for our continued existence. Unfortunately, we are currently in the midst of one of the largest and most dramatic extinction events in the history of our planet, caused in large part by us. Being informed and aware of the biodiversity on this planet and its current status contributes to our knowledge and understanding of the world we live in.

CRITICAL THINKING

1. How is it that natural selection acts on an individual organism but evolution can be seen only at the level of the population? Do the other evolutionary processes happen at the individual or population level? How so?

2. Why is there contention over the definition of *species*? Why is it not surprising that some species can interbreed with one another?

3. If biological changes can occur via epigenetic or developmental pathways, what are the implications for our understanding of genotype–phenotype interactions (as laid out in this chapter and chapter 3)? Is it possible that some of the traits that characterize human beings are not the result of natural selection and adaptation? Can you think of any examples? What about behaviors? What is the significance of this issue?

4. Does it matter whether species arise via phyletic gradualism or punctuated evolution? What implications might each of these views have for understanding our own evolution?

5. Some people think that the species living on earth today will eventually become extinct and be replaced by others and that it is therefore not important to protect biodiversity. Others think conservation is a critically important undertaking for humans today. What do you think?

RESOURCES

EVOLUTION AND BIODIVERSITY

Gould, S. J. (1980). *The panda's thumb.* New York: Norton.
This highly readable and entertaining set of essays by the late Stephen Jay Gould focuses on issues of adaptation and evolution.

Otte, D., & Endler, J. A. (Eds.). (1989). *Speciation and its consequences.* Sunderland, MA: Sinauer.
This excellent compilation of professional papers deals with the multitude of issues surrounding species and speciation.

Oyama, S., Griffiths, P. E., & Gray, R. D., (Eds.). (2001). *Cycles of contingency: Developmental systems and evolution.* Cambridge, MA: MIT Press.
A variety of articles argue for a more complex approach to evolution. Chapters range from easily understandable at a college level to very complex.

Wilson, E. O. (Ed.). (1988). *Biodiversity.* Washington, DC: National Academy Press.
This edited volume by the renowned biologist E. O. Wilson includes a wealth of essays about biodiversity and its importance.

REFERENCES

Gould, S. J., & Eldredge, N. (1977). Punctuated equilibria: The tempo and mode of evolution reconsidered. *Paleobiology, 3,* 115–151.

Gould, S. J., & Vrba, E. S. (1982). Exaptation: A missing term in the science of form. *Paleobiology, 8*(4), 4–15.

Ho, M. (1984). Where does biological form come from? *Revista di Biologi, 77*(2), 147–179.

Ho, M., Saunders, P., and Fox, S. (1986). A new paradigm for evolution: Standard evolutionary theory sees little beyond the natural selection of random variation, yet there is more to life. *New Scientist, 27,* 41–43.

Jablonka, E., & Lamb, M. (2005). *Evolution in four dimensions: Genetic, epigenetic, behavioral, and symbolic variation in the history of life.* Cambridge, MA: MIT Press.

Lewontin, R. C. (1978). Adaptation. *Scientific American, 239*(9), 156–169.

Odling-Smee, F. J., Laland, K. N., & Feldman, M. W. (2003). *Niche construction: The neglected process in evolution.* Princeton, NJ: Princeton University Press.

Oyama, S., Griffiths, P. E., & Gray, R. D. (Eds.). (2001). *Cycles of contingency: Developmental systems and evolution.* Cambridge, MA: MIT Press.

Templeton, A. R. (1999). Human races: A genetic and evolutionary perspective. *American Anthropologist, 100*(3), 632–650.

CHAPTER 5

Primate Behavioral Ecology

This chapter addresses the following questions:

▲ What is comparative primatology, and how can it tell us about human behavior?

▲ What is behavioral ecology, and how does it help us understand the evolution of behavior?

▲ What are the general behavioral patterns in the living primates?

▲ What kinds of societies do primates have, and how can we use specific examples (macaques and chimpanzees) to help us understand primate patterns present in humans?

▲ How are human societies similar to and different from those of other primates?

We humans have long wondered what lies at our innermost core. What part of us is contributed by "nature," and what is the result of "nurture"? If a child were raised in isolation, without human contact, would we see in that child raw "human nature," untainted by education or culture? Of course we could not carry out such an experiment, but the folklore and literature of many cultures include tales of human children raised by wolves, apes, bears, or other animals. A few actual cases have also been recorded that offer insight into these questions.

In 1799 a "wild boy" was discovered in the French countryside in a forest of Aveyron. He seemed to be mute and behaved as though he had been raised by wild animals. Victor, as he came to be called, was taken to an institute for deaf-mutes in Paris and placed in the care of a physician named Jean Itard. Dr. Itard took the boy under his wing and tutored him in French culture, language, and manners. Victor never learned more than a few phrases, but he did learn to behave in a somewhat "normal" manner for his time. The French film director Francois Truffaut was so taken with this story that he made a movie about it in 1969, *The Wild Child,* using the boy's experience to explore the larger human experience.

In 1970 a "wild girl" was discovered in California. This girl, given the pseudonym Genie, was about 13 years old. For unknown reasons, her parents had isolated her in a small room and never spoke to her. She was restrained by a harness and at night put in an enclosed, locked crib (Curtiss, 1977). When she was discovered and rescued, she could not stand erect or speak. Genie was eventually treated and tutored by a battery of researchers who tried to teach her to speak English and behave in ways considered "normal" for an American child. Genie never learned to speak at more than a rudimentary level—she could not learn how to combine words in sentences—but she was able to effectively use tools, succeed at complex spatial tests, and easily master cause-and-effect tasks.

These two cases make it clear that human behavior results from the complex interaction of our morphology and physiology; our exposure to other humans, cultural patterns, and language; and our individual life histories. We cannot discover what it means to be human by stripping away any of these components to see what is left.

There is another place to look for answers to our questions, however. We can learn something about human behavior by determining what aspects of our behavior result from our evolutionary heritage as mammals, as primates, as anthropoids, and as hominoids. We can especially look to our primate relatives to understand what we all have in common and what patterns and processes in the past have influenced both general primate and specific human behavioral patterns.

In the previous four chapters we have focused on genetics, anatomy, and the processes of evolution, establishing a baseline for understanding how our bodies function, what forces have shaped the evolutionary history of our species, and how some aspects of behavior may be related to genetics and biology. In upcoming chapters, we will delve into the evolutionary history of the human species, from the earliest primates to modern *Homo sapiens*. We will explore in detail the evolution and characteristics of mammals and primates (chapter 6) and the emergence of humans and their ancestors (chapters 7–9). In this chapter, we examine our closest living relatives, the primates, to understand aspects of our own behavior. We call this approach **comparative primatology.**

Comparative primatology provides insights into modern human behavior

In chapter 2 we described humans as belonging to the order Primates, the suborder Simiiformes (anthropoids), the family Hominoidea (hominoids), and the genus *Homo*. We also discussed the phylogenetic principles that biological anthropologists use to talk about the appearance and relationships of morphological traits, that is, ancestral, derived, and shared derived traits. Comparative primatology is based on these same principles, but here we are talking about behavior rather than morphology. Thus, instead of asking if brachiator anatomy (arm and shoulder morphology adapted to swinging through tree branches) is a shared derived trait for apes relative to other primates, we will be looking at behavioral patterns and asking about their relative presence among the living primates or subgroups within the primates.

The Living Primates Are Widespread and Diverse

The living primates represent nearly 300 species in two major suborders and about 15 families. The two suborders in the order Primates are the **Strepsirrhini** (also known as the prosimians) and the **Haplorrhini** (also known as the tarsiers, monkeys, apes, and humans). Primates live throughout the tropical and neotropical areas of the world (Figures 5.1, 5.2).

comparative primatology
the study of our closest living relatives, the primates, for the purpose of understanding aspects of our own behavior

Strepsirrhini
primate suborder that includes the Lemurs, Lorises, and Galagos (the prosimians)

Haplorrhini
primate suborder that includes the Tarsiers, monkeys, apes, and humans

■ **FIGURE 5.1**
The primates are a diverse
group of animals.

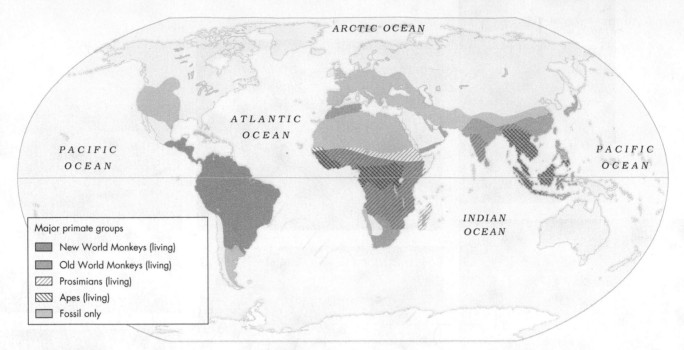

■ FIGURE 5.2
Geographic distribution of the living primates. Except for a few species of Old World monkeys and humans, primates live in tropical regions.

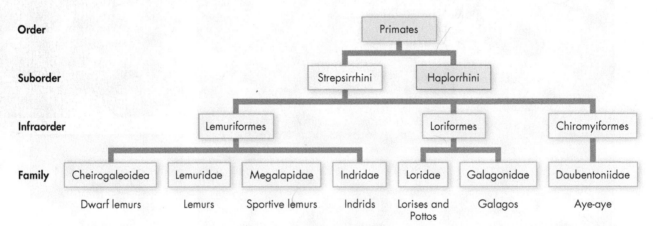

■ FIGURE 5.3
Taxonomy of the strepsirrhines to the family level. The strepsirrhines include lemurs, lorises, pottos, and galagos.

The Strepsirrhini, or Prosimians

The Strepsirrhini are divided into the lemurs of Madagascar and the galagos and lorises of Africa and Asia (Figures 5.3 and 5.4). The lemurs are a diverse group of primates that exist solely on the island of Madagascar. Like most strepsirrhines they have a special nail on their feet called a grooming claw and a modified set of lower incisors called a tooth comb that are used for cleaning their own and others' fur. Because there are no other primates (such as monkeys) on Madagascar, the lemurs have spread out and adapted to many available environments. This resulted in lemurs that fill the same environmental roles as some monkeys do on the African mainland. Before the arrival of humans a few thousand years ago, there were lemurs the size of bears and a diverse array of forms. Today, human hunting and forest conversion

(a)

(b)

(c)

(d)

■ **FIGURE 5.4**
Strepsirrhines. Shown are: slender loris (a); indri with young (b); adult male crowned lemur (c); ringtailed lemurs (d).

have caused the extinction of a large number of lemur forms, but many species are still found in the forested areas of Madagascar.

The galagos are a group of small, nocturnal (nighttime active) strepsirrhines found across central African forested environments. They have specialized lower limb morphology that results in a great leaping anatomy. The galagos are largely fruit and insect eaters and spend a lot of their time involved in vocal and olfactory communication. Many researchers have argued that the galagos are nocturnal to avoid competition with the larger bodied diurnal (daytime active) monkeys that share the same forests and overlap in diet and habitat use.

The lorises consist of the Asian lorises (usually called slow and slender lorises) and the African pottos. Like the galagos, these strepsirrhines are mostly nocturnal and fully arboreal. However, the lorises tend to have diets that are made up largely of insects and other small animals. Unlike the galagos, the lorises do not leap in the trees; rather they move (usually slowly) by using all four limbs to grasp branches and "clamber" through the trees. The

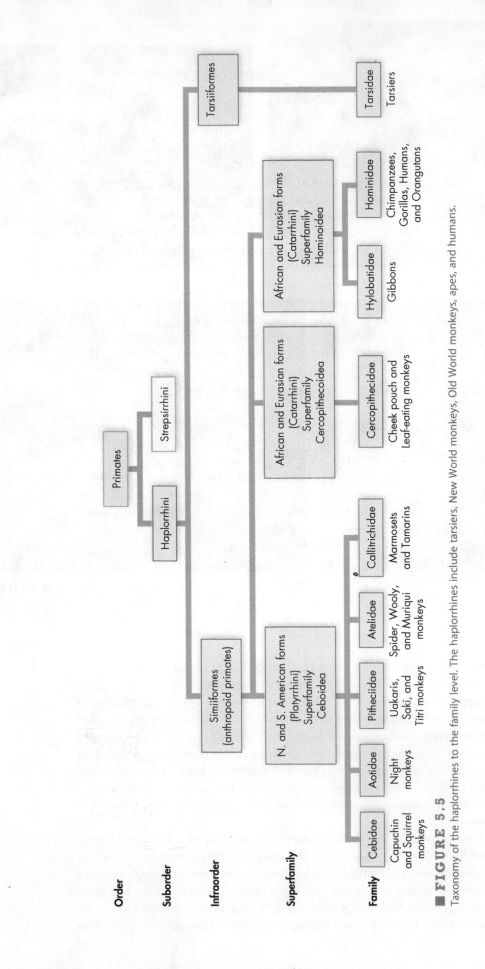

■ FIGURE 5.5

Taxonomy of the haplorrhines to the family level. The haplorrhines include tarsiers, New World monkeys, Old World monkeys, apes, and humans.

lorises are the most widespread of the strepsirrhines and are found across Africa and into southern and Southeast Asia.

The Haplorrhini, or Tarsiers, Monkeys, Apes, and Humans

The Haplorrhini are divided into two infraorders: the Tarsiiformes and the Simiiformes. The Tarsiiformes are made up of the tarsiers (family Tarsiidae). The Simiiformes are made up of three superfamilies: **Ceboidea**, or monkeys of the Americas; the **Cercopithecoidea**, or Asian and African monkeys; and the Hominoidea, or apes and humans (Figure 5.5). In this book, we use two specialized terms to refer to the Simiiformes: **anthropoid** refers to all monkeys, apes, and humans, and **hominoid** refers to all apes and humans. We reserve the term **hominin** for the hominoid lineage that produced our own species, *Homo sapiens.*

The tarsiers are a group of small-bodied, nocturnal primates found in Southeast Asia. They get their name from having very elongated tarsal bones (see chapter 2) and lower limbs adapted for incredible leaping abilities (greater even than galagos). The tarsiers live in small groups, usually consisting of two adults and some young. They hunt small animals and insects and use a diverse array of vocal sounds to communicate. The tarsiers have extremely large eyes and are well suited to moving about through dense tropical forests at night. Tarsiers are particularly interesting, as they share traits with both the strepsirrhines and the Simiiformes and may even represent a third branch of primates outside of the haplorrhine/strepsirrhine dichotomy (Figure 5.6).

The Ceboidea, or New World monkeys, are a large and diverse group found in forested environments from southern Mexico to southern Argentina. The vast majority of Ceboid forms are fully arboreal and relatively small compared to the Old World monkeys and apes. The smallest Ceboids are as small as or smaller than the tiniest strepsirrhines (less than 250 g, or half a pound), and the largest are about the size of a middle-sized anthropoid (about 12 kg, or 26 lb). The Ceboidea share a set of dental and anatomical characteristics that differentiate them from the other anthropoids and unite them as a group. However, among the Ceboidea there are many morphological and behavioral variants. A group of small-bodied Ceboidea known as the Callitrichids always give birth to twins, and one genus, *Aotus,* is the only nocturnal monkey. Additionally, a few genera of Ceboids are the only primates with truly prehensile (or grasping) tails (Figure 5.7).

The Cercopithecoidea, or Old World monkeys, include all of the monkeys found in Asia and Africa. These monkeys are divided into two subfamilies: the colobinae and the cercopithecinae. The cercopithecines are the baboons, macaques, and related forms of both Africa and Asia. These range in size from a few pounds (~1 kg) to over 60 pounds (~28 kg). They include both terrestrial (ground using) and arboreal species. All, however, are diurnal. The cercopithecines are also called "cheek-pouch" monkeys, as they have small pockets inside their cheeks in which they can store food. The other subfamily of Cercopithecoidea, the colobines, are more arboreal than the cercopithecines and do not have cheek pouches. However, they do have large "sacculated" stomachs with multiple folds that act as reservoirs for special bacteria that help the colobines digest leafy matter. For this reason the colobines are also known as the leaf-eating monkeys,

Ceboidea
primate superfamily that includes all monkeys found in the Americas

Cercopithecoidea
primate superfamily that includes all monkeys found in Africa and Asia

anthropoids
all monkeys, apes, and humans

hominoid
member of the super-family Hominoidea

hominin
the division (called a tribe) in the superfamily Hominoidea that includes humans and our recent ancestors

■ **FIGURE 5.6**
A tarsier. Notice the large eyes and elongated tarsal bones.

(a)

(b)

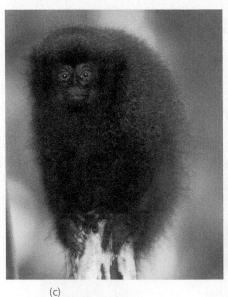
(c)

(d)

(e)

■ FIGURE 5.7
New World monkeys, or Ceboidea. Shown here are: spider monkey (a); capuchin monkey (b); titi monkey (c); cotton-top tamarin (d); and wooly monkey (e).

and many species specialize in hard-to-digest leaves and plant matter that other primates cannot eat (Figures 5.8).

The Hominoidea include the African and Asian apes and the humans. The African apes include the chimpanzees and gorillas; the Asian apes are the orangutan and the gibbons. Relative to the other primates (especially the monkeys), the living Hominoidea have very few species that have survived into the modern era. As you will see in chapter 6, the Miocene period (~22–5 million years ago) was a time of great diversity of hominoid forms. The hominoids are mostly large bodied (except for the gibbons) and have relatively large brains (much larger relative to body size than other primates or most mammals). The apes

(a)

(b)

(c)

(d)

■ **FIGURE 5.8**
Old World monkeys, or Cercopi-thecoidea. Shown here are: black and white colobus (a); olive baboons (b); hanuman langurs (c); and guenon (d).

and humans also lack external tails and have adaptations in the upper body that allow a wide range of movement in the arms and hands (Figure 5.9).

Comparing the Primates Helps Us Understand Behavior

Studying primates is interesting in itself, and it teaches us a great deal about our own species. In comparative primatology we are looking for three things: primate-wide trends, hominoid-wide trends, and unique hominin or human characteristics. *Primate-wide trends* are those behaviors or behavior patterns that occur in all, or most, primates. We assume that their universal presence in members of the order Primates indicates that they are ancestral traits that have maintained themselves in all cases due to their selective benefits. In other words, behaviors that have some genetic basis and have done well for

(b)

(c)

(d)

(a)

(e)

 FIGURE 5.9
Hominoids. The hominoids include apes (gibbons, orangutans, gorillas, chimpanzees) and humans. Shown here are: gorilla (a); orangutan (b); chimpanzees (c); gibbon (d); and humans (e).

Monkey See, Monkey Do, and Humans Too?

If chimpanzee groups fight each other, is it the same as human war? When two gibbons live together for a long time, is it like human marriage? No; in both cases these are not homologous behaviors. While we have made a big deal about how similar humans and other primates are, we have to be careful not to fall into the trap of superficial similarity when it comes to complex social and behavioral scenarios. Human biocultural reality is more complex than that of other primates. Our evolutionary and social histories have created a whole range of options for us that are not available to other primates (see chapters 6–11). Wars occur for reasons that are simultaneously economic, political, and philosophical—all reasons that other primates do not have. A war is never simply about two groups fighting when they encounter one another (as chimpanzees will do). When two gibbons form a small group and mate together, they are not entering into a social, legal, and religious association (marriage). They are pair-bonding, as many primates do, and living in a small group that usually has only two adults and their offspring. There are no vows, no parties, no societal expectations of the pair. There are many behavioral overlaps between humans and other primates, but these tend to be in basic trends and patterns, not complex culturally defined events. Comparisons between us and other primates are as likely to show us what is unique about humans as they are to show us what is common among all primates.

primates are expected to be favored by natural selection and maintained across primate species.

Hominoid-wide trends are those behavior patterns that we see in all, or most, hominoids but not in other anthropoids or other primates. We assume that these behavior patterns arose since the evolutionary split between the hominoids and other anthropoids in the earliest Miocene, about 22 million years ago (as we will discuss in chapter 6). These behaviors are those that distinguish the apes and humans from other primates. Finally, looking at our primate relatives and ourselves, we will find that many behaviors occur only in humans, not in other primates. These behaviors are *unique to humans* and thus have arisen since our split with the apes in the terminal Miocene, about 6 million years ago (as will be discussed in chapter 7). Looking at these trends allows us to begin to reconstruct the evolution of our behavior.

CONNECTIONS

See chapter 7, pages 206–209, to read about some of the hominoid behavior patterns and how our early ancestors modified them.

To Study Behavior, We Have to Measure It

To scientifically investigate behavior we have to be able to test hypotheses about it; to do that, we have to define it, quantify it, translate it into units of data, and develop tools to record it. Most broadly, behavior is defined as all the actions and inactions of an organism. It may seem counterintuitive to include inactions in this definition, because we tend to think of behaving as engaging in an active state, such as running, talking, fighting, eating, and so on. However, sleeping is also a behavior (a very important one), as are not running, not talking, not fighting, and not eating. In other words, inactions can be as important as overt actions. All are forms of behavior, especially in such complex social organisms as primates.

Specific Methodologies Are Used to Measure Primate Behavior

A *methodology* is a set of means used for data collection. Both quantitative and qualitative methods are used in comparative primatology. In *quantitative methods*, data are recorded in a standardized format such that actual numbers (individual data) can be compared across time and place. This type of data can be analyzed statistically and therefore tested most effectively. In *qualitative methods*, data are not collected in specific, standardized formats. These data may enlighten the observer about the behavior of a particular organism, but they cannot readily be used to test hypotheses across different studies. Qualitative data are valuable because they can frequently fill in gaps in more standardized data by adding context and offering a glimpse of the "bigger picture" (Figure 5.10).

To collect quantitative data, researchers use a specific sampling protocol, a fixed pattern for data collection. For example, they might follow a single individual, record the behavior of a whole group, or take snapshots of behavior every 5 minutes of the day. Such studies can be long term (some chimpanzee studies have lasted more than 40 years) or short term (some studies last only a few weeks), depending on the questions being asked and the methods used. Primate studies are done both in captive situations (laboratories, zoos, captive colonies of primates) and in free-range situations, where the researchers go to the locations where the primates live naturally.

■ FIGURE 5.10
The author observes a macaque in the field. Both qualitative and quantitative methods are used to study primate behavior.

A Behavior Can Be Viewed from Five Perspectives

Once you have recorded a behavior, you will want to ask questions about it. A useful approach is to think about behavior from five different angles: phylogeny, ontogeny, proximate stimulus, the behavior itself, and its function (Bernstein, 1999; Tinbergen, 1963). As an example, let's consider the behavior of eating. When you are hungry, a set of chemical and nerve responses stimulates you to look for food. When you obtain food, you use your hands and mouth to process it. These are observations we might make about eating if we are considering it in terms of *phylogeny,* its evolutionary history. The behaviors of using your hands to get your food to your mouth and then chewing it have an evolutionary past that includes the morphology and anatomy of your digestive system (recall chapter 2), hands, fingers, mouth, teeth, and so on. The combination of these features is not unique to you or to humanity; rather, it arose among the earliest primates, who used their hands to manipulate food items, and it is common to all primates.

In contrast to the phylogeny of a behavior, the *ontogeny* of a behavior includes all the factors that have influenced an organism since its conception, that is, learning and life experience. For example, when you are hungry, you go to certain places to get food—if you are at home, you go to the refrigerator or cupboard—and you eat certain sets of food but not others—you select specific items to consume. Food preferences and knowing where to go for food are learned behavior patterns and important parts of ontogeny.

If we think about eating from the perspective of *proximate stimulus,* we consider the trigger event that initiated the behavior. For example, you may be out and about and pass a hot dog stand, which smells quite good (assuming you have learned to like hot dogs). The aroma stimulates your hunger and you move toward the stand to feed. If we think about eating from the perspective of the *behavior itself*, we look at the behavior of feeding: Once you have the hot dog, you eat it. Finally, and importantly from an evolutionary perspective, we are also interested in the *function* of a behavior, that is, its impact on fitness (or lifetime reproductive success, as discussed in chapters 1 and 4). The function of a behavior, its evolutionary consequences, can be significant when we are trying to understand why a behavior is common or rare or even why it appears at all. From this perspective, we might consider the effects on overall fitness of relying on a diet of fast food.

When we collect behavioral data, then, we ask one or more of these five questions in an attempt to better understand the behavior itself. In the overall picture of biological anthropology, we are most interested in behaviors that seem to serve some function and therefore add to potential lifetime reproductive success. Just as in our earlier discussions of Darwin's finches, we are interested in what facets of our behavior have evolved over time—behaviors that have at least some genetic basis such that natural selection would have favored them over the last several million years, influencing the patterns we see in humans today.

Behavior and Genetics Are Interconnected

In chapter 3 we saw that all aspects of an organism have some genetic component. When it comes to behavior, however, identifying the underlying genetic basis is extremely difficult, because behavior is not directed by one or two genes or a few chemical or neurological impulses (although we assume that there is some heritable component to at least some behavior). Most, if not all, behavior is a complex series of interactions among morphology, learning, experience, circumstance, and chance events. This complexity makes it difficult to assess the function (or evolutionary impact) of any behavior and to understand the biological basis or genesis of a behavior. Many behaviors may also reflect exaptations, the use of certain behavioral capabilities in novel ways. These complex factors do not mean that we cannot attempt to answer these questions.

CONNECTIONS

See chapters 3, pages 88–89, and 4, pages 106–108, for discussions of genetics and behavior.

Some behavior patterns that are widespread in a taxonomic group serve clear functions. These patterns are easily observed, described, and tested, and we assume that they are adaptations. The flight/fight/startle response in mammals is an example of such a behavior. We see this response when a zebra standing on the savannah looks up from the grass it is eating to see a lion charging at it, mouth open and teeth glistening. The zebra immediately stops eating and starts moving. Its heart beats faster, the blood flows away from its stomach and intestines toward its legs, and it sprints away as fast as it can. If successful, it escapes the lion and then slowly calms down and returns to eating. If the situation is slightly different—for example, the lion has cornered the zebra and her offspring—the zebra may choose to stand and fight. Either way, the physiological response (changing heartbeat and blood flow) is the same and is part of the zebra's phylogeny. The decision to flee or fight is based on experience/learning and is part of the zebra's ontogeny.

A similar pattern happens in humans. If a friend (or foe) sneaks up on you and scares you, your heart pumps faster, your stomach feels queasy, and you may yell or jump. A whole genre of movies (suspense/slasher movies) relies on

STOP & THINK

What does it mean for us that modern humans can induce these stress responses just by worrying about jobs, moneys, families, and other aspects of our lives?

this startle response for its success. The fight/flight/startle physiological pattern and its generalized behavioral response are very old and are found in most animals. Why? It stands to reason that those individuals who did not respond to predators in this way with relative frequency did not do well in the overall evolutionary picture. We hypothesize that this combined physiological and behavioral response pattern is an adaptation because it is widespread and potentially results in a selective benefit for an organism.

There are several such behaviors common to mammals and other organisms. In this chapter we are going to focus specifically on the nonhuman primates and their general behavior patterns. From assessment of these general patterns and a look at a few groups of primates, we stand to learn something about human behavior.

Behavioral ecology provides the basis for evolutionary investigations of behavior

behavioral ecology
the study of behavior from ecological and evolutionary perspectives

foraging
the act of seeking and processing food

Behavioral ecology is the study of behavior from ecological and evolutionary perspectives (Strier, 2006). In later chapters we will be looking at how ecological pressures and evolutionary patterns have shaped morphology, but in this chapter we examine how these pressures and processes affect behavior. By obtaining a general understanding of how aspects of ecology challenge organisms, we can model ways in which organisms might deal with these pressures through behavior as well as morphology. In other words, the behavioral ecological approach seeks to understand the selective pressures on organisms and hypothesize about how the behaviors they exhibit today have arisen in response to current and past ecological pressures.

Foraging/nutrition

Habitat locomotion

Predation

Interspecific competition

Intraspecific competition

Socioecological Pressures Affect Organisms in Five Areas

General socioecological pressures can be divided into five main arenas: nutrition, locomotion, predation, intraspecific competition, and interspecific competition (Figure 5.11). *Nutritional ecology* refers to the pressures that organisms face in obtaining sufficient food and water. Whether a primate feeds on fruits, leaves, insects, or other mammals makes a substantial difference in how it forages— that is, how it goes about finding food, where it looks for food, and how it captures and processes food. This pattern is an important element in the primate's behavioral ecological profile.

The challenges of *locomotion* involve how an animal moves about. Generally, primates are arboreal, terrestrial, or both. Within each of these categories there is a great deal of variation. One arboreal primate may use the lower limbs of trees and move about in dense foliage, while another arboreal primate may use the upper extremes of the forest, moving by leaping between trees and using the smaller terminal branches as its pathways. Both of these primates are arboreal, but the pressures on their bodies and behavior are substantially different, based on the surfaces they use in their arboreal environment (Figure 5.12).

Predation is another important selective force. If an organism is eaten, its reproductive success is drastically diminished, to say the least. If there are predators in the environment, we would expect primates to deal with this

FIGURE 5.11
Socioecological pressures. All animals are subject to five basic kinds of challenges: the need to obtain food, to move around their habitat, to protect themselves from predators, and to compete for resources both with members of their own species and with other species.

threat in some way. Most primates have very little defensive morphology (aside from large canine teeth), so we would expect to see some behavioral means of avoiding predators. In fact, that is what we find. Most primates have vocalizations and specific behaviors that they use to respond to predators. Sometimes, primates will mob predators as a group. The pressure of predation is thought to be so important in the evolution of behavior that it is often proposed as one of the reasons that many animals live in groups. This idea is referred to as the *selfish herd concept.* If an individual is in a group, the odds of its being eaten are reduced by the number of other individuals in the group. Additionally, with more eyes and ears, predator detection increases. On the other hand, the larger the group, the easier it is for predators to detect it. Clearly, there are trade-offs in the evolution of behavior, just as there are trade-offs in the evolution of morphology, as we will see in upcoming chapters.

There are many ways that competition can be an important selective force on primates. *Intraspecific competition* refers to contests among members of the same species or even the same group. *Interspecific competition* refers to contests between different species for the same resources (for example, competition between monkeys and birds over the same fruit source). A distinction is also made between contest competition and scramble competition (Sterck, Watts, & van Schaik, 1997; van Schaik, 1989). *Contest competition* occurs when the resource being fought over can be monopolized by one or more individuals. For example, if there is a relatively small prize fruit tree, one or a few individual monkeys can potentially dominate access to it and keep others away. The contest is then between individuals or groups to see who can hold the tree and defend it from others. *Scramble competition* occurs when a resource is not effectively defensible by one or a few individuals (for example, a whole orchard of fruiting trees), and thus all individuals are really racing against time to see how much fruit they can gather before it is all gone. Each of these types of competition exerts slightly different pressures on organisms. Consequently, we would expect that behavioral adaptations to these pressures would also vary. Figure 5.13 illustrates these two types of competition.

■ FIGURE 5.12
Modes of locomotion. These two arboreal primates move very differently. The prosimian (indri), top, moves by leaping between branches and clinging. The anthropoid (baboon), bottom, moves by quadrupedal walking along the branches. Note the anatomical differences in their upper bodies and lower legs.

Success of a Behavioral Adaptation Is Measured in Terms of Energy Costs and Benefits

Primatologists use the concept of costs and benefits to describe an organism's behavioral responses to ecological pressures. In chapters 1 and 4, we discussed the concept of *fitness,* which we can define here as a genotype's contribution to net lifetime reproductive success relative to other genotypes. In terms of behavioral ecology, we seldom actually measure an organism's

STOP & **THINK**

Do humans today still have to worry about these basic pressures?

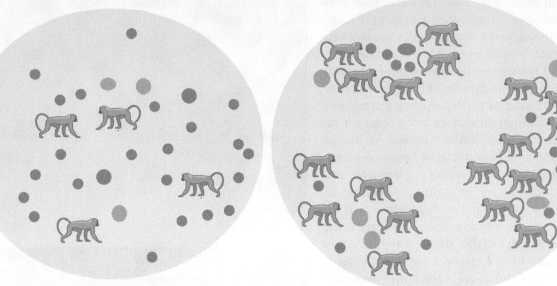

■ FIGURE 5.13

Scramble competition: dispersed food, difficult to monopolize

Contest competition: clumped and defendable food sources

overall lifetime reproductive output; rather, we model the amount of energy that an organism uses in any given behavior and try to determine whether the organism gets back what it expended (neutral behavior), loses energy in the behavior (a cost to the organism), or gains energy in the behavior (a benefit to the organism).

Because it costs energy to reproduce and to live from day to day, the core assumption of behavioral ecology is that organisms will try to maximize their net energy gains and minimize their costs. Those organisms that do this most effectively will hypothetically have the most success in reproducing and thus leave more copies of their unique genotype in the next generation (the process we call natural selection). Notice that we assume that natural selection will favor those behavior patterns with the highest net fitness returns (as measured by energetic benefits and, ostensibly, reproductive output).

If a set of behavior patterns becomes prominent in a population as a result of natural selection, we call this pattern a **strategy.** Thus, competition among behavioral variants leads, over time, to the overrepresentation of the better-fit strategies in subsequent generations. Of course, this process is only possible via natural selection if the behavioral patterns in question are heritable, that is, they have a genetic component (or, as noted by Jablonka and Lamb in chapter 4, have epigenetic, behavioral, or symbolic inheritance).

Certain predictions about how animals should behave emerge from these basic notions of behavioral ecology. One of the most significant predictions is **kin selection,** the behavioral favoring of your close genetic relatives (Hamilton, 1964). Kin selection was proposed to explain the dilemma posed by altruism. **Altruism,** or acts that have a net loss of energy to the actor but a net gain in energy to the receiver, does not make sense if organisms only benefit by maximizing their own fitness. However, the idea of kin selection offers a simple equation that should predict when an organism might behave in a manner that looks altruistic. If the individual who receives the benefit from a behavior that costs you energy is your relative, then a certain percentage of your genotype (depending on the degree of relatedness) is still benefiting. Because

See chapter 4, page 103, to tie this into modern evolutionary theory.

CONNECTIONS

strategy
set of behavior patterns that has become prominent in a population as a result of natural selection

kin selection
behavioral favoring of one's close genetic relatives

altruism
acting in a way that has a net loss of energy to the actor and a net benefit in energy to the receiver

close relatives (parents and offspring, siblings) share much of their genotype, we would expect behaviors among them to be seemingly altruistic, as they frequently are. As individuals are more distantly related, we would expect to see less and less seemingly altruistic behavior among them.

Alternatively, even if organisms are not related to each other, we might still expect to see reciprocal altruism. In *reciprocal altruism*, an individual behaves in a way that benefits another at a cost to itself, and the other individual in turn benefits the original actor, either immediately or at some time in the future. These basic assumptions serve as a set of predictors that researchers use in attempts to explain the types and patterns of behavior they observe.

Reality Is More Complex Than Suggested by Cost-Benefit Analyses

Organisms are constellations of traits, and often there are conflicting pressures on different traits. For example, if an organism used both arboreal and terrestrial environments, we might expect that arboreality would exert pressure favoring curved phalanges for better movement in the trees, while terrestriality would exert counterpressures favoring straighter phalanges (at least on the feet) for more efficient bipedal walking. The situation is even more complex when we try to understand behavior, especially complex social behavior.

Because there are no known direct gene–behavior links, it is likely that ecological pressures set up ranges of selection within which many behaviors can function, some better than others. Imagine a spectrum of potential behaviors influenced by a variety of factors (Figure 5.14). Natural selection (fitness costs/benefits) and other limitations (such as body size and shape) determine the ends of the spectrum—the limits of practical behaviors—and particular environmental stimuli or experiences elicit behavior from a specific part of the spectrum. As a simple example, think of femur length. In the fetus the mass of tissue that is eventually going to be the femur is controlled in part by genetic instructions, and during fetal development the general shape of that bone is influenced by cell–cell interactions and the interactions of proteins and tissues—epigenetic and developmental factors. After the individual is born, however, the rate at which the bone grows is powerfully influenced by the amount and quality of nutrition received. So although the potential spectrum of femur length for two individuals might be the same (especially if they were identical twins), different stimuli and experiences would result in different actual femur lengths.

We can refer to the spectrum as the **potential** for a trait and to the actual phenotype as the **performance** of that trait. As a behavioral example, consider physical aggression in humans. There is a range of possible types and patterns of physical aggression that any individual can exhibit. This broad potential is influenced by body

potential
the spectrum of possible expression created by morphology, evolutionary history, and other aspects of a genotype

performance
the actual expression of a trait or behavior

CONNECTIONS

See chapter 4, pages 16–108, and think about how this relates to epigenetic inheritance and niche construction.

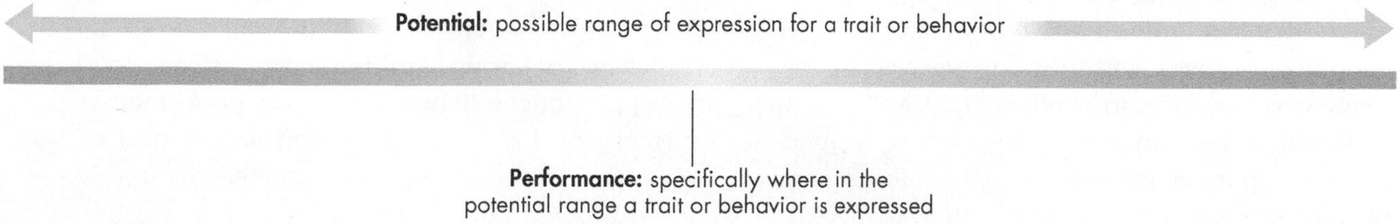

Potential: possible range of expression for a trait or behavior

Performance: specifically where in the potential range a trait or behavior is expressed

■ **FIGURE 5.14**
The spectrum of behavior. Natural selection and other limitations create the potential range of the spectrum. Particular environmental stimuli, experience, and physiological conditions determine where on the spectrum the behavior or trait occurs.

size, muscle density, and health, among other things. However, cultural patterns, life experience, and the availability of weapons or other tools can dramatically influence where in the potential spectrum an individual actually expresses physical aggression.

This example is simplistic, but it illustrates the complexity of understanding even one behavior. Although a behavioral ecological approach can be useful in modeling the function and thus the evolution of behavior, we need to remember that it is not individual behaviors or traits but whole organisms that face environmental challenges on a day-to-day basis. It is the overall lifetime reproductive success of those organisms that affects the next generation; our estimates of energy costs and benefits can easily oversimplify or miss the mark on lifetime patterns.

Adding to this complexity, factors other than natural selection affect behavior. Chance events (such as in genetic drift) can influence an individual's life in ways that we cannot predict based on energy models, giving rise to new behaviors. Some behaviors may be exaptations (behaviors that are co-opted for a new purpose); thus, a behavior that functions in a particular way today may have arisen for an entirely different purpose. And some behaviors may be by-products of other behaviors. The evolutionary biologist Stephen Jay Gould introduced the notion of **spandrels**—by-products of structural change— to account for some anatomical structures. The example he gave was the arch, which by its very structure creates two open spaces, or spandrels, in either corner (Figure 5.15). In terms of behavior, a spandrel pattern could mean that a given behavior produces other side behaviors that in themselves are not the result of selection. It might be very difficult for a primatologist to tease out the causes of such a behavior.

Morphological constraints on organisms also limit the spectrum of potential behavior expression. For example, human morphology will not allow us to see certain wavelengths of light or hear certain ranges of sound; our behavior could not evolve in response to detection of those elements outside the ranges

spandrels
by-products of structural change

CONNECTIONS

Are All Men Jerks?

Chimpanzee males often attack females just to keep them in line. Certain types of baboon males will bite and attack females to keep them from wandering toward other males. Human males in many societies occasionally attack and abuse women. Are male primates just jerks? No, but they have the potential to be very aggressive. In many societies, human and other primates, social cooperation keeps within-group aggression relatively low. However, in some species and in some contexts males can use aggression to influence other group members, including females. In many primate species males are larger than females and thus have an advantage when it comes to physical

conflict. So in these species there is the potential for males to use physical aggression as a social tool, but they do not always do so. The difference between males having evolved aggressive responses and males using those aggressive responses is a good example of the potential and performance concept. The body size difference between males and females sets up the possibility that such behavioral patterns could emerge. However, many other factors, such as type of social system, makeup of the group, and tendency for coalitionary support in conflicts, all affect the performance (or emergence) of such aggression on the part of males. So, when it comes to aggression, males have the potential to be jerks, but they are not evolved to be that way.

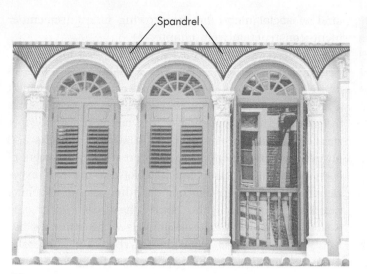

Spandrel

■ FIGURE 5.15
The spandrel is the by-product of arch building. Just as building an arch creates spandrels, natural selection creates some behaviors that are merely by-products.

accessible to us. Finally, there are **phylogenetic constraints** on behavior, which are limits on our current behavior due to patterns and trends in our evolutionary past. Just as humans have five fingers because they are primates, they also have other morphological and possibly behavioral patterns that have been inherited from their distant ancestors.

General behavior patterns in the living primates

If we look across the primate order, we see that some behavior patterns are found in nearly all primate species. When we identify such widespread patterns, we assume that they represent ancestral characteristics and successful adaptations. Most of these behavior patterns stem from living in groups and negotiating the social relationships that group living creates.

Mother-Infant Bonds Are the Core of Primate Societies

In all primates, and in many mammals, the behavioral interactions between a mother and her infant establish the parameters for the offspring's later social relationships. Compared to other mammals, primates have a very long **infant dependency period,** the period during which the infant is wholly reliant on others for nutrition, movement, thermoregulation, and protection. Obviously, it is in the mother's evolutionary interest to enable her offspring to mature successfully. In primates, due to the long dependency period, this interest results in a patterned set of behavior we refer to as the *mother-infant bond.* This bond is characterized by very close spatial association (for years in human, ape, and some monkey societies), frequent physical and vocal contact, and the exposure of the infant to the mother's behavior and association patterns. The infant not only gains nutrition and protection from the mother but also acquires information about other group members, foods, ranging patterns, and behavior habits (Figure 5.16). We can see this as one of the major aspects of behavioral inheritance in primates. We might even consider the intense closeness of primate mothers and infants as building a

phylogenetic constraints
limits on current behavior or traits due to patterns and trends in an organism's evolutionary past

infant dependency period
period during which the infant is wholly reliant on others for nutrition, movement, thermoregulation, and protection

■ FIGURE 5.16
A female primate and her infant. These are macaques (*Macaca fascicularis*).

STOP & THINK

If we do not automatically know how to parent, then how do we learn?

home range
area used by a primate group or community

affiliative
bond enhancing or prosocial ("friendly")

agonistic
aggressive or combative ("unfriendly")

kind of social niche for the growing infant (remember niche construction from chapter 4).

Specific mothering behavior is not coded for by particular genes; rather, all female primates (and males in many species) have the behavioral capability to exhibit a set of caretaking behaviors. What type of behavior an individual exhibits depends on her or his previous experience (ontogeny). Infants act as a strong stimulus and always seem to generate much interest from members of a group; however, if a female has not had previous experience observing her mother or other group members handle infants, or if she herself has never interacted with young individuals, she may feel the stimulus but not be able to exhibit behavior that results in successful infant caretaking. We can hypothesize that the evolution of a set of physiological and behavioral patterns that predispose individuals to caretaking behavior (caretaking potential) exists as a result of natural selection. Life experience then enables the differential expression of those behaviors (caretaking performance). We could also expect that in many species the selection pressures for successful caretaking potential would be stronger on females than on males due to the fact that females give birth and must lactate and provide food if the offspring is to survive.

There Are a Few Primary Grouping Patterns in Primates

Most primates live year-round in relatively cohesive groups, typically consisting of more than two adults and related offspring. Frequently, there are multiple adult females and males, although sometimes there is only one male and multiple females. In a few species there are groups with one adult female and multiple adult males. In about 3% to 5% of primate species, groups typically consist of one female, one male, and their offspring (Fuentes, 1999). Some primates, primarily prosimians and a few anthropoids, are also found in what is referred to as a *dispersed social group*. In this pattern, individuals rarely gather in the same place at the same time, but their individual **home ranges**, the areas they use regularly, overlap substantially. These individuals know each other and frequently interact via scent marking or vocalizations but rarely engage in face-to-face behavioral interactions (Figure 5.17).

Affiliation and Grooming Are Important in Primate Societies

Because primates live in groups and interact with one another frequently, social tolerance is extremely important. One way that individuals establish relationships with one another is through the use of space and a type of contact behavior called *grooming*. Space use is an indicator of the type of relationship between individuals. If individuals are frequently in close spatial association, we can say they have a tolerant and probably **affiliative** ("friendly") relationship. If two individuals avoid one another or engage in conflict over the use of the same area, we can say that they are less tolerant of one another and have an **agonistic** ("unfriendly") relationship.

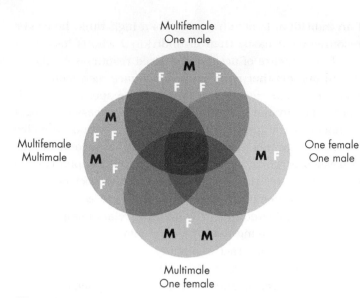

■ FIGURE 5.17

Basic primate grouping patterns. Much of primate behavior stems from living in groups.

Primates establish and cement affiliative relationships through mutual grooming (Figure 5.18). Grooming is the movement of the hands and/or mouth through the fur to clean out particles of dirt, insects, and other debris. Obviously, this behavior has a hygienic function, but primates groom far more frequently than would be required for simple hygiene (McKenna, 1978). The physical contact involved in grooming appears to have a beneficial effect on both the groomer and the groomee. Especially in times of tension or strife, grooming can reduce stress and cement relationships. Individuals may spend more time grooming those with whom they want to associate, or they may refuse to groom those with whom they have agonistic relationships. The directionality of grooming can also be important. Who grooms whom and who initiates and terminates grooming sessions can reveal a great deal about the relationship between individuals.

Because grooming involves both morphological components (hands, mouth) and physiological components (the changes caused by touch and the effect that cleaning has on health), we can see the importance of selection in creating the parameters for its expression. At the same time, an individual learns during its lifetime which other individuals to groom, how to groom, and when to start and stop grooming. All primates groom—it is a primate-wide behavior pattern—but they vary in how they use social grooming.

Hierarchies and Dominance Help Structure Primate Societies

Most primate species exhibit a pattern of differential access to resources within a social group—in other words, some individuals get better food or more food, or better sleeping areas, than others. The set of relationships that results in different relative abilities to acquire desired goods is

■ FIGURE 5.18

Three macaque adults and a juvenile relaxing. The adult female on the right grooms the young juvenile.

STOP & THINK

Do humans groom each other? Is physical touch the only way we might groom?

dominance
set of relationships that results in different relative abilities to acquire desired resources

philopatric
staying in one's natal group

CONNECTIONS

See Chapter 7, page 208, and 8, page 226, to see how human ancestors might have changed the relationship between the sexes relative to other primates.

called **dominance.** If an individual is dominant, or has a high rank, he or she can gain a favored resource more easily than an individual who is less dominant or lower ranking. The measure of access to desired resources by different individuals relative to one another is called a *dominance hierarchy.*

Dominance hierarchies can take a variety of forms. Some species have relatively linear hierarchies, wherein one individual has priority access over most or all of the other members of the group. This dominant individual is called the *alpha* animal. In such a system there would also be a second-ranked individual who has access over all other members except the alpha, and a third-ranked individual, and so on. However, in most primate societies there is another level of complexity to dominance relations: They are contingent on coalitions and alliances (predictable and mutually invested relationships). Even in relatively linear systems, high-ranking individuals usually have one or more allies in the group with whom they interact frequently and who provide social support in contests for resources or even in direct physical fighting.

In many primate species, adult males and adult females have separate dominance hierarchies. Frequently, in one-on-one contests for resources, males are dominant over females, especially if the males are larger (sexually dimorphic). However, environmental and social selective pressures do result in systems in which females are dominant, in which males and females are co-dominant, or in which measuring dominance is difficult because individuals do not compete overtly with one another. Dominance is not a trait inherent in an individual; rather, it is a role that he or she occupies for a time. Primates move through different dominance ranks and roles throughout their lives, and each primate species has a different pattern according to which individuals attain dominance or interact with one another in competition for resources. Because dominance hierarchies are found primarily in adult primates, the system is one that young individuals have to learn to negotiate as they mature (Figure 5.19).

Dispersal and Life History Patterns Are Important to Social Behavior

When we want to understand the behavior of primates in an evolutionary context, we have to take into account the genetic makeup of the group they live in and the types of experiences they have across their life span. Understanding dispersal patterns is key to understanding these aspects of group living. For example, in most primate species, members of one sex disperse (leave their natal group, the group they were born into), and members of the other sex are **philopatric** (stay in the natal group). Members of the philopatric sex then have genetic relatives (siblings, parents, cousins) who live in the same group and theoretically have an investment in their survival (according to the kin selection hypothesis). Members of the dispersing sex have to enter a group in which they have no relatives and thus must forge relationships with nonkin. They cannot expect the "built-in" alliances and assistance that having kin around would provide. In some primate species, both sexes leave their natal groups, resulting in few kin bonds except those between mothers and offspring. Dispersal also has another cost: time spent alone, outside of a group. It is highly likely that dispersal can be very costly in an evolutionary sense, because the individual does not get the

■ FIGURE 5.19
Dominance. A male macaque displays his canine teeth in a mild display of dominance.

benefits of living in a group and may be more susceptible to predation and less able to compete for access to food.

In some primate species, individuals of one or both sexes move among multiple groups during their lifetime, making and breaking alliances and relationships across groups and time. In some species, different types of groups exist within the same population. Hanuman langurs of India (*Semnopithecus entellus*), for example, have multifemale/multimale groups, multifemale/one-male groups, and all-male groups living in the same area. A male could move among three distinct types of group throughout his lifetime. His experiences in each of these group types would be very different and might require different social skills and patterns. We would expect to see a range of behavioral potential in species with this pattern, because the specific behaviors any individual would need to exhibit could change across the different social situations.

Cooperation and Conflict Are Integral to Primate Societies

Both cooperation and conflict play major roles in the lives of primates. Alliances and coalitions are core in social groups, and primates use social negotiation to establish, reinforce, and disrupt these relationships. Very few primates spend most of their time alone; therefore, they are constantly interacting with their group-mates. Because dominance relationships are pervasive in primate societies, serious fighting for resources usually does not occur. There are fights, but the overall time and energy spent engaging in serious aggression tend to be quite low (Sussman & Garber, 2007). This is not to imply that conflict is not important. It has been argued that social relationships between individuals are so important that the potential damage caused by conflict is serious and must be repaired. Many primate species display some form of reconciliatory behavior wherein they repair damage to relationships caused by conflict (Aureli & de Waal, 2000).

STOP & THINK

Do humans spend more time cooperating or fighting?

Social organization in two nonhuman primate societies: macaques and chimpanzees

It is evident that social organization is complex in primate societies. That is, their systems of living together, interacting with one another, acquiring sufficient nutrition, and ensuring safety from predators are quite intricate. We can envision social organization as being made up of the mating patterns, group structure, and individual behaviors of members of a species. Researchers generally agree that these constituent components of social organization have been, and are being, shaped by evolutionary pressures. Thus far in this chapter we have considered general patterns of primate behavior and briefly introduced the core aspects of behavioral ecology. In this section we examine two nonhuman primate societies—macaques and chimpanzees—and then briefly compare them with modern humans. Using the comparative approach, we hope to identify some behavioral patterns in humans that are primate-wide, some that are hominoid-wide, and others that are uniquely human.

Macaques: A Widespread Primate Genus

Macaque monkeys (members of the genus *Macaca*) are among the most widespread of any primate genus. In fact, of all the primates, only humans have a more extensive distribution on the planet (Figure 5.20). The genus *Macaca*

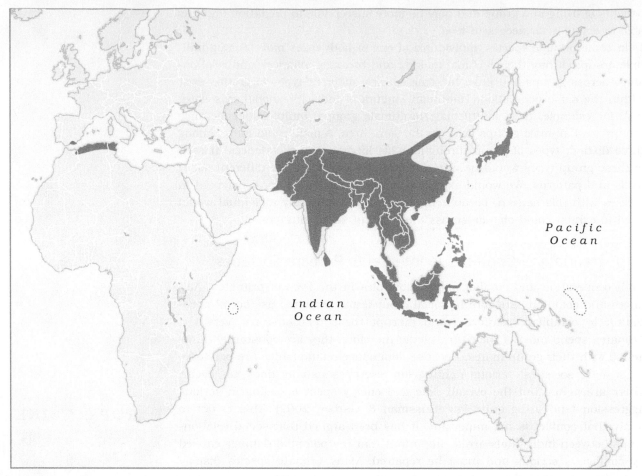

■ FIGURE 5.20
The distribution of the genus *Macaca*. Of all nonhuman primates, macaques have the widest geographical distribution.

is an excellent group to examine in a comparative perspective because the *nasa* radiation of the genus in the Plio-Pleistocene, about 2 million years ago, is similar to that of the genus *Homo* at the same time. The macaques spread across much of Asia and into central Eurasia and even northern Africa. Today, their distribution remains widespread throughout eastern and southern Asia and into northern Africa. Macaques have encountered many diverse habitats. As a result, they reflect responses to a broader range of environmental pressures than nearly any other nonhuman primate group.

There are about 19 macaque species, but they tend to cluster into a few major species groups. The rhesus-fascicularis group (primarily *Macaca mulata*, the rhesus macaque, and *Macaca fascicularis*, the long-tailed macaque) represents an extremely widespread species group wherein the different species can and do interbreed when they overlap in the wild (Figure 5.21). This occasional cross-breeding between species suggests that their speciation is relatively recent or that the species never diverged dramatically either behaviorally, ecologically, or physiologically.

Social Organization in Macaques
Female macaques range in body size from about 3 to 4 kg in some species to more than 12 kg (~27 lb) in others. Males are roughly 20% to 40% larger

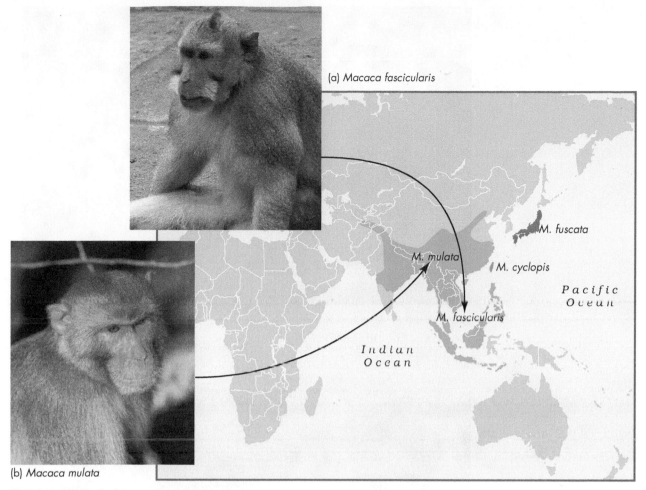

(a) *Macaca fascicularis*

M. fuscata

M. mulata

M. cyclopis

Pacific
Ocean

M. fascicularis

Indian
Ocean

(b) *Macaca mulata*

■ FIGURE 5.21

The combined ranges of *Macaca fascicularis* (a) and *Macaca mulata* (b). The rhesus-fascicularis group is a widespread species group of macaques.

than females (Rowe, 1996; Figure 5.22). Macaques are generalists in their feeding patterns, preferring fruit but eating a wide variety of foodstuffs, including leaves, insects, and occasionally vertebrates. They are full quad-rupeds and spend a good deal of time in the trees; however, most macaque species also use the ground for foraging and moving about.

The majority of macaques live in multifemale/multimale groups that can number from 10 to more than 100 individuals; the most usual group size is between 20 and 50. There are usually more adult females than adult males in these groups, and social activity revolves around clusters of related females (Thierry, 2010). In macaque societies, males tend to leave their natal groups and seek out other groups to join. Females, on the other hand, are philopatric and therefore are surrounded by their female relatives (sisters, cousins, aunts, mother, grandmother, and so on) throughout their lives. As we would expect, female macaques spend a great deal of time and energy associating and interacting with their maternal kin. Clusters of females and young can be seen in macaque groups huddling together in close proximity, grooming one another, and occasionally fighting (Figure 5.23). These clusters are called *matrifocal units* (Wheatley, 1999), indicating that they are generally made up of related females. A few adult males may be seen near and/or in the midst of the matrifocal units, but most males are relatively solitary, remaining on

■ FIGURE 5.22
Sexual dimorphism in *M. fascicularis.*

■ FIGURE 5.23
A macaque matrifocal unit. Female macaques spend a great deal of time interacting with maternal kin.

the outskirts of the groups and occasionally interacting with females and other males. Subadult (teenage) males may be seen together.

An explanation for these social differences between males and females can be found in the dispersal and dominance patterns that characterize macaque societies. Although there is a range of dominance patterns, from very strict linear (sometimes called "despotic") dominance systems to relaxed, "egalitarian" ones, the pattern of the rhesus-fascicularis group tends toward strict dominance patterns in females and males (Thierry, 2010).

Life for Female Macaques

The main arena of social interactions for female macaques involves female maternal kin. Depending on the size of the group, it will usually contain from two to six matrifocal units. There is a set of dominance relationships within and between each of these units. The more dominant matrifocal units usually displace the others from prime food sources, sleeping sites, and other preferred resources. This is partly because the dominant matrifocal units are also the largest. With more individuals in a cluster, they have a better chance of intimidating or outcompeting other, smaller clusters of individuals. This can often confer a slight advantage to infants born into higher-ranking matrilines.

Although there is strength in numbers, individuals are not always dominant on their own. Macaque females rely heavily on alliances with female relatives to gain access to resources and win competitions. A lone female from a dominant matrifocal unit may not be dominant when her relatives are far way (in another tree) and she has to contest with five or six females from a subordinate cluster. Usually, however, females do not stray far from their kin. Female dominance disputes typically involve vocalizations and threats and occasionally some physical fighting, but only rarely are participants seriously wounded.

In addition to the dominance relationships between units, there are dominance relationships within such a cluster. Generally, a prime-age female (about 8 to 14 years old) holds the highest rank within a cluster. In a system unique to macaques, youngest daughters inherit their mother's rank. It is not uncommon to see the 2-year-old daughter of a high-ranking female taking resources from a fully adult female who ranks lower than her mother. This rank relationship always transfers to the youngest daughter. Therefore, when the 2-year-old's mother has another female offspring, this youngest daughter will outrank her older sister. Why do we see this system of rank-reversal in macaque female social dominance? Probably partly because the youngest individuals are most in need of resources and partly because the mother offers greater protection to her youngest daughter than to other kin and intervenes more frequently on her behalf.

Life for Male Macaques

Life for male macaques is quite different from that of females. Males have clear linear dominance relationships that can change frequently. Because they leave their natal groups, they cannot rely on kin to assist them in conflicts and need to form associations with other males and with females in order to negotiate dominance disputes. High-ranked males often form coalitions with other, slightly lower ranked males, to defend their position and gain access to preferred resources. Because males may transfer groups multiple times during a lifetime, they can be exposed to risks, especially when they are between groups and on their own. This may be why there tend to be more adult females than males in macaque groups, despite the fact that the sex ratio is generally equal in young individuals.

There appear to be many ways for males to attain a high rank. Some males are extremely aggressive and use fighting and conflict to move up the dominance hierarchy. They rely on winning fights and intimidating others, including females, to gain access to preferred resources. Fighting in male macaques can result in substantial injuries; however, it is not clear how often these injuries result in deaths. Other males use association with females to form coalitions to create strong social bonds with other individuals. These males engage in a lot of grooming and other calm social interactions with females and young, even including holding infants. In a sense they rely on the assistance of others to attain and maintain high rank. Because of the varied ways in which males attain rank, their ranks are fragile, and males may spend anywhere from a few months to many years at high rank (Berkovitch & Huffman, 1999).

Sexual Behavior in Macaques

Although sexual behavior can be varied, generally female macaques mate with more than one adult male and sometimes with all the males in a group. Many macaques are seasonal breeders, that is, females are receptive only during certain times of the year. During this period of **estrus,** or behavioral and physiological sexual receptivity, females actively seek males and solicit copulations with them. In some groups, high-ranking males can restrict access to females by fighting with other males or staying very close to the females (sometimes referred to as *mate guarding*), but in large groups, restricting access is very difficult. In slightly over half the macaque groups in which researchers have determined genetic relationships, high-ranking males fathered the majority of infants born during their tenure.

estrus
behavioral and physiological sexual receptivity

Other Patterns of Social Interaction

Interactions between groups of macaques are frequently aggressive. Disputes over favored resources (such as areas with food trees) are usually resolved by one group displacing the other. In areas where food resources are not limited, however, groups may tolerate one another's presence on occasion. It may be that the degree of territoriality and the way in which a group views a neighboring group are related to the relative abundance of food and the type of habitat in which they live.

Throughout Asia there are many sites, such as temples and even cities, where macaque monkeys live in and around areas also occupied by humans. In these groups, the macaques tend to exhibit high rates of object manipulation. They manipulate food and nonfood items in a variety of ways, such as rubbing objects together, rubbing them on the ground, and stacking and playing with stones. Some researchers suggest that these kinds of behavior arise in groups with very little food stress. Macaques have occasionally been observed using behavioral innovations to clean or access foodstuffs and even, in a few isolated cases, using tools.

Chimpanzees: Our Closest Relatives

When researchers ask comparative questions about the evolution of human behavior, the primate genus they probably use the most is chimpanzees. Along with the gorilla, the chimpanzee is our closest relative and therefore shares many ancestral (primate-wide) and shared derived (hominoid and hominine) morphological and, probably, behavioral traits with humans.

There are two species of chimpanzee: *Pan troglodytes,* frequently called the common chimpanzee, and *Pan paniscus,* frequently called the bonobo (Figure 5.24). They are found across central Africa (Figure 5.25). Chimpanzees are large primates, with female *P. troglodytes* weighing between 35 and 50 kg (~75–110 lb) and female *P. paniscus* between 32 and 40 kg (~70–90 lb). Males are about 10% to 20% larger than females in *P. troglodytes;* the sexual dimorphism is somewhat less pronounced in *P. paniscus.* All members of the genus *Pan* are heavily frugivorous (fruit-eating), and their lives are substantially affected by seasonality and fruit abundance.

(a)   (b)

■ FIGURE 5.24
The two chimpanzee species, *Pan troglodytes* (a), and *Pan paniscus* (b).

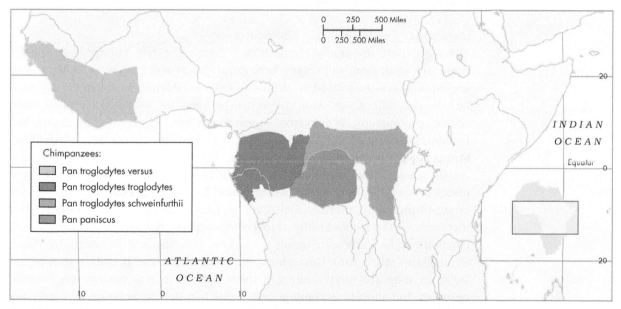

■ FIGURE 5.25
Distribution of the two chimpanzee species and the subspecies of *P. troglodytes*. They are found across central Africa.

Social Organization in Chimpanzees

Both species of chimpanzees live in multifemale/multimale communities ranging in size from 20 to more than 150 individuals. All these individuals are rarely, if ever, in the same location at the same time, however. This is because chimpanzee communities are characterized by a *fission-fusion* social pattern, meaning that individuals spend their time in various subgroups, which have variable compositions across space and time. Both species are characterized by female dispersal and male philopatry, although there is some female philopatry in at least a few eastern chimpanzee populations (Stumpf, 2010).

Subgroups generally consist of mixtures of age and sex classes. Mother-offspring subgroups are made up of an adult female and her dependent offspring (usually a youngster under 7 years of age). Multifemale subgroups consist of multiple adult females and their offspring. Subgroups made up of clusters of related individuals consist of females and their offspring, some of whom may be adult or at least independent of the mother. All-male subgroups are made up of multiple adult and sometimes subadult (teenage) males. Heterosexual subgroups consist of adult males and females and frequently, young individuals. Consort pairs are two adult individuals (usually one male and one female) who separate themselves from other individuals in the community and spend a good deal of time mating. Finally, individual chimpanzees occasionally move around the range of their community by themselves.

The specific sizes of the different subgroups and the relative frequency of their occurrence vary by chimpanzee species, subspecies, and population. This variation is geographically pronounced, with the eastern populations of *Pan troglodytes* (*schweinfurthii*) having, on average, smaller parties than the other subspecies and than *Pan paniscus*. Overall subgroup size appears to be closely correlated with the availability of fruit and, in heterosexual subgroups, with the number of estrus females (females who are sexually receptive and have visibly swollen sexual organs, as discussed in more detail later in this section). The more fruit available and/or the more sexually active females present, the larger the subgroups tend to be.

Dominance Relationships in Chimpanzees

Although there are many similarities between the two chimpanzee species, there are also some important behavioral differences. Because both species are equally closely related to humans, it is worthwhile to examine the similarities and differences. One difference between the two species is in dominance relationships. In *Pan troglodytes*, males are, on average, dominant over females; however, both males and females compete with others of their sex and establish hierarchical ranks (McGrew, Marchant, & Nishida, 1996; Stumpf, 2010). Males attain high rank by forming alliances and coalitions with other males (frequently those of similar ages) and by using spectacular displays and other intimidation tactics, including serious fighting, to manipulate other members of their community into ceding access to favored resources. Male competition for rank can result in serious injuries and occasionally death. Some males attain rank through extreme aggression and maintain that behavior once they are high ranking. Others appear to rely heavily on coalition partners and mutual grooming and social bonding to achieve and maintain dominance status.

For females, dominance is associated with substantially improved access to food sources and high infant survivorship (especially in east African populations). High-ranking females tend to have a large number of offspring in the group, and occasionally mother-daughter pairs act together to achieve or maintain high rank. Females do achieve dominance via aggressive displays and occasionally fighting, but they do not do so as frequently or intensely as males (Figure 5.26).

In east African *P. troglodytes*, both males and females who are high ranking gain access to favored food sources and social partners and therefore have increased reproductive success. In west African forms, rank does not always result in increased reproductive success (Boesch, et al., 2002).

In *Pan paniscus*, dominance contests, dominance relationships, and the overall tenor of rank are different from those in *Pan troglodytes*. In this species, females are generally dominant to males and put on substantial dominance displays in which they drag tree branches or other objects behind them. However, dominance interactions rarely result in serious fighting. Rather, many of the dominance interactions and other conflicts in this species are resolved via genital–genital rubbing and other **sociosexual behavior** (nonreproductive sexual behavior that serves to resolve conflicts and/ or reinforce alliances and coalitions) (Figure 5.27). Male bonobos also have an intrasexual dominance hierarchy, but they are seldom dominant over females. A male's rank is frequently tied to that of his mother. Males do compete with one another aggressively at times, but compared with *Pan troglodytes*, bonobos show lower overall rates of aggression (Stumpf, 2010).

Although females disperse in both species, strong bonds between unrelated females are common in *Pan paniscus* and less so in *Pan troglodytes*. This difference may have to do with the differences in dominance systems and in the way that community members treat recent migrants in the two species.

■ **FIGURE 5.26**
Chimpanzees engaging in an aggressive encounter. This is one way to achieve dominance.

Sexual Behavior in Chimpanzees

Female members of the genus *Pan* display distinct and easily observable signs of fertility. Their anogenital region becomes filled with fluid and very large and turgid during estrus. These sexual swellings provoke interest from other individuals in the community. Before, during, and after the period of peak swelling, females actively seek males and solicit copulations. In both species females mate with multiple males during these periods. In *Pan troglodytes*

sociosexual behavior
nonreproductive sexual behavior that serves to resolve conflicts and/or reinforce alliances and coalitions

■ **FIGURE 5.27**
Sociosexual behavior by *Pan paniscus*. Serious fighting is rare in this species.

males may attempt to mate-guard females. This usually takes the form of one or two high-ranking males staying very close to an estrus female and chasing away other males who try to approach her. *Pan troglodytes* males have also been reported to display high rates of aggression toward females. Some suggest that this aggression may be a coercive strategy to get females to mate with them. This is not the case in *Pan paniscus*. Female choice plays an important role in both species, but to date there is no evidence that bonobo males are able to effectively mate-guard or restrict females' mating choices. Some researchers have suggested that female chimpanzees mate with multiple males to confuse paternity and reduce the likelihood that any given male will treat them aggressively.

Although most copulation occurs during female estrus, members of the genus *Pan* do engage in sexual activity outside of estrus, especially in *Pan paniscus*. Bonobo females and males engage in frequent genital contact and stimulation as a means of social interaction. Conflicts among females are frequently followed by intensive sociosexual behavior. There are also indications that favored food sources (a kind of giant fruit) are shared among females and that the process of food distribution and sharing is mediated by sociosexual behavior.

Hunting and Meat Eating

Both species of the genus *Pan* hunt and eat other mammals, but *Pan troglodytes* do so more frequently than *Pan paniscus* (Boesch, et al., 2002; Stumpf, 2010). In some populations chimpanzees hunt frequently and have a high success rate; in other populations hunting is less frequent. Animal matter can make up 5% or 6% of a chimpanzee's diet. Hunting appears to coincide with times of fruit abundance, suggesting that meat may not be merely a nutritional supplement. *Pan troglodytes* across Africa appear to prefer hunting and eating red colobus monkeys (subfamily Colobinae), but they eat a variety of other mammals as well. Although females hunt in both species, it is an activity performed predominantly by males in *Pan troglodytes*.

Researchers report that populations of *Pan troglodytes* in western Africa hunt in a more coordinated manner than those in eastern Africa (Stanford, 1998). Hunting success rates seem to be related to the size of the subgroup doing the hunting, with larger parties being more successful. When kills are made, the meat is frequently shared among a few individuals, usually the coalition partners and allies of the successful hunter. There is great excitement in the community when kills are made, and many individuals beg for meat, but only a few receive any. Occasionally, if the kill is made by a low-ranking individual, a high-ranking male may steal the kill and not share any with the actual hunter. Interestingly, infanticide (killing of infants) and cannibalism are both reported for *Pan troglodytes*. There are cases in which adult females and males have captured, killed, and eaten infants from their own community and from females of neighboring communities. When an infant is killed and consumed, it is treated very much like a colobus monkey that has been hunted and captured.

Group Aggression

In populations of *Pan troglodytes* (especially Eastern Africa), researchers have reported incidents of intercommunity conflict that resulted in deaths. "Border patrols," or groups of males moving along the communities' geographic boundaries, are reported for most populations of chimpanzees. Researchers hypothesize that these patrols are subgroups of males searching for small subgroups or lone individuals from neighboring communities. Occasionally, when these subgroups encounter individuals from another community, they attack as a mob. Some researchers have hypothesized that these attacks are an effort to increase the community's access to desired resources and that chimpanzees strategically assess the relative "power" of their neighbors in attempts to increase their ranges (Wilson & Wrangham, 2003).

Tool Use and Social Traditions

Tool use was once thought to be a hallmark of humanity, but we now know that many organisms use *extrasomatic* (outside the body) means to get food. Of all organisms other than humans, chimpanzees appear to exhibit the widest variety of tool use and tool modification. Across their range, chimpanzees use many types of tools, including stone hammers and anvils for cracking nuts, carefully selected sticks and blades of grass for extracting termites from mounds, and forked branches for skimming moss off the top of ponds (Figure 5.28). Although all chimpanzee populations use tools, different groups seem to have different ways of using similar tools, and some don't use certain tools at all. The behavior of tool use is a learned one that, in some cases, takes years to acquire. Both male and female chimpanzees use tools, but it seems that females, at least in *Pan troglodytes,* are the more prolific tool users.

It is not only patterns and styles of tool use that vary across chimpanzee populations; there are also stylized differences in social traditions. *Social traditions* are behaviors that have a learned component and are frequently nonfunctional. For example, in some communities chimpanzees raise their arms above their heads in a hand clasp when they groom each other. In some communities this takes the form of hand holding; in others the chimpanzees simply lean their wrists against one another. Individuals also appear to take their own traditions with them when they move into new groups. At least 39 distinct social traditions have been documented in chimpanzee populations. Some argue that this is evidence for chimpanzee culture (Whiten, et al., 1999). Regardless of what we call it, evidence clearly shows that a substantial component of chimpanzee behavior is passed on through learning and that these behaviors vary regionally and by community. Tool use and possibly some social traditions are excellent examples of Jablonka and Lamb's ideas about behavioral inheritance (remember chapter 4) and are a goal indicator that such patterns are ancestral for at least chimpanzees and humans.

Humans are also primates, and human behavior has an evolutionary history

In this chapter we have reviewed some general, primate-wide behavioral trends and briefly described specific patterns of behavior in two nonhuman primate societies. What can this tell us about humans? As mentioned earlier, the comparative approach asks questions about similarities and differences between us and our close evolutionary relatives with the assumption that some of the patterns we see are the result of natural selection. We know that behavior is complex and that humans have a long and varied evolutionary

■ **FIGURE 5.28**
Tool use in chimpanzees. At Gombe Stream National Park in Tanzania, chimpanzees use specially prepared twigs to fish for termites from a termite mound.

history. We can gain some insight into human behavior when we combine our knowledge of human evolution with observations from comparative primatology.

Social Organization and Behavior in Humans

Like macaques and chimpanzees, humans can be characterized as living in primate societies. For most of our evolutionary history, humans lived in small foraging groups consisting of some related and some unrelated individuals. All individuals cooperated in food collection, defense, and possibly, to some extent, rearing of young. By 2 million years ago or so, our ancestors were moving around and out of Africa, encountering new environments and new organisms. Humans appear to have met these challenges in groups, both by developing increasingly complex tools and other extrasomatic techniques and by forming social coalitions and alliances with other individuals and groups.

These small bands of humans most likely did not exceed a few hundred individuals and probably were much smaller than that until the appearance of our species, *Homo sapiens*. Bands would have moved about within home ranges and met other such bands, sometimes interacting peacefully, maybe exchanging members, other times fighting, and probably frequently just avoiding one another. After the initial spurt of movement 2 million years ago, humans probably moved fairly frequently. This means that over time, individuals lived in semisedentary groups, periodically encountered new groups and occasionally joined them, and sometimes moved far away from other groups.

With the appearance of anatomically modern *Homo sapiens sapiens* (discussed in detail in chapter 9), we begin to see substantial changes in the fossilized evidence of social behavior. Groups appear to get larger, more sedentary, and probably more diversified in terms of roles and divisions of labor within the group. By 20,000 to 40,000 years ago, there is evidence of larger aggregates of groups and, soon thereafter, relatively permanent settlements. By the time agriculture began to flourish, population sizes were dramatically greater, manipulation of the environment was substantially different, and the ways in which humans interacted in groups were probably more diversified. Additionally, disease may have become a more important selective force as population densities increased and became more settled.

Given our evolutionary history, what can we conclude about the basic characteristics of human behavior? We live in multifemale/multimale groups with varied subgroup patterns. We have both male and female philopatry depending on the culture and demography. We have an omnivorous diet, much of which we now grow or raise as domestic animals and plants. We form very strong social bonds both heterosexually and homosexually with both kin and nonkin. Sometimes these bonds are related to mating behavior, and sometimes they are not. Human females do not appear to have a visible signal of estrus. Mating patterns vary a great deal, but humans appear to mate with multiple individuals and exert both male and female choice. Although many of these behaviors may be common to other primates, there is one behavior that humans display that no other primate (as far as we can tell) does: We use symbol and language to interact with one another.

Comparisons with Macaques

Humans and macaques share some general characteristics, such as the existence of multifemale/multimale groups, the importance of biological kin in social interactions, and the ability to coexist in a wide variety of habitats. We also overlap in the general sense of having dominance hierarchies and having many ways in which dominance is attained and maintained. There are critical differences in our morphologies, however, especially locomotion patterns, relative and absolute brain size, and the size and complexity of our social organization. Another difference is that adult male and adult female macaques have life trajectories that are very different from each other, and such an extreme difference is not characteristic of human societies (at least not many).

It is interesting that macaques and humans can (and do) coexist in many areas, perhaps because both species have great flexibility in the face of environmental challenges. Both spread across much of the planet during about the same time periods, and perhaps the two species' shared ways of foraging and behaving became increasingly flexible, and overlapping, to meet the environmental challenges they encountered.

Comparisons with Chimpanzees

Although humans have some things in common with macaques, we have more in common with chimpanzees. One commonality is the type of community living we practice. Modern human communities are larger and much more complex than those of chimpanzees, but the patterns of subgrouping and the types of relationships between individuals in communities, especially among those who know one another but do not interact or see one another on a daily basis, may be a common element between our two genera.

The use of sex in a social context and the male–male bonding related to aggression may also be patterns of behavior that we share with our close relatives. The active acquisition of meat and subsequent sharing among selected group members in both species of chimpanzee, and the similar behavior with large fruit sources in bonobos, bear a resemblance to the acquisition and social distribution of prestige goods in human societies.

What about sexual aggression, mate guarding, and intercommunity aggression in chimpanzees? Could they be related to rape, marriage laws, and war in humans? Although such behaviors may bear a superficial resemblance across species, there is currently a great deal of debate over whether human patterns and chimpanzee patterns are analogous, homologous, or not comparable as the same types of behavior.

As noted earlier, the two species of chimpanzee appear to use aggression and social sex quite differently. In fact, *P. troglodytes* groups in different parts of Africa differ in these behaviors as well. Are some groups more similar to humans than others? Probably not. Humans and chimpanzees have spent more than 6 million years evolving separately from one another, so all chimpanzee species and subspecies are more evolutionarily similar to one another than any are to humans. Humans have encountered many more environments and, at least for the last 2 million years, have relied much more heavily on extrasomatic adaptations, and they have a substantially larger relative and absolute brain size than chimpanzees.

It is not surprising that there is considerable overlap in the kinds of behavior exhibited by the genus *Pan* and the genus *Homo*, considering our evolutionary proximity and a shared range of underlying potential variation in behavior. It appears that behavioral flexibility in social traditions and the ability to use and manipulate extrasomatic elements are important adaptations of both chimpanzees and humans. Because humans are more widespread and are theoretically more flexible in their behavior (due to their larger brain and use of symbols and language), we should expect to see in humans more behavioral complexity than we see in chimpanzees and bonobos. It might just be that our potential expression of behavior is much broader than that of our closest relatives.

What is Uniquely Human?

Making direct comparisons between human behavior and the behavior of other organisms is difficult because we interact with our environment through a substantial interface that affects both behavior and morphology: human culture. Culture structures all aspects of our lives. This is not to say that culture overrides or negates any biological facets of our existence. Rather, just as the social traditions of chimpanzees affect the way individuals from different groups behave, human culture interacts with our biology and the varying environments in which we live to create a myriad of behavioral results.

For example, language enables us to communicate content not accessible to other organisms and, combined with our use of symbolic representation (including writing), allows us to acquire, manipulate, and broadcast knowledge more quickly and thoroughly than other organisms. Language and the ability to use symbolic representation, which have been around for at least 60,000 years, have dramatically changed our species' environment in the recent past (recent, that is, in evolutionary terms). Our population sizes have grown by thousands-fold in just the last millennium; our ability to grow and manipulate our own food has changed the types and patterns of foraging we can exhibit; and our ability to alter the face of the planet is so dramatic that we are one of the driving forces in ecological change on the earth. In short, humans are able to undertake more dramatic and far-reaching niche construction than any other primate. Such complexity in everything we do makes it quite difficult, but not impossible, to use comparative primatology to attempt to understand the evolution of human behavior. If done carefully and systematically, comparative primatology can give us insight into those patterns of behavior that have arisen through natural selection and other mechanisms of evolution.

It is also worth emphasizing that the evolutionary changes that make us human arose over time and continue to arise. For example, the lower body anatomy that allows us to be bipedal emerged several million years ago. The dramatic

CONNECTIONS

Why We Never Shut Up

Language makes a difference. It separates humans from other animals on this planet; even from our closest relatives, the primates. Language allows humans to construct real and imagined niches and scenarios and gives us the power to do things that nothing else can do. Language gives us the ability to share information about the past and the future as well as to lie, to create fantasies, to explain thoughts and emotions—all things that are not possible for other animals. You are reading this right now and I am transferring ideas and information to you without my even being there. We see that the other primates have complex social lives, but that they do it without languages. They do have many ways to communicate, but none of them are as information-rich and temporally complex as language. Even humans who cannot speak can still use language (sign language or writing). To understand how important this is, try to go a few hours using words that represent only things in your immediate line of sight, that refer only to the present moment, and that contain no adjectives or representations of your inner thoughts. It will not be easy. We take the importance of language for granted because we are so totally reliant on it. That is why we never shut up.

What We Know

Much behavior is the result of evolutionary adaptation over the history of our species. Examining our closest relatives can give us insight into primate-wide behavior, anthropoid-wide behavior, and even hominoid-wide behavior.

Questions That Remain

Although it is relatively easy to identify general patterns as adaptations, it is not so easy to sort out the evolutionary aspects of specific behaviors in humans. What parts of behaviors like our choice of sexual partner, our decision to stay or leave home, or the kinds of relationships we have with members of the other sex can be traced to specific adaptations? Human culture makes it very difficult to answer these questions. However, the comparative approach offers careful and methodical ways of investigating these issues.

What We Know

There are five aspects of a behavior that we can investigate scientifically: phylogeny, ontogeny, proximate stimulus, the behavior itself, and the function of the behavior. A behavioral ecological approach can assist in understanding the pressures that affect a behavior and the outcomes of the behavior.

Questions That Remain

For each behavior, which of the factors impacting it is more important? Not all behaviors have equal input from the five factors, and it is not always clear what the most important questions to ask in a given context might be. If not all behavior is functional, and if we do not know all of the possible constraints on, or life experience of, an individual, our examinations can sometimes be misdirected. For this reason, investigations into the behavior of human evolution need to proceed very cautiously.

What We Know

Kin selection has been proposed to explain many apparently altruistic (selfless) acts. We can hypothesize that altruism should be rare because of its potential costs to the individual.

Questions That Remain

Does true altruism exist? Without a way of measuring actual costs to individuals, this question is hard to answer accurately. It is possible that in social organisms, such as primates, the costs and benefits of many behaviors are deeply imbedded in long-term complex social relationships between individuals. These relationships, coalitions, and alliances may be a very important arena for continued primatological research.

What We Know

Members of the genus *Pan* are among our closest evolutionary relatives on this planet. Some behavior of both species in this genus appears to be similar to human behavior and may offer insight into shared adaptive histories.

Questions That Remain

Because the two species of *Pan* differ in some key behavioral patterns, which one is a better model for humans? It is possible that neither are good models or that all three of our species (*Pan troglodytes, Pan paniscus,* and *Homo sapiens*) have some commonalities in behavioral potentials. It is also possible that differing ecologies, evolutionary histories, and morphologies have resulted in a patchwork of behavioral similarities and differences across the three species. Future study, especially long-term studies on all three species, may help to disentangle these relationships.

increase in brain size that distinguishes us from other primates occurred over a period of about 1 million years and then leveled off in our archaic ancestors. The chin, unique to humans, began to appear in the fossil record about 200,000 years ago. These and innumerable other characteristics of our species arose over time as pieces in a larger system. It is inaccurate to think of humans as big-brained geniuses trapped in bodies adapted to evolutionary pressures that existed hundreds of thousands of years ago or, put another way, that we are caught in a completely new realm of cultural complexity such that our biology is being outpaced and rapidly rendered irrelevant. Rather, humans are organisms whose main adaptation is a biocultural one and who exist in a dynamic interconnection of biology, behavior, history, and culture—and who have done so for a very long time. In chapters 9 and 11 we will go into more detail about current ways researchers investigate the evolution of human behavior.

Conserving the Nonhuman Primates Is a Critical Challenge

This chapter ends with a cautionary note. We gain valuable insight into human nature by studying our primate relatives, but comparative primatology may not be a viable field of research for much longer. All of the African apes, the orangutan, and many monkey and prosimian species are severely threatened with habitat loss and possible extinction. As of 2009, more then 30% of primate species and subspecies were considered to be threatened or endangered. Modification of the planet for human use is currently driving many of our closest evolutionary relatives to the brink of extinction. To ensure that 60 million years of shared evolutionary history does not come to an end in our lifetime, we need to seriously consider how best to reduce and manage these threats.

SUMMARY

▲ The study of the nonhuman primates can provide information from which we can attempt to reconstruct aspects of human evolution, especially the evolution of our behavior.

▲ Behavior may be defined as all the actions and inactions of an organism.

▲ Both quantitative and qualitative research methods enrich our study of behavior.

▲ A behavior may be viewed from five different perspectives: phylogeny, ontogeny, proximate stimulus, the behavior itself, and the function of the behavior.

▲ Behavior that is widespread in a taxonomic group is frequently considered to be an adaptation.

▲ Behavioral ecology is the study of behavior from ecological and evolutionary perspectives.

▲ Basic ecological stresses on organisms fall into the following five general areas: nutrition, locomotion, predation, intraspecific competition, and interspecific competition.

▲ We measure the success of behavioral adaptation generally in terms of estimated energy costs and benefits in the sense of how these could potentially impact lifetime fitness (reproductive success).

▲ Kin selection, the favoring of close genetic relatives, has been proposed to explain apparent altruistic acts in organisms.

▲ Genetic, morphological, and phylogenetic characteristics set the basic potential for any given behavior; the particular expression of that behavior (called performance) is elicited by a myriad of factors including ontogeny, health, and type of proximate stimulus.

▲ Not all behavior is functional.

▲ Primate-wide trends in behavior include strong mother-offspring bonds, certain primary grouping patterns, an important role for use of space and grooming, the establishment of dominance hierarchies, an important role for life history and dispersal patterns, and an important role for coalitions and alliances in both conflict and cooperation.

▲ Macaques live in multifemale/multimale societies with male dominance, distinct male and female hierarchies, matrifocal clusters, female philopatry, and flexible male strategies for attaining dominance.

▲ Chimpanzees live in multifemale/multimale communities characterized by a fission-fusion social pattern. The species *Pan troglodytes* exhibits clear male dominance and more serious intercommunity aggression and conflict than does the species *Pan paniscus*, which is characterized by female dominance and a higher frequency of sociosexual behavior, with both aggressive and affiliative intercommunity interactions. All chimpanzees have complex social lives characterized by female dispersal, sharing of favored food sources (including hunted meat), tool use, and the passing of learned social traditions within different communities.

▲ No other primate is a perfect model for human evolution; even the members of the genus *Pan* have millions of years of separate evolution from us. However, both *Macaca* and *Pan* can provide some insight into aspects of human behavior and evolution.

▲ Humans are similar to other primates in a number of ways, yet specific aspects of our evolutionary history have resulted in a distinct trajectory of biocultural adaptation. The complexity of culture can make it difficult, but not impossible, to untangle the evolutionary history of human behavior.

▲ Many primate species are currently endangered, in large part due to human alteration of the environment. We are responsible for ensuring that our relatives continue to exist on this planet.

CRITICAL THINKING

1. What kinds of different information are gathered by qualitative versus quantitative methods? Why is this difference important, and how can each approach contribute to a better overall understanding of behavior?

2. How can a behavior not have a function? Doesn't everything "cost" energy? How could behaviors that do not have a cost or a benefit arise?

3. Is altruism incompatible with natural selection? Is it feasible to measure all reciprocal altruism? Considering that not all of our cultural kin are biological kin, how might kin selection impact humans?

4. Why are chimpanzees frequently held up as a good model for understanding human evolution? What morphological and behavioral similarities might they have with early humans? If we see extreme male aggression such as lethal fighting, sexual coercion, and group attacks in both chimpanzees and humans, is it not reasonable to explain it as a common adaptation in both species? Why or why not?

5. What does it mean to say "culture is biological"? How can something be abstract and symbolic and yet be impacted by biology? Think about each of the following human behaviors: language use, mate choice, eating habits, and sleeping patterns. How is each one impacted by both morphology and evolutionary history, on the one hand, and cultural patterns, on the other?

RESOURCES

PRIMATOLOGY BOOKS

Campbell, C., Fuentes, A., Mackinnon, K. C., Bearder, S. K. & Stumpf, R. M. (Eds.). (2010). *Primates in perspective 2nd Ed.* New York: Oxford University Press.
The first in-depth overview of the field of primatology in nearly 20 years, this volume provides extensive coverage of all the major primate groups and a review of current issues in theory and methodology in primatology.

de Waal, F. B. M. (Ed.). (2001). *Tree of origin: What nonhuman primate behavior can tell us about human social evolution.* Cambridge: Harvard University Press.
This edited volume contains essays focusing specifically on understanding human social evolution by examining the nonhuman primates.

Dolhinow, P., & Fuentes, A. (Eds.). (1999). *The nonhuman primates.* New York: McGraw-Hill.
This collection of short essays deals with the behavioral and evolutionary diversity in nonhuman primate behavior and ecology.

Rowe, N. (1996). *The pictorial guide to the living primates.* East Hampton, NY: Pogonias Press.
An overview of all the living primates, this guide contains stellar photos and brief summaries of their behavior, ecology, distribution, and conservation status.

Strier, K. B. (2006). *Primate behavioral ecology* (3rd ed.). Boston: Allyn & Bacon.
This textbook is a rich source of information about the nonhuman primates and the evolution of primate behavior.

Sussman, R. W. (1999, 2000, 2003). *Primate ecology and social structure,* Vols. 1–3. Needham Heights, MA: Pearson Custom Publishing.
These three books provide in-depth coverage of the behavior and ecology of the prosimians (Vol. 1), the neotropical primates (Vol. 2), and the Old World forms, the monkeys and apes (Vol. 3).

PRIMATES ON THE WEB

www.asp.org The home page of the American Society of Primatologists has a variety of educational links on the study and conservation of primates.

pin.primate.wisc.edu/ The home page of the Primate Information Network hosted by the Wisconsin Primate Research Center and the National Primate Research Centers Program at the University of Wisconsin-Madison is the gateway to hundreds of links exploring the diversity of primates, the field of primatology, and all things primate.

www.internationalprimatologicalsociety.org This is the home page of the International Primatological Society.

REFERENCES

Aureli, F., & de Waal, F. B. M. (Eds.). (2000). *Natural conflict resolution.* Berkeley, CA: University of California Press.

Bernstein, I. (1999). The study of behavior. In P. Dolhinow & A. Fuentes (Eds.), *The nonhuman primates* (pp. 176–180). New York: McGraw-Hill.

Boesch, C., Hohmann, G., & Marchant, L. F. (Eds.). (2002). *Behavioural diversity in chimpanzees and bonobos.* Cambridge: Cambridge University Press.

Curtiss, S. (1977). *Genie: A psycholinguistic study of a modern-day "wild child."* New York: Academic Press.

Fuentes, A. (1999). Re-evaluating primate monogamy. *American Anthropologist, 100*(4), 890–907.

Hamilton, W. D. (1964). The genetical evolution of social behavior, I and II. *Journal of Theoretical Biology, 7,* 1–52.

McGrew, W. C., Marchant, L. F., & Nishida, T. (1996). *Great ape societies.* Cambridge: Cambridge University Press.

McKenna, J. (1978). The biosocial function of grooming behavior among the common langur monkey (*Presbytis entellus*). *American Journal of Physical Anthropology, 48,* 503–510.

Stanford, C. B. (1998). *Chimpanzee and red colobus: The ecology of predator and prey.* Cambridge, MA: Harvard University Press.

Sterck, E. H. M., Watts, D. P., & van Schaik, C. P. (1997). The evolution of female social relationships in nonhuman primates. *Behavioral Ecology and Sociobiology, 41,* 291–309.

Strier, K. B. (2006). *Primate behavioral ecology* (3rd ed.). Boston: Allyn & Bacon.

Stumpf, R. (2007). Chimpanzees and bonobos: inter- and intraspecies diversity. In Campbell, C., Fuentes, A., MacKinno, K. C., Bearder, S. K. & Stumpf, R. M. (Ed.), *Primates in perspective 2nd Ed* (pp. 340–356). New York: Oxford University Press.

Sussman, R. W., & Garber, P. (2007). Cooperation and competition in primate social interactions. In Campbell, C., Fuentes, A., MacKinnon, K. C., Panger, M., & Bearder, S. K. (Eds.), *Primates in perspective* (pp. 636–651). New York: Oxford University Press.

Thierry, B. (2010). The Macaques: a double-layered social organization. In Campbell, C., Fuentes, A., MacKinnon, K. C., Bearder, S. K. & Stumpf, R. M. (Eds), *Primates in Perspective 2nd Ed* (pp. 229–240). New York: Oxford University Press.

Tinbergen, N. (1963). On aims and methods of ethology. *Zeitschrift Tierpsychologic, 20,* 410–433.

van Schaik, C. P. (1989). The ecology of social relationships among females. In V. Standen & R. A. Foley (Eds.), *Comparative socioecology: The behavioral ecology of humans and other mammals* (pp. 195–218). Oxford: Blackwell Scientific Press.

Wheatley, B. (1999). *The sacred monkeys of Bali.* Long Grove, IL: Waveland Press.

Whiten, A., Goodall, J., McGrew, W. C., Nisshida, T., Reynolds, V., Sugiyama, Y., et al. (1999). Cultures in chimpanzees. *Nature, 399,* 682–685.

Wilson, M., & Wrangham, R. W. (2003). Intergroup relations in chimpanzees. *Annual Reviews in Anthropology, 32,* 363–342.

CHAPTER 6

Early Primate Evolution

This chapter addresses the following questions:

▲ What is a fossil, and how can we tell how old a fossil is?

▲ What are the characteristics of a mammal? Of a primate?

▲ When and where do we see primates in the fossil record, and how do we know they are primates?

▲ What are the relationships among the early fossil primates?

Who are we, as a species? Where do we come from? These are questions that human beings have pondered for a long, long time. One way to answer them, in a biological sense, is to ask them from an evolutionary perspective: When did our most distant direct ancestors arise, and who were they? A growing body of evidence suggests that part of the answer to this question lies in an event in the distant past that spelled bad luck for many life-forms on the planet.

Seventy million years ago, the dinosaurs (reptiles active on land), pterosaurs (reptiles active in the air), and icthyosaurs (reptiles active in the water) were the predominant vertebrate life-forms on the planet. They came in all sizes and shapes and sat comfortably at the top of the food chain in most environments. They first arose from other reptilian forms more than 100 million years earlier and had diversified into numerous orders, families, genera, and species. Then, about 65 million years ago, a giant asteroid struck the earth, producing dramatic changes in climates and ecologies worldwide and resulting in massive waves of extinction. All of the pterosaurs and ichthyosaurs, nearly all the dinosaurs, and many other forms of life disappeared from the planet. These extinctions left gaping holes in ecosystems and food chains and led to the appearance of a multitude of empty niches, or ecological roles. One group of fairly small and primarily nocturnal organisms did quite well through all the climatic and ecological changes and began to rapidly diversify and radiate into all the empty niches. This group was the mammals.

In a broad sense, this sequence of events is the beginning of the story of human evolution. Mammals had started to expand in form and range more than 70 million years ago, so they were poised to explode in a myriad of structures and functions when the extinctions occurred. One group of mammals began to undergo selective pressures that resulted in changes to their hands and feet, their eyes, and most importantly, their brains. They spread rapidly and successfully to many areas of the planet, living in trees and consuming fruits, leaves, and insects. This group of mammals is known in taxonomy as the order Primates, and it is the group to which you and I, as humans, belong.

Sixty-five million years is a long time; since that cataclysmic event, dramatic and substantial changes have occurred in all primate lineages. No organism closely resembling us shows up until about 20 million years or so ago. Nevertheless, as strange as it seems, these earliest forms—small mammals that ran around in the trees eating insects more than 60 million years ago—do include our most distant ancestors. Examining the evolutionary history of these early and distant relatives will give us a better foundation to talk about humans, both as primates in general and as a unique and fascinating lineage within the primate order.

This chapter provides a general framework for what we know about the primate fossil record. First we take a look at why humans are placed in the group of mammals called primates, and then we take a brief journey through the fossil history of the primates and try to pin down the fossils and lineages that are most directly related to us. This process will take us through nearly 65 million years of history and leave us at the doorstep of our immediate ancestors.

Fossils provide direct evidence of an organism's existence

STOP & THINK

If so very little of past life becomes fossilized, how can we hope to accurately reconstruct the past?

In the right environment, some of the organic matter in an organism that has died will slowly be replaced by inorganic compounds. In other words, tissues such as bones slowly turn to stone. This is the process of *fossilization*. Usually it is the hard parts of an organism, such as teeth or bones, that are fossilized, but sometimes the impressions of soft tissues such as skin or feathers, or even footprints, can be left embedded in rocks. One example of the fossilization process is petrified wood. When you see or hold petrified wood, you can tell that it is not wood anymore; it is more like a rock that has faithfully taken over the shape of the wood.

Fossilization happens very slowly; sometimes fossils we find are still in transitional phases between organic and mineral states. Most organisms that die do not become fossils. Only a very small percentage of anything that has lived on this earth will ever become a fossil (Figure 6.1).

You may have heard reports of fossil discoveries dating to millions of years ago and wondered how researchers determine the age of fossils. Several dating methods are used, but a primary consideration for all of them is the *provenience*, or precise location, of the fossil. If the exact location of a fossil find is not known, it is generally not possible to determine its age. The exact location offers information about the fossil's context—the type of rock it was found in, what other fossils were found nearby, and what nonfossil items surrounded it. This information is needed to draw inferences about the fossil and to use it in reconstructions of past life and environments. Once researchers know the provenience and the context, they can attempt to calculate the fossil's age.

(a) Living animal.

(b) Animal dies.

(c) Postmortem modification by scavengers.

(d) Postmortem modification by trampling.

(e) Postmortem modification by the elements.

(f) Accumulation of sediment on bones.

(g) Internment in earth layers and fossilization of bones.

(h) Erosion or movement of earth layers, revealing fossil-bearing region.

(i) Discovery of fossils by researcher.

■ **FIGURE 6.1**
The process of fossilization.

Dating methods can be divided into two broad categories, relative and chronometric. **Relative dating techniques** provide us with assessments of a fossil's age relative to other fossils (Table 6.1). For example by using *stratigraphy,* the study of the layers of the earth, we can assess the age of a fossil relative to its surroundings. Because more recent layers of rock are laid down, or superimposed, over older ones, we can make relative statements about fossils. If we find one fossil deeper in the earth than another at the same site, we can say that the fossil closer to the surface is more recent (younger) than the deeper one. Unfortunately, this assumption does not always hold true, because a number of different geological disturbances can affect layering of the earth.

relative dating techniques methods of dating that provide us with assessments of a fossil's age relative to other fossils

Another relative dating technique is *faunal correlation*. In this situation we need to have a good existing database of when certain fossil animals lived. For example, if we know that a certain species of pig lived in East Africa from 1.5 to 1 million years ago, we can use its fossil remains as a guideline to get relative dates. If the fossil we are interested in was found in the same layer of rock as a fossil of this particular pig species, then we can say that the fossil is probably between 1 and 1.5 million years old.

Fluorine dating can also be used to assess a fossil's age. Fluorine is an element that is found in most groundwater sources. When bones are buried and begin to degrade in the earth, groundwater can seep into the bones, leaving a mineral mark. This mark can then be used to compare bones found at the same or nearby sites, to see if they were buried at the same time. If the fluorine level in the bones varies, then they were not exposed to the same water influences at the same time, suggesting that they had not been in the ground for the same length of time.

chronometric dating techniques
methods of dating that provide a specific age of a fossil based either on analysis of a piece of the fossil itself or analysis of the rocks surrounding the fossil

Unlike relative dating, **chronometric dating techniques** give us a specific age for a fossil, based either on analysis of a piece of the fossil itself or on analysis of the rocks surrounding the fossil (thus, knowing the exact location of a fossil find is important). Many of the chronometric dating techniques are radiometric methods, which use the patterned decay of radioactive elements to reconstruct the age of the object being measured. Many elements found in organic matter (such as carbon in bones or potassium and argon in volcanic rocks) contain radioactive components that slowly change, or decay, into another element at a constant rate over time. Measuring the amount of decay of the element in the rock or bone allows us to get a numeric value (number of years) for an object's age. For example, we know that living things absorb C14 (an isotope of the element carbon) into their bodies. When they die, that C14 begins to decay at a constant rate (it has a half-life of 5,730 years; that is, one half of it decays in that time period). By using radiocarbon dating (also known as C14 dating), we can measure the amount of C14 in a bone we find (or any organic matter) by the radiation it gives off and then calculate how much time has elapsed, giving us an age since death. Unfortunately, this method is only good for things that died less than 100,000 years ago; by that time all the C14 would be decayed.

For older items we can use other decay ratios such as potassium to argon (40K/40Ar) and Argon to Argon (40Ar/39Ar). These elements decay at a much slower rate (~1.3-million-year half-life). They are not usually found in fossilized bones, but rather in rocks that are in the layers around the bone. Many rocks trap argon gas as they are being formed, and so we can measure the ratio of potassium to argon, or one 40Ar to 39Ar, in the sample to establish how long the rock has been there. If a fossil is between two layers of rocks that have been dated, then the fossil dates to the time between the two rock layers. Other chronometric methods include dendrochronology, the study of tree rings, and thermoluminescence, the relationship between the heating of crystalline rock and the pattern of electron release associated with it.

Many effective dating technologies are in use today; different methods are chosen depending on the matter being dated and the type of information sought. It is also common to use multiple methods on the same item to increase the validity of our re-creation of past timelines and sequences.

Humans are members of the order of mammals called primates

A Very Brief History of the Mammals

The origin of the primates lies near the beginning of the radiation of placental mammals in the Cretaceous period and seems to be tied to the diversification and radiation of the flowering plants (angiosperms). Before the Cretaceous-Tertiary boundary, about 65 million years ago (sometimes abbreviated "mya"), there were four major groups of mammals: the monotremes, the marsupials, the multituberculates, and the placentals (Figure 6.2). These four groups shared a number of traits that allow us to classify them as mammals, in distinction from reptiles. These traits are **homiothermy** (the ability to generate and regulate internal temperature); **heterodontism** (having different types of teeth); a set of specific reproductive patterns (**lactation,** the production of milk for young, and **internal gestation,** the carrying of the embryo/fetus inside the female's body until birth); and a set of unique brain structures (Figure 6.3).

homiothermy
ability to generate and regulate internal body temperature

heterodontism
having different types of teeth

lactation
internal production of a nutrient-rich milk by the female to feed young offspring

internal gestation
retention of the fetus inside the body of the female through the course of its prenatal development

After the mass extinction event 65 million years ago, the multituberculates quickly became extinct, both the monotremes and marsupials dramatically decreased in numbers, and the placentals underwent an adaptive radiation. Today, the vast majority of mammals are placentals, a few are marsupials, and three species are monotremes. To find large populations of marsupials or monotremes, you must go to areas of the world that were not well colonized by placentals, such as Australia.

How does all of this relate to humans? In chapter 2, we saw the similarity across mammalian anatomy and physiology. In chapter 3, we saw the ubiquity of DNA and the genomic systems across all forms of life. In chapter 4, we learned about the processes of evolution and saw that closely related organisms have more traits in common than do distantly related forms. By understanding the evolution of mammals, we understand a little more about ourselves. Why do we have hair? Because we're mammals. Why do we have different types of teeth? We're mammals. Why do we have a system of internally produced and maintained heat? Again, because we're mammals. Understanding what we have in common with other mammals lays the groundwork for understanding how we are unique.

Kangaroo: Marsupial

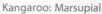

Platypus: Monotreme

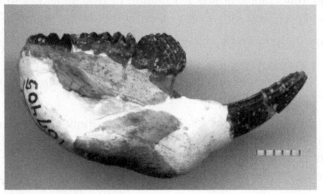

Fossil Jaw: Multituberculate

Dog: Placental

■ FIGURE 6.2
The four groups of mammals before the Cretaceous-Teriary boundary (about 65 mya). Today, only marsupials, placentals, and monotremes exist.

■ FIGURE 6.3
Characteristics of mammals. These include homiothermy, or the ability to regulate the body temperature; heterodontism, or having different types of teeth; lactation and internal gestation; and unique brain structures, such as the neocortex (the gray covering on the cerebrum).

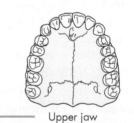

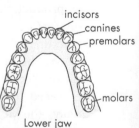

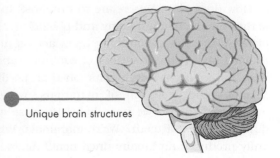

Homiothermy (the abiltity to generate and regulate your internal temperature)

incisors
canines
premolars

molars

Upper jaw   Lower jaw

Heterodontism (having different types of teeth)

Unique brain structures

Specific reproductive patterns (**lactation** and **internal gestation**)

Homiothermy Is Cool!

The fact that mammals produce their own heat makes our lives simultaneously awesome and difficult. Generating and regulating your own heat takes a lot of energy. This means that mammals need more calories and have to eat them more often than reptiles do; thus we face a greater challenge of finding and consuming food regularly. On the bright side, we can live in colder places than reptiles, and we can be active day and night regardless of temperature. We can deal with cold weather by making more heat (of course that costs more energy). That is what happens when you shiver. Shivering is just your body's way of ratcheting up the thermostat. When it is too hot we have to find some way to cool down such as sweating, to keep our temperatures in the correct range of functioning. So homiothermy lets mammals do more in more places than reptiles, but it means that mammals' lives are more active and energy-intensive than reptiles. This is a good case of evolutionary trade-offs in action. An added bonus about being a human is that we can use our ability to modify the environment to deal with regulating our homiothermy. For example, today when you are cold, you can put on more clothing, or better yet, make a warm fire and sit in front of it. As humans, we can readily use a wide array of things outside our bodies to help our bodies do their jobs.

Primates Are Mammals with Specific Characteristics

There are several different ways to describe and define primates. Linnaeus initially lumped all primates (prosimians, monkeys, apes, and humans) together with bats (Chiroptera) in the order Primates (although we no longer use that early association). Although we can identify and classify living primates fairly easily, our definitions do not always work when we are trying to identify early primate forms. This is because most characteristics we use to define mammals have arisen over the last 60 million years and not all at once (as we will see in the next section of this chapter).

We do, however, have a set of characteristics that generally tell us whether or not the mammal we are looking at is a primate. Very few of these characteristics are confined to primates; rather, the specific association of these traits in the same organism defines it as a primate. These traits are the following:

- A bony ring around the eye socket (postorbital bar) or a bony, enclosed eye socket

- Hands (manus) and/or feet (pes) that are constructed such that they can grasp objects (that is, they exhibit *prehension*)

- Nails instead of claws on the ends of the digits (this is referred to as *unguiculate*)

- Binocular, or 3-D, vision (providing extensively overlapping visual fields)

- Large brain relative to body size (known as a high **encephalization quotient, or EQ**)

- Long gestation period and slow postnatal growth compared to maternal body size

Taken together, these characteristics define the living primates—you and me as well as the lemurs and monkeys and apes (Figure 6.4). How did this set of characteristics evolve in a particular group of organisms, and why? To answer these questions, we need to look back to the fossil record.

STOP & **THINK**

Can you think of other mammals with some of these traits?

encephalization quotient (EQ) ratio of brain to body size; an EQ of 1 indicates a brain size expected for that mammalian body size

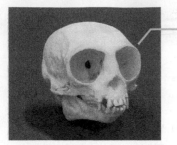

Visual cortex

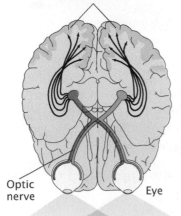

Optic nerve   Eye

Bony ring around the eye socket (postorbital bar) or a bony enclosed eye socket

Hands (manus) and/or feet (pes) that are constructed such that they can grasp objects (they exhibit prehension)

Nails instead of claws on the ends of the digits (unguiculate)

Long gestation period and slow-post natal growth rate compared to maternal body size

Large brain relative to body size (high encephalization quotient)

Binocular, or 3–D, vision (overlapping visual fields)

■ FIGURE 6.4
Characteristics of primates. These traits help define what a primate is.

The fossil primates

The Earliest Possible Primates Are Found in the Paleocene

Our primate story begins somewhere in the late Cretaceous period or earliest Paleocene epoch with a group of mammals placed in the infraorder **Pleseadapiformes.** This group first shows up in the fossils of the Cretaceous (Table 6.2). During the Paleocene: (65–53 million years ago) Pleseadapiformes underwent an adaptive radiation throughout the areas that are now Europe and North America; they make up as much as 30% of the fossils found at some sites. The Pleseadapiformes are part of a large superorder called **Archonta** (Figure 6.5). This taxonomic group includes the now extinct Pleseadapids as well as the living orders Primates, Scandentia (the tree shrews), Chiroptera (the bats), and Dermoptera (the colugos—large gliding mammals of Southeast Asia).

The Pleseadapids were very successful, but they did not exhibit any of the characteristics we generally associate with primates today. Why are they considered potential primate ancestors? As you know, the earliest forms of a given lineage may resemble the current members of that lineage very little, if at all. They do, however, exhibit morphological characteristics that are similar to those of current forms, or that have the basic structural potential (form) to act as raw material for later modifications.

Although no Pleseadapiform can be held up as an ancestor to the primates, a few branches of the Pleseadapiformes appear to have the constellation of traits that we would expect to see in a basal primate form. For example, some groups within the Pleseadapiformes had molar teeth and outer ear skeletal

Pleseadapiformes
a group of early mammals thought to be peripherally related to primates

Archonta
superorder of mammals made up of the extinct Pleseadapiformes and the living orders Primates, Scandentia (the tree shrews), Chiroptera (the bats), and Dermoptera (colugos)

TABLE 6.2 A Geological Timeline of Major Events in Primate Evolution

Geologic Epoch (millions of years)	North America	Europe	Asia	Africa	South America
Pleistocene (1.8 mya–10,000 years ago) Genus *Homo* present worldwide		Old World monkeys diminish, hominoids go extinct.	Old World monkeys persist and ultimately colonize insular Southeast Asia; giant hominoids found in southern China and Vietnam.	Old World monkeys proliferate on the continent; giant prosimians found on Madagascar; hominoids limited to tropical belt.	Unusual fossil monkeys found on Caribbean Islands; large fossils resembling spider and howler monkeys found in Brazil.
Pliocene (5–1.8 mya)		Great diversity of Old World monkeys and a few surviving hominoids that resemble living apes and early hominoids.	Presumed loss of hominoid diversity in temperate areas (very few fossil deposits of this age are known).	Old World monkeys greatly diversify; no fossil evidence of hominoids except for earliest known hominins.	
Miocene (23–5 mya)		Hominoids flourish in the middle and late Miocene, including the earliest known definite brachiator.	Hominoids flourish in the middle and late Miocene, including a probable direct ancestor of living orangutans; no known Old World monkeys.	Emergence and diverse radiation of hominoids In sub-Saharan Africa; first evidence of distinct Old World monkeys.	Diverse radiation in southern South America in early Miocene; very diverse radiation of modern-looking forms in northern South America in middle and late Miocene.
Oligocene (35–23 mya)	Primates go extinct.	Remaining Adapoid and Omomyoid primates go extinct.	Fragmentary anthropoid fossils in Myanmar.	Proliferation of early anthropoids and possibly the earliest distinct catarrhine.	Earliest known (35–23 mya) fossil New World monkeys.
Eocene (53–35 mya)	Two different types of prosimian-like primates, Adapoids and Omomyoids, flourish. Clear evidence of the Haplorrhine/Strepsirrhine lineages appears.	Two different types of prosimian-like primates, Adapoids and Omomyoids, flourish.	Several fragmentary jaws of potential early anthropoids in China and Southeast Asia.	Appearance of early anthropoids in Fayum deposits.	
Paleocene (65–53 mya)	Possible origin of primates, but fossil record offers no definitive evidence.		A logical tropical area for primate origins, but no evidence yet in the fossil record.	A logical tropical area for primate origins, but no evidence yet in the fossil record.	

Based on "Primate Evolution," by W.C. Hartwig, 1999, *The Nonhuman Primates* (p. 11), P. Dohlinow and A. Fuentes (Eds.). New York: McGraw-Hill.

■ FIGURE 6.5
The Pleseadapiformes. This group, which arose during the late Cretaceous, includes a wide variety of forms; this reconstruction shows four different species adapted to different niches. The Pleseadapiformes include the ancestors of the primates as well as other mammalian orders.

arrangements that appear to be similar to those we see in the earliest true primates. Therefore, somewhere within the Paleocene Pleseadapiform radiation, one or more lineages began a long, complex series of adaptive steps that eventually resulted in the set of morphological characteristics we currently identify as "primate."

By the beginning of the Eocene; (53–35 million years ago) many of the Pleseadapiformes were extinct, and by the time we begin to see true primates in Europe, Africa, and Asia, the Pleseadapiformes were almost completely gone. There are many hypotheses about why this successful group of mammals became extinct. Among the most popular is the notion that competition from newer mammals (primarily rodents, bats, and maybe even early primates) drove these more primitive forms into marginal areas and eventually extinction.

We do have a few fossils from the Paleocene that may be our earliest primates. The fossil teeth of a genus named *Purgatorius* show up in some deposits dating to the early Paleocene in what is now Montana. These teeth look very much like what we might expect of our earliest primate ancestors. In the mid-Paleocene a small set of fossils called *Decoredon elongatus* (or *anhuiensis*) from what is now southern China, and some teeth from a form we call *Altiatlasius koulchii* in what is now Morocco, are also possible candidates for the earliest primates (Fleagle, 1999). All of these forms are very small (all estimated to be under 100 g, or about 3.5 oz, in body weight) and are represented primarily only by some teeth; so until we recover a broader set of fossil evidence, the jury will remain out on the first primates.

Why Did Primates Evolve Out of Early Mammalian Groups?

What accounts for the appearance of a set of primatelike traits in the fossil record? Given what we know about evolutionary processes, we can hypothesize about the kinds of selective pressures that would result in the divergence of primates from a general mammalian form. Currently there are three main sets of ideas about why this divergence occurred.

The *arboreal hypothesis* suggests that because early primate ancestors were arboreal, they developed a cluster of traits, such as specializing in herbivorous foods and a leaping/clinging type of locomotion. Recognizably primate traits eventually developed from this cluster (Szalay, 1972). The *visual adaptation hypothesis* (proposed by Matt Cartmill) suggests that the cluster of primate traits arose as a result of the visual nature of primate insect predation. According to this view, accurate 3-D vision, grasping hands and feet, and nails rather than claws would seem to be adaptations that fit well for an active, nocturnal, arboreal insect predator (Cartmill, 1992). The *angiosperm radiation hypothesis* (proposed by Robert Sussman) suggests that the changing structure and composition of forests during the radiation of the angiosperms (flowering plants) provided the selective pressures resulting in primates. The exploitation of a new and diverse set of foodstuffs (flowers, fruit, and the insects that prey on them) in a variable and multicolored environment may have favored the constellation of traits we see in primates (Sussman, 1991).

Any attempt to reconstruct the exact conditions under which primates diverged from the Archontan stock is quite difficult. We can really only model hypotheses, most of which are equally difficult to test. D. T. Rasmussen did attempt to test some of these hypotheses by looking at a living mammal that is convergent with primates (a small possum called *Caluromys*). His results could not refute any of the hypotheses and in fact appear to support each of them to a small extent (Rasmussen, 1990).

True Primates Appear in the Eocene

The Eocene epoch (approximately 53–35 million years ago) was generally warm and humid. Most land environments were tropical and subtropical forests (Figure 6.6). At the beginning of the Eocene, North America and Europe were still joined, so there was an extensive overlap in animals and plants. Many early forms of modern mammals show up in the Eocene: Cetaceans (the whales, porpoises, and dolphins), Perissodactyla (horses, tapirs, and rhinoceroses), Rodentia (rodents), and, of course, the Primates. It is in the Eocene that we first find fossil forms that meet all of the criteria for a true primate.

Early in the Eocene we see a diversification of primates into two, or possibly three, distinct groups. These groups are the Adapoids, the Omomyoids, and possibly the Simiiform anthropoids (Figure 6.7). The **Adapoids** are known to us by hundreds of fossils representing more than 37 genera and nearly 90 species, ranging from the tiny *Donrusselia* (weighing less than 200 g, or half a pound) to the large *Notharctus* (weighing more than 6000 g, or ~12 lb). They are found in Africa, North America, Europe, and Asia from the Eocene through the Oligocene (and a few into the Miocene). Interestingly, the fossil histories of the Adapoids in North America become very different from those in Europe as the epoch progresses.

On average, these primates were fairly large (many weighing more than 2000 g, or about 4 lb) and arboreal. They had relatively long legs, a long trunk, and a long tail. Their hands and feet had nails and displayed grasping

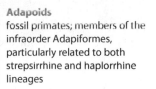

Adapoids
fossil primates; members of the infraorder Adapiformes, particularly related to both strepsirrhine and haplorrhine lineages

■ FIGURE 6.6
Eocene fossil primate sites. These locations represent the known geographic spread of Eocene primates.

(a)

(b)

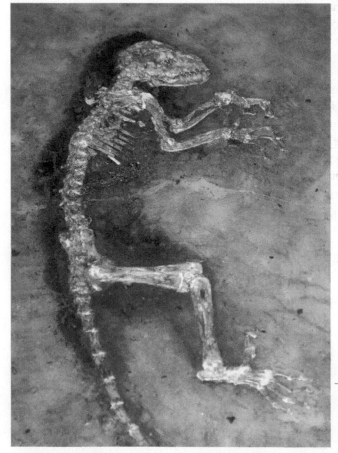

(c)

Omomyoids
fossil primates; members of the infraorder Omomyiformes, suborder Haplorrhini

■ FIGURE 6.7

The Omomyoids (a), Adapoids (b), and the adapoid fossil *Darwinius massillae* (c). These forms arose during the Eocene.

morphology. In many aspects of their morphology, the Adapoids are similar to some modern lemurs (strepsirrhines from the island of Madagascar), and a few were even similar to modern anthropoids (haplorrhines, monkeys), but the exact link between these primates and modern forms remains unclear. One recent, very complete find from deposits in Messel, Germany, does suggest links between Adapoids and Haplorrhines. The complete fossil, *Darwinius masillae* shows some Haplorrhine traits and gives us great insight into the life of an early arboreal, fruit- and leaf-eating nocturnal primate (Franzen et al., 2009).

The **Omomyoids** show up in the Eocene fossil record of North America, Europe, and Asia. Like the Adapoids, the North American and European forms display quite different evolutionary histories as the Eocene progresses toward the Oligocene. Many of the Omomyoid fossils show a strong resemblance to a modern primate lineage, *Tarsius* (the tarsiers), but whether they share a direct relationship remains unclear. The Omomyoids are represented by more than 44 genera and nearly 100 species; they constituted a substantial component of the Eocene mammalian fauna, especially in North America. They generally had short, narrow snouts and large eyes. Skeletal remains suggest that many Omomyoids moved about by leaping arboreally.

Until relatively recently, the story of anthropoid primates (monkeys, apes, and humans) was thought to begin in the Oligocene epoch. An accumulation of fossil finds over the past few decades has changed that view. We now have a number of presumably anthropoid fossils from the mid- to late Eocene. We say "presumably" because most of the fossils are teeth; thus, we are unable to say whether there was a bony, enclosed eye socket. The teeth themselves are primate teeth and are relatively distinct from those of the Adapoids and Omomyoids; most are similar to those of the Oligocene anthropoids. Therefore, we can call these mid- to late Eocene primates the earliest anthropoids.

The early forms are found in Africa (genera *Algeripithecus*, *Catopithecus*, *Moeripithecus*, and *Oligopithecus*) and Asia (*Amphipithecus*, *Eosimias*, *Pondaungia*, *Siamopithecus*, and *Wailekia*) (Ducrocq, 1998; Simons & Rasmussen, 1994). It is interesting to note that the radiations of both the Adapoids and the Omomyoids appear to have been primarily in North America and Europe with some forms reaching more broadly, whereas the earliest anthropoids are found only in Africa and southern and Southeast Asia. This distribution of fossils suggests the possibility that neither the Adapoids nor the Omomyoids may be ancestral to living anthropoids; the three Eocene primate lineages may share a more distant common ancestor well back in the Paleocene or even the Cretaceous.

Anthropoids (Simiiformes) Radiate in the Oligocene

In the Oligocene period (35–23 million years ago), we find fossils that clearly fit not only our notions of what a primate is but, more specifically, our notions of what an anthropoid primate is (monkeys, apes, and humans). Those characteristics are a reduced snout/nasal area; a bony, enclosed eye socket; and generally small orbits (eye sockets) (Figure 6.8).

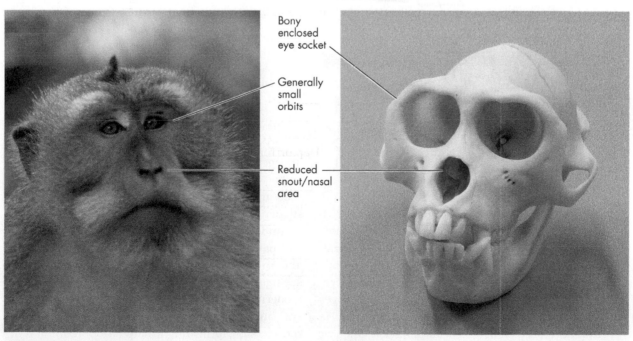

■ FIGURE 6.8

Characteristics of anthropoids. This male macaque displays the bony, enclosed eye sockets; small orbits; and reduced snout area that are characteristic of anthropoids.

■ FIGURE 6.9

Anthropoid forms during the Oligocene. This reconstruction of the Fayum during the Oligocene shows three anthropoid species.

Compared with the Eocene epoch, the Oligocene *era* was generally characterized by cooling global temperatures, an expansion of grassland environments, and a reduction in global forest cover. North American and European vertebrates were still similar to one another at the beginning of the epoch, but that similarity decreased dramatically by the end of the Oligocene *era* as the land areas became more separated. During this epoch there was an expansion in the number and diversity of herbivorous mammals and a related increase in the number and types of carnivorous predators as well.

A good deal of the best fossil remains from the Oligocene, and much of the fossil interpretation, come from a region in northern Africa (in present-day Egypt) called El Fayum. Today this great stretch of land is a desert, but between 40 and 30 million years ago it was filled with lush tropical forests and swampy regions dotted with lakes and rivulets. Most of the Fayum fossils come from a section of strata of earth called the Jebel Qatrani formation. This formation includes nearly 400 m (~1250 feet) of sediments ranging in date from the upper Eocene (40 mya) through the earliest Miocene (about 24 mya). In addition to primate fossils it has also yielded fossils of rodents, bats, porcupine-like and guinea-pig-like mammals, early hippopotamuses, early elephants, and a wide array of aquatic forms (Figure 6.9).

In the early Fayum deposits, we find two main groups of anthropoid primates, the Parapithecids and the Propliopithecids. The Parapithecids are well known from fossils representing the genera *Apidium, Qatrani,* and *Parapithecus.* All of the Parapithecids share a common dental formula of 2-1-3-3 and a collection of primitive and derived primate traits. Some of the better

CONNECTIONS

Why Care about 30-Million-Year-Old Dead Primates?

Understanding early primate evolution actually helps us understand why we are the way we are. We can see from the early primate fossils that vision, specifically color vision, and hand-eye coordination are very deep in our evolutionary past. One of the first things that began to differentiate the primates from other mammals was our eyesight and coordination. This then led to changes in our brain, setting the stage for a more complex brain and more complex social behavior. Once we have the bigger brain (relative to other mammals)

and the beginnings of complex social behavior (by 20–30 million years ago) we can see the basis for lineages that have all the traits needed to possibly begin our own evolutionary line. If we did not have the early primate fossils we would not know the sequence of these patterns nor would we be able to understand the kinds of evolutionary forces and patterns that shaped our ancestors' evolution and thus laid the baseline for our own. It's like seeing the very first cars. A model T Ford and a modern-day Ford Mustang are extremely different, but the earlier form is the basis for the current version, providing a better understanding of how the system and its parts work.

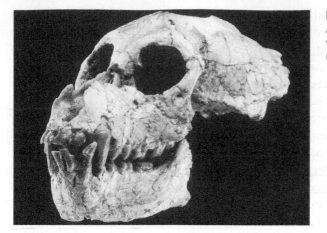

known forms, such as *Apidium*, show some adaptations to arboreal quadrupedal locomotion, perhaps including leaping.

The Propliopithecids are the best-known group of early anthropoids at the Fayum, and many researchers believe they are directly linked to the modern monkeys and apes found in Africa and Asia today. This group of primates has the dental formula 2-1-2-3 (as humans do) and a generalized dental morphology more like that of the living apes than that of the living monkeys (they lack a kind of molar tooth called bilophodont that characterizes the monkeys of Africa and Asia today). Postcranially, the Propliopithecids were fairly primitive and did not directly resemble any living primate forms. The best-known Propliopithecid fossil is a genus called *Aegyptopithecus*, the largest of the Fayum primates (Figure 6.10). The largest species of *Aegyptopithecus* reached an estimated 7 kg (about 15 lb) in weight. This genus is also believed to have been sexually dimorphic in body and canine size. **Sexual dimorphism** is a difference between the sexes in body size or shape, and **canine dimorphism** is a difference between the sexes in the size of canine teeth.

Aside from El Fayum, we also find fossils of anthropoid primates elsewhere in northern Africa, in parts of southern Asia, and, by about 28 to 26 million years ago, in South America.

Note that although we do have fossils of early prosimian primates (Adapoids and Omomyoids) in North America during the Eocene and a few in the Oligocene, we have absolutely no fossil primates of any sort from South or Central America until the appearance of anthropoid primates in the mid-Oligocene. From approximately 28 to 26 million years ago, we see a steady radiation of anthropoid primates throughout most of South and Central America. These primates (called Platyrrhines or neotropical monkeys) have the dental formula 2-1-3-3 (except for a more recent group called the Callitrichids that have lost a molar and have the formula 2-1-3-2) and a number of other skeletal traits in common.

One of the most vexing questions in primate evolution is how anthropoids got to South America. There are three main possibilities. The first is that neotropical primates evolved convergently with African and Asian forms from a common ancestor in the Paleocene. The second suggests that neotropical primates are derived from North American forms that migrated into South America. The third hypothesis suggests that neotropical primates arose from Parapithecids, or Parapithecid-like ancestors, in Africa and migrated, somehow, to South America.

CONNECTIONS

See chapter 7, pages 199, 201, 204, 206, and 208, for an example of how sexual dimorphism might change in early human evolution.

sexual dimorphism difference between the sexes of a species in body size or shape

canine dimorphism difference between the sexes of a species in the size of the canine teeth

All three of these hypotheses can be addressed, to some extent, with data currently available. Regarding the first hypothesis, no fossil anthropoids are found in the Americas until the mid-Oligocene, meaning either that no anthropoids were there before then or we just have not found their fossil remains. We do have a solid fossil record from these areas for the Eocene, and we might expect that if anthropoids were around during the Oligocene, we might find some evidence. Thus, it seems unlikely that anthropoids evolved convergently with African and Asian forms from a Paleocene ancestor. Regarding the second hypothesis, the only primates in North America are probably strepsirrhine forms (Adapoids and Omomyoids), and they are distinct from the neotropical anthropoids (which are Haplorrhines). We would be hard pressed to construct a hypothesis that would explain a transition from North American Adapoids or Omomyoids toward the neotropical anthropoids. Regarding the third hypothesis, the Oligocene anthropoids of South America share a number of traits in common with the other anthropoid Simiiformes of Oligocene Africa. It is probably most realistic to envision the neotropical monkeys deriving from, or sharing a recent common ancestor with, the African forms, rather than explaining all of the similarities through convergent evolution.

How did these primates get to South America from Africa? The rafting scenario is a commonly proposed explanation. The basic rafting hypothesis states that early Oligocene forms (probably Parapithecids) were swept out to sea on floating chunks of vegetation and moved from island to island until they reached the South American mainland. During the early Oligocene the continents of South America and Africa were much closer together than they are today (but still hundreds of miles apart), and evidence indicates that a chain of small islands dotted the central Atlantic between the continents. This hypothesis is tentatively supported by the above-mentioned similarities between South American and African anthropoids and by the fact that a particular form of rodent appears in South America at roughly the same time as the anthropoids do. This type of rodent is most closely related to the African porcupine group and has no apparent precursor forms in the Americas (Figure 6.11).

Hominoid Primates Radiate During the Miocene

By the early Miocene epoch (22–5 mya), the cluster of structural traits that we now use to define the hominoids (apes and humans) begins to appear in some of the anthropoid primates in Africa. These traits include modifications to the shoulder and arm (**brachiator anatomy**); low, rounded molar teeth (with a tooth morphology called Y5 molar pattern); lack of a tail; and, eventually, larger body and brain size (higher EQ). This entire constellation of traits is not seen fully until approximately the mid-Miocene. In fact, the earliest hominoids are called "dental apes," because it is really only in the teeth that we see true hominoid characteristics—the rest comes later. Again, this is an excellent example of the pattern of evolutionary processes in the fossil record: various traits appear gradually over time, eventually reaching a stage at which the trait constellation is different enough from previous forms to allow us to call it something new (Figure 6.12).

At the beginning of the Miocene, temperatures were warm, and tropical forests covered much of the middle latitudes. By about 17 to 16 million years ago, global temperatures began to cool, and woodlands, bushlands, and savannas spread. During this time (about 17–16 mya), Africa was connected to Eurasia, and many forms, including various forms of hominoids, migrated

brachiator anatomy
the ball-and-socket shoulder joint and the positioning of the scapula on the back allowing for 360° rotation of the arms

STOP & THINK

If we never fully determine how primates got to South America, does that negate evolutionary hypotheses about them?

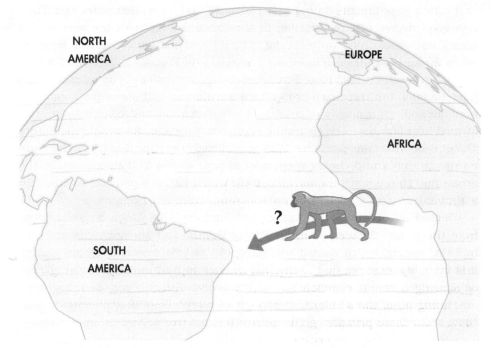

FIGURE 6.11

The rafting hypothesis: Early Oligocene primates most likely reached the Americas on rafts made of floating vegetation.

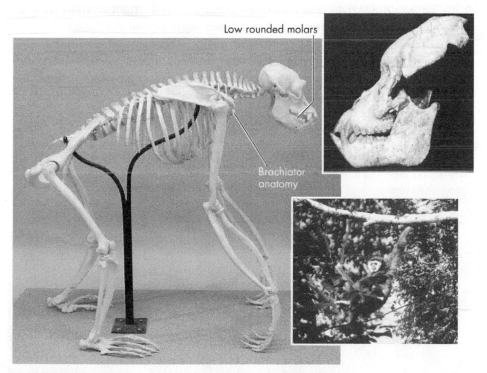

Low rounded molars

Brachiator anatomy

FIGURE 6.12

Characteristics of hominoids. These traits define the apes and humans.

out of Africa into different areas of Eurasia. Currently, most fossil evidence points to Africa as the place of origin for the hominoids.

The Earliest Forms Appear in Africa

The earliest hominoids belong to an extinct family called **Proconsulidae**, known by a number of genera. These early hominoids are found primarily in

Proconsulidae
the earliest family of hominoids (apes), dating to the Miocene

east Africa in sediments dating to between 23 and 17 million years ago. There is a good degree of size variation in the Proconsulids, with the largest (*Proconsul major*) weighing up to 50 kg (110 lb) and the smaller forms weighing 15 to 20 kg (~30–40 lb) (Figure 6.13). Skeletally, Proconsulids exhibit a mixture of generalized anthropoid and hominoid morphology. For example, they have no tails, but their limb proportions are similar to those of many modern, nonhominoid anthropoids (monkeys). Their shoulders and elbows show signs of modifications that are clearly apelike, but they are not truly brachiators. The Proconsulids were relatively un-specialized; they lived both in trees and on the ground and probably spent a lot of time eating fruit. Interestingly, this genus had thin enamel on its molar teeth much like two modern African apes (chimpanzees and gorillas) but unlike orangutans and humans.

We find other families and genera of hominoids in Africa as well. Forms from the genera *Nyanzapithecus*, *Morotopithecus*, and *Micropithecus* are common in eastern Africa during the early and middle Miocene. By the middle and later Miocene, we find forms that appear to have potential relationships with modern hominoids. Members of the genera *Afropithecus*, *Kenyapithecus*, and *Samburupithecus* all exhibit aspects of morphology that potentially align them with the modern African hominoids (chimpanzees, gorillas, and humans).

Eurasian Forms Appear After the Mid-Miocene

Several hominoid forms appear in the fossil record of southern Europe and Asia beginning about 17 million years ago. Although hominoids disappear, briefly, from Europe during the Pliocene, they remain in Asia right through modern times. The genus *Dryopithecus* is well known from several European localities. These apes have thick enamel on their teeth (like humans and orangutans) and a number of skeletal traits that resemble those found in modern hominoids (especially the Hominidae: gorillas, chimpanzees, orangutans, and humans).

■ **FIGURE 6.13**
Reconstruction of *Proconsul*. This family is considered among the first hominoids. Here we see *Proconsul* leaping from tree to tree.

Found throughout much of southern Europe and Asia, the fossil family Pliopithecidae includes at least four distinct genera of hominoids. Of these forms, the genera *Pliopithecus* (dating from the middle Miocene in Europe and Asia) and *Laccopithecus* (dating from the late Miocene in Asia) have been proposed as possible ancestors to the modern hominoid family Hylobatidae (the siamangs and gibbons). Existing fossils are in varying states of intactness, however; so debate remains about how direct the relationships are between these forms and modern gibbons.

There are three interesting forms from the middle Miocene in southern Europe. One is the fossil genus *Oreopithecus*, found in late Miocene sediments in northern Italy. This fossil bears many similarities to the earlier African hominoid forms (such as *Nyanzapithecus*), to earlier European forms (*Dryopithecus*), and to later, modern Hominidae (African apes and humans). Another late Miocene form, *Ouranopithecus*, known from several sites in Greece, also exhibits strong similarities to the modern hominoids. Many researchers suggest that, based on facial morphology, this genus has very close affinities with the modern African hominoids (chimpanzees, gorillas, and humans). *Ouranopithecus* may be one of the best links between Miocene and modern hominids. Another possible link between Miocene and modern African hominoids (chimpanzees, gorillas, and humans) is the recently discovered *Pierolapithecus catalaunicus* (Figure 6.14). This middle Miocene (~12–13 mya) fossil ape from

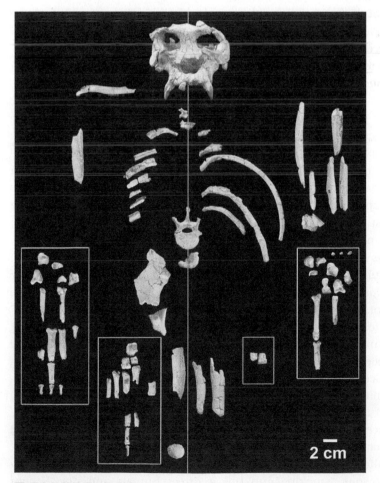

■ FIGURE 6.14
Pierolapithecus catalaunicus. This middle Miocene fossil ape from Spain is a possible ancestor to the African hominoids.

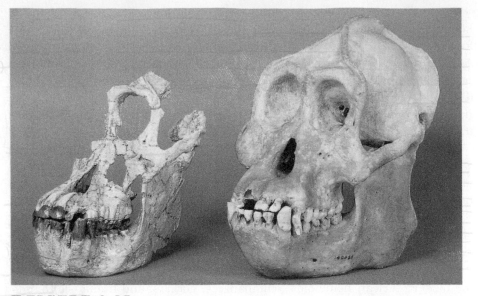

■ FIGURE 6.15

Sivapithecus (left) with the skull of a modern orangutan (right). *Sivapithecus* is a good candidate for ancestor of modern orangutans.

Spain also has a number of traits that suggest it as a possible ancestor to the African apes (Moya-Sola et al., 2004).

The majority of the hominoid fossils from southern and Southeast Asia are found in mid- to late Miocene sediments. Three main genera are *Gigantopithecus, Lufengpithecus,* and *Sivapithecus. Sivapithecus* is a very well known collection of fossils representing three species, found in the Siwalik hills of India and Pakistan. These fossils bear a striking resemblance to the modern orangutan. The small canine dimorphism, thick-enameled molars, and specific characteristics of the skull morphology make *Sivapithecus* a strong candidate for a direct (or very close) orangutan ancestor (Figure 6.15).

Based on morphology, *Gigantopithecus* appears to be closely related to *Sivapithecus.* This genus is found in late Miocene sites in India and Pakistan and in Pleistocene sites in China and Vietnam as recently as 300,000 years ago. The three species in this genus are the largest primates ever to have lived. The largest of the three, *G. blacki,* probably exceeded 300 kg (640 lb) in body weight—nearly twice the size of living gorillas (Figure 6.16).

Lufengpithecus is known from more than a thousand dental fragments and a number of skulls. The morphologies of this late Miocene form are similar to those of *Dryopithecus* of Europe. *Lufengpithecus* displays a greater degree of sexual dimorphism than any living ape.

The primate fossil record of the Miocene provides us with a strong, but incomplete, picture of the evolutionary history of the hominoids. The early and middle Miocene deposits in Africa are rich in fossils, as are the middle and late Miocene sites in Eurasia. However, three of the five living hominoid genera (chimpanzees, gorillas, and humans, the subfamily Homininae) probably started to appear in Africa at the end of the Miocene or the beginning of the Pliocene. Unfortunately, researchers have successfully explored very few fossil localities of that age (between about 8 and 5 mya) in Africa.

The current Miocene record gives us a number of clues and possible candidates but no obvious "smoking gun" for a direct human ancestor. Recent advances in fossil collection from late Miocene locales and increasingly precise molecular research conducted on the living hominoids continue to provide

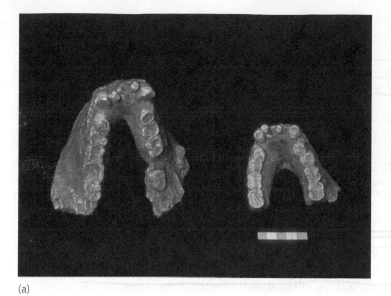

■ FIGURE 6.16
Gigantopithecus fossil jawbone (left). The reconstruction, made by Russell Ciochon and Bill Munns, is shown with Munns (right).

CONNECTIONS

Ok, So Is *Gigantopithecus* Bigfoot?

Most people laugh at anyone who believes that big, hairy, apemen exist. But what about if something like bigfoot existed and, although they are extinct today, people still have deep cultural memories of them? If you look at the estimated range of *Gigantopithecus*, it fits very nicely with the range of the mythical Yeti, the most documented of the giant ape-like creatures purported to still roam the globe. We know that, even though it was at least 100,000–200,000 years ago, early humans and *Gigantopithecus* probably overlapped in parts of South and South East Asia. Maybe, tales have been passed down across the ages about the big furry humanlike folk, and those tales are still around as part of cultural lore. It's possible. Ok, but what about Sasquatch,

the "bigfoot" of the U.S. Pacific Northwest? We have no evidence that any apes lived in the Americas prior to the arrival of modern humans, so it is more likely that bigfoot is a myth not based in ancestral lore. However, there are two points that make the whole bigfoot scenario a bit more interesting. The first is that we know that the peoples who first colonized the Americas came from Asia . . . maybe they brought the stories about Yeti with them. Second, the recent discovery of the "hobbit," *Homo floresiensis*, a new dwarf species of human who lived as recently as 12,000 years ago in South East Asia reminds us to be humble about pronouncing that we know all there is to know. Are there undiscovered humanlike creatures still out there? Probably not, but until actually tested and refuted, it remains a valid hypothesis.

insight into the relationships between Miocene and subsequent forms (as discussed in the next chapter). As fieldwork continues at sites with Miocene exposures, we expect to build a greater understanding of the exciting and complex evolution of the hominoids. We also hope to be able to address the question of why there were so many hominoids in the Miocene and so few today.

Nonhominoid Anthropoid Primates Radiate During the Pliocene and Pleistocene

During the Pliocene (5–1.8 million years ago) and Pleistocene (1.8 million to about 10,000 years ago), most of the modern primate forms show up in the fossil record. As the Miocene drew to a close, the overall number of hominoid species and genera underwent a dramatic reduction, and the diversity and number of monkeys increased. In Africa and Asia the major modern Cercopithecidae groups such as baboons, macaques, and colobines appeared. By the end of the Pliocene and beginning of the Pleistocene, most modern species are found (in more or less modern form) in the fossil record.

Evolutionary relationships among these fossil primates are a matter of debate

Now that we have sped through more than 60 million years of evolutionary history, we need to stop and ask, How are all these forms related? That is, what are the evolutionary connections, or phylogenies, that characterize primate evolution from the Paleocene to the late Miocene? One such phylogeny is presented in Figure 6.17.

Currently, researchers argue about the specific relationships among primate taxa across some of the time periods. Although there are no certain "right" answers at this point, some proposed phylogenies have more support than others. Many paleoanthropologists think that some Adapoids probably aligned with, but possibly not directly ancestral to, the modern lemurs (Lemuriformes). There are also many who place the Omomyoids in the general early haplorrhine lineage, possibly ancestral to the tarsiers (Tarsiiformes), and *Darwinius*, an Adapoid, is likely related to Haphorrhines as well.

The most debate occurs over the ancestry of the Simiiform (anthropoid) primates—the monkeys. Some researchers consider Omomyoids to be their ancestors; some give that spot to Adapoids; and an increasing number think the late Eocene Asian forms, such as *Eosimias*, are the most likely candidates for anthropoid ancestry. The debate centers on determining exactly which specific characteristics the earliest Simiiform primates would exhibit. It should not be surprising that all three of the Eocene primate lineages—Adapoid, Omomyoid, and early anthropoid (Simiiform)—are considered possibilities, since they are the earliest true primates and therefore exhibit all of the primitive traits we would expect to find in such a primate ancestor. The trick is to figure out which few morphological changes heralded a shift in selection pressures that eventually resulted in the forms that gave rise to the structures we see in monkeys, apes, and humans today.

Currently, the best representations of primate evolution are those that depict general morphological trends as revealed in the fossil record without explicitly tying one form to the next in a linear fashion unless there is extremely convincing evidence. When we view primate evolution this way, without having to link individual fossils to one another, we see the trends and patterns of change over time.

STOP & THINK

Is there likely to be one correct answer to these questions about relationships in the foreseeable future? Why or why not?

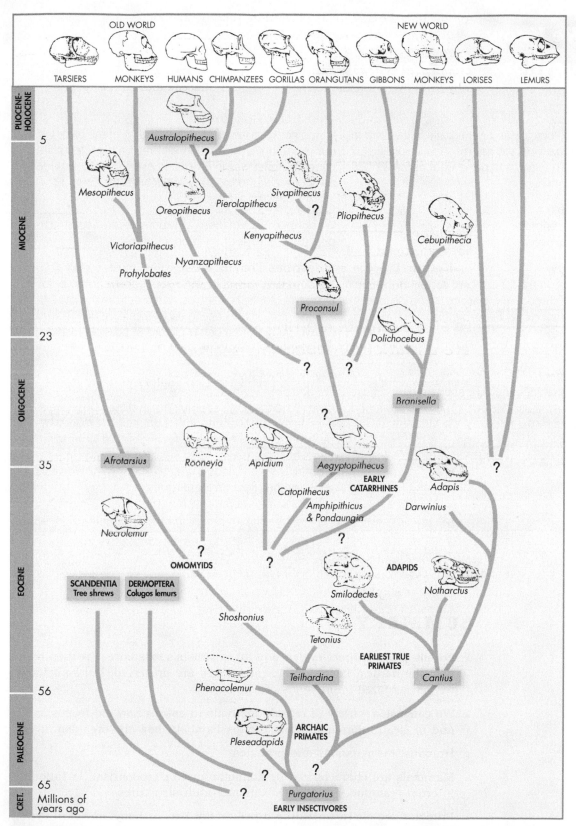

OLD WORLD

NEW WORLD

TARSIERS MONKEYS HUMANS CHIMPANZEES GORILLAS ORANGUTANS GIBBONS MONKEYS LORISES LEMURS

PLIOCENE-HOLOCENE

5

MIOCENE

23

OLIGOCENE

35

EOCENE

56

PALEOCENE

65

CRET.

Millions of years ago

Australopithecus

Mesopithecus

Oreopithecus

Pierolapithecus

Sivapithecus

?

Pliopithecus

?

Cebupithecia

Kenyapithecus

Victoriapithecus

Nyanzapithecus

Prohylobates

Proconsul

Dolichocebus

?

?

Branisella

?

Afrotarsius

Rooneyia

Apidium

Aegyptopithecus

EARLY CATARRHINES

Adapis

Catopithecus

Amphipithicus & Pondaungia

Darwinius

?

Necrolemur

?

OMOMYIDS

?

ADAPIDS

Smilodectes

Notharctus

SCANDENTIA Tree shrews

DERMOPTERA Colugos lemurs

Shoshonius

Tetonius

EARLIEST TRUE PRIMATES

Phenacolemur

Teilhardina

Cantius

Pleseadapids

ARCHAIC PRIMATES

?

?

?

Purgatorius

EARLY INSECTIVORES

■ FIGURE 6.17

A possible phylogeny for the primate order. There is much debate over specific relationships among primate taxa across some time periods.

What We Know

Humans morphologically and genetically fit well within the group of organisms we call mammals. Specific aspects of the morphology and genetics of humans place us in the order Primates.

Questions That Remain

We do not yet have a full understanding of the pieces of our evolutionary history. Several research projects are currently under way in Africa and Asia that may provide additional clues to the story of our ancestry.

What We Know

Fossils of true primates first show up in the late Paleocene/early Eocene.

Questions That Remain

We don't yet know if these early primates are ancestral to only some or to all of the modern primates.

What We Know

Primates show up in the fossil record continuously from the Eocene right through the present. By the Oligocene, there are fossils that clearly fit the definition of Simiiform anthropoids.

Questions That Remain

We don't know which lineage of Oligocene anthropoids is ancestral to the hominoids. As fossils from the late Oligocene to early Miocene in east Africa continue to turn up, we are getting a better picture of possible relationships between Oligocene and Miocene forms.

What We Know

The first fossils that look truly like apes (hominoids) are found in Africa in the early Miocene. They spread around Eurasia and Africa by the middle of the Miocene.

Questions That Remain

We don't know which of these fossil hominoid lineages gave rise to the hominins (humans and their closest relatives) in the late Miocene. Although there are several hypotheses, we still have very few hominoid or hominin fossils from the period 10 to 5 million years ago in eastern Africa. Recent finds dating to about 6 million years ago may shed light on these issues.

SUMMARY

▲ Fossils provide direct evidence of an organism's existence. Frequently only the hardest tissues (bones and teeth) are preserved, but sometimes we get fossilized impressions of soft tissues.

▲ We can use a variety of reliable methods to assess how old fossils are and to glean information from the fossils about how the organism lived.

▲ Humans are mammals and primates.

▲ Mammals are characterized by homiothermy, heterodontism, lactation, internal gestation, and a set of unique brain structures.

▲ Primates are characterized by a postorbital bar, or bony, enclosed eye socket; hands and feet capable of grasping; nails instead of claws on the ends of the digits; extensively overlapping visual fields; a large brain relative to body size; and long gestation and slow postnatal growth compared to maternal body size.

▲ The earliest primates are thought to be derived from a group related to the Pleseadapids sometime in the late Cretaceous or early Paleocene.

- There are three main hypotheses for the evolution of primates from Archontan stock; they center on arboreality; visual adaptation; and fruit, flower, and insect predation.

- Three main primate groups show up in the fossils of the Eocene age: the Omomyoids, the Adapoids, and the Simiiform anthropoids.

- The Oligocene fossils reveal a radiation of anthropoid forms and the colonization of South America by anthropoid primates.

- By the Miocene, a new set of primates, the hominoids, began to radiate out of Africa. These primates exhibit a set of morphological characteristics that characterize the living apes.

- The hominoids experienced a decrease in diversity by the terminal Miocene, at the same time that the number and diversity of nonhominoid anthropoid primates (monkeys) increased.

- The best representations of primate evolution are those that reveal general patterns and trends over time.

CRITICAL THINKING

1. Why do the hypotheses for the evolution of early primates center around selective elements imposed by arboreal and fruit/flower/insect-eating lifestyles? Why not terrestriality, or quadrupedalism, or predation pressure?

2. Why do we call the early primates "primates" if they do not have all the characteristics of modern primates? Why are the early "dental apes" considered apes? What does this have to do with the processes of evolution?

3. Is the rafting hypothesis scientific? How can we test it? What are other possible explanations for the appearance of Simiiformes in South America?

4. What kind of selective environments might have favored the adaptations that led to the different primate groups (for example, hominoids versus cercopithecoids)?

5. Why is it not a problem for scientists to propose multiple possible ancestors for modern apes from the Miocene hominoid fossils? Shouldn't we look for one perfect missing link?

RESOURCES

PRIMATE EVOLUTION IN DETAIL

Conroy, G. C. (1990). *Primate evolution.* New York: Norton.
This book provides an advanced discussion of the topic for students interested in looking more intensively at our origins.

Fleagle, J. (1999). *Primate adaptation and evolution* (2nd ed.). New York: Academic Press.
This is another advanced book on the primates for interested students.

MAMMALS AND MAMMALIAN EVOLUTION IN DETAIL

Vaughan, T. A. (1999). *Mammalogy* (4th ed.). New York: Harcourt.
This book provides an introduction to the diverse array of mammals on our planet.

www.ucmp.berkeley.edu/mammal/mammal.html This link to the Web site of the University of California Museum of Paleontology focuses on mammals.

REFERENCES

Cartmill, M. (1992). New views on primate origins. *Evolutionary Anthropology, 1*, 105–111.

Ducrocq, S. (1998). Eocene primates from Thailand: Are Asian Anthropoideans related to African ones? *Evolutionary Anthropology, 7*, 97–104.

Fleagle, J. G. (1999). *Primate adaptation and evolution* (2nd ed.). New York: Academic Press.

Franzen, J. L., Gingerich, P. D., Hubersetzer, J., Hurum, J. H., van Koenigswald, W., & Smith, H. (2009). Complete Primate Skeleton from the Middle Eocene of Messel in Germany: Morphology and Paleobiology. PLoS ONE 4(5): 1–26.

Moya-Sola, S., Kohler, M., Alba, D. M., Casanovas-Vilar, I., & Galindo, J. (2004). *Pierolapithecus catalaunicus,* a new middle Miocene great ape from Spain, *Science, 306*, 1339–1344.

Rasmussen, D. T. (1990). Primate origins: Lessons from a neotropical marsupial. *American Journal of Primatology, 22*, 263–277.

Simons, E. L., & Rasmussen, T. (1994). A whole new world of ancestors: Eocene Anthropoidean from Africa. *Evolutionary Anthropology, 3*, 128–139.

Sussman, R. W. (1991). Primate origins and the evolution of angiosperms. *American Journal of Primatology 23*, 209–223.

Szalay, F. S. (1972). Paleobiology of the earliest primates. In R. Tuttle (Ed.), *The functional and evolutionary biology of the primates* (pp. 3–36). Chicago: Aldine.

CHAPTER 7

Early Hominin Evolution

This chapter addresses the following questions:

▲ What are the hominins, and why do we call them our ancestors?

▲ What hominin fossils do we have for the late Miocene through the mid–late Pliocene (6–3 million years ago)?

▲ What are the evolutionary relationships between the early hominins?

▲ What do these fossils tell us about the behavior and lifeways of these hominins?

▲ Why did the hominins become bipedal?

In 1911 amateur prehistorian Charles Dawson claimed to have found part of a fossilized human skull in a gravel pit at Piltdown in southern England. Between 1911 and 1912 a few more bone pieces were discovered at the site. With the help of Sir Arthur Smith Woodward of the British Museum of Natural History and Sir Arthur Keith of the Royal College of Surgeons of London, Dawson produced a reconstruction of what came to be considered the link between modern humans and the brutish, apelike creatures before them, **Piltdown Man** (Figure 7.1). The Piltdown skull was startling because its cranium (braincase) was essentially modern in form, but its jaw was entirely apelike, with protruding canine teeth and no chin. It appeared to show that the early ancestor of modern humans was not a small-brained, ape-like creature, but rather a large-brained creature with an apelike jaw.

Many thought that the so-called Piltdown Man was the "missing link" between apes and humans, and for 40 years, even though many anthropologists and other scientists doubted its authenticity, it played a prominent role in hypotheses about human evolution. By 1953 the Piltdown skull had been proven to be a fake: A modern human cranium and the jaw of an orangutan had been planted at the site. In fact, it was through the use of fluorine dating that the jaw and skull were shown to be of different ages

CONNECTIONS

See chapter 6 for further discussion of fluorine and other dating technologies.

■ FIGURE 7.1
The Piltdown skull. The cranium is that of a modern human and the mandible is an altered orangutan jawbone. This "find" confirmed the then-current idea that the "missing link" between apes and humans would be a creature with a large brain and an apelike jaw.

Piltdown Man
fossil find considered an important link in human evolution until it was shown to be a fake in 1953

bipedality
use of two legs rather than four for locomotion

bipedal anatomy
a set of anatomical adaptations that make it possible for an animal to use two legs for locomotion

CONNECTIONS

See chapter 2, pages 50–55, for discussion of the skeleton and muscles associated with bipedalism.

than the materials around them (see chapter 6). The hoax raises several questions: First, why was it perpetrated, and by whom? To this day, no one has definitive answers to these questions. More important, why was the hoax so successful? Here we can offer a number of reasons. One is that the Piltdown skull conformed to an idealized version of the ancestor of humans as being big brained and therefore not "apelike" (Feder, 2002). The Piltdown fossil fit nicely into an ideology that viewed humans as unique. It reinforced the notion of human dominance over all other animals and the Great Chain of Being by making brain size, and thus intelligence, the dividing line between both modern humans and other organisms and human ancestors and other organisms. It implied that humans had been unique and distinct in their intelligence for a long time, and it showed that the earliest evidence of intelligent humanity occurred in Europe, specifically in England. These elements fit well into the worldview of many scientists involved in the study of human evolution at the time (see chapter 10).

Since the 1920s, some researchers had suggested that our earliest ancestors did not have big brains, and by the late 1960s and 1970s, a number of significant fossil finds in Africa supported this interpretation. These relatively small-brained fossils demonstrated that the real difference between early human ancestors and other apes was **bipedality**, the fact that they walked on two legs instead of four. Walking on two legs across open ground (*terrestrial bipedality*) served as a marker, or reinforcer, of the uniqueness of our ancestors, because no other mammal shares this trait. It also carried a strong message: Humans strode across the ground and stood tall while other primate lineages stayed in the trees or lumbered across the ground on all fours. Reading popular magazines (and many scientific ones) today, we continually encounter descriptions of the "missing link" as very apelike, but bipedal. For example, *Time* published this description on July 23, 2001:

> It was in eastern Africa at about this time that a new type of primate arose—an animal not so different from its apelike ancestors except in one crucial respect: it stood on two legs. . . . Its knuckle walking cousins would stay low to the ground and never get much smarter . . . this new primate's evolutionary descendents would eventually develop a large complex brain. And from that would spring all of civilization, from Mesopotamia to Who Wants to Be a Millionaire. (pp. 55–56)

As this popular interpretation demonstrates, most people assume that there is a strong linkage between bipedalism and increased brain size (and hence intelligence). In the popular imagination today, terrestrial bipedality was the necessary precursor to big-brained modern humans.

Over the last few decades our understanding of the last ancestor shared by humans and other apes has become more complex. We once thought that a large brain separated humans and our ancestors from the rest of the animal kingdom. Then we focused solely on bipedalism as the distinguishing characteristic. Now, as you'll see in this chapter, many researchers consider that bipedal anatomy, not necessarily full terrestrial bipedal behavior, may be the key. **Bipedal anatomy** is a set of anatomical adaptations that allows an organism to use its hind limbs (legs) as primary support and exhibit a locomotory pattern on the ground, in trees, or a mix of the two. These adaptations include changes to the pelvis, legs, and feet that we will discuss later in the chapter. However, having bipedal anatomy does not require that terrestrial bipedalism is the organism's only, or even primary, mode of locomotion.

Why Walking On Two Legs Makes Birth Painful for Mom

Bipedality, standing erect and walking on the hind legs, is complicated (as discussed in this chapter and chapter 2), but one thing that most people don't consider is that having a big brain and being bipedal present a bit of a problem: giving birth. Late in human evolution brains get really big relative to body size. That brain (and the head it is inside of) has to pass between the bones of the pelvic girdle during birth. In modern humans a newborn's head is larger than the opening in the pelvic girdle, presenting a significant problem in getting the baby out of the womb. The human body deals with this in two ways. The infant's cranial bones are unfused and flexible so its head can squeeze in a bit as it passes through the birth canal. In mom, right around the moments of birth, a hormone called relaxin courses through her body affecting her cartilage. It turns out that the connections between the various bones in the pelvic girdle (chapter 2) are with cartilage. As the cartilage loosens the bones making up the birth canal (specifically the two parts of the pubis) are able to spread apart a bit increasing the diameter of the birth canal. So, birth can be painful as the mother's and infant's bodies compensate for the conflict between those two very important aspects of being humans: big brains and bipedality.

Humans seem driven to find the key that will explain our existence, whether it be a philosophy or a fossil. In our search we look for something clear, distinctive, and unique that not only separates us from all other organisms but also ties us to our closest relatives. Could there really be a single organism, or species—a modern Piltdown Man—that would fulfill this role? What would its characteristics be? In an evolutionary sense, defining such characteristics may be impossible, because most of the characteristics we use to distinguish ourselves from the other apes are not necessarily apparent in our oldest common ancestors. As the anthropologist Pat Shipman (2001) wrote, "Paleoanthropologists must seriously reconsider the defining attributes of apes and Hominids ["hominins" in this text] while we wait for new fossils. In the meantime, we should ponder our complicity, too, for we have been guilty of expecting evolution to be much simpler than it is." In short, the earlier assumptions of a single missing link—a creature with a big brain or one who walked upright across the ground—that would set us apart from other apes were erroneous. The evolution of the human lineage is a much more complicated reality.

In this chapter we examine the fossils that anthropologists and others have discovered in their search for the earliest direct human ancestor. Having sped through the first 60 million years or so of primate evolution in chapter 6, we find ourselves now in the late Miocene epoch (about 6 million years ago) with the appearance of a new branch of hominoids in east Africa. The background information on mammals and early primates presented in chapter 6 sets the stage for our discussion of human evolution. In this chapter and the next, we meet our immediate evolutionary family and review the different facts (fossils) and hypotheses (testable explanations of the fossils and their relationships to one another) concerning the evolution of humankind.

Classification of hominids/hominins is a subject of debate

In the traditional, commonly used taxonomy, the living hominoids (superfamily: Hominoidea) are divided into three families: Hominidae (hominids or humans), Pongidae (pongids or great apes), and Hylobatidae (gibbons). In this taxonomic system the pongids consist of the African genera *Gorilla* (gorillas)

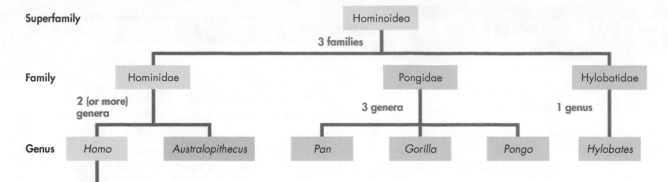

Superfamily		Hominoidea			

3 families

Family	Hominidae		Pongidae		Hylobatidae

2 (or more) genera   3 genera   1 genus

Genus	*Homo*	*Australopithecus*	*Pan*	*Gorilla*	*Pongo*	*Hylobates*

Species	*sapiens*

■ FIGURE 7.2

Traditional taxonomy of apes and humans (superfamily Hominoidea). This classification places humans and their direct ancestors in a different family from the great apes (Pongidae) and gibbons (Hylobatidae).

CONNECTIONS

Compare taxonomy today with Linneaus classification discussed in chapter 2, pages 48–49.

hominid
member of the family Hominidae

pongid
member of the family Pongidae (not used by the author of this book)

tribe
taxonomic classification placed below subfamily and above genus

CONNECTIONS

See chapter 6, pages 168–183, for an overview of possible ape and human ancestors.

and *Pan* (chimpanzees) and the Asian genus *Pongo* (orangutans) (Figure 7.2). The assumption is that these three great apes share closer evolutionary relationships with one another than any of them does with the human lineage. This taxonomy assumes that human ancestors (**hominids**) separated from great ape ancestors (**pongids**) before the pongids differentiated into African and Asian forms. In this system the hominoids that lived in eastern and southern Africa between 5 and 2 million years ago have generally been referred to as hominid (Hominidae) and considered part of the human lineage.

Over the last 35 years accumulated molecular and fossil evidence suggests that the traditional taxonomy should be revised. Current knowledge of morphological and molecular relationships among the living apes and humans indicates that chimpanzees, gorillas, and humans are more similar, and thus more closely related, to one another than any of them is to the orangutan (Begun, 1999). Therefore, the traditional classification of humans by ourselves (hominids) and chimpanzees, gorillas, and orangutans lumped together (pongids) is not an accurate reflection of evolutionary histories. In line with current data, a modified taxonomy has been proposed (see Figure 7.3). In this new taxonomy, all great apes and humans are placed together in the family Hominidae, and the family Pongidae is discarded. Within the Hominidae, chimpanzees, gorillas, and humans are lumped together as the subfamily Homininae (an African-derived branch of Hominidae), and orangutans are placed by themselves as the subfamily Ponginae (an Asian-derived branch of Hominidae). This creates only two families within the superfamily Hominoidea; Hominidae (humans and great apes) and Hylobatidae (gibbons). The distinction between the chimpanzees, gorillas, and humans is placed at the taxonomic level of **tribe** (just under subfamily and just above genus). Humans and direct human ancestors are then classed as representatives of the tribe Hominini and referred to as hominins.

Not all researchers agree with this classification, and it remains controversial despite its growing usage by paleoanthropologists and other researchers (Begun, 1999; Leakey et al., 2001; Lieberman, 2001; Wood & Collard, 1999; Wood & Lonergan, 2008). We need to consider several lines of evidence, both fossils and living forms. The molecular data suggest that humans and chimpanzees are slightly more closely related than are humans and gorillas or gorillas and chimpanzees and that the most recent common ancestor for these three forms existed about 7 to 8 million years ago (summarized in Begun, 1999). These data also demonstrate that the orangutan lineage separated from the

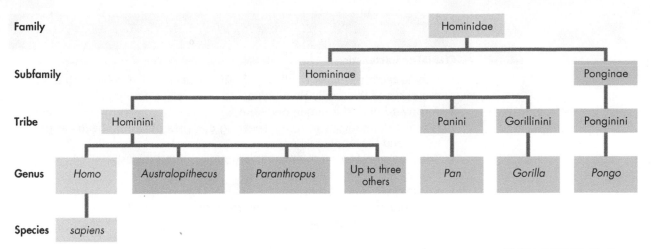

Family					Hominidae				
Subfamily			Homininae					Ponginae	
Tribe		Hominini				Panini	Gorillinini	Ponginini	
Genus	*Homo*	*Australopithecus*	*Paranthropus*	Up to three others		*Pan*	*Gorilla*	*Pongo*	
Species	*sapiens*								

■ **FIGURE 7.3**
Modern taxonomy of apes and humans (family Hominidae). This classification places humans and great apes in the same family. Compare with Figure 7.2.

African apes and humans about 10 to 12 million years ago (Pilbeam, 1996). These genetic data seem to fit with the available fossil evidence (see chapter 6). Given that the African forms (chimpanzees, gorillas, and humans) form a clear genetic cluster and that the Asian form (orangutan) falls out as a separate group, it does not make sense to lump the orangutan, chimpanzee, and gorilla together in one category (called family Pongidae) and the humans in another (family Hominidae). In other words, this type of classification does not fit with the available data, even though it has been in use for many years. Under the methodology of science, when data do not support a hypothesis (such as the Pongidae/Hominidae taxonomy), we must alter our hypothesis to fit the current data sets. That is why in this book we use the classifications Homininae (chimpanzees, humans, and gorillas), Ponginae (orangutans), and Hominini (humans and ancestors in our lineage since the split with the other African apes).

In this book we refer to humans and all their ancestors and relatives *after* the split with any other ape lineage as the hominins. We refer to our closest African ape cousins (the gorilla and chimpanzees, the other members of the subfamily Homininae) as **hominines** and the orangutans as *ponginines* (members of the subfamily Ponginae). This is not the most widely used naming system—at least not yet. Some books (even introductory textbooks like this one) still call all humans and human ancestors after the split with the African apes *hominids*. We will not use that system here because the current genetic, molecular, and fossil data do not support it.

All the hominins share a number of unique physical traits (see Table 7.1). These include modifications in the pelvic girdle and lower limbs that make them capable of effective bipedal locomotion. Changes in the upper arm and vertebral column indicate that weight is borne by the legs. Hominins also have smaller canine teeth than do other members of the family Hominidae and subfamily Homininae, a forward-placed foramen magnum, and no (or a dramatically reduced) **shearing complex** (a condition in which the lower first premolar is somewhat sharpened or flattened from rubbing against the upper canine as the mouth closes). In other words, you and I are hominins, and the fossils that show many or all of these morphological traits are considered hominin as well (Figure 7.4). While most of these traits were developed in hominins by about 5 million years ago, the large brain that characterizes modern hominins (us), did not develop until about 2 million years ago.

hominine
member of the subfamily Homininae, which includes the African apes and humans

shearing complex
condition in which the lower first premolar is somewhat sharpened or flattened from rubbing against the upper canine as the mouth closes

STOP & **THINK**

Are there any philosophical or ethical issues created by making humans and African apes part of the same subfamily?

TABLE 7.1 — Characteristics of the Hominins

Cranial characteristics

▲ Canine teeth relatively small and incisiform (incisor-like) relative to other members of the family Hominidae and subfamily Homininae
▲ A forward placed foramen magnum
▲ No, or a dramatically reduced, shearing complex between the lower premolar and the upper canine
▲ The first premolar on the mandible double rooted (bicuspid)
▲ Molars with thick enamel
▲ Mastoid process present
▲ Temporal origins forward on cranium
▲ Parabolic dental arcade

Postcranial characteristics

▲ Modifications to the pelvic girdle and lower limbs making hominins capable of effective bipedal locomotion, changes in the upper arm and vertebral column indicating that weight is borne by the legs

  – Angled femur, center of gravity medial and forward, distal end indicates "knee-locking"

  – Foot (pes) double arched

  – Big toe (hallux) relatively nonabductable

  – Phalanges of pedal digits 2–5 shortened

  – Wide flaring iliac blade, os coxae broad and short

■ FIGURE 7.4
Characteristics of hominins. Hominins are distinguished from other apes by bipedal anatomy (a) and unique characteristics of the teeth (b) and jaw (c).

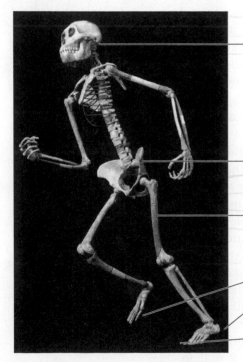

Forward placed foramen magnum

Wide flaring iliac blade; os coxae broad and short

Angled femur, center of gravity medial and forward, distal end indicates "knee locking"

Hallux (big toe) relatively nonabductable

Foot double-arched

Phalanges of toes 2–5 shortened

(a) Bipedal anatomy

Canines are relatively small

Thick enamel on molars

(b) Mandible

Dramatically reduced shearing complex between the lower premolar and upper canine

(c) Jaws

Early hominins evolved primarily in east Africa

Although we have plenty of access to rocks from the **Plio-Pleistocene** age in Eurasia and the Americas, it is only in Africa that we find any fossil evidence of hominins before about 2 million years ago. If we look back to the late Miocene, we find that hominoid forms that look most like the hominins are found principally in eastern Africa (*Afropithecus, Kenyapithecus,* and *Samburupithecus*), with a few forms found in the Mediterranean region (*Ouranopithecus* and *Pierolapithecus*) near north Africa (see chapter 6). This suggests that the transition by one or more hominoid lineages toward a hominin form took place in these areas (Benefit & McCrossin, 1995).

An especially important area for hominin fossils in Africa is the Rift Valley, a massive geological feature characterized by active volcanoes, earthquakes, and mountain-building over the last several million years (Figure 7.5). This huge series of canyons and land rifts extends over 1200 miles across the countries of Ethiopia, Kenya, and Tanzania in east Africa. Due to the geological activity, many different layers of sediments and ages of rock are exposed across its length. The high frequency of volcanic

Plio-Pleistocene
boundary between the Pliocene and Pleistocene epochs, about 1.8 mya

See chapter 6, pages 176–182, for more info on hominoid and hominin fossils.

■ FIGURE 7.5
The east African Rift Valley. The photo shows Little Magidi, one of the numerous lakes in the valley, which stretches 5600 km (3500 miles) from the Red Sea to Mozambique. In some places the valley is over 600 m (2000 feet) deep.

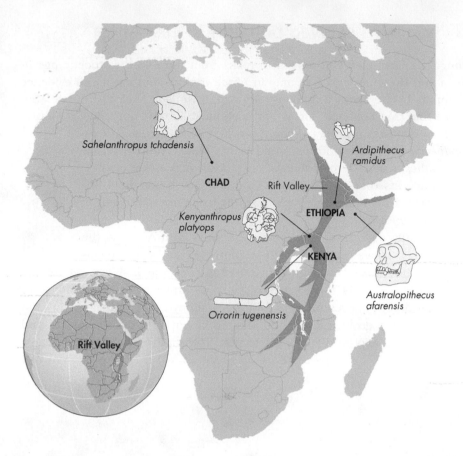

activity in the region has allowed for accurate dating of many of the fossil finds (Figure 7.6).

Early Possible Hominins

Some fragmentary fossils that are very likely hominin have been dated to as early as the late Miocene (6–5 mya). A partial mandible dated to approximately 5.7 mya was found at Lothagam, Kenya, and another mandible dated to approximately 5 mya was unearthed at Tabarin, Kenya. At Mabaget, Kenya, researchers uncovered a section of a young individual's humerus dated to approximately 5 mya. Precisely what groups these fossils belong to remains unclear, but they appear to share structural similarities with later hominin finds (see Table 7.2).

Orrorin tugenensis: Root of the Ape-Human Split?

In December 2000, fossils of postcranial bones (bones of the body below the cranium) said to be hominin were unearthed in Kenya and dated to approximately 6 mya (Figure 7.7). Whether this find, named *Orrorin tugenensis* (Senut et al., 2001), is a hominin remains unclear however. There are some teeth, a jaw fragment, a partial humerus, a phalange (finger bone), and three partial femurs. As evidence that these fossils are hominin, the scientists who found them point to the thick molar enamel on the *Orrorin* teeth. Most hominins have thick enamel on the molars, but chimpanzees and gorillas do not. However, the one canine fossil of *Orrorin* appears to be relatively large and apelike. The team that found *Orrorin* contend that the size of the heads of the fossil femurs and the angle of the femoral neck indicate that *Orrorin* was at least frequently bipedal (Galick et al., 2004). They also note that elements of its bipedal anatomy are similar to those found in modern humans but somewhat different from those found in some later hominins (such as those to be

TABLE 7.2	Early Hominine and Hominin Fossils		
Species	**Location**	**Date (mya)**	**Main Characteristics**
Orrorin tugenensis	E. Africa	~6	Thick molar enamel, hominine but not undoubtedly hominin
Sahelanthropus tchadensis	N. central Africa	~7–6	Relatively small canines with no shearing complex and thick molar enamel, hominine but not undoubtedly hominin
Ardipithecus ramidus	E. Africa	5.8–4.4	Thin molar enamel, reduced canines, forward placed foramen magnum, hominine but not undoubtedly hominin
Australopithecus anamensis	E. Africa	4.5–3.9	Large molars with thick enamel, relatively large canines and sectorial premolar, likely biped, long arms
Australopithecus afarensis	E. Africa	3.9–3.0	Large molars with thick enamel, relatively large canines and semisectorial premolar, bipedal anatomy, long arms
Australopithecus bahrelghazali	N. central Africa	3.3	Mandible fragment only
Kenyanthropus platyops	E. Africa	3.5	Single cranium, relatively small teeth, thick molar enamel

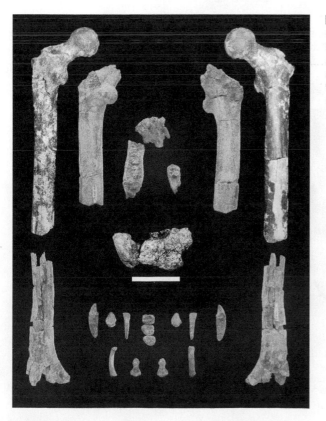

■ FIGURE 7.7

Orrorin tugenensis fossils from Kenya. *Orrorin tugenensis* lived approximately 6 million years ago. Finds include portions of the limb bones, mandible fragments, and teeth.

discussed shortly), suggesting that *Orrorin* might be a direct ancestor of humans. In fact, the fossil's name actually means "original man." It is difficult to support such a sweeping claim with only 13 fossil fragments. As the fossil record from the 5–6 mya period becomes more complete, we will have a better understanding of this potential early hominin form.

Sahelanthropus tchadensis: Earliest Hominin or Something Else?

In summer 2002, the published report of a fossil cranium found in Chad, northern central Africa, added a new twist to the search for human origins. Dated to between 6 and 7 mya and very different from the few other late Pliocene potential hominin finds, *Sahelanthropus tchadensis* expands the range of the earliest possible hominins outside of eastern Africa (Brunet et al., 2002) (Figure 7.8). This badly crushed and relatively deformed cranium displays a remarkable and confusing mix of hominine-like and potentially hominin-like features. The canines are relatively small and the enamel on the molars relatively thick. The cranium has very prominent supraorbital torus (boney ridges above the eyes) a feature associated with later hominins, yet a

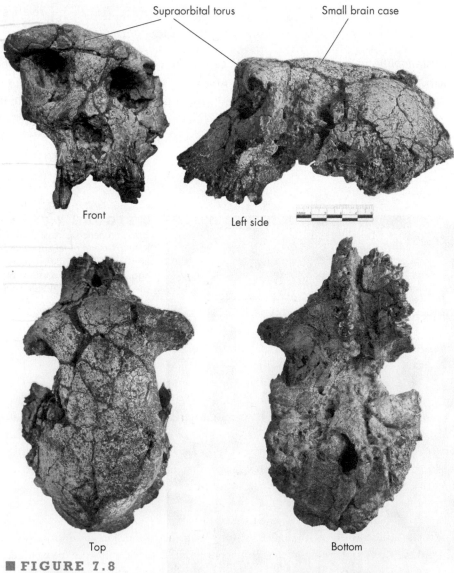

Supraorbital torus   Small brain case

Front   Left side

Top   Bottom

■ **FIGURE 7.8**
Cranium of *Sahelanthropus tchadensis*. This species, best known from a cranium found in Chad, lived approximately 6–7 million years ago. It shows a mix of hominine and hominin traits.

small, "apelike" brain case. The researchers who discovered the fossil propose that the way in which the neck muscles probably attached to the occipital bone and other basal cranial areas suggest that this organism moved bipedally. Because of the limited sample size (the cranium published in 2002 and a partial mandible and some teeth found in 2004) and the time it probably lived (6–7 million years ago), this fossil is hard to place relative to the later hominins. It could be a hominine whose descendants are either African apes or hominins, or it could be the remnant of an extinct lineage. However, recent finds demonstrate a lack of a shearing complex, which weakens the potential for *Sahelanthropus* to be ancestral to the gorilla or chimpanzee lineages (Brunet et al., 2005; Wood and Lonergan, 2008). If and when more fossils from this species are found, we will have a much better idea of what it is and how it may or may not relate to living humans.

Ardipithecus ramidus: The First Hominin?

Since 1992 an international research team has uncovered a number of fossils at the Aramis site along the Awash River in northern Ethiopia, and in 2009 a comprehensive analysis was published (Figure 7.9). This site has produced 110 fossils, representing multiple individuals, dated to approximately 4.4 mya (White, Suwa, & Asfaw, 1994). These fossils include many dental fragments, upper limb bones, some cranial remains, and a partial skeleton. Unfortunately, many of the fossils are embedded in a limestone matrix and are very difficult to extract, so it took 17 years for a full description to become available.

Initially, these fossils were placed in the genus *Australopithecus.* However, in 1995, Tim White and colleagues argued that the Aramis fossils are significantly different from those of the genus *Australopithecus* and may belong to an earlier hominin with many ancestral traits. Consequently, the Aramis fossils have been placed in their own genus and species, *Ardipithecus ramidus* (literally, "ground ape at the root"). They may indeed represent a species near the base of the hominin divergence from the other African hominine lineages (chimpanzees and gorillas). Interestingly, in assessing fossil pollens and other fossil remains associated with these finds, researchers have also concluded that 4.4 million years ago Aramis was a woodland, or forested, environment, suggesting that *Ardipithecus* was a forest dweller.

The *Ardipithecus* fossils are characterized by a number of late Miocene hominoid traits, such as a flat cranial base and thin molar enamel, but also show some derived traits such as reduced canines, little canine dimorphism between the sexes, and relatively reduced facial **prognathism.** The hands are large, the arms are long, and the feet have grasping large toes (White et al., 2009). The foramen magnum is much farther forward under the skull than we would expect in a quadruped, and the humerus does not demonstrate the specific structures associated with weight bearing that are common to quadrupedal hominoids. Therefore, researchers have concluded that *Ardipithecus* most likely used a form of bipedal locomotion. Given the forested environment and the overall morphology of the *Ardipithecus* skeleton, it is likely that *Ardipithecus* moved bipedally on the ground but was very adept at moving in trees as well

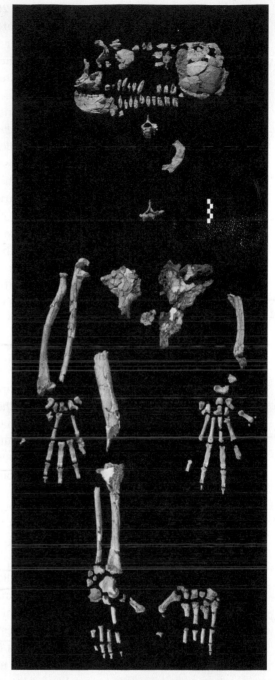

■ FIGURE 7.9

Fossils of *Ardipithecus ramidus.* The Aramis site in northern Ethiopia has produced numerous fossils, representing several individuals, and dating from 4.4 million to as much as 5.8 million years ago. This species was originally placed in the genus *Australopithecus* but is now thought to belong to an earlier hominin.

prognathism
condition in which the jaw projects beyond the upper parts of the face

(White et al., 2009). The one near-complete skeleton suggests that this species weighed about 50 kg and stood nearly 120 cm tall.

In summer 2001, Yohannes Haile-Selassie and coworkers (Haile-Selassie, 2001) published a remarkable set of finds: an earlier and older subspecies of *Ardipithecus ramidus*, which they named *Ardipithecus ramidus kadabba* (Figure 7.9). These finds, uncovered at a location near the earlier *Ardipithecus* site of Aramis, consist of fossils from at least five different individuals. They include mandible fragments, at least 20 teeth, finger and toe bones, pieces of the arm bones, a partial clavicle, and several other fossil fragments. Most surprisingly, all of these fossils date to between 5.8 and 5.2 mya. Although only preliminary results have been published, it is clear that *Ardipithecus ramidus kadabba* had anatomical structures that suggest bipedality and that it lived (as did its later relative, now called *Ardipithecus ramidus ramidus*) in a forested environment (Haile-Selassie, 2001). Haile-Selassie and colleagues (Haile-Selassie, et al., 2004) also suggest that canine morphology changes from *A. r. kadabba* to *A. r. ramidus*, and that this change is in line with the type of canine we see in subsequent hominins of the genus *Australopithecus*. This find gives us at least three possible hominin species and two genera from the period between 4.4 and 6.0 mya.

Hominins of the Middle and Late Pliocene Were Bipedal and Sexually Dimorphic

Dating to approximately 4.2 million years ago we begin to find hominin fossils of *Australopithecus* species—undoubtedly bipedal forms that have large molars with thick enamel and eventually slightly larger brains than those of earlier hominines (Table 7.3). Australopithecines lived in eastern and southern Africa for over 2 million years. The australopithecine fossils provide the majority of information on how the early hominins lived.

Australopithecus anamensis: The First Australopithecine

Seventy-eight fossils from two sites near Lake Turkana in Kenya (Kanapoi and Allia Bay) are described as *Australopithecus anamensis* (Figure 7.10). These fossils, dated to approximately 4.5–3.9 mya, represent the first species in the genus *Australopithecus*. The *A. anamensis* fossils are primarily dental fragments and some cranial and postcranial remains (skull, arm, finger, and leg bone fragments). Based on the articulation of the lower limbs, Maeve Leakey and colleagues have suggested that this species was bipedal, like later species of this genus (Leakey et al., 1995, 1998; Ward, Leakey, & Walker, 2001). In addition, the molars in these fossils are large and have thick enamel, like the molars of later members of this genus. However, *A. anamensis* displays some ancestral characteristics, such as a slight canine/premolar shearing complex,

TABLE 7.3	Differences Between Australopithecines and Earlier Hominins	
Early hominins (*Ardipithecus**, Orrorin, and *Sahelanthropus*)		**Australopithecus anamensis and *A. afarensis***
Possibly bipeds		Bipedal anatomy
Thin and thick molar enamel		Thick molar enamel
Reduced canines		Small canines and reduced shearing complex

*Ardipithecus was bipedal when on the ground.

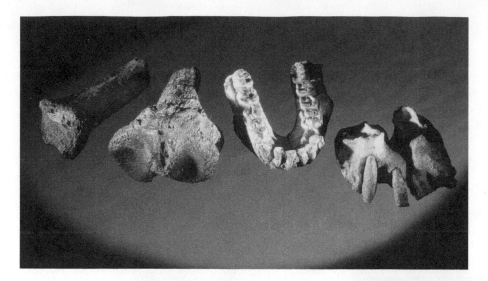

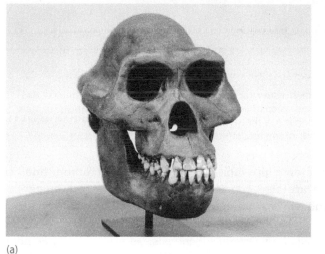

(a)

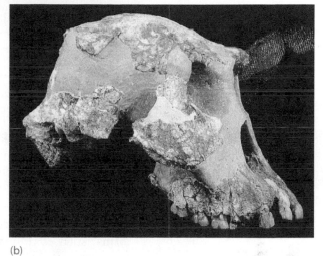

(b)

■ **FIGURE 7.11**
Australopithecus afarensis. This species, which lived from approximately 3.0–3.9 million years ago, is known from numerous sites in Africa. (a) Artist's composite. (b) Reconstructed fossil.

and a **sectorial premolar** (a lower premolar that exhibits side-to-side compression due to its role as a shearing surface for the upper canine tooth). The fossils also suggest that there was a large range in body size in this species; there may have been sexual dimorphism with males being larger than females, and there may also have been canine dimorphism, again with males having larger canines than females.

Australopithecus afarensis: The Best-Known Early Hominin

By far the best-known early hominin is *Australopithecus afarensis*. Represented by fossils making up over 70 individuals from at least six different sites in east Africa, this species existed from about 3.9 to 3.0 million years ago (Figure 7.11).

   A. afarensis shares a number of primitive traits with *Ardipithecus* and *A. anamensis.* The canines are fairly large compared to those of later hominins; the lower first premolar is semisectorial (partially compressed side to side); and the tooth rows are quite parallel (as in *Ardipithecus ramidus* and *A. anamensis* but unlike those of modern humans, which are slightly divergent from one another) (see Figure 7.12). The canines of *A. afarensis* are slightly smaller than those of earlier hominins, however, as is the canine/premolar shearing complex

CONNECTIONS

See chapter 5, pages 144–146, for more on sexual dimorphism and primates.

sectorial premolar
first lower premolar that exhibits lateral (side-to-side) compression due to its role as a shearing surface for the upper canine tooth; related to the shearing complex

STOP & THINK

Why is it so difficult to link these early forms with later hominins and the human lineage?

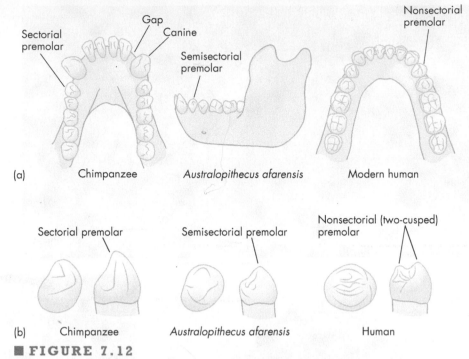

■ **FIGURE 7.12**

Teeth of chimpanzee, *Australopithecus afarensis*, and modern human. In (a), note the parallel tooth rows in the australopithecine, as compared to those of the modern human. In (b), note the sectorial premolar of the chimpanzee, the semisectorial premolar of *A. afarensis*, and the nonsectorial, two-cusped premolar of the modern human.

(producing a less sectorial lower pre-molar). The base of the cranium and the relatively prognathic face are also considered to be primitive commonalities between *A. afarensis* and earlier hominin forms. The large size and thick enamel of the molars are characteristics that reflect similarities to earlier forms, such as *A. anamensis* and *Orrorin tugenensis*, as well as to later hominins. The size of the cranium in this species remains fairly small, with a brain about 420 cc (25.6 cubic in.) in volume. This is only slightly larger than we would expect for a generalized hominoid with the body size of *A. afarensis*.

Postcranially, *A. afarensis* is somewhat different from earlier hominin forms. A reconstruction of the bones in the lower body shows a highly modified pelvic girdle as well as femur, tibia, and feet that indicate frequent, if not constant, bipedal locomotion (Figure 7.13). The arm bones are longer than in later hominins, however, and some researchers suggest that the phalanges (finger and toe bones) are relatively curved (see Stern, 2000), as in the earlier hominins (such as *Ardipithecus* and *A. anamensis*). Long arms and curved phalanges are associated with arboreal movement in hominoids. We also have a set of fossil footprints from Laetoli in Tanzania that date to nearly 3.6 mya. Most researchers have attributed these footprints to *A. afarensis* (however, see the discussion of *Kenyanthropus platyops* later in this section). These prints are found at a fantastic site where an ashfall and a light rain combined to create a 3.5-million-year-old snapshot of the movement of many organisms across a savanna. Analyses of the hominin footprints in a 23-meter (~75-foot) stretch suggest that two (and maybe a third) individuals strolled, bipedally, across this open area with short, slow strides. It is also evident that the two individuals differed in height and body size (Figure 7.14).

A. afarensis was bipedal, but we do not know how much time it spent on the ground. It lived in a savanna and woodland environment, and it has anatomical indications of both bipedal walking (the lower limbs) and possibly

STOP & THINK

Is it possible to have an anatomy that allows you to walk on the ground but still spend a lot of time in the trees? Why might early hominins want to be in trees as opposed to on the ground?

Big Guys with Small Teeth Rock!

For many primate species, having big males and small females usually means that the social relations between the sexes are conflictual, with males dominating and with lots of male-male competition. These primate species usually have dimorphic canines as well, with large canines in males being used for displays and fights. On the other hand, primate species where males and females are more or less the same-size and have similar-sized canines tend to live in groups with more egalitarian relationships and strong bonds between males and females. Is it possible that *Ardipithecus ramidus* or *Australopithecus afarensis* are the start of a new type of relationship between males and females? Could it be that some degree of dimorphism in body size but little differences in canines between the sexes reflects a new version of primate intersexual relationships? Reduced male-male conflict and stronger bonds between males and females? Different researchers have very different takes on this, but it would make sense that at some point in the early hominins a real change in sociality occurred. Modern humans have inter- and intrasexual relationships that are quite different from other living primates, and thus the early forms of those changes had to show up in prehuman hominins. Maybe the changing dimorphism we see in these fossil hominins is one of the early indications of humanness.

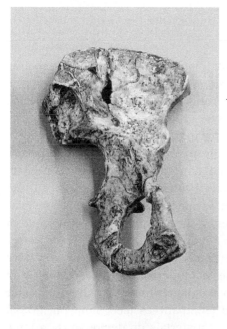

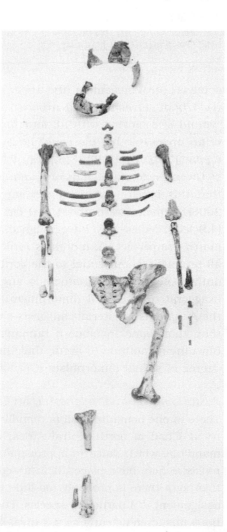

■ FIGURE 7.13
Bipedal aspects of *Australopithecus afarensis*. The skeleton shows the wide pelvis, the angled femur, and the tibia surface reflective of bipedality. The pelvis is a modern reproduction.

■ FIGURE 7.14

The Laetoli footprints. This diorama shows one possibility for the creation of the footprints, which were made by at least two individuals of different sizes who walked side by side.

some arboreal movement (the upper limbs). It is very possible that this species used both terrestrial and arboreal environments, walking bipedally on the ground and moving with all four limbs through the trees (although the lack of an opposable big toe could limit the type of arboreality exhibited by this species) (Conroy, 1997; Simpson, 2002; Stern, 2000).

Given the fossil remains of *A. afarensis*, most (but not all) researchers believe that this species exhibited extreme sexual dimorphism (Wood & Lonergan, 2008). Females were about 110 cm (3.6 feet) tall and males nearly 150 cm (4.9 feet). Males may have weighed twice as much as females. If these estimates are correct, *A. afarensis* ranks among the most sexually dimorphic of all primates (about equal to the gorilla in this respect). However, some paleoanthropologists and anatomists suggest that analyses of *A. afarensis* have exaggerated its sexual dimorphism. At least one comprehensive overview of the *A. afarensis* materials suggests a degree of dimorphism just slightly greater than that found in modern humans and chimpanzees (see Simpson, 2002), but others continue to argue that the same materials do demonstrate a large degree of sexual dimorphism (Gordon et al., 2008).

Australopithecus bahrelghazali: An Early Hominin in North-Central Africa

There is one hominin fossil (a mandible) from the site of Koro Toro in the country of Chad in north-central Africa. Although some experts suggest that this mandible, which dates to approximately 3.3 mya, is a representative of *A. afarensis*, others have placed it in a separate species named *A. bahrelghazali*. At this point there is probably too little information available to make an accurate assignment to a particular species. The find indicates, however, that not all early hominins (even as early as 3.3 mya) lived in eastern Africa. It is very likely that future finds will demonstrate a much broader African distribution for early members of the genus *Australopithecus* (Figure 7.15).

Kenyanthropus platyops: A Contemporary of A. afarensis

In the late 1990s, fieldwork in the Lomekwi region west of Lake Turkana, Kenya, turned up a series of fossil remains (a nearly complete cranium, a maxilla, and some teeth) dating to approximately 3.5 million years ago. Maeve Leaky and her coworkers have named these fossils *Kenyanthropus platyops* (Leakey et al., 2001) (Figure 7.16). They contend that this fossil material is significantly different from any of the *A. afarensis* materials and therefore should be assigned to a new species. The relatively small size of the teeth and the flatness of the face suggest that this is not a member of the genus *Australopithecus*, but something new. This find could indicate that there were at least two or three, if not more, types of hominins living in Africa between 3 and 4 million years ago (Leakey et al., 2001). This early hominin also could have made the fossil footprints at Laetoli. Until further information on the postcranial anatomy of *Kenyanthropus* is available, the debate over the type and quality of hominin bipedality between 4 and 3 million years ago is likely to continue (Lieberman, 2001).

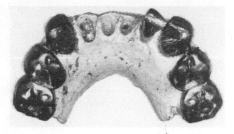

■ FIGURE 7.15
Australopithecus bahrelghazali. This mandible is the only fossil found to date of this species, which lived in north-central Africa (Chad) approximately 3.3 million years ago.

Were There Early Hominins in Southern Africa?

There is a large and complex set of hominin fossils from sites in southern Africa. These are generally dated as younger than 3 million years old and attributed primarily to *Australopithecus* species that are assumed to be derived from *A. afarensis*. Recent challenges to the dating of these sites suggest that some of these hominins may be as much as 4–3.5 million years old. The new dates are still being assessed and are not yet fully accepted. We review the southern African forms in the next chapter, but keep in mind that some of these early hominins may have been around at the same time as *A. afarensis*.

Evolutionary Relationships Are Unclear

A significant amount of debate remains over the specific relationships among early hominin taxa. There are no "right" answers; there are just several different possible phylogenies, some with more support than others. What we do know for certain is that we find a multitude of fossils in eastern Africa between 3 and 6 mya that, for the most part, can be called hominins. The relationships between *Orrorin tugenensis*, *Sahelanthropus tchadensis*, and both *Ardipithecus* subspecies, on the one hand, and later hominins, on the other, are currently a subject of debate. Recently, White et al. (2009) suggested that *Orrorin*, *Sahelanthropus* and *Ardipithecus* are all members of the genus *Ardipithecus* and that they are likely ancestral to *Australopithecus*. However, this remains contentious. Although the available data support the notion that *A. anamensis* is ancestral to *A. afarensis*, we cannot be 100% certain that this is the case either. And we do not yet know where *A. bahrelghazali* fits into the picture (Figure 7.17). The bottom line is that we do not know how many early species existed or how the early species are related to later ones. We have a few fascinating fossils that may represent early members of our lineage, but until *A. afarensis*, we can say little about their relationships with any certainty.

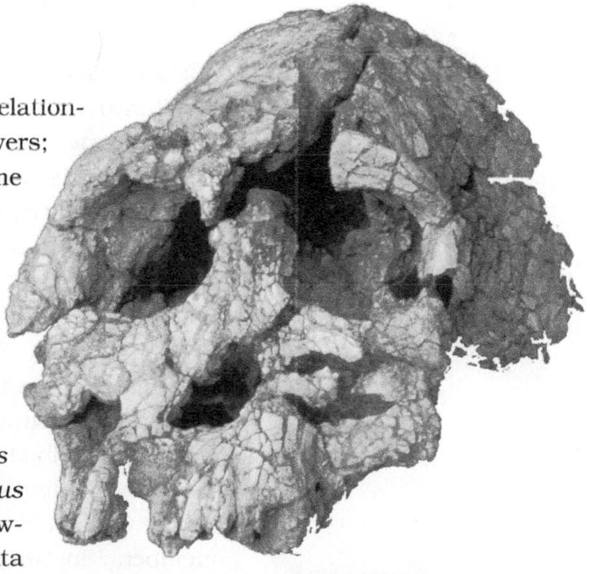

■ FIGURE 7.16
Skull of *Kenyanthropus platyops.* This hominin lived approximately 3.5 million years ago in east Africa. It was a contemporary of *A. afarensis*, but the researchers who found it claim that it belongs to a different genus.

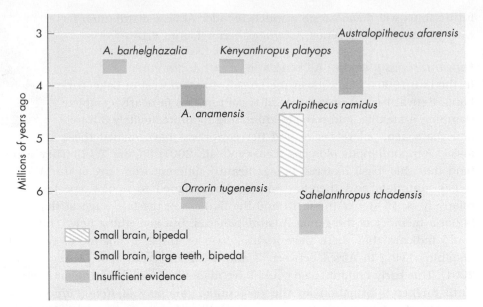

■ FIGURE 7.17

Temporal relationships between early hominin species. This diagram shows the time relationships among fossil species that lived between 6 and 3 million years ago.

Fossils give us clues about early hominin behavior

One of the great challenges in the study of paleoanthropology is the attempt to understand how fossil organisms lived. Recent advances in the study of fossil pollens and research into ancient environments have allowed us to create models of the general habitat, ecology, and climatic conditions in which these early hominins lived. The **Pliocene** epoch was characterized by a significant change in the assemblages of animals across different areas of the planet. During this period, climatic changes led to geological events that affected wide areas. North and South America became connected, and the Mediterranean basin began to fill up after having largely dried out during the late Miocene. Overall, the Pliocene was generally warmer than the Miocene, and sea levels were higher.

Because of the extremely fragmentary fossil record for the hominins before *A. afarensis,* it is difficult to say much about their behavioral patterns. We know that *Ardipithecus ramidus* lived in a forested environment, and therefore it seems likely that they used the trees extensively (as do all modern primates living in forests). The near-complete skeleton and the many and diverse fossil fragments tell us that *Ardipithecus* was probably equally at home in the trees and on the ground. Their teeth and jaws indicate a general omnivorous diet, collecting its food from trees and the ground. In many primates large canine teeth and large dimorphism in size between males and females implies a high degree of conflict and competition between the sexes and between some group members. In *Ardipithecus,* the relatively small canine teeth (compared with earlier Miocene ape forms) and the small amount of dimorphism between males and females suggest that there may have been strong social and bonding relationships between the sexes (White et al., 2009) and between individuals in social groups. Currently, we know very little about *Orrorin tugenensis, Sahelanthropus tchadensis,* or *A. bahrelghazali. A. anamensis* appears to have lived in habitats very much like those of *A. afarensis.* Most of the information we have relates to this latter species, *A. afarensis.*

Pliocene
epoch that occurred between 5.0 and 1.8 mya

FIGURE 7.18
Mixed savanna and woodland.
Early hominins shared their
environment with a variety of
other animals. They probably
used watering holes like
this one.

Habitat: Where They Lived

A. afarensis fossils are found in areas that were primarily mixed savanna and woodland environments 4 to 3 mya. This means that these hominins shared their habitat with a range of herbivorous bovids (such as zebras and giraffes), a number of medium-sized and smaller mammals (antelope and monkeys, for example), and several carnivores (including very big cats and hyenas). These environments were rich in grasses (some up to 1 m, about 3 feet, in height), shrubs, root and tuber plants, and fruiting and nonfruiting trees. Temperatures varied across the year but were never as cool as those of the temperate world today. Rainfall probably totaled about 50 to 80 cm (~20–32 in.) per year, with the possibility of a dry season (or seasons) in which there was little or no rain for months (Figure 7.18).

Diet: What Did They Eat, and How Did They Get It?

The teeth of *A. afarensis* tell us a great deal about its diet. Microscopic analyses of the fossil molars reveal a combination of tiny pits, striations, and smooth areas that reflects a diet composed of fruits, leaves, nuts or grains, and a variety of tubers and roots. The thick enamel on the molars and the relatively large size of the incisors also support these general dietary assumptions.

It is probable that *A. afarensis* also took advantage of the animal foodstuffs available in its environment, including insects, birds' eggs, small mammals, and reptiles. There were probably some opportunities to scavenge the remains of carnivore kills as well. Whether animal matter made up a very large portion of the diet of these early hominins is unclear; most researchers would argue that it did not.

Tools: Did They Use Bone, Wood, or Stone Tools?

We do not have any direct evidence that these early hominins modified stone, bone, or wood to use as tools, but there is strong comparative evidence for at least some tool use. All the living apes except the gibbons use modified

STOP & THINK

We used to think tool use separated humans from everything else, but that is no longer the case. But do we do different things with tools than other animals do?

objects in foraging. Modern humans exhibit the most complex tool use, but both chimpanzees and orangutans modify sticks to forage for insects and fruit, and chimpanzees use unmodified rocks to crack open nuts (see chapter 5). Given that all hominids (humans and apes) use tools of some sort, it is very likely that tool use is a primitive characteristic shared by a recent common ancestor of modern primates (from the late Miocene possibly) that was an ancestor of *A. afarensis* as well. *A. afarensis* may have used sticks and grasses to forage for insects and may have used stones to crack nuts. These assertions remain speculative (but strong) because it is very difficult to find evidence for this type of tool use in the fossil record.

Social Life: How Did They Live Together?

There is considerable debate about the grouping patterns and general behavior of *A. afarensis*. Because these elements do not fossilize, the only way we can reconstruct social life is through comparative assessment of behavior.

Most (but not all) researchers agree that this hominin exhibited significant sexual dimorphism in body size, as mentioned earlier. Interestingly, although the males are thought to have been much larger than the females, the canine teeth of both sexes are very similar in size, much like in *Ardipithecus*. This combination of traits is rare in living primates. Generally, large males and small females are found in species that exhibit grouping patterns in which either one adult male lives with many adult females and offspring or many adult males and females and young live in the same group. The latter type of group is the most common in primates today. Similar-sized canines are most often found in modern primates that live in small groups (usually averaging one male and one female plus young), but they occasionally show up in multiadult groups as well. If we add to this the fact that one of the main fossil finds of *A. afarensis* (AL-333 at Hadar) may consist of up to 13 individuals (including 4 infants) at a single site, we can see tentative support for a multiadult grouping pattern in this species.

CONNECTIONS

See primate grouping patterns in chapter 5, pages 138–139.

We know that many kinds of behavior are found among all primates (see chapter 5), and we can assume that many of these patterns characterized *A. afarensis.* They probably moved as a group, ranging over large areas of their environment. Most likely they engaged in mutual grooming and a good deal of socializing that may or may not have involved various kinds of gestural and vocal communication. Given that there were many predators capable of consuming these hominins on the savannas and in the trees, it is likely that predation was a significant selection pressure and that some form of antipredator strategy was practiced. The strategy may have been simply to run away, or it may have involved individual or group defense. Either way, avoiding predation may have been a very important element in the life of *A. afarensis* (Hart & Sussman, 2005). Although attempts to reconstruct the daily events and patterns that characterized our early ancestors are frustrating at times, anthropological investigations continue to make progress in the quest to understand the roots of human behavior.

The Bipedalism That Wasn't

Bipedalism is a major component of being human. It is one of the determining traits of the hominins and is directly linked with our emergence and separation from the apes. Our brief review of the early fossil record in this chapter shows that the full-blown modern bipedality that we have today was not present in the early hominins.

Hyenas, Wolves, and Saber-Toothed Cats, Oh My!

Early hominins had to deal with a pretty harsh set of environmental challenges; among the dominant of those was predation. Think about it—small body size, lack of natural weapons, and bipedal but probably not great at running. Hominins did not have much in the way of purely physical responses to fend off attacks. As we might expect, evidence of predation appears to be common in *Australopithecine* fossils, with many skulls and bones showing the marks of large carnivores (and even some large eagles!). From about 4 to 1 million years ago there were many, many types of potential hominin predators in southern and eastern Africa. There were large and small saber-toothed cats, large and small Hyena species, wolves and other dog-like species, and both the lion and leopard groups were appearing on the scene. Could this possibility of predation have had an impact on our ancestors' evolutionary trajectories? Predation, as a strong selection pressure, might have driven these hominins to come up with innovative ways to avoid threats. Without horns, big teeth, or fast legs, hominins may have used group coordination, sharing information about threats, and group defense as possible responses to predation threats. It might be that the threat of being eaten helped drive the increase in cooperation and trends of social reliance on group members that is characteristic of modern humans. So in these early hominins, before they were hunters, rather than eat or be eaten, maybe it was cooperate or be eaten.

Both *Ardipithecus* and *Australopithecus afarensis* have longer arms than would be expected for a biped. They also have long hands with curved fingers suggesting. *Ardipithecus* even had a divergent big toe. These characteristics are good indications that these forms could move through the trees as well as bipedally on the ground. In other words, evidence suggests that early hominins walked on two feet, but not in a modern way, and that moving about in the trees still played a core role in their daily lives. If this is the case, then what we call bipedal anatomy in early forms is really "bipedal-allowing" anatomy, not bipedal-enforcing anatomy (as modern humans have). Having a flat broad chest, hands that can grab and hold, and strong hind legs can be beneficial when moving in trees as well as on the ground. Such an anatomy could have emerged from a more basic hominoid anatomy (a general ape-like form) even while individuals still spent a majority of time in arboreal environments.

The capacity for full terrestrial bipedality is probably not the determinant of the earliest hominins, since their anatomy mixed terrestrial bipedal and arboreal traits. So our aim is not so much to explain the initial anatomy associated with the emergence of bipedality as to answer the question of why the "bipedal-allowing" anatomy evolved toward a "bipedal-enforcing" anatomy. In other words, what is so great about being a full-time biped?

The evolution of bipedality has several possible explanations

Bipedality is a central component in discussions of hominin evolution. It is apparent from the fossil record that between about 6 and 2 million years ago, a substantial set of changes occurred in the hominin lineage that eventually

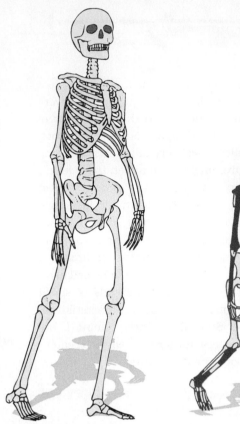

■ FIGURE 7.19
Bipedality in modern humans and *Australopithecus afarensis*. Compared with modern humans, *A. afarensis* had longer arms and curved fingers. Actual fossils are shown in black; the remainder are reconstructed.

resulted in a very different kind of primate: humans. One of these major changes was the transition from a mixed terrestrial bipedal and arboreal climbing existence to an obligate, exclusively terrestrial bipedal one (Figure 7.19). This move toward full terrestrial bipedality was followed (at least in one lineage of hominins) by a substantial increase in the size and complexity of the brain. Given that bipedality is quite important for the hominins and is rare in mammals, we are led to ask this question: What kind of selective pressures could have favored the move from a generalized hominoid quadruped to a sometimes biped to a full terrestrial biped in the hominin lineage? Currently, there are several ideas about the evolution of bipedality. The following are some of the more popular ones:

- *Bipedality is beneficial for carrying objects.* Being upright frees the arms to carry a variety of things, such as tools, foods, and offspring, and thus can confer an advantage over organisms that cannot carry items. Many scientists (including Charles Darwin) have made this argument. However, the benefits of carrying don't come into play until the organism is a biped. Thus, carrying can favor bipedality when it is already there but probably does not explain why it arose.

- *Bipedality is beneficial for hunting.* Because it frees the hands to carry weapons and provides an efficient means of long-distance locomotion, bipedality greatly increases the effectiveness of hunting. Unfortunately, good archeological evidence for increased hunting comes much later than the appearance of bipedal locomotion (see chapter 8).

- *Bipedality is derived from a foraging pattern favoring upright reaching.* The erect posture that leads to bipedality might have resulted from a dietary adaptation. This hypothesis suggests that a feeding specialization favored structural changes in the upper and lower body that resulted in bipedality.

- *Visual surveillance, or vigilance, favored bipedality.* Standing up (bipedally) provided better opportunities to see predators, especially in savanna environments. This in turn may have selected for structural changes that favored standing and moving in a bipedal fashion.

- *The benefits of long-distance walking or running favored bipedality.* Hominin bipedal locomotion is a highly effective way of moving across long distances. This ability to move across large areas with energetic efficiency in search of food or mates may have conferred benefits on the early hominins. Again, the problem here is that this assessment of bipedalism is based on bipedality in modern hominins; it is not clear that early hominins had a kind of bipedalism as efficient or effective as that of later hominins.

- *Male provisioning and female infant carrying resulted in bipedality.* This hypothesis suggests that there were selective pressures on hominins for males to forage and bring back food to females and young at a central home base. Bipedality then was favored for many of the reasons just

What We Know

Accumulated fossil and genetic evidence suggests that humans, chimpanzees, and gorillas share a more recent common ancestor with each other than any of them do with the orangutans.

Questions That Remain

Does this evidence justify changing our current naming system? The current usage, in which the family Hominidae describes humans and human ancestors and the family Pongidae describes a group consisting of chimpanzees, gorillas, orangutans, and their ancestors does not reflect recent analyses. Some, but not all, researchers consider the use of *hominin* (tribe Hominini) for humans and human ancestors and Hominidae for all living great apes and humans to be an appropriate solution. However, it is not clear whether this nomenclature is the most accurate. We can expect that further investigation and continued scientific debate will eventually result in a consensus on the best system of nomenclature.

What We Know

Fossils that fit the definition of hominin show up in east Africa at least 5 million years ago or earlier.

Questions That Remain

Are these fossils part of the modern human ancestral lineage? In all likelihood these early forms are basal hominins and are ancestral to all subsequent forms. Ongoing research in east Africa by a number of teams continues to uncover late Miocene/early Pliocene fossils, and we can expect that we will soon have a better understanding of hominin diversity between 6 and 4 mya.

What We Know

Hominin fossils from more than 70 individuals spanning the time between 4 and 3 mya in east Africa display small brains coupled with morphologies that reflect both bipedal adaptations and possibly some retention of arboreal behavior patterns.

Questions That Remain

Do these bones make up one species, *A. afarensis*, that is ancestral to many later hominins, or do they represent two or more species and possibly two genera, one of which may be ancestral to modern humans? A majority of paleoanthropologists continue to favor the one-species model; however, recent finds such as *Kenyanthropus platyops* suggest that there may have been more diversity in hominins in this period than we currently envision.

What We Know

We have been able to reconstruct a good deal of the environment in which *A. afarensis* lived. We know that it ate a good deal of vegetation, had opportunities to eat meat, and used simple tools (much as modern apes do). We have found at least one fossil site where a group of mixed ages and sexes were fossilized at the same time.

Questions That Remain

If *A. afarensis* ate meat, how much did it eat? How did it get it? What size groups did these hominins live in? How did they deal with predators? How did they deal with other groups of hominins (of the same species or possibly different ones) if they encountered them? Because of the great chasm of time separating *A. afarensis* from us, and the incompleteness of the fossil record, answering any of these questions will be a long and difficult process.

listed, and it additionally allowed females to carry their young effectively. This hypothesis implies that early hominins exhibited a monogamous mating pattern and lived in small, pair-bonded groups. There is little evidence to support the assertions of grouping patterns and pair bonding implicit in this hypothesis however.

- *Bipedality confers benefits in thermoregulation.* Bipedality is said to increase the rate of heat loss and minimize the amount of surface area directly exposed to the sun. If the early hominins lived on open savannas, ultraviolet radiation and heat stress may have been important factors. However, evidence suggests that the earliest hominins lived in forested or mixed forest/ savanna environments where heat dissipation may not have been as critical to survival.

Whatever the explanations, over time hominins became progressively better at bipedality. As we approach the end of the Pliocene and the beginning of the Pleistocene epoch, we see that one branch of effectively bipedal hominins did some pretty amazing things.

SUMMARY

▲ Hominins are members of the family Hominidae, subfamily Homininae, and tribe Hominini. The subfamily Homininae is made up of the African forms, of which the living representatives are chimpanzees, gorillas, and humans. Some researchers continue to use the term *hominid* to represent only the hominins; however, this practice is not supported by the genetic, molecular, or fossil evidence.

▲ The earliest potential fossil hominins come from north-central and eastern Africa and date to approximately 6–7 and 5–6 million years ago, respectively. Among these early forms are at least three species: *Ardipithecus ramidus kadabba, Orrorin tugenensis,* and *Sahelanthropus tchadensis.* It is not clear that these species were bipedal, but they show some skeletal indications of bipedal anatomy.

▲ Two subspecies of *Ardipithecus ramidus* lived across a span of nearly 1 million years in east Africa. They combine hominin-like lower anatomy with apelike cranial and dental anatomy.

▲ The species *A. anamensis* is the first member of the genus *Australopithecus* and is well known from fossils dating to between 4.5 and 3.9 million years ago. This hominin displays adaptations to bipedality but shares some upper-body arboreal adaptations and dental features with earlier possible hominin forms.

▲ Fossils of *A. afarensis* date from approximately 3.9 to 3.0 million years ago. This hominin was bipedal but may have used arboreal environments as well. It shares many anatomical similarities with *A. anamensis* but has smaller canine teeth and a reduced canine/premolar shearing complex relative to previous hominins.

▲ *Kenyanthropus platyops* and *Australopithecus bahrelghazali* are two hominin species that lived at the same time as *A. afarensis. Kenyanthropus* may have lived in the same area as well. We have little information about either of these fossil species.

▲ Although researchers have a good understanding of when and where the fossil hominins lived, there is no full consensus on the evolutionary relationships among these forms.

▲ *A. afarensis* had a varied but primarily vegetarian diet, probably used wood and other minimally modified tools, displayed significant variation in body size, may have displayed significant sexual dimorphism, and probably lived in social groups consisting of multiple adults and young.

▲ Bipedality is a core adaptation in the hominins. Exactly when, how, and why bipedality arose is the subject of many diverse hypotheses.

CRITICAL THINKING

1. Some people think that researchers will eventually find the "missing link"—one organism or species that will clearly tie humans to the other apes and show how they evolved into a new species. Why is it unlikely, from an evolutionary standpoint, that a fossil or set of fossils that perfectly fit the "missing link" scenario will be found?

2. Should we be surprised that there are a number of early hominin forms dating to between 6 and 3 million years ago? Does the Miocene ape information from chapter 6 contribute to your answer? Should we expect many of the earliest hominins to look similar to one another? Why or why not? Do you think *Ardipithecus* is our ancestor?

3. What do you think the relationships among the hominin fossils from between 4.2 and 3.0 million years ago are? How does the find of *A. bahrelghazali* affect our ideas about hominins? If *Kenyanthropus* and *Australopithecus* are the only two genera of hominins we currently know from between 4 and 3 mya, does that make one or both of them our ancestors? Why or why not?

4. How can fossil bones tell us about past behavior? What kinds of fossil finds and related scientific information would help answer the following questions: What type of groups did the organisms live in? What did they eat? How did they move around? What did they look like? Were they predators or prey? Did they use tools?

5. From an evolutionary standpoint, is it logical to expect to find one selective pressure primarily responsible for the appearance of bipedality? Why or why not? What types of selection pressures could affect an organism's locomotary pattern? Could other evolutionary forces (mutation, gene flow, genetic drift) have influenced the evolution of bipedality in hominins? How?

RESOURCES

HOMININ FOSSILS

Conroy, G. C. (2004). *Reconstructing human origins: A modern synthesis* (2nd ed.). New York: Norton.
This midlevel text will familiarize you with the hominin fossils in greater depth.

Feder, K. L. (2002). *Frauds, myths, and mysteries: Science and pseudoscience in archeology* (4th ed.). New York: McGraw-Hill/Mayfield.
A chapter on the Piltdown hoax provides details on the fossils, an exploration of possible reasons for the hoax, and a "whodunit?" section describing nine different people who might have been the perpetrators.

Lieberman, D. E. (2001). Another face in our family tree. *Nature, 410,* 419–420.
This brief overview discusses the finding of *Kenyanthropus* and what it might mean to our understanding of the early hominins.

Shipman, P. (2001). Hunting the first hominid. *American Scientist, 90*(1), 25–27.
This short commentary discusses and compares the early potential hominins *Orrorin* and *Ardipithecus*.

Wood, B., & Lonergan, N. (2008). The fossil record: taxa, grades and clades. *Journal of Anatomy, 212,* 350–376.
A good overview of the different interpretation, of the hominin fossils.

www.boneclones.com This Web site belongs to Kronen Osteo, the company whose hominin and other skeletal casts are featured throughout this book and Interactive Anthropology segments. The site contains information and images of all of their casts and bone collections.

THE AUSTRALOPITHECINES

Simpson, S. W. (2002). *Australopithecus afarensis* and human evolution. In P. N. Peregrine, C. R. Ember, & M. Ember (Eds.), *Physical anthropology: Original readings in method and practice* (pp. 103–123). Upper Saddle River, NJ: Prentice-Hall.
This piece reviews the history of *A. afarensis* finds and takes a stance opposite to that of Stern (below), namely, that *A. afarensis* was conclusively a terrestrial biped.

Stern, J. T. (2000). Climbing to the top: A personal memoir of *Australopithecus afarensis. Evolutionary Anthropology, 9,* 113–133.
This relatively advanced overview of the changing ideas that have been proposed about the anatomy and lifeways of *A. afarensis* favors the idea that the species retained some arboreal adaptations.

HOMININ EVOLUTION

www.talkorigins.org This well-known Web site deals with the ideas and disputes surrounding human evolution.

www.becominghuman.org This site is sponsored by the Institute of Human Origins and has video, news, and information about human evolution and hominin fossils.

REFERENCES

Begun, D. R. (1999). Hominid family values: Morphological and molecular data on the relations among the great apes and humans. In S. T. Parker, R. W. Mitchell, & H. L. Miles, *The mentalities of gorillas and orangutans* (pp. 3–42). Cambridge: Cambridge University Press.

Benefit, B. R., & McCrossin, M. L. (1995). Miocene hominoids and hominid origins. *Annual Reviews in Anthropology, 24,* 237–257.

Brunet, M., Guy, F., Pilbeam, D., Mackaye, H. T., Ahounta, D., Beauvilain, A., et al. (2002). A new hominid from the upper Miocene of Chad, Central Africa. *Nature, 418,* 145–151.

Brunet, M., Guy, F., Pilbeam, D., Mackaye, H. T., Ahounta, D., Beauvilain, A., et al. (2005). New material of the earliest hominid from the upper Miocene of Chad. *Nature, 434,* 752–755.

Conroy, G. C. (1997). *Reconstructing human origins: A modern synthesis.* New York: Norton.

Feder, K. L. (2002). *Frauds, myths and mysteries: Science and pseudoscience in archeology* (4th ed.). New York: McGraw-Hill/Mayfield.

Galick, K., Senut, B., Pickford, M., Gommery, D., Treil, J., Kuperaunge, A. J., et al. (2004). External and internal morphology of the BAR 1002_00 *Orrorin tugenensis* femur, *Science, 305,* 1450–1453.

Gordon, A., D., Green, D. J., & Richmond, B. G. (2008). Strong postcranial size dimorphism in *Australopithecus afarensis:* Results from two new multivariate resampling methods for multivariate data sets with missing data. *American Journal of Physical Anthropology 135,* 311–328.

Haile-Selassie, Y. (2001). Late Miocene hominids from the middle Awash, Ethiopia. *Nature, 412,* 178–181.

Haile-Selassie, Y., Asfaw, B., & White, T. D. (2004). Hominid cranial remains from upper Pleistocene deposits at Aduma, Middle Awash, Ethiopia, *American Journal of Physical Anthropology 123,* 1–10.

Hart, D. L., & Sussman, R. W. (2005). *Man the hunted: Primate predators and human evolution.* New York: Basic Books.

Leakey, M. G., Feibal, C. S., McDougall, I., & Walker, A. (1995). New four-million-year-old hominid species from Kanapoi and Allia Bay, Kenya. *Nature, 376,* 565–571.

Leakey, M. G., Feibal, C. S., McDougall, I., Ward, C., & Walker, A. (1998). New specimens and confirmation of an early age for *Australopithecus anamensis. Nature, 393,* 62–67.

Leakey, M. G., Spoor, F., Brown, F. H., Gathogo, P. N., Kiarie, C., Leakey, L. N., & McDougall, I. (2001). New hominin genus from eastern Africa shows diverse middle Pliocene lineages. *Nature, 410,* 433–440.

Lieberman, D. E. (2001). Another face in our family tree. *Nature, 410,* 419–420.

Pilbeam, D. R. (1996). Genetic and morphological records of the Hominoidea and Hominid origins: A synthesis. *Molecular phylogenetics and evolution, 5,* 155–168.

Senut, B., Pickford, M., Gommery, D., Mein, P., Cheboi, C., & Coppens, Y. (2001). First hominid from the Miocene (Lukeio Formation, Kenya). *C. R. Academy of Science Paris, 332,* 137–144.

Simpson, S. W. (2002). *Australopithecus afarensis* and human evolution. In P. N. Peregrine, C. R. Ember, & M. Ember (Eds.), *Physical anthropology: Original readings in method and practice* (pp. 103–123). Upper Saddle River, NJ: Prentice-Hall.

Stern, J. T. (2000). Climbing to the top: A personal memoir of *Australopithecus afarensis. Evolutionary Anthropology, 9,* 113–133.

Ward, C. V., Leakey, M. G., & Walker, A. (2001). Morphology of *Australopithecus anamensis* from Kanapoi and Allia Bay. *Journal of Human Evolution, 41* (4), 255–368.

White, T. D., Asfaw, B., Beyene, Y., Haile-Selassie, Y., Lovejoy, C. O., Suwa, G., WoldeGabriel, G. (2009). *Ardipithecus ramidus* and the paleobiology of early hominids. *Science 326,* 75–86.

White, T. D., Suwa, G., & Asfaw, B. (1994). *Australopithecus ramidus,* a new species of early hominid from Aramis, Ethiopia. *Nature, 371,* 306–312.

Wood, B., & Collard, M. (1999). The changing face of the genus *Homo. Evolutionary Anthropology, 8,* 195–207.

Wood, B., & Lonergan, N. (2008). The fossil record: taxa, grades and clades. *Journal of Anatomy, 212,* 354–376.

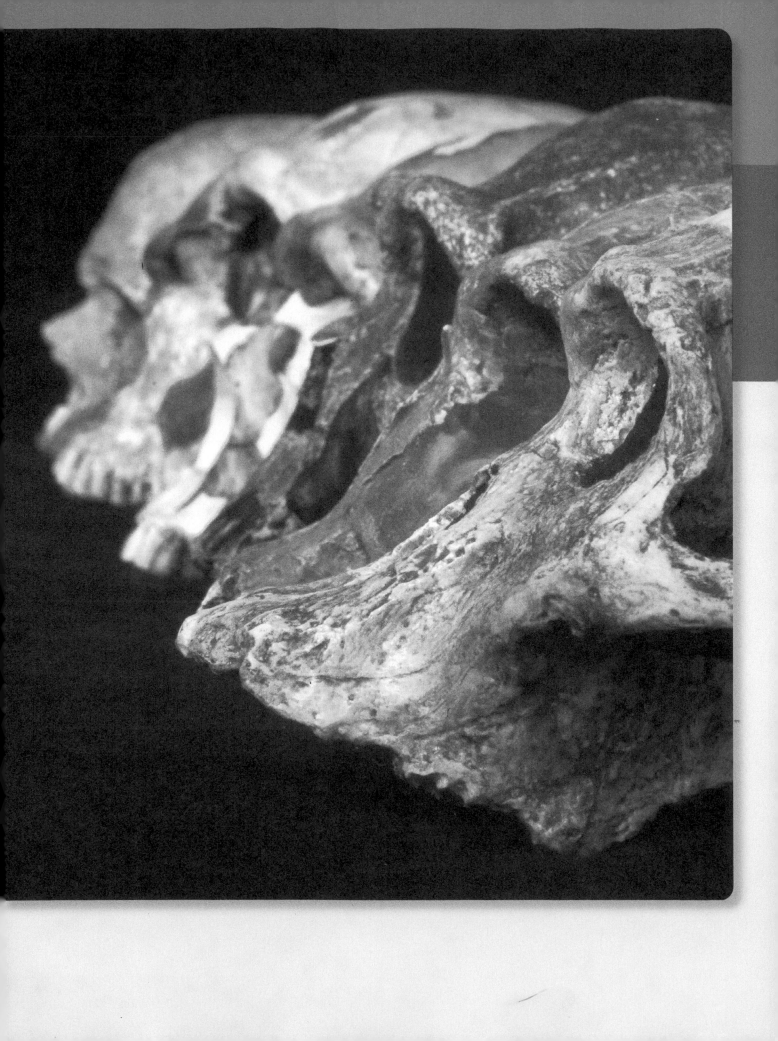

CHAPTER 8

Plio-Pleistocene Hominins and the Genus *Homo*

This chapter addresses the following questions:

▲ What changes emerge in the fossil record beginning about 2.7 million years ago?

▲ Who were the robust hominins, and how were they different from other Plio-Pleistocene hominin forms?

▲ Who are the two gracile hominins? Are they related to later forms?

▲ What major changes happened in the human lineage about 2 million years ago, and how did humans of this time period live?

I n summer 2002, a group of anthropologists reported an exciting new find in west Africa: an archaeological site with evidence of long-term tool use by chimpanzees (Mercader, Panger, & Boesch, 2002). These researchers concluded that generations of chimpanzees had cracked nuts at this site, using unmodified stones as tools, for more than a hundred years (Figure 8.1). The evidence the chimps left behind allowed archaeologists to recognize and identify the site as easily as they would an early human site. This was a case in which nonhuman primates left a material record of their behavior.

In a related set of findings, a group of scientists compared the social traditions of different groups of chimpanzees, including greeting gestures, tool use patterns, and other behavioral habits (Whiten et al., 1999). These scientists argue that such variations in tradition are not purely biological or genetic in origin but rather reflect a set of learned and socially transmitted behaviors. In short, they argue that chimpanzees have culture.

If other primates use tools, leave an archeological record, and have culture, what is distinct about early humans? How were they different? The answer to this question is the subject of this chapter. Human beings are biological organisms adapting and evolving under the same conditions and patterns—natural selection, gene flow, genetic drift, and mutation—as other organisms on this planet. However, some of our biological characteristics, or adaptations, distinguish us from these other organisms. In chapter 7, we saw that bipedal anatomy is an adaptation that distinguishes the

■ FIGURE 8.1
Tool use in chimpanzees.

hominins (including humans) from other hominoids. In this chapter, we will see that increased brain size and increasingly complex behavior are adaptations that distinguish humans from other hominins.

On a nonbiological level (or a level that is not *purely* biological), we know that humans are group-living, social organisms—we are primates, after all—and much of our adaptation involves social behavior. However, certain aspects of the ways in which we use behavior to adapt to environmental challenges are different from those of the other primates and even the other hominins. As humans, we exhibit an extremely complex form of culture and language. This allows us to construct fantastical ideas and images in our minds, share them with one another, and turn them into reality. By doing this we can alter the very patterns of environmental pressures we face. This creates a kind of niche construction with ecological and symbolic inheritance, which, you remember from chapter 4, are significant processes in evolution.

For example, have a look around your house and marvel at even the simplest of appliances, such as a can opener. Creating such a device is far beyond the capabilities of any other organism on this planet. This ability to modify our environment by imagining, envisioning, and creating complex material items sets us apart from other species. We interact with and construct our surroundings more than any other organism. It also affects us biologically. As we alter our environment through cultural behavior, whether cooking and processing our food, thus making it easier to digest, or creating stronger bacteria through the overuse of antibiotics, we alter the challenges and selective pressures with which our environment confronts us. This way that humans construct niches and deal with complex evolutionary pressures is called **biocultural evolution**—evolutionary change and adaptation through both somatic (biological) and extrasomatic (material/cultural) means—and it is the hallmark of humanity.

Toward the end of the Pliocene period, a little more than 2 million years ago, the earliest hints of biocultural evolution begin to appear in the fossil record. By the end of the Pliocene, about 1.8 million years ago, our ancestors were well immersed in biocultural change. In the time period covered in this chapter, the amount and quality of the fossil data increase dramatically over earlier periods. This chapter therefore contains more detailed information about the fossils and their interpretations and treats the fossil record in a more complex manner. In this chapter we explore basic information about the first humans—our direct ancestors—and the other hominins that shared the earth with them for a time.

biocultural evolution
evolutionary change and adaptation through both somatic (biological) and extrasomatic (material/cultural) means

■ FIGURE 8.2
A mosaic habitat. This type of mixed habitat creates many different ecological niches.

Changes at the late Pliocene–Pleistocene boundary

The end of the Pliocene and the start of the **Pleistocene** (a time known as the Plio-Pleistocene) was a time of climate change in Africa. Temperature fluctuations and changing seasonal patterns created mixed habitats of forests, grasslands, and open woodlands. This **mosaic habitat,** or pattern of mixed habitat types, and the frequent climatic fluctuations are associated with diversification of many animal lineages, including that of the hominins (Figure 8.2). As the changing habitat created new ecological niches, new species evolved to exploit them, including new species of hominins.

As described in chapter 7, *Australopithecus afarensis* and at least one or two other forms (*Kenyanthropus platyops* and *Australopithecus bahrelghazali*) represented the hominin lineage in east and central Africa in the mid-Pliocene (3 to 4 million years ago). In the last million years of the Pliocene epoch (about 3 to 1.8 mya), the fossil record reveals a diversification of hominin forms in east and south Africa. It is likely that these forms were descendants of *Australopithecus afarensis* or one of the other earlier forms. These new hominins shared many general structural similarities, but they varied greatly in the shapes and structures of their skulls. There are two morphological groups of late Pliocene fossils: a robust group with stout mandibles, massive teeth, and large chewing adaptations, and a gracile (or slightly built) group whose teeth are large but who do not have the massive skull and jaw adaptations that characterize the robust group (Figure 8.3). It is possible that some of these gracile forms were, in fact, the first members of the human lineage, the first representatives of the genus *Homo.*

By about 2 million years ago, near the beginning of the Pleistocene, we find fossils of members of the genus *Homo,* humans. These early humans differed from the hominins that preceded them in a number of ways. They were taller, had bigger brains, and behaved in a very humanlike fashion: They expanded into new lands. At the start of the Pleistocene we see the beginning of an amazing journey of discovery that characterizes humanity to this day.

Our goal in this chapter is to describe the diversity of hominin forms in the late Pliocene and into the Pleistocene and to hypothesize about which among

CONNECTIONS

See chapter 4, pages 107–108, for a discussion of niche construction.

Pleistocene
epoch dating from 1.8 million to 10,000 years ago

mosaic habitat
area that consists of two or more habitat types

Homo
the hominin genus to which humans belong; characterized by bipedal locomotion, large brains, and biocultural evolution

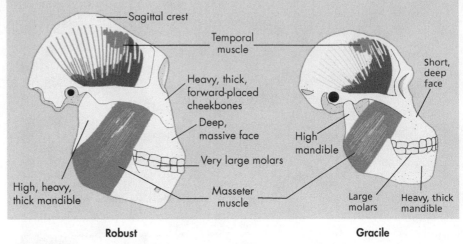

■ FIGURE 8.3

Skulls of robust and gracile hominins. Robust hominins had thicker, heavier bones to support their more massive musculature. Some robust species developed a sagittal crest to support their massive temporal muscles.

them gave rise to the earliest humans, true members of the genus *Homo*. Once we have examined the early human fossils, we will explore how they differed from the earlier hominins in both biology and culture, and how these differences translated into a new way of being.

The robust hominins had unique cranial and dental anatomy

In 1938, physician and avid paleontologist Robert Broom purchased a unique fossil skull that had been extracted from the ground at Kromdraai, South Africa. This skull had a mix of characteristics that were considered, at the time, to be both humanlike and apelike. A small braincase held a brain that could not have been larger than 500 cc (30.5 cubic in.). This is about a third the size of a modern human's brain, which is about 1450 cc (88.5 cubic in.). The top of the skull had a **sagittal crest** running between the parietal bones like the skull of a gorilla (see Figure 8.3). But the face, elements of the teeth, and the location of the foramen magnum were all humanlike. This fossil was the first of many to be discovered in both east Africa and what is now South Africa, representing the group we call the robust hominins.

Currently, there is debate about whether these fossils belong in their own genus (genus *Paranthropus*) or are best included in the well-established and long-lived genus *Australopithecus*. In this book we treat them as belonging to the genus *Paranthropus*, but we refer to all species of both *Australopithecus* and *Paranthropus* as "australopithecines" for practical purposes. Here, then, australopithecines are those hominins in the Plio-Pleistocene fossil record that are not members of the genus *Homo*. We refer to all members of the genus *Homo* as "human." Table 8.1 provides an overview of the fossils discussed in this chapter.

The Genus *Paranthropus*: Hominins with Massive Chewing Adaptations

The robust hominin fossils are currently grouped into three species dating to between 2.7 and about 1.0 million years ago. The two east African forms,

| TABLE 8.1 | Plio-Pleistocene Hominin Fossils |

Species	Location	Date (mya)	Main Characteristics
Paranthropus aethiopicus	E. Africa	2.5–2.3	Hyper-robust, few fossil fragments
Paranthropus boisei	E. Africa	2.3–1.3	Robust, MQ of 2.7, canines that look like incisors (incisiform)
Paranthropus robustus	S. Africa	2–1.5	Robust, MQ 2.2, brain >500 cc (30.5 cubic in.)
Australopithecus africanus	S. Africa	3–2.4	Gracile, MQ 2.0, slightly prognathic face
Australopithecus garhi	E. Africa	2.5	Large incisors, long femur, possible tool association
Australopithecus sediba	S. Africa	1.95–1.78	Brain ~420 cc, *homo*-like tooth size, *Australopithecus*-like tooth shape
Homo habilis	E. and S. Africa	2–1.6	Large incisors, MQ 1.9, brain ~600 cc (36.6 cubic in.), Olduwan tools
Homo rudolfensis	E. Africa	2.4–1.6	Large body size, MQ 1.5, brain ~700 cc (42.7 cubic in.), Olduwan tools
Homo erectus	Africa, Eurasia	1.8–~.25	Brain 727–1251 cc (avg. 883 cc, or 54 cubic in.), increasingly complex tools (Achulean) Moved out of Africa Robust compared to modern humans
Other possible forms:			
Homo ergaster	Africa	1.8–2.6	same as *Homo erectus*
Homo antecessor	Europe (Spain)	~.8	same as *Homo erectus*

Paranthropus aethiopicus and *Paranthropus boisei*, and the South African form, *Paranthropus robustus*, are represented by hundreds of fossils. All of these fossils display **megadontia**, meaning that they have larger postcanine teeth (molars and premolars) than would be expected for the size of their bodies (measured as MQ—megadontia quotient). These forms also have cranial adaptations for pronounced masticatory (chewing) structures (see Figure 8.3).

P. aethiopicus: The Earliest Robust Form

In 1985, a hyper-robust fossil hominin was found on the west side of Lake Turkana in east Africa. This fossil was called the "black skull" because of the coloration of the rock in which it was found (Figure 8.4). Dating to between 2.5 and 2.3 million years ago (based on ash layers above and below the fossil), this fossil cranium shows a number of derived characteristics relative to earlier hominins (such as *Australopithecus afarensis*), but it has strong similarities to a later east African form (*Paranthropus boisei*) (Walker, Leakey, Harris, & Brown, 1986). It has a broad, dish-shaped face, almost no forehead, widely flared **zygomatic arches** (the cheekbones, made up of the maxilla and the temporal bones), a pronounced sagittal crest, extreme facial prognathism, and very large molar teeth. In addition to the black skull, this species is also represented by a few mandibles and numerous teeth found at three sites in east Africa, ranging from 2.5 to 2.3 million years in age. The single cranial fossil of *P. aethiopicus* has a braincase of approximately 410 cc (25 cubic in.), no larger than those of earlier hominins.

Because *P. aethiopicus* is the earliest robust hominin fossil, it may be ancestral to the two subsequent robust forms. Nothing is known about the postcranial skeleton of this species. However, postcranial material from the other

megadontia
the characteristic of having larger postcanine teeth than would be expected for body size, measured as megadontia quotient (MQ)

zygomatic arches
cheekbones; arches created by the meeting of extensions of the temporal and zygomatic bones in the cranium

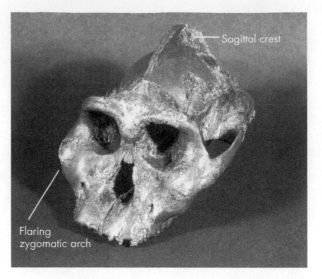

■ FIGURE 8.4
The "black skull": *Paranthropus
aethiopicus*. This fossil dates to
about 2.6 million years ago.
The sagittal crest and flaring
zygomatic arches are considered to be hyper-robust
characteristics.

Sagittal crest

Flaring
zygomatic arch

two members of the genus *Paranthropus* suggest that it retained many ancestral hominin characteristics—it looked a bit like *A. afarensis*—except for the
possibility of changes in the hands and feet, evident in both *P. boisei* and
P. robustus.

Other East African form

~~P.~~ boisei: The Famous Zinjanthropus

In 1959, paleoanthropologist Mary Leakey discovered a fossil cranium in Olduvai Gorge in Tanzania (Figure 8.5). One of the best known hominin fossils,
this skull was assigned to a species initially known as *Zinjanthropus boisei*
and now known as *Paranthropus boisei.* The find was of substantial initial
interest because of the massive chewing adaptations on the cranium and the
tantalizing possibility that it was the potential maker of some rudimentary
stone tools found in the same area.

This species is known from multiple fossils, all from east Africa, dating to
about 2.3 to 1.3 million years ago. Most of these fossil finds are of cranial and
dental remains; only a few postcranial bones are associated with the species.
However, there are enough skeletal elements to allow researchers to calculate
some general anatomical characteristics. *P. boisei* appears to have been somewhat sexually dimorphic, with males weighing about 49 kg (108 lb.) and

STOP & THINK

Sexual dimorphism seems
to shift across different
hominin species—is it
possible that this reflects
different behavioral
patterns and evolutionary
trajectories?

■ FIGURE 8.5
Paranthropus boisei cranium and
mandible. This species lived in
east Africa approximately 2.3 to
1.3 million years ago. Note the
adaptations for chewing: the
massive molars (a), as well as
the sagittal crest and zygomatic
arches (b).

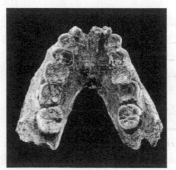

Reduced incisors, large molars
and premolars
(a)

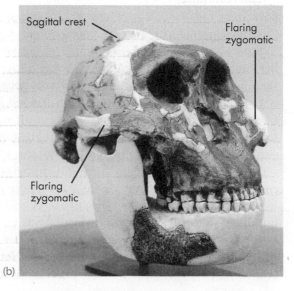

Sagittal crest

Flaring
zygomatic

Flaring
zygomatic

(b)

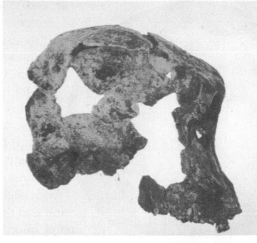

standing nearly 137 cm (4.5 feet) tall and females weighing about 34 kg (75 lb) and standing about 124 cm (~4 feet) tall (McHenry & Coffing, 2000). The dimorphism in this species appears to be less dramatic than in earlier hominin forms and more like what we find in modern humans (Figure 8.6).

P. boisei displays many of the same chewing adaptations as *P. aethiopicus*, including a sagittal crest, flaring zygomatic arches, a broad face, and very large teeth. Measures of the **megadontia quotient (MQ)**—a measure of premolar/molar tooth area relative to body size—suggest that *P. boisei* had the largest relative molar and premolar teeth to body size of any hominin. Their MQ is 2.7, indicating that their postcanine teeth are more than two and a half times larger than we would expect for their size (modern humans have an MQ of about .09) (McHenry & Coffing, 2000). Because we have a number of cranial fossils for this species, we also have a relatively good idea of their brain size and **encephalization quotient (EQ)**—a measure of the brain size relative to body size. Estimates place the brain size of *P. boisei* between 410 and 530 cc (25–32 cubic in.), giving them an EQ of about 2.7 (slightly higher than earlier hominins).

A major difference between *P. boisei* and *P. aethiopicus* is in their degree of facial prognathism: *P. boisei*'s face was quite flat and protruded very little at the jaw compared to *P. aethiopicus* (compare Figures 8.4 and 8.5). In part, this shape was due to the dramatic reduction in the size of the incisors and canines. Unlike earlier hominins, *P. boisei* (and *P. robustus*, as we will see shortly) had very small incisors and canines that were highly incisiform (incisorlike; see Figure 8.5). These characteristics are more like those of later hominins and humans than like those of any of the earlier forms. In addition, unlike earlier forms, *P. boisei* had a relatively parabolic tooth row, with the tooth rows diverging slightly at the back of the mouth. This characteristic is shared with humans and not with earlier hominins (see Figure 7.12).

P. robustus: A Robust Hominin with Hands Like Ours

Broom's publication of his South Africa find initiated a series of fossil discoveries, many of which are placed in the species *Paranthropus robustus*. *P. robustus* is found at four major sites in South Africa dating to between 2 and 1.5 million

megadontia quotient (MQ) measure of premolar/molar tooth area relative to body size

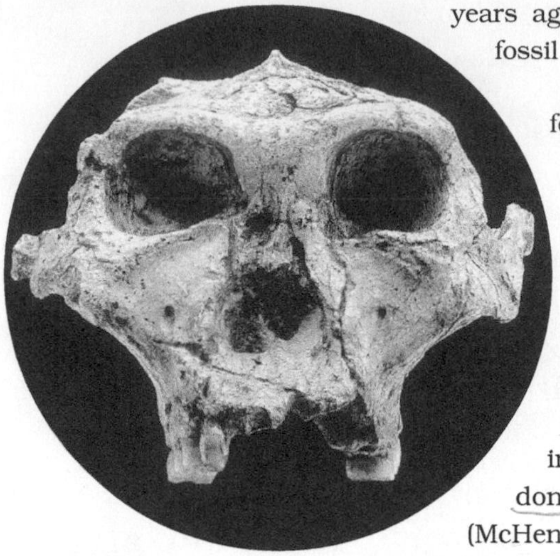

■ FIGURE 8.7
Paranthropus robustus. This species, which lived between 2 and 1.5 million years ago in South Africa, may have been a tool user.

years ago and is well known from many cranial and some postcranial fossil elements representing more than 100 individuals (Figure 8.7).

P. robustus females were approximately 110 cm (just over 3.5 feet) tall and weighed about 32 kg (70 lb). The males were about 132 cm (~4 feet, 4 in.) tall and weighed approximately 40 kg (88 lb) (McHenry & Coffing, 2000). Sexual dimorphism in this species was very similar to that in *P. boisei* and in later hominins. Members of this species share many cranial features with *P. boisei.* They have a flat face, small incisors and canines, a sagittal ridge, a small forehead, and pronounced zygomatic arches. However, the *P. robustus* braincase appears to have been slightly larger than that of *P. boisei,* about 530 cc (32 cubic in.), and the resulting EQ is also higher (3.0). *P. robustus*'s megadontia quotient of 2.2 is slightly smaller than that of *P. boisei* (McHenry & Coffing, 2000).

Because of the richer pool of postcranial fossils for members of this species of *Paranthropus,* we have a better understanding of their morphology. The arms of *P. robustus* were longer than the legs (a primitive characteristic), but the feet and hands displayed remarkable similarities to those of later hominins (humans). While there is no doubting they were bipedal, there is some debate as to how often they moved bipedally on the ground as opposed to other movement in trees (Wood & Lonergan, 2008). Because *P. robustus* is found in areas where we also find stone tools and because their hands are quite similar to modern human hands, this robust hominin may also have been a tool user, maybe even a tool maker.

STOP & THINK

Does it make sense, given what we know about natural selection, that something as major as teeth size would be shaped by extreme pressures not regularly encountered by *Paranthropus?*

Significance of the Robust Hominins' Specialized Chewing Adaptations

Despite their megadontia and the massive structures on the crania, the bodies of the robust australopithecines were fairly small. When we refer to these fossils as robust, we are really referring only to their cranial anatomy and dental adaptations. Why did they have such remarkable jaws and teeth? Most researchers agree that these structures were adaptations to particular dietary patterns, and judging by the fact that *P. boisei* and *P. robustus* were both around for about 1 million years, these structures appear to have been successful adaptations. It is likely that *Paranthropus* could rely on difficult-to-chew foods such as seeds and grasses in times of food stress. Their adaptations were to times of extreme pressure, not necessarily an indication of their regular everyday diet (which was omnivorous).

How do these adaptations work? The changes to the cranium resulted from increased ability to exploit hard-to-process foods. The features of the skull are affected by the use and structure of chewing muscles, and, over time, increasingly robust muscles and skull features in turn assist in the processing of tough foods by enhancing the power of each bite (see Figure 8.3). The sagittal ridge acts as an attachment for the muscles that connect to the mandible, giving them much more "pull" with each bite. The flaring zygomatic arches act in the same way. Other mandibular muscles attach to the broad surfaces provided by large zygomatic arches, further contributing to the increased power and effectiveness of each bite. As the molars and premolars expand in size over time, the incisors and canines shrink, thus changing the shape of the face. As the surface area of the molars increases, they become more effective processing surfaces for hard substances such as nuts, grasses, and seeds. More surface area combined with more powerful bites results in a very successful way to process highly nutritious foods. So when other food sources are scarce, *Paranthropus* could "fall back" on these food types for survival when perhaps some of their competitors could not.

Robust Hominin Behavior

Just as we are able to draw some inferences about behavior from the *Australopithecus afarensis* fossil record, we are able to gain insight into the lives and habits of the robust hominins from the *Paranthropus* fossils.

Habitat: Mixed Grasslands, Woodlands, and Forests

Since members of the genus *Paranthropus* are found in both southern and eastern Africa, they may have lived in a broader set of climates and habitats than did earlier hominins. Fossil pollen data, along with assessment of the nonhominin mammalian fossils found with the *Paranthropus* fossils in east Africa, suggest that *P. boisei* lived in a mosaic grassland and woodland environment with numerous lakes. Interestingly, this puts them in areas with many large carnivores who may have been predators of animals about the size of *Paranthropus*. It has also been suggested that beginning in the terminal Pliocene, about 3 to 2 million years ago, the global climate began to fluctuate more rapidly and a general cooling trend emerged. If this suggestion is true, then large forested areas may have shrunk and mosaic habitats may have become more common in east Africa during the terminal Pliocene and throughout the Pleistocene. The South African sites suggest *Paranthropus* lived in both forested environments and mixed grassland habitats (mosaic habitats) and that there was indeed a cooling trend from about 3 to 1 million years ago. Interestingly, research by Lockwood et al. (2007) on 35 South African *Paranthropus* specimens suggests that predation was an important pressure on them.

A Diet of Tough Vegetarian Foodstuffs

On the basis of the chewing adaptations evident in all of the *Paranthropus* fossils, they could rely on a tough vegetarian diet of seeds, roots, nuts, and hard-to-process leafy matter if needed. Examination of the tiny marks left on the fossil teeth of these hominins indicates that they did indeed consume hard-to-process foods (Figure 8.8). Therefore, the extreme morphologies we see in their skulls and teeth may have been the result of natural selection favoring the variants who could most effectively exploit these particular foodstuffs. However, this does not mean that *Paranthropus* was exclusively vegetarian. The chemical makeup of *Paranthropus* fossil bones strongly suggests that

■ **FIGURE 8.8**
Scanning electron microscope images of hominin teeth surfaces. Compare the marks on the teeth of *Australopithecus africanus* (a) and *Paranthropus* (b). The rough, pitted surface of the *Paranthropus* teeth suggests that this species could eat tough, gritty foods.

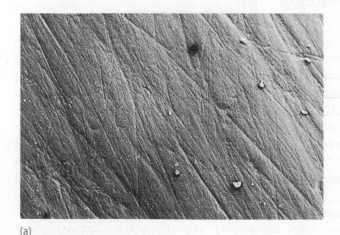

(a)

(b)

they did eat meat (Stewart, 1992). Additionally, animal bones with processing marks (cut marks on the bones made by stone flakes) found in both east Africa and South Africa at the times and locations where *Paranthropus* species existed leave open the possibility that they hunted for meat, or at least scavenged for it. (It is also possible that another hominin left the marks on those bones; see the later section on the gracile hominins). Recent work (Wood & Strait, 2004) indicates that their diets were relatively omnivorous.

CONNECTIONS

See chapter 5, page 151, for chimpanzee tool use.

Did *Paranthropus* Make Stone Tools?

Like the earlier hominins, members of the genus *Paranthropus* probably used tools (as do modern chimpanzees and other apeys). They may have used unmodified stones in an opportunistic fashion, as in picking up a rock and hitting something with it. However, unlike the earlier hominins (and unlike chimpanzees and other apes), *P. boisei* and *P. robustus* may have made stone tools (Susman, 1994). Simple modified stone tools are found in the same general time and vicinity as both *P. boisei* and *P. robustus* fossils. We also have fairly good evidence that their hands were suitable for the manipulation required to construct these tools, as mentioned earlier. However, because at least two other types of hominins were around at the same time, and because there has never been a find in which the tools are associated exclusively with *Paranthropus* fossils, we cannot say for certain that *Paranthropus* was the maker or user of these tools.

Inferences about Social Life

Because the members of the genus *Paranthropus* did not leave behind much, if any, material remains aside from bones, we cannot effectively reconstruct their social lives. It is likely, however, that they lived in mixed-sex groups of multiple adults and young. The reduced dimorphism relative to earlier hominins might suggest that male-female relationships were somewhat different than in *A. afarensis*. Because their hands and feet were more similar to those of modern humans, they perhaps spent less time in trees than previous hominins, even though their arms remained slightly longer than their legs (a primitive trait for hominins). If they did make and use simple stone tools, the process of collecting the stones and crafting and using the tools was probably a social one that involved many group members.

The gracile hominins shared characteristics with both earlier and later groups

Genus *Australopithecus:* Three Plio-Pleistocene Forms

At the same time that the members of the genus *Paranthropus* were roaming around eastern and southern Africa, at least three other australopithecine forms were sharing those areas with them. These other forms were gracile hominins—they did not have the super-robust chewing apparatus—and members of the genus *Australopithecus:* They were *A. garhi* in east Africa, *A. africanus* in South Africa, and *A. sediba*, the later South African form. These species shared traits with earlier hominins, especially *A. afarensis*, as well as with later hominins (the earliest potential humans). Because fossils of these hominins did not exhibit the derived chewing morphology of the robust *Paranthropus*, and because they seem to fill the gap between the disappearance of *A. afarensis* and the appearance of members of the genus *Homo*, they are frequently thought of as possible human ancestors.

A. africanus: The Early South African Form

There is significant debate about the exact dates of *Australopithecus africanus'* tenure. There is little dispute that they existed between 3.0 and 2.4 million years ago, but some researchers have proposed dates as old as 3.5 million years ago for some of the finds. If these older dates are supported, then *A. africanus* was a contemporary of *A. afarensis* and is not likely to be a link between the earlier hominins and humans.

First reported by Raymond Dart in 1925 with the publication of a description of the famous "Taung child" fossil, *A. africanus* has long held a central role in the understanding of hominin evolution (Figure 8.9). The species is known from fossils representing more than 50 individuals from at least three sites in South Africa. *A. africanus* exhibited sexual dimorphism similar to, or slightly greater than, that seen in members of the genus *Paranthropus*. Females stood approximately 115 cm (~3 feet, 8 inches) tall and weighed about 29 kg (64 lb), and males reached 138 cm (4.5 feet) in height and weighed about 41 kg (90 lb). Cranial capacity ranged from the low 400s to the low 500s cc, with a mean of about 454 cc (28 cubic in.). These figures give *A. africanus* an EQ of about 2.7, making them comparable to *P. boisei*.

The face of *A. africanus* is more prognathic than that of *P. boisei* or *P. robustus*, but less so than *A. afarensis*. The incisors are small, as are the canines, and the premolar and molar teeth are substantially smaller (both relative to body size and in actual area) than those of *Paranthropus*, giving *A. africanus* an MQ of 2.0 (McHenry & Coffing, 2000). The arms of this species are longer than the legs, as in other early hominins, and the big toe is slightly divergent and mobile (less so than in apes, but in a similar vein). These characteristics suggest that *A. africanus* may still have moved around in trees. Interestingly, the vertebral column appears to have a curve similar to that in modern humans, and the pelvic region is very similar to that of *A. afarensis* (Conroy, 1997). *A. africanus* was probably primarily bipedal but also capable of some arboreal locomotion.

A. sediba: The Later South African Form

In 2010, researchers published an exciting and important new find from the Malapa site in South Africa: fossils that shared both gracile Australopithecine and *Homo*-like characteristics. This new species, dated between 1.95 and 1.78 million years ago, is called *Australopithecus sediba*, with "sediba" meaning *wellspring* or *fountain* in the local Sesotho language. The species is represented by both adult and juvenile cranial and post-cranial elements from two individuals. Most striking about this find is that it appears to share many characteristics with *Australopithecus africanus* and early members of the genus *Homo* (Berger et al., 2010). The brain size is small, at ~420 cc, and the skull shares features in common with both genera, such as tooth size and pelvic shape similar to *Homo* but tooth cusp morphology and foot structure similar to *Australopithecus africanus*. The post-cranial materials (including sections of upper and lower limbs, plus the pelvic girdle) appear to represent a sort of intermediate stage between more arboreally adapted hominin and a totally terrestrial one. The discoverers of *A. sediba* suggest that it might be a link between *A. africanus* and early members of the genus *Homo* (Berger et al., 2010). However, the exact relationship between this species and later fossils, and the

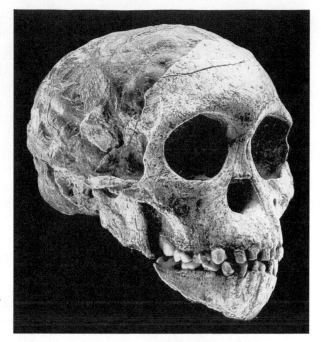

■ FIGURE 8.9
The "Taung child," an example of *Australopithecus africanus*. This fossil, the first of its species to be discovered, includes a partial cranium and a natural endocast of the brain. The species lived between 3.0 and 2.4 million years ago and perhaps earlier.

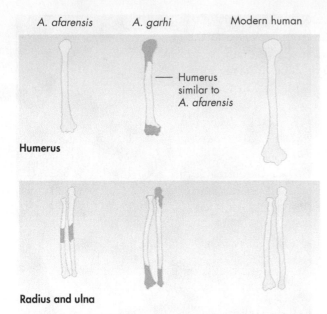

A. afarensis   A. garhi   Modern human

Humerus

— Humerus
similar to
A. afarensis

Radius and ulna

Femur

— Longer femur
more similar
to later
hominins

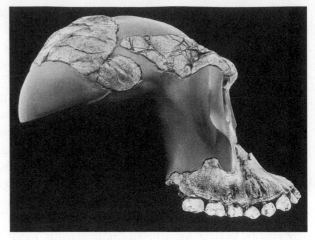

■ **FIGURE 8.10**

Australopithecus garhi. This "surprise" species, dated to about 2.5 million years ago, has extremely large teeth. Its lower limbs are suggestive of later hominins.

types of tools it might have used, are still unclear and wait on further discoveries and analyses.

A. garhi: The East African Form

In 1999, a group of scientists reported the discovery of a new form of australopithecine at the Hata area in the Bouri geological formation of Ethiopia (Figure 8.10) (Asfaw et al., 1999). They called this striking find *Australopithecus garhi* (*garhi* means "surprise" in the local Afar language). This set of fossils, dating to 2.5 million years ago, represents at least a few individuals and includes cranial and dental fragments. Upper and lower limb bone fossils were also found in the same general area and dated to approximately the same time. No other hominin species are currently known in this area and time.

Numerous characteristics of this species set it apart from other known fossil hominins. *A. garhi* has extremely large premolars and molars; in fact, they are at the upper end in size even for *Paranthropus* postcanine teeth. However, because the incisors are also very large, the relative size of the postcanine teeth is smaller than in *Paranthropus*. Despite the large molar teeth, *A. garhi* does not have all the facial features shared by all members of the genus *Paranthropus* (as described earlier). Instead, *A. garhi* shares a set of primitive traits in the face and palate with *A. afarensis* (large molars with thick enamel, relatively large canines, parallel tooth rows, relatively prognathic face), but it is distinguished from that species by its distinct dentition (Asfaw et al., 1999).

If the limb bones found in rocks of the same age at nearby sites belong to the same species, then A. garhi also displayed a longer femur relative to the humerus than earlier hominins (a characteristic of humans), but an upper arm–to–lower arm ratio very similar to that of A. afarensis. Although represented by only a few fossils, this australopithecine appears to exhibit a constellation of traits not seen in any other hominin. As mentioned, its location and dates of existence place it in a time and place when no other hominin fossils are found.

In addition to the surprising morphology of A. garhi—very large teeth, specific facial traits, upper limbs similar to A. afarensis, and lower limbs resembling those of later hominins—this fossil hominin is found in association with evidence of tool use and meat eating. Several fossils of mammalian bone with cut marks clearly made by stone tools were found by another group of researchers in rocks of roughly the same age as the A. garhi finds and at locations near the finds (de Heinzelin et al., 1999) (Figure 8.11). Unfortunately,

STOP & THINK

If A. garhi is accurately associated with the femur fossils and stone tools, does that make it the best candidate for human ancestor? How might we compare and contrast A garhi and A. sediba to determine which might be a more likely ancestor to humans?

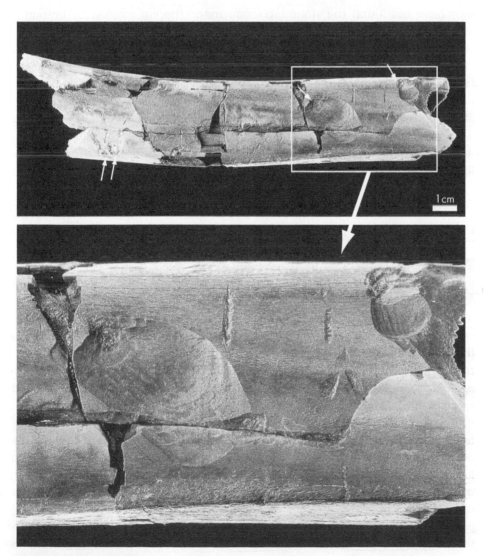

1cm

■ FIGURE 8.11
Evidence of tool use from approximately 2.5 million years ago, possibly by A. garhi. The arrows show the direction of the hammerstone's impact. Note the cut marks on the bone in the lower photo. These marks are clear evidence that a hominin was using stone tools to deflesh the carcass. Because A. garhi was in this area at this time, many researchers assume that this species created these marks.

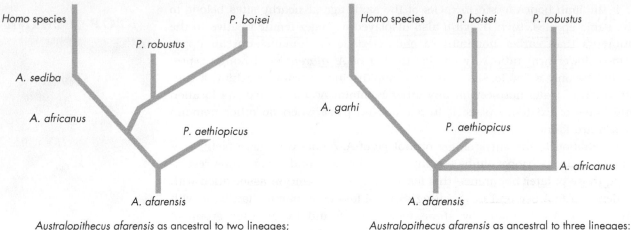

Australopithecus afarensis as ancestral to two lineages; Australopithecus africanus ancestral to Paranthropus and Homo.

Australopithecus afarensis as ancestral to three lineages: Homo, the East African Paranthropus and the South African Australopithecus, and Paranthropus.

■ FIGURE 8.12

Hominin phylogenies propose linear relationships between early hominin and modern *Homo sapiens,* but not enough information is available to fully support such detailed ideas about ancestry.

they have not found the stone tools that made the cut marks on the bones at this site. About 100 km (62 miles) to the north, however, at the Gona site, researchers have found simple stone tools dated to 2.6 million years ago. Pointing out that natural outcrops of raw materials for stone making appear to be limited at the Hata site, they suggest that the users of the stone tools may have transported them over large distances rather than discarding them at the site (de Heinzelin et al., 1999). Regardless, if the cut marks on the bones at Hata are the work of the only hominin known from that site (*A. garhi*), it would be the earliest example of cultural processing of animal food in the fossil record.

Are These Australopithecines Ancestral to Humans?

Until the mid-1990s, most anthropologists hypothesized that the genus *Homo* evolved in a relatively linear way from earlier hominins. They proposed that a two- or three-way split occurred after *A. afarensis,* with separate lineages leading to the robust *Paranthropus* species, to *A. africanus,* and to humans. Figure 8.12 shows two different versions of this traditional phylogeny.

The specific sequence of hominin evolution has become progressively less clear, however, as a result of the multiple new fossil finds published during the last 12 or so years (*Sahelanthropus tchadensis, Orrorin tugenensis, Australopithecus anamensis, Australopithecus bahrelgazalia, Kenyanthropus platyops, Australopithecus sediba,* and *Australopithecus garhi*) and the increased number of discoveries of fossils from already known species (Lieberman, 2001; Wood, 2002). In fact, many representations of the possible phylogenies of the hominins no longer draw direct links among most forms. That is what this book does—we simply describe the location, timing, and morphologies of the fossil finds and suggest some potential relationships. Figure 8.13 displays major traits of the hominin species that are known to have lived from 6 to 1 million years ago.

Because of the extremely derived features (the massive chewing adaptations) of the species in the genus *Paranthropus,* most scholars believe this genus could not have given rise to humans. However, the *Paranthropus* species do appear to be extremely similar to early humans in many postcranial aspects, suggesting that *Paranthropus* may be a sister group to the genus *Homo.* Given the current state of knowledge, it is highly probable that if *A. garhi, A. sediba,* and *A. africanus* were the only gracile australopithecines

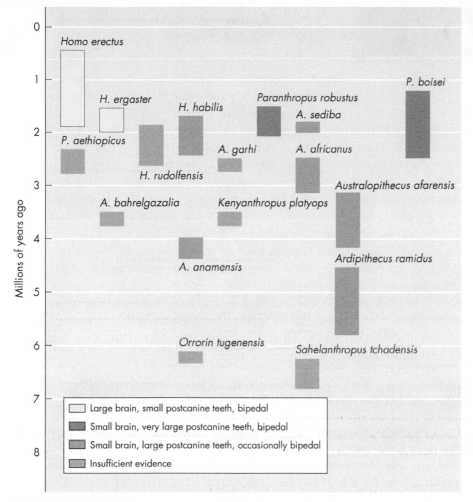

■ FIGURE 8.13

Characteristics and dating of known hominin species. This chart displays selected character-istics of known hominin species, which are arranged according to the dates each species is known to have lived. It suggests certain broad relationships among early species but does not make assumptions about which species were direct human ancestors.

in existence during the period of about 2.9 to 2.4 million years ago, one of them is ancestral to humans.

There is also the possibility that early humans overlapped with these aus-tralopithecines and that our lineage may be derived directly from earlier hom-inins, such as *A. afarensis* or *Kenyanthropus platyops*, without intermediate forms. Alternatively, the intermediate forms may still be undiscovered. The bottom line is that we currently do not know with a high degree of certainty what the specific lineage of humans looks like. We do have some good ideas, but a definitive statement cannot currently emerge without further fossil data.

CONNECTIONS

See *Homo floresiensis* on page 242 of this chapter.

Early *Homo:* A New Genus Emerges

In the 10th edition of his *Systema Naturae*, published in 1758, Linnaeus placed humans in genus *Homo,* species *sapiens.* Over the last two and a half centuries, researchers have added more species to the genus *Homo* as fossil finds emerged. Anthropologists, biologists, anatomists, and other researchers generally agree that a set of hominin fossils found in Africa and around the planet, all dating to less than about 1.8 million years ago, are members of

Where Is the Missing Link?

It does not exist. The concept of a missing link is that a single form in the fossil record is a true intermediate between the human lineage and other hominins (or even the other apes). Having one clear ancestor would make our discussion and description of the fossil past much easier. Drawing lines of relationship between fossil species is not easy, and in fact might not even be scientific. How do we really test the hypotheses with such a limited data set? But the search for a missing link is not even what we want. If we remember all that we have discussed about the way evolution works, a true intermediary fossil is not really possible. You won't find a 50% bipedal, 50% large brain, decreasing tooth size, almost stone-tool-using fossil hominin filling

the connecting space perfectly. Evolutionary change does not always work in a linear fashion and different parts of the body change in different ways at different times. As we can see from the fossil record between 4 and 2 million years ago there were a number of forms, and they have a mixed bag of characteristics—some good candidates for the human lineage, others less so. Evolution is best described as a densely branching tree, not a clear line. It is much easier to say what is *not* on the human branch than to specify which forms are our direct ancestors. So forms like *Ardipithecus* and the Australopithecines are not missing links but rather parts of branches on the tree. Our task is to try to assess whether they are parts of the branches that lead to us or just nearby branches that share the same part of the tree.

the genus *Homo*, although there is substantial disagreement about how many species they represent.

There is less clarity and more debate about early humans between the dates of about 2.5 and 1.8 million years ago. What characteristics would a hominin have to exhibit to be placed definitively in genus *Homo*? As we saw with the early primate fossils (chapter 6) and the early hominin fossils (chapter 7), the earliest forms of a lineage do not necessarily share all the features currently found in that lineage. Because evolution is change over time, descendant species and their ancestors (or even the same species at two very different time periods) may be quite different. However, a key determinant of distinction for the genus *Homo* is that characteristic that continues to differentiate us from all other hominins: a large brain relative to our body size. The EQ in modern humans is roughly 6.0. In the largest-brained australopithecine it was 3.0.

Hominins with large brains, differently shaped faces, and slightly smaller teeth begin to appear in the fossil record between 2.5 and 1.5 million years ago, and modified stone tools appear alongside them. Because of certain morphological elements, there is significant debate over whether these fossils should be assigned to the genus *Homo* or the genus *Australopithecus* (Wood & Collard, 1999; Wood & Lonergan, 2008). The fossils attributed to early *Homo* are frequently classified as two separate species, *Homo habilis* and *Homo rudolfensis*. Both display a mix of primitive and derived characteristics, but each one does so differently.

H. habilis: Anatomical Change and Possible Tool Use

In 1964 Louis Leakey and colleagues (Leakey, Tobias, & Napier, 1964) published a description of a new member of the genus *Homo*, which they called *Homo habilis*, the "handy man." These fossils were found in Olduvai Gorge in east Africa in association with simple stone tools. Fossils attributed to this species date from a little more than 2 million years ago to about 1.6 million

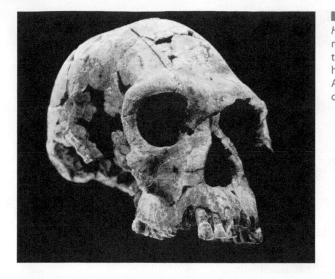

■ FIGURE 8.14
Homo habilis skull. The "handy man" lived approximately 2.0 to 1.6 million years ago. Fossils have been found in both east Africa and South Africa in association with stone tools.

years ago; they have been found at sites in both east Africa and South Africa where fossils of *Paranthropus* were also found. The fossils include both cranial and postcranial material, including elements of both the upper and lower limbs (Figure 8.14).

From these fossils we know that *H. habilis* females stood nearly 100 cm (3.2 feet) tall and weighed about 32 kg (70.4 lb). Males reached about 131 cm (4.3 feet) in height and weighed about 37 kg (81 lb)—slightly smaller than the contemporary australopithecines. These fossils display a relatively prognathic *look up* face, no sagittal ridge, large incisors, smaller postcanine teeth (MQ = 1.9), and a narrower tooth row than are seen in the australopithecines (Conroy, 1997; McHenry & Coffing, 2000). The phalanges in the hand are slightly curved and strongly built, and other aspects of the hand suggest the ability to use a **precision grip**, an important requirement for making tools. Some suggest that the arms of *H. habilis* are relatively primitive (showing similarities to those of *A. afarensis* and *A. garhi*), but other researchers argue that there is too little fossil information to support such an assessment (Asfaw et al., 1999). The pelvic girdle and legs of *H. habilis* display clear bipedal adaptations similar to those seen in the contemporary australopithecines. However, the one fossil foot associated with this species is a mix of primitive and derived traits and appears to retain some potential climbing adaptations (Wood & Collard, 1999; Wood & Lonergan, 2008).

Six cranial remains attributed to *H. habilis* provide estimates of brain size, which range from 503 to 661 cc with a mean of 601 cc (37 cubic in.) (McHenry & Coffing, 2000). The smaller-bodied *H. habilis* thus has both a relatively and an absolutely larger brain than the *Paranthropus* species.

precision grip
ability to grip objects forcefully with the phalanges of the hand and yet exert fine-tuned control of the movement of the objects; includes the ability to grip items between the thumb and any of the fingers

H. rudolfensis: A Larger Body and a Larger Brain

In addition to the fossils attributed to *Homo habilis* found in east Africa, there is another set of similar, yet distinct, fossils belonging to a larger hominin dating to between 2.4 and 1.6 million years ago (Figure 8.15). At first, these fossils were grouped with *H. habilis*, with the idea that the species might be highly variable or extremely sexually dimorphic. They have since been moved out of *H. habilis* and placed in their own species, *Homo rudolfensis* (Wood, 1992). Unfortunately, the majority of *H. rudolfensis* material comes from about 12 fossils, with very little postcranial material, and researchers are still debating whether the postcranial material that does exist belongs to this species or to *Paranthropus* (McHenry & Coffing, 2000; Wood & Lonergan, 2008). If this is

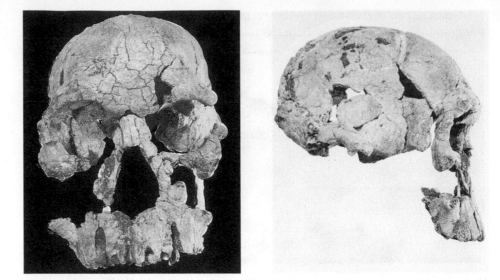

■ FIGURE 8.15

The sole fossil cranium for *Homo rudolfensis*. Researchers originally classified this specimen as *Homo habilis* but later placed it in a new species. If *H. rudolfensis* is a true species, it was the largest of the early hominins.

a true species, its members are much larger than members of *H. habilis*, and they present a very different picture of an early member of the genus *Homo*.

H. rudolfensis females may have been as tall as 150 cm (nearly 5 feet) and weighed as much as 51 kg (112 lb), making them larger than any previous hominins and putting them well within the size range of modern humans. Males were probably taller (160 cm, or 5.3 feet) and heavier (up to 60 kg, or 132 lb). The one relatively complete cranial remain for this species suggests a brain size of 736 cc (45 cubic in.), by far the largest for any hominin living before 1.8 mya. The face is broad and flat, there is no distinct **supraorbital torus** (a robust projection at the front of the frontal bone), and there is a sagittal ridge. The postcanine teeth exhibit megadontia and are absolutely larger than those of *H. habilis*, but because of the larger skull size of *H. rudolfensis*, the premolars and molars are relatively smaller (MQ = 1.5) (McHenry & Coffing, 2000).

If the postcranial material associated with this species does not belong to it, the overall weight (which would be based solely on the one fossil cranium) goes down and the MQ goes up. Despite the very large brain, the EQ of *H. rudolfensis* (3.1) is slightly lower than that of *H. habilis* due to its assumed large body size. The pelvic girdle fossils potentially attributed to *H. rudolfensis* exhibit distinct modifications that might align it more with later members of the genus *Homo* than with *H. habilis*.

Which Fossils Are in Our Lineage?

Homo habilis has the smaller body size, the pelvic and limb anatomy, and the relatively flexible feet of the australopithecines, but it also has absolutely smaller teeth than the australopithecines and an absolutely and relatively larger brain, similar to *A. sediba*. *Homo rudolfensis* exhibits megadontia similar to *Paranthropus* and *Australopithecus garhi*, but it has relatively smaller teeth due to its larger size, an absolutely larger but relatively similar brain, and pelvic anatomy that is more like that of later humans than that of the australopithecines. In other words, *H. habilis* has the right head and the wrong body for a human ancestor, and *H. rudolfensis* has the wrong head and the right body.

supraorbital torus
a robust projection at the front of the frontal bone on the cranium

STOP & THINK

It is likely that there were many species of hominin 3–2 million years ago. What could have happened that nudged one of them, evolutionarily, along a specific path that resulted in humans?

In looking at these two species, we are reminded again of the difficulty of understanding complex evolutionary patterns from limited fossil samples. It remains unclear whether these fossils represent one species or two and whether they are *Homo* or *Australopithecus*. What *is* clear is that they reflect a trend toward an increase in brain size and a greater ability to use tools and possibly to modify the environment in other ways. Whatever we choose to call these fossils, they appear to represent the earliest glimmer of humanness—but they are probably not the first true humans.

Gracile Hominin Behavior and the Advent of Biocultural Evolution

Habitat: Savannas, Woodlands, and Forests

The distribution of early *Homo* fossil finds is nearly identical to that of the gracile australopithecines and *Paranthropus*. In fact, many sites that have yielded *Paranthropus* fossils also turn up fossils attributed to *H. habilis* or *H. rudolfensis*. Like these other hominins, early members of the genus *Homo* lived in a variety of habitats, including lakesides, savannas, woodlands, and semiforested areas. *H. habilis* may have slept in trees and possibly foraged and moved about arboreally, but it is more likely that terrestrial bipedality was the primary mode of locomotion. It is unlikely that *H. rudolfensis* used the arboreal environment much, given the structures of the pelvic girdle and the lower limbs. Given these lifestyles, it is likely, as for the *australopithecus*, that threats from predaters such as lions, leopards, and hyenas were important in shaping the behavior of these hominins.

Evidence of Increased Meat Eating?

In modern humans the brain requires approximately 20% of the entire energy intake of the body, and as the body gets larger, the amount of energy required to run the brain increases. It appears that the absolute and relative size of the brain increased in the early members of the genus *Homo* compared to other early hominins. This size increase in the brain, and possibly in the body as well for *H. rudolfensis*, would have come with an increase in the metabolic cost of keeping the body running. The cost appears to rise dramatically in later members of the genus *Homo* (as discussed later in this chapter), but it may have its beginning in *H. habilis* and *H. rudolfensis*. If this is the case, we would expect to see the diets of these early members of the genus *Homo* improving in quality and increasing in calorie content. The fastest way to implement such changes is to increase the amount of animal protein in the diet.

There is ample evidence that many types of large carnivores lived in east and south Africa, and several fossil sites have revealed the processed remains of bovids (antelopes and antelope-like mammals) and other animals in association with the types of tools we think early *Homo* made; in fact, the earliest of these sites may be associated with *Australopithecus garhi*. At these sites, researchers have found animal bones (primarily limb bones) with indications that meat was cut off them, as well as bones that have been crushed and had their marrow extracted (marrow is the nutrient-rich, blood-cell-producing substance inside long bones). Increasing the amount of meat and marrow in the diet could have helped solve the problem posed by larger brains and bodies.

However, there is little evidence that meat made up more than a small portion of the diet for early *Homo*. A larger portion was probably made up of high-quality vegetable sources of proteins and carbohydrates, such as underground storage organs (roots and tubers) and nuts and other fatty fruits. It remains unclear exactly how these early members of the genus *Homo* foraged, but it is likely that they revisited food-rich sites, engaged in some hunting, and used tools to enhance their ability to process animal and plant foods. It is also quite possible that they collected meat by scavenging the kills of large predators.

The Olduwan Tool Kit

On the basis of comparisons with all the living apes, it is assumed that simple tool use is common to all the hominins. However, we do not see any evidence that hominins actually *modified* stone to change its structure and function until approximately 2.5 million years ago. Modified stones, referred to as **Olduwan** (sometimes also spelled "Oldowan") after their initial discovery in the Olduvai Gorge, have been found at numerous sites in east Africa and South Africa. In the Olduwan tool industry, very simple modifications were made to certain types of rocks to produce sharp flakes and edged choppers (Figures 8.16, 8.17). There is no evidence that any animal other than hominins has ever independently produced such tools.

The earliest tools were unearthed about 96 km (58 miles) north of a site where we find *A. garhi*, and slightly later tools have been found at many sites that we know were occupied by *H. habilis*, *H. rudolfensis*, *P. boisei*, or *P. robustus*. However, we have not actually found an Olduwan tool in a fossil hand. The closest thing to a "smoking gun" is a mandible assigned to *H. habilis* found in very close spatial association with Olduwan tools at Hadar, dated to about 2.3 million years ago. Many researchers assume that early members of the genus *Homo* made Olduwan tools because of their increased brain size and hand morphology, but there is no evidence to counter the hypothesis that *Paranthropus*, and possibly *A. garhi*, also made Olduwan tools. Remember, all of these hominins were more or less sympatric with one another (that is, they lived in the same area) and may have shared elements of material culture or at least imitated or stolen from one another.

If early members of the genus *Homo* did make these tools, we can see how the tools could have enhanced their ability to acquire and process foods and otherwise modify their surroundings. In a sense, this tool use could be a type of niche construction as they shaped the environmental pressures by innovating and modifying the world around them. These dietary and environmental modifications, in turn, may have facilitated the ongoing changes that led to the later forms of *Homo*. If this ability to make and use tools to modify their environment

Olduwan
relating to the first stone tools in the archaeological record, dating to about 2.5 million years ago and consisting of relatively simple flakes and choppers

STOP & THINK

Even though we see these stone tools as simple, they require intense planning and communication to make. Is this what differentiates the human lineage from others?

■ FIGURE 8.16
Olduwan tools. The stone shown in the upper left was used unmodified; it is a little larger than a tennis ball. At the bottom right are two flake tools. The remaining tools shown are core tools from which flakes have been removed, leaving sharp edges.

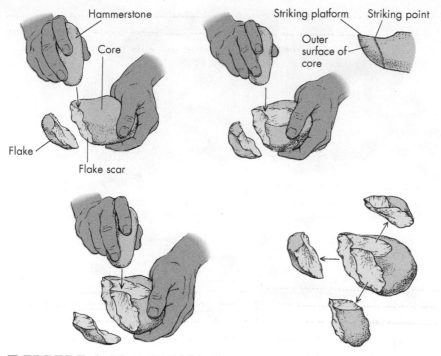

■ FIGURE 8.17
Making Olduwan tools. The toolmaker strikes a hard stone in just the right place to remove thin, sharp flakes.

and meet its challenges was successful, as we think it was, then it is here, with these early members of the genus *Homo*, that we see the advent of biocultural evolution—the interaction of biology and culture to meet selective challenges.

An Increasingly Complex Social Life

It seems likely that *H. habilis* and *H. rudolfensis* lived in social groups, as did the other hominins. As their brains grew in size over time and their ability to use and modify more and more objects in their environment increased, it is likely that the level and quality of their social interactions became more complex. Such activities as making stone tools, searching for and gathering the raw material for those tools, hunting or scavenging for meat, and extracting nutrient-rich tubers and other plants from the ground are more effectively conducted in social groups. Additionally, coordinating these types of activities across time and among a number of individuals requires a fairly advanced communication system, probably more than grunting and pointing. This suggests that we might be seeing the beginnings of the complex social community that characterizes all humans.

In sum, we now know that sometime between 2.5 and 1.8 million years ago, members of the genus *Homo* began to move along a morphological trajectory leading to modern humans. That trajectory included bigger brains, larger bodies, and more modern bipedal anatomy. Given the record of stone tools and the evidence of food processing, it appears that these hominins began to behave like humans as well.

The genus Homo diversifies: the first humans

In the late 1800s, a Dutch physician and early paleoanthropologist named Eugene DuBois set out in search of humanity's ancestors. DuBois was convinced that our true ancestors were to be found in Southeast Asia, and he

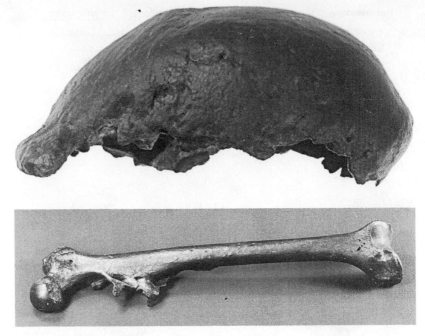

■ FIGURE 8.18

Homo erectus. The skull and femur from DuBois's first discovery of this species, which he called *Pithecanthropus erectus.*

took a position as an army surgeon in the Dutch East Indies (modern-day Indonesia) in order to find them. During the 1890s, on the island of Java, he found his fossils: a skullcap (including part of the frontal bone, both parietals, and part of the occipital), a femur, and some other bone fragments (Figure 8.18). These fossils seemed human and very old, but they suggested a creature with a smaller brain and thicker bones than modern *Homo sapiens*. DuBois named his discovery *Pithecanthropus erectus*, "the ape man who stood erect." Since the 1800s, hundreds of fossils belonging to this or closely related species have been recovered throughout Asia, parts of Europe, and Africa. Today we call the fossils DuBois discovered *Homo erectus*.

CONNECTIONS

See species concepts and definitions in chapter 4, pages 108–111.

A Classification Debate: One Genus but How Many Species?

Between 1.8 and 0.3 million years ago, the fossil record for the genus *Homo* began to diversify and became increasingly complex (Figure 8.19). No longer are we focused only on Africa, nor are there only a few simple stone tools. Rather, beginning about 1.8 million years ago, the fossil record shows a growing "humanness" in our ancestors, as they move into new geographical regions, change in morphology, and demonstrate a wider and richer array of material culture.

There is currently significant debate over the classification of the fossils of the genus *Homo* dating to between about 1.8 and 0.5 million years ago (Rightmire, 2008; Wood & Lonergan, 2008). All scientists agree that these fossils come from members of the genus *Homo*, but they disagree about how many species are represented and how they are related to modern humans. There are three main perspectives in this debate:

- All members of the genus *Homo* occurring between roughly 1.8 and 0.3 million years ago are one species (*H. erectus*). This species originated in Africa at the end of the Pliocene and dispersed throughout Africa, Eurasia, and

■ **FIGURE 8.19**
Major *Homo erectus* sites. Beginning about 1.8 million years ago, hominins, represented by *H. erectus*, spread throughout the Old World.

eastern Asia. In this model some gene flow occurred in *Homo erectus* populations as they moved around the Old World, and all of these populations are generally ancestral to modern humans.

- The genus *Homo* included at least three or four species between 1.8 and 0.3 million years ago, and there were repeated movements out of Africa. In this model, Asian forms (*H. erectus*) are a sideline to modern human evolution and are not ancestral to modern humans.

- All fossils of the genus *Homo* from about 1.8 million years ago through the present day are members of the same species, *Homo sapiens*. Here the assumption is that this species has been quite variable over time and that we (*Homo sapiens sapiens*) are its current representatives.

This debate centers around two main issues: interpretations of the fossil evidence and concepts of the pattern of evolution. The three perspectives reflect two main orientations: *lumpers*, who see one or a few species in the *Homo* fossil record, and *splitters*, who see many species. If we use a splitters category we have as many as eight species of human (genus *Homo*) during this time period (1.8 million to ~300,000 years ago), but only 1 or 2 if we are lumpers. What

CONNECTIONS

See chapter 4, pages 108–111, for a discussion of species concepts in greater detail.

is the difference between these views? Basically, it is what one considers as the defining characteristics of a paleospecies. That is, how different must fossil members of the genus *Homo* be in order to be considered a separate species? Since the majority of our fossil information comes from crania, most of the measurable differences come from comparing different skulls' shapes and structures. We also have to take into account the timing of fossils and the geographic locations in which we find them, and determine if there are clear continuities between fossils from different time periods but in similar locations. This would be a continuity of form, suggesting that the changes are in one lineage over time, but probably not representing different species (a lumper perspective). We also can ask if there are easily distinguishable measurements of fossil crania or post-cranial elements that enable us to divide the fossils into discrete clusters, and if so then into how many clusters? If we can divide the fossils into such discrete clusters consistently and clearly across space and time, then they can be considered different species in the genus *Homo* (a splitter perspective).

In this book we will refer to all the genus *Homo* fossils between 1.8 million and about 300,000 years ago as *Homo erectus* (the lumper perspective). However, we will also point out which of these fossils are considered to possibly be different species and give some indication as to why this is the case (the splitter perspective). Keep in mind that even though we can identify differences in clusters of fossils, it does not automatically mean that they are true biological species as we use the term for living organisms.

Physical Characteristics of *H. erectus*

In general, all of the fossil *Homo* material dating from between about 1.8 and about 0.3 million years ago is differentiated from the late australopithecines and the earlier forms of *Homo* by larger brains, larger bodies, less sexual dimorphism in size, shorter arms relative to legs, longer legs relative to the body, reduced absolute and relative postcanine tooth size, and a diversification in the material record left behind, including more tools and other extrasomatic material. Although there is some debate over the pace and pattern of change these fossils represent, there is agreement on the general pattern of decreasing tooth size and increasing average brain size (Figure 8.20).

The *Homo* fossils from this period can be generally described as follows: Females weighed, on average, about 51 kg (112 lb) and stood about 160 cm (5.3 feet) tall; males weighed about 66 kg (145 lb) and stood about 180 cm (5.9 feet) tall. Measurements of 26 fossil crania from Africa and east Asia indicate that *H. erectus* had an average cranial capacity of about 883 cc (54 cubic in.), with a range of 727 to 1251 cc (44–76 cubic in.) (Conroy, 1997). Their postcranial anatomy was similar to modern humans in many respects, although bone density was higher and the skeleton was more robust. There are only a few fossils of hand bones, but those available do not show strong curvature of the phalanges; rather, the fingers appear to be long and straight like those of modern humans. The thorax is broad and barrel shaped as in modern humans, and the toes are shorter than in earlier forms (Conroy, 1997; McHenry & Coffing, 2000; Wood & Lonergan, 2008). The shape of the cranium is long and low, with a fairly robust projection at the front of the frontal bone, a supraorbital torus. Some of the fossils have a **sagittal keel (ridge)**, a raised area where the parietals meet midcranium, and most have an **occipital (or nuchal) (torus)**, or pronounced ridge, at the rearmost point on the occipital bone. The mandibles are robust compared to those of modern humans, and there is a receding chin (Figure 8.21).

sagittal keel (ridge) raised area, much less pronounced than a sagittal crest, where the parietals meet on top of the cranium

occipital (or nuchal) torus pronounced ridge at the rearmost point on the occipital bone

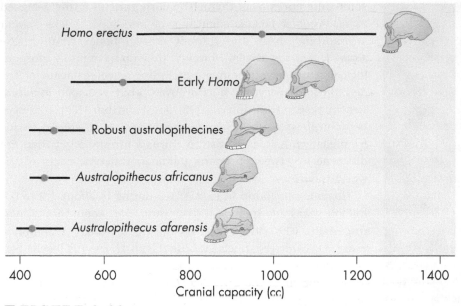

■ FIGURE 8.20

Brain size in australopithecines and early *Homo*. The dots show the average cranial capacity for each species.

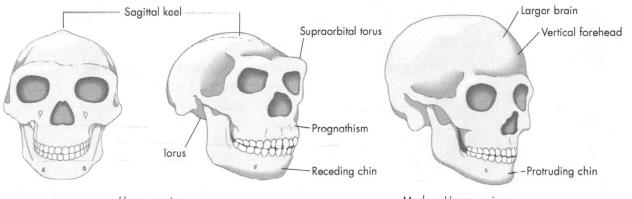

Homo erectus

Modern *Homo sapiens*

■ FIGURE 8.21

Cranial features of *Homo erectus*. Compared with modern *Homo sapiens*, *H. erectus* had a smaller brain, pronounced brow ridges, a prognathic face, and a receding chin.

Geographic Distribution of *H. erectus*

H. erectus Finds in Africa

A series of fossils found in east Africa and South Africa dating from about 1.8 to 1.6 million years ago have been attributed alternatively to the species *Homo erectus* or *Homo ergaster*. The best known of these fossils are a cranium dating to about 1.8 million years ago, assumed to be a female, and the nearly complete skeleton of a young teenage boy, known as "Turkana boy," dating to about 1.65 mya, from east Africa and standing just under 180 cm (5.9 feet) tall (Figure 8.22). These fossils suggest that there might have been more sexual dimorphism in these early African forms than in later *H. erectus*. Their overall build may have been slighter, with some retention of primitive characteristics (those found in earlier hominins), such as six lumbar vertebrae (modern humans have five and *A. africanus* had six) and a smaller canal for the passage of the spinal cord (Walker & Leakey, 1993).

The crania and postcranial material that have been assigned to *H. ergaster* exhibit some similarities with the *H. erectus* fossils of Asia and Eurasia and

STOP & THINK

In an evolutionary sense, how would moving around and out of Africa have changed *Homo erectus*?

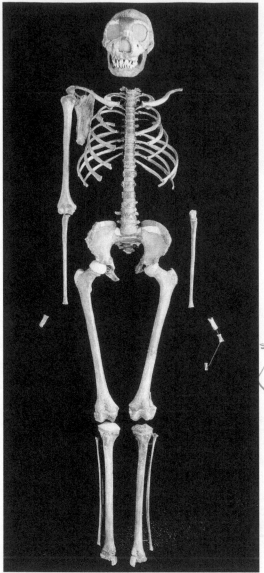

■ FIGURE 8.22

"Turkana boy," a nearly complete *H. erectus* skeleton. This individual, who lived in east Africa approximately 1.65 million years ago, was a very tall teenage male who would have been just a few inches under 6 feet in height at maturity.

shovel-shaped incisors
incisor teeth with a shovel-like grooved inner surface

some differences from them. The early African forms assigned to *H. ergaster* lack a sagittal keel and have a less robust supraorbital torus and thinner cranial bones than do the Asian *H. erectus* fossils. However, they do have many morphological features in common, including specific facets of the dental morphology, such as grooved, **shovel-shaped incisors**. Recent research (Kramer, 2002) suggests that the differences between these early African forms and other *H. erectus* fossils from eastern Asia and western Eurasia are no larger than the differences between humans living in different parts of the world today.

Homo fossils found in east Africa dating to about 1.2 to 0.6 million years ago include a few crania and some mandibular fragments. The earlier crania (dating to about 1.2 million years ago) are very much like the Javan *H. erectus* fossils (see the following section), and the later east African finds appear to be somewhat more gracile. *H. erectus* finds in north Africa include mandibles and a cranium dating to between 0.7 and about 0.25 mya.

H. erectus Finds in Asia

The first fossils attributed to *Homo erectus* were found on the island of Java, as mentioned earlier. Along with the Chinese *H. erectus* fossils, they make up the typical or "classic" description of *Homo erectus*. Dating to between about 1.8 and about 0.3 million years ago, the Java sample consists of a number of partial crania, a few complete crania, and some postcranial elements (Figure 8.23). The fossil crania display the classic *H. erectus* characteristics; thick cranial bones; a strong sagittal keel; a pronounced occipital (nuchal) torus; a strong supraorbital torus; broad, flat nasal bones; large mandibles with no protruding chin; and shovel-shaped incisors. Fossils of *H. erectus* and stone tools dating to about 0.9 to 0.8 million years ago were also found on the eastern Indonesian island of Flores (Arribas & Palmqvist, 1999). Flores is also the site of a startling recent find: a very small *erectus*-like hominin that dates to between 95,000 and 12,000 years ago! These fossils, named *Homo floresiensis* by their discoverers (Brown et al., 2004), are approximately 1 m (3 feet, 3 in.) tall with a brain of around 380 cc (23.2 cubic in.). There is much contention as to whether these fossils represent a dwarfed version of *H. erectus* or are a separate species.

Recent overviews of the cranial and postcranial fossils attributed to this species and comparisons with modern humans and *Homo* fossils strongly suggest that these diminutive hominins are closely related to early *Homo erectus* (those called *Homo ergaster*) or possibly *Homo habilis* (Gordon et al., 2008). In fact, the *H. floresiensis* fossils seem to share many characteristics with the very early *H. erectus* forms found at the site of Dmanisi in Eurasia (see the next section). A solid association between these forms, if verified, would suggest that *H. floresiensis* and the other *H. erectus* fossil found in Southeast Asia are probably representative of two distinct lineages of early humans moving out of Africa (Aiello, 2010). It would also show that modern humans (us) and representatives of *H. erectus* or non-modern human *H. erectus* descendant hominins lived concurrently in at least some parts of the world.

Is That You Frodo? Ardi?

The discoveries of *Homo floresiensis* and *Ardipithecus ramidus* show us that science works and that truth can be stranger than fiction. Both of these fossils challenged current assumptions by most scientists about what human evolution looks like. They demonstrated that many of our hypotheses (even favored ones) were not correct. New data has forced us to rethink our hypotheses and even admit that those we really liked are just wrong. Science works. At the same time, these discoveries also demonstrate that reality is often as fascinating as anything we could make up. The challenge of the *Homo floresiensis* fossils on Flores, and the possibility of *Homo erectus* at up to 25–30,000 years ago (at the same time that *Homo sapiens* are here), force us to consider that many types of humanlike organisms shared the planet up until recently. Not quite *Lord of the Rings*, but maybe closer than most researchers want to admit (how does humans, Hobbits, and Orcs at 25,000 years ago sound?). Even the form of *Ardipithecus's* arms, feet, and teeth also make us change our hypotheses about when changes occurred in the human lineage. It is now likely that much of our important early evolution took place much more in the trees than nearly anyone was willing to hypothesize (not really Tarzan, but definitely in the trees). The landscape of our past is as rich and amazing as any science fiction or fantasy book, but even better because it really happened.

Recently, some skulls assigned to *H. erectus* found at two sites on Java have been estimated to be only 27,000–53,000 years old (Swisher et al., 1996). Although there is some contention over the characteristics used to classify these skulls as *H. erectus*, there is no argument that they do display *erectus*-like morphology. If these dates are accurate (as they seem to be), then either two species of *H. erectus*-like hominins coexisted with modern humans on Java, or some populations of modern humans displayed many primitive traits up until very recently.

Many *H. erectus* fossils have been discovered in China, but the cave site of Zhoukoudian has provided the most in-depth information on this fossil hominin in east Asia. The remains of about 45 individuals, dating to between about 0.7 and 0.25 million years ago, were found at this site (Conroy, 1997). Most of the material comes from layers that date to between 0.5 and 0.25 million years ago, suggesting that *H. erectus* inhabited this cave off and on for approximately 250,000 years. All of the original material from pre-1941

■ **FIGURE 8.23**
H. erectus cranial fossils from Java. Note the sagittal keel.

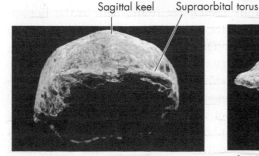

Front

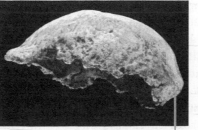

Left side

Right side

Sagittal keel   Supraorbital torus

Supraorbital torus

Nuchal torus

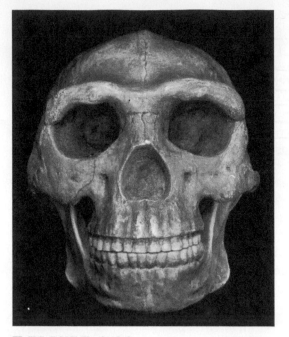
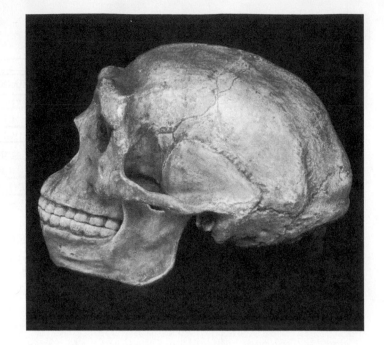

■ FIGURE 8.24

Homo erectus from Zhoukoudian. Note the prominent nuchal torus and supraorbital torus.

excavations was lost during World War II, but excellent casts and diagrams were made of that material, so it can still be used for comparative and research purposes (Figure 8.24).

In general, the material from Zhoukoudian is similar to the *H. erectus* fossils from Java, with the cranial fossils sharing many characteristics. The fossils from the Zhoukoudian site show two trends over time: an increase in incisor size and a decrease in postcanine tooth size. In addition to the rich hominin fossil record at Zhoukoudian, there are many stone tools, processed animal and plant remains, and indications of the use of fire.

At least seven other sites in China have yielded *H. erectus* fossils. The earliest are a mandible and associated teeth found at Longgupo cave, estimated to date from 1.9 to 1.7 million years ago. Crania have been found at Lantian, Hexian, and Yunxian, dating, respectively, from 1.0 to 0.7 million years ago, 0.7 to 0.2 million years ago, and about 0.3 million years ago. The Yunxian fossils are especially interesting because they are some of the most recent fossils and appear to share some specific characteristics both with *H. sapiens* and with earlier *H. erectus*.

The Indian subcontinent has yielded few clear hominin fossils from the early to mid-Pleistocene, but there are at least two sites where stone tools associated with *H. erectus* have been found. Each of these sites is reported to be about 1.8 million years old, but there is some contention over the dates.

H. erectus Finds in Central and Western Eurasia

In central Eurasia, the earliest hominin finds come from a site in the Republic of Georgia called Dmanisi and date to about 1.7 million years ago (Gabunia et al., 2001; Lordkipanidze et al., 2005). The finds consist of a mandible, a metatarsal, a number of complete and partial crania, and a collection of stone tools. The crania are very similar in morphology to the early African forms (those assigned by some to *H. ergaster*) except in aspects of the dentition and parts of the mandible; in these respects they bear more resemblance to the east Asian forms (Gabunia et al., 2001). Interestingly, at least one of the crania from Dmanisi is that of an aged individual who lived long after losing most of his/her teeth (Lordkipanidze et al., 2005).

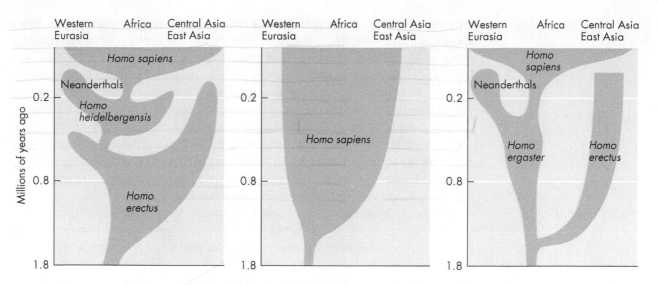

(a) Late African origin for *Homo sapiens.*

(b) Early African origin for *Homo sapiens.*

(c) Asian *H. erectus* as a dead end, *H. ergaster* giving rise to both modern humans and Neanderthals.

■ **FIGURE 8.25**

Expansion out of Africa—three hypotheses. Scenario (a) proposes a late origin in Africa, with *H. erectus* in Asia going extinct. Scenario (b) posits a single origin for the species *Homo sapiens* in Africa approximately 1.8 million years ago. Scenario (c), in contrast, proposes that *H. ergaster* and *H. erectus* were separate species, with *H. erectus* in Asia not leading to humans.

The site of Ubeidiya in Israel has produced some hominin teeth and stone tools dating to about 1.4 million years ago. Two other sites in Israel have yielded Olduwan-type stone tools reported to date to about 2 million years ago; however, these dates are under dispute.

In Spain, the site of Gran Dolina in Atapuerca has recently produced a rich fossil collection dating to between 0.8 and about 0.25 million years ago. The older levels have produced Olduwan-type tools and hominin fossils that researchers say may represent a new species, one that evolved from the early African *H. erectus* (*H. ergaster*) and gave rise to subsequent species (early *H. heidelbergensis*, also called archaic *Homo sapiens*; see chapter 9). The researchers proposed naming these fossils *Homo antecessor*, arguing that they share specific morphological features with both the early African *H. erectus* and the later African and Eurasian *H. heidelbergensis* (Bermudez de Castro et al., 1997). A few other sites in Spain and Italy, dating to between 1.0 and 0.7 million years ago, have also produced fragmentary hominin remains that can be assigned to *H. erectus* (or *H. antecessor* or *H. heidelbergensis*, depending on the lumper/splitter perspective of the researcher).

When Did Hominins Expand Beyond Africa?

After reading this brief overview of hominin fossils dating from between 2.5 and 0.3 million years ago and distributed around Africa, Asia, and Eurasia, you may be wondering which hominins moved out of Africa, when they did so, and why. Different researchers answer the first part of this question in three different ways, as shown in Figure 8.25. In Scenario A, early members of the genus *Homo* (*H. habilis* or *H. rudolfensis*) expanded throughout, and out of, Africa approximately 2 million years ago, taking their Olduwan tool technology with them. Over time, populations moved around Eurasia and Africa, gradually evolving into the morphologies we associate with *H. erectus* and then into early *H. sapiens* (*H. heidelbergensis* to some). In this scenario, the east Asian branch of *H. erectus*, and *H. floresiensis*, became relatively isolated and did not contribute significantly to the more modern forms. As we will see in chapter 9, this scenario claims that modern *H. sapiens* evolved about 200,000 years ago in Africa.

In Scenario B, the species that expanded throughout and out of Africa about 1.8 million years ago was *Homo sapiens*, giving our species a very ancient origin in Africa. These theorists claim that all the fossils found in Africa, Asia, and Eurasia dating to 1.8 million years ago or later belong to a single species, *Homo sapiens*, although splitters who take this view claim that there were variations within the species, identified as *H. erectus*, *H. heidelbergensis*, and so on. However, the presence of *H. floresiensis* makes this scenario the least likely of the three.

Scenario C suggests that *H. ergaster* evolved in Africa and subsequently gave rise to *H. antecessor* and *H. heidelbergensis* in western Eurasia. In this scenario *H. erectus* and its descendants existed exclusively in Asia and, as in Scenario A, did not contribute to the modern forms at all.

Which of these three scenarios is correct? As mentioned earlier in this chapter, researchers do not agree on how many species are represented by the fossil record between 2.5 and 0.3 million years ago. We have a diverse set of fossils from this period, exhibiting numerous similarities and differences. Some argue that the morphological differences are not great enough to justify placing the fossils in different species, and others argue that these differences, in combination with the disparate locations of the finds, are sufficient to warrant species-level distinctions. It depends on how you classify species in the fossil record and how you envision the evolution of many populations over large geographical distances.

What is certain is that by approximately 1.8 million years ago hominins had expanded from east and south Africa into new areas of Africa and Eurasia. Further, members of the genus *Homo* were doing this with Olduwan (or Olduwan-type) tools, and their brains were getting a bit larger and their postcanine teeth a bit smaller. In chapter 9 we discuss all three of these scenarios in greater depth, adding the hominin fossils from the period beginning 0.5 million years ago.

Why Did Hominins Expand Beyond Africa?

Why did members of the genus *Homo* (whatever species we call them) begin to move around so much about 2 million years ago? Previous hypotheses were based on the advent of a new type of stone tool (the Acheulean, discussed in the next section), which allowed for greater manipulation of the environment and thus movement into more areas. These tools do not show up regularly in the fossil record until about 1.5 million years ago however, and they infrequently show up at the Southeast Asian fossil sites. Others have argued that population pressure may have been a factor, but there is currently no evidence to support this claim.

We do have indications that hominins were not the only organisms to move out of Africa and around Eurasia during the early Pleistocene. Sites in central and western Europe where we find *H. erectus* fossils have yielded evidence of fauna (animal remains) from both western and eastern Eurasia and Africa. There is also strong evidence that a group of nonhuman primates, the macaques, moved into Southeast Asia at roughly the same time as *H. erectus*. It may be that global climatic and habitat changes at this time caused widespread movement by many types of mammals, of which hominins were just one group.

H. erectus Material Culture and the Expansion of the Biocultural Evolution

Although we see the advent of biocultural evolution in early *Homo*, it is in *H. erectus* that material cultures expand and begin to play an ever more important role in human evolution. Because of changing body morphologies in *H. erectus* and the new environments these hominins encountered, cultural patterns of food acquisition and social behavior were probably more complex than in earlier hominins, lending to expanded niche construction.

◄ CONNECTIONS ►

See chapter 4, pages 106–108, to consider inheritance and niche construction in the context of this section.

Moving Beyond Simple Tools: The Acheulean Tool Kit

When members of the genus *Homo* first spread from east and south Africa, they used a simple but effective mix of tool types referred to as the Oluwan tool kit, as described earlier. With these sharp flakes and stout-edged choppers they were able to process both animal and plant matter rapidly and effectively, although they probably did not use them in hunting, if in fact *H. erectus* hunted at all.

About 1.6–1.4 million years ago, a new type of stone tool begins to show up in the fossil record, first in east Africa and then throughout the rest of Africa, in western and central Eurasia, and in at least one location in east Asia. These new tools, named **Acheulean** after a site in France, were more complex and diverse than earlier Oluwan tools. The main characteristic of the Acheulean tool kit was bifacial flaking, a process that produced strong, sharp edges. The most typical tool was the bifacial "hand axe," so named not because it was hafted like a modern axe but because it was a good-sized stone flaked on both sides (Figure 8.20). The Acheulean tools were made in a variety of forms and sizes and included bifaces, flakes, and sometimes choppers similar to those of the earlier Oluwan tradition. Analyses indicate that the Acheulean tools were used to process meat and hides and possibly to modify wood and bone.

Interestingly, although the Acheulean tools show up in many (but not all) *H. erectus* sites from southern Africa to the British Islands to the Indian subcontinent, so far in eastern and Southeast Asia, they have been uncovered at only a few *H. erectus* sites (Figure 8.27). Areas where Acheulean tools are rare are set off from areas where they do appear by an imaginary line referred to as the *Movius line*.

There are a few hypotheses for why this difference exists. It may be that the members of the genus *Homo* who moved out of Africa and into Asia some 1.8 million years ago did so before the invention of Acheulean tools, and the subsequent innovations in tool types did not reach the relatively isolated Far Eastern populations. Alternatively, it may be that the Acheulean tools were an adaptation for hunting large game animals in an open environment and the prey animals in east and Southeast Asia were smaller, making the Acheulean tools unnecessary or ineffective. A third hypothesis is that *H. erectus* populations in east and Southeast Asia relied heavily on high-quality vegetable matter (like bamboo) for tools; which would leave little or nothing in the fossil record. It is highly likely that all *H. erectus* populations used biodegradable material such as wood, bamboo, and probably bone to make tools; but since there is so little evidence in the fossil record, we do not know what these tools were or how they were used.

The Controlled Use of Fire

Another biocultural innovation associated with *H. erectus* is the controlled use of fire. Near the end of *H. erectus*'s tenure as a species, we have evidence of the use of fire from sites in France, Spain, China, and Hungary, dating to between 0.5 and 0.3 million years ago. There is also some very controversial evidence of fire use from before 1 million years ago in east Africa and about 1 million years ago in south Africa, but it is not clear that hominins used

Acheulean
relating to the type of stone tool that follows the Olduwan in the archaeological record, dating to about 1.5 million years ago and consisting of bifaced tools (flaked on both sides) that are more complex to make and allow more kinds of manipulation than the earlier types

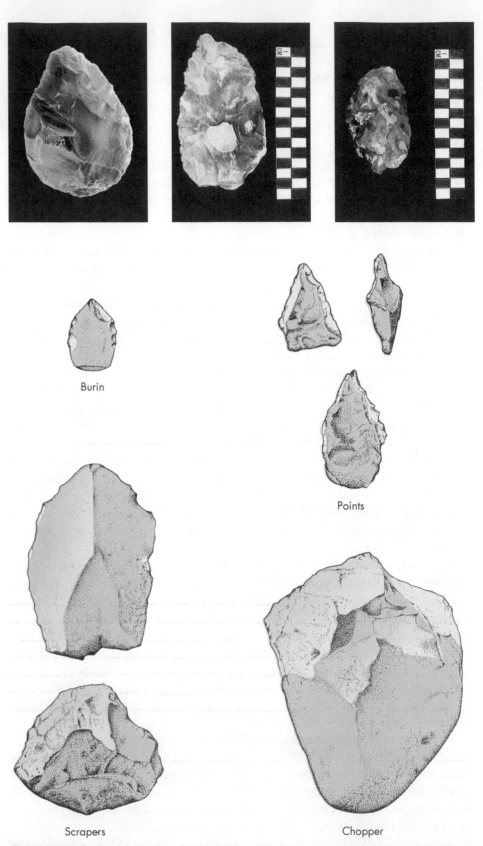

Burin

Points

Scrapers

Chopper

■ **FIGURE 8.26**

Acheulean stone tools. More complex than Olduwan tools, Acheulean tools first appeared 1.6–1.4 million years ago. They have been found at many sites, from Africa to western Europe and into central Asia. They are characterized by bifacial flaking, which produces a sharp edge. The color images represent actual "hand axes" used primarily as chopping and cutting tools. The line drawings reflect the different types of tools in the Acheulean tradition.

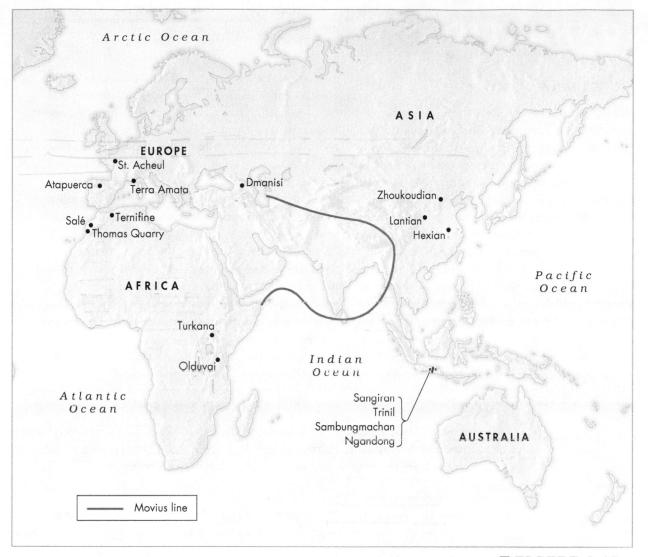

Movius line

■ FIGURE 8.27
The Movius line. The majority
of Acheulean tools have been
found southwest of the Movius
line. For the most part,
researchers have found stone
choppers but no hand axes in
eastern and Southeast Asia.

and controlled these fires. It is possible that *H. erectus* began to use fire before
0.5 million years ago, but we currently do not have firm factual support for
this conjecture. Since fire use does show up regularly in the archeological
record by about 0.5–0.3 million years ago, we can hypothesize that in at least
some locations, *H. erectus* was using fire earlier than that. Some researchers
have even suggested that it was fire and the cooking of food that set the stage
for many important social and behavioral changes in humans (Wrangham, 2009).

The Construction of Shelters

Many *H. erectus* fossils are found in caves, suggesting that these hominins
used caves for shelter. There is no direct evidence of the construction of shelters before about 0.3 million years ago or so (see chapter 9). Given the widespread distribution of *H. erectus*, some of the formidable obstacles they had
to face, and some of their other likely innovations, it is not unreasonable to
hypothesize that they may have built temporary shelters in times of cold or
wet weather. An example will testify to their resourcefulness. Until recently,
it was thought that any water barrier was secure against *H. erectus*. However,
the dates for the tools and fossil remains found on the Indonesian island of
Flores suggest otherwise. Even at the lowest sea levels between islands in
Southeast Asia, at 0.9–0.8 million years ago, *H. erectus* would have had to

What's the Deal with Fire?

Recently, some researchers have even argued that it was the control of fire and cooking that helped nudge earlier hominins on the path to humanity. While the super-early control of fire is a little farfetched (and not supported by current data), the concept of a core role for fire is correct. Anyone who thinks about it recognizes how important fire is and has been for humans. Today, we equate using fire, cooking, heat production, and light with being human. Think about what the world would be like for people if we had no access to light outside of the daytime? Think about how important food is for all humans . . . imagine the world's cuisines without cooking? Think about the protection from predators and other animals fire can provide. Think about steam engines and even electricity (made from burning coal). A huge chunk of what we consider typical for humanity is not possible without fire; the use and control of it was a major turning point in our evolutionary, especially niche constructive, history. It is very difficult to pinpoint the first control of fire. Across the savannas of Africa wildfires are common, and when a tree burns to the ground it is hard to differentiate it from a fire pit a million years later. Wildfires could have even given our ancestors access to cooked meat long before they used fire themselves. So, we know fire is core to being human, and that by at least a half million years ago, our ancestors were controlling it. But how deep in our past do humans and fire really connect, and in what ways did it change our evolutionary trajectories? These remain two of the great questions in biological anthropology.

cross at least 19 km of water to get to the island from its nearest neighboring land mass (Arribas & Palmqvist, 1999). If they could get across a small ocean strait, they could probably also build a lean-to for shelter.

A Need for Higher Quality Food Sources

Recently, researchers have made models of the changes in metabolic rates that must have occurred between earlier hominins and the early African *H. erectus* (*H. ergaster*), given the larger body and larger brain, both relatively and absolutely, of *H. erectus.* These researchers report that because of increases in size, especially in females, *H. erectus* would have had much higher energetic, or caloric, requirements—perhaps as much as 35% higher—than earlier hominins (Aiello & Wells, 2002). Larger brain and body size conferred advantages on *H. erectus*—they enhanced the ability to exploit and modify a wider range of habitats, creating new niches, increased the effectiveness of prey collection, allowed females and other group members to carry infants to an older age, and resulted in more effective thermoregulation and water utilization—and thus can be seen as adaptations. This also carried costs, namely, the higher energy requirements to "run" the larger body and brain. *H. erectus* simply had to consume more calories than earlier hominins.

The increase in energy requirements suggests that a change in dietary patterns accompanied (or arose just prior to) the appearance of *H. erectus.* Aiello and Wells (2002) hypothesize that this dietary change took the form of greater reliance on animal protein and other high-energy food resources. Their hypothesis has been supported by recent overviews of animal fossils and stone tool assemblages in east Africa from around the time that early *H. erectus* (*H. ergaster*) fossils begin to show up in the record (O'Connell, Hawkes, Lupo, & Blurton-Jones, 2002).

Supporting this hypothesis is the fact that estimated gut sizes are smaller in *H. erectus* than in earlier hominins. The same is true for modern humans:

What We Know

By approximately 2.5–2.0 million years ago, at least three lineages of hominins were represented in east and south Africa. One lineage had a huge chewing apparatus, and at least one of the others demonstrates the beginning of a significant increase in brain size.

Questions That Remain

Which of these lineages is ancestral to modern humans? Although we think it is probably one of the gracile forms (*A. garhi*, *A. sediba*, *A. africanus*, *H. habilis*, or *H. rudolfensis*), we are currently not sure of the specific relationships.

What We Know

The robust lineage (*Paranthropus*) was extinct by 1 million years ago.

Questions That Remain

We don't know if the extinction of *Paranthropus* was due to competition from members of the genus *Homo* or to an inability to adapt to changing environments.

What We Know

Olduwan stone tools were being made and used approximately 2.5 million years ago.

Questions That Remain

Although we know that later members of the genus *Homo* made and used stone tools, we are not certain which of the hominins made these earliest tools.

What We Know

The earliest evidence of genus *Homo*, found in east Africa and South Africa, dates to between 2.4 and 1.8 million years ago.

Questions That Remain

We do not yet know which, if any, of these fossils are ancestral to modern humans.

What We Know

True members of the genus *Homo* existed by at least 1.8 million years ago, spreading rapidly around Africa and Eurasia. *Homo* fossils demonstrate increased brain and body size relative to earlier hominins.

Questions That Remain

We do not know how many species of *Homo* there were between 1.8 and about 0.3 million years ago.

Our guts (digestive organs) are smaller and our brains much bigger than would be expected for a mammal of our size. Because digestion and gut tissue are relatively expensive in terms of energy expenditure, there may have been an evolutionary trade-off between gut size and brain size in *H. erectus*. In other words, as brain size increased, gut size decreased, partially offsetting the higher calorie requirements of the brain. But having a smaller gut, in addition to having smaller dental apparatus (teeth and jaws), makes it more difficult to process low-quality, easily available foods (namely, plants), giving added impetus to the shift toward meat eating.

If *H. erectus* did shift to a better quality diet of meat protein and high-quality plant material, such as roots and tubers with high caloric values, we would expect to see evidence of such a shift in the fossil record. What we do see is evidence of an increasing reliance on stone tools for food processing and evidence of an apparent ability to increase hunting and/or scavenging activities, alongside the appearance of the Acheulean tool industry. All of this evidence appears to support the hypothesis about the changing dietary patterns of *H. erectus* (O'Connell et al., 2002). It is also possible that in many areas where the Acheulean tools do not show up in the fossil record, as in much of Asia, this shift in behavior was made possible, in part, by biodegradable tools.

Social Life: Small Cooperative Social Groups

If *H. erectus* was indeed shifting to a greater reliance on hunting and on gathering high-quality plant material, the pressures for cooperative social living would have been even greater than they were for earlier hominins. As caloric requirements go up, the costs of reproduction, especially lactation (producing milk for an infant), skyrocket. Researchers estimate that the energy cost of lactation was as much as 45% greater in *H. erectus* than in earlier hominins (Aiello and Key in Aiello & Wells, 2002). If this is the case, we might see increased infant caretaking responsibilities shared among members of the social group, or at least more collaboration in hunting, scavenging, and other food-gathering activities. The toothless aged cranium from Dmanisi also suggests that cooperative assistance to the elderly may have been present in even relatively early members of the genus *Homo*. There is no real evidence indicating how large these social groups may have been, but the assumption is that they were relatively small and mobile.

In sum, members of *H. erectus* were armed with a material culture and a repertoire of behaviors that allowed them to exploit a wide array of food sources and to modify stones, wood, and other items. They had relatively large brains and large bodies. We know these early humans moved over great geographical distances and ventured into new lands, habitats, and climates. We do not, however, know how they thought, whether they spoke to one another, or how they communicated. They were the first humans, but they were not yet us.

SUMMARY

- Between 2.5 and about 1.8 million years ago, the fossil record reveals an adaptive radiation of hominins. At least three lineages emerge: the robust forms (genus *Paranthropus*), the gracile members of the genus *Australopithecus*, and the genus *Homo*, which may or may not be derived from one of the gracile *Australopithecus*.

- The robust australopithecines, genus *Paranthropus*, existed from about 2.5 to 1.0 million years ago. They are characterized by massive chewing adaptations that result in robust skulls. They were bipedal and had hands similar to human hands. Their brains were slightly larger than those of earlier hominins.

- Three kinds of gracile australopithecines occurred at the end of the Pliocene. *Australopithecus africanus*, a biped with a slightly divergent big toe, occurred in South Africa between about 3.0 and 2.4 million years ago. *Australopithecus garhi*, associated with animal bones that show evidence of modification by stone tools, is found at about 2.5 million years ago in east Africa. *Australopithecus sediba*, existing between 1.78 and 1.95 mya, is a mix of ancestral and more *Homo*-like characteristics.

- Fossils of hominins with absolutely and relatively larger brains than earlier forms are found in east Africa and South Africa between 2.4 and about 1.6 million years ago. These forms are classified as early members of the genus *Homo* and are placed in two species, *H. habilis* and *H. rudolfensis*.

- The first stone tool industry, the Olduwan, appears in the archeological record about 2.6 million years ago. Olduwan tools are simple choppers and flakes; they added substantially to their users' ability to process foods.

- Approximately 2 million years ago, members of the genus *Homo* began to move around Africa and out of Africa into Eurasia. Compared with earlier hominins, these first humans have larger brains, larger bodies, reduced sexual dimorphism, shorter arms relative to legs, longer legs relative to the body, and reduced absolute and relative postcanine tooth size.

▲ There is a great deal of contention over the number of species represented by fossils in the genus *Homo* between 1.8 and about 0.3 million years ago, but there is no debate that these fossils represent members of the genus *Homo*.

▲ It is not fully clear why humans spread around Africa and into Eurasia about 1.8 million years ago, but they were probably able to do so because of their anatomy, cognitive abilities, social cooperation, and material culture.

▲ From at least about 2 million years ago—maybe as early as about 2.5 million years ago—biocultural evolution and its subsequent extensive niche construction became a primary mechanism by which members of the genus *Homo* coped with environmental challenges.

CRITICAL THINKING

1. What evolutionary pressures could have resulted in the morphological adaptations shown by *Paranthropus*? What about for early members of the genus *Homo*? Could these two hominin lineages reflect two different ways to adapt to the same pressures?

2. Why has the general assumption been that it was *Homo* who made the Olduwan tools and not *Paranthropus*? Could both *Paranthropus* and *Homo* have used them? How would you test these hypotheses?

3. Do you think *Paranthropus* and *Homo* interacted? What sort of evidence could you use to answer this question?

4. Why did *Homo* successfully expand around and out of Africa? Why do you think *Paranthropus* became extinct?

5. Does it matter how many species of the genus *Homo* there were between 2.5 and 0.5 million years ago? Why or why not? If there are many species, what might that imply for modern humans? If we belong to the same species as *H. erectus*, what does that say about our evolutionary patterns?

RESOURCES

RELATIONSHIPS BETWEEN THE FOSSIL FORMS

Lieberman, D. E. (2001). Another face in our family tree. *Nature, 410,* 419–420. This brief essay provides an excellent overview of the current status of the fossils on the human evolutionary tree and the issues surrounding them.

Wood, B. A. (2002). Hominid revelations from Chad. *Nature, 418,* 133–135.
Like the Lieberman essay, this article offers an up-to-date summary of the current understanding of human evolution.

Wood, B., & Lonergan, N. (2008). The hominin fossil record: taxa, grades and clades. *Journal of Anatomy 212,* 354–376.

OVERVIEW OF THE GENUS *HOMO*

Wood, B., & Collard, M. (1999). The changing face of genus *Homo. Evolutionary Anthropology, 8*(6), 195–208.
This review essay summarizes the history of genus *Homo* and introduces the debate about nomenclature and the evolution of our genus.

REFERENCES

Aiello, L. C. (2010). Five years of *Homo floresrensis*. *American Journal of Physical Anthropology,* March 12, 2010.

Aiello, L. C., & Wells, J. C. K. (2002). Energetics and the evolution of the genus *Homo*. *Annual Review of Anthropology, 31,* 323–338.

Arribas, A., & Palmqvist, P. (1999). On the ecological connection between saber-tooths and hominids: Faunal dispersal events in the lower Pleistocene and a review of the evidence for the first human arrival in Europe. *Journal of Archeological Science, 26,* 571–585.

Asfaw, B., White, T., Lovejoy, O., Latimer, B., Simpson, S., & Suwa, G. (1999). *Australopithecus garhi:* A new species of early hominid from Ethiopia. *Science, 284,* 629–635.

Berger, L. R., De Ruiter; D. J., Churchill, S. E., Schmid, P., Carlson, K. L., Dirks, P. H. G. M., & Kibii, J. M. (2010). *Australopithecus sediba:* A new species of *Homo*-like Australopith from South Africa. *Science 328;* 195–204.

Bermudez de Castro, J. M., Arsuaga, J. L., Carbonell, E., Rosas, A., Martinez, I., & Mosquera, M. (1997). A hominid from the lower Pleistocene of Atapuerca, Spain: Possible ancestor to neanderthals and modern humans. *Science, 276,* 1392–1395.

Brown, P., Sutikna, T., Morwood, M. J., Soejono, R. P., Jatmiko, Wayhu Saptumo, E., et al. (2004). A new small-bodied hominin from the Late Pleistocene of Flores, Indonesia. *Nature, 431,* 1055–1061.

Conroy, G. C. (1997). *Reconstructing human origins: A modern synthesis.* New York: Norton.

de Heinzelin, J., Desmond Clark, J., White, T., Hart, W., Renne, P., WoldeGabriel, G., et al. (1999). Environment and behavior of 2.5 million year old Bouri hominids. *Science, 284,* 625–629.

Gabunia, L., Anton, S. C., Lordkipanidze, D., Vekua, A., Justus, A., & Swisher, C. C. (2001). Dmanisi and dispersal. *Evolutionary Anthropology, 10(5),* 158–170.

Kramer, A. (2002). The natural history and evolutionary fate of *Homo erectus*. In P. N. Peregrine, C. R. Ember, & M. Ember (Eds.), *Physical anthropology: Original readings in method and practice* (pp. 140–154). Englewood Cliffs, NJ: Prentice-Hall.

Leakey, L. S. B., Tobias, P. V., & Napier, J. R. (1964). A new species of the genus *Homo* from Olduvai Gorge. *Nature, 202,* 7–9.

Lieberman, D. E. (2001). Another face in our family tree. *Nature, 410,* 419–420.

Lockwood, C. A., Menter, C. G., Moggi-Cecchi, J., & Keyser, A. W., (2007). Extended male growth in a fossil hominin species. *Science 31,* 1443–1446.

Lordkipanidze, D., Vekua, A., Ferring, R., Rightmire, G. P., Agusti, J., Kiladze, G., et al. (2005). The earliest toothless hominin skull. *Nature, 434,* 717–718.

McHenry, H. M., & Coffing, K. (2000). *Australopithecus* to *Homo:* Transformations in body and mind. *Annual Review of Anthropology, 29,* 125–146.

Mercader, J., Panger, M., & Boesch, C. (2002). Excavation of a chimpanzee stone tool site in the African rainforest. *Science, 296,* 1452–1455.

O'Connell, J. F., Hawkes, K., Lupo, K. D., & BlurtonJones, N. G. (2002). Male strategies and Plio-Pleistocene archeology. *Journal of Human Evolution, 43,* 831–872.

Rightmire, G. P. (2008). *Homo* in the middle Pleistocene: Hypodigms, variation, and species recognition. *Evolutionary Anthropology 17* (1), 8–21.

Stewart, I. (1992). Real Australopithecines do eat meat. *New Scientist, 134*.

Susman, R. L. (1994). Fossil evidence for early hominid tool use. *Science, 265*, 1570–1573.

Swisher, C. C., Rink, W. J., Anton, S. C., Schwarcz, H. P., Curtis, G. H., Surpijo, A., et al. (1996). Latest *Homo erectus* of Java: Potential contemporaneity with *Homo sapiens* in Southeast Asia. *Science, 274*, 1870–1874.

Walker, A., & Leakey, R. E. (Eds.). (1993). *The Nariokotome Homo erectus skeleton*. Cambridge, MA: Harvard University Press.

Walker, A., Leakey, R. E., Harris, J. M., & Brown, F. H. (1986). 2.5 myr *Australopithecus boisei* from west of Lake Turkana, Kenya. *Nature, 322*, 517–522.

Whiten, A., Goodall, J., McGrew, W. C., Nishida, T., Reynolds, V., Sugiyama, Y., et al. (1999). Cultures in chimpanzees. *Nature, 399*, 682–685.

Wood, B. A. (1992). Origin and evolution of the genus *Homo*. *Nature, 355*, 783–790.

Wood, B. A. (2002). Hominid revelations from Chad. *Nature, 418*, 133–135.

Wood, B. A., & Collard, M. (1999). The changing face of genus *Homo*. *Evolutionary Anthropology, 8*(6), 195–208.

Wood, B. A., & Lonergan, N. (2008). The hominin fossil record: taxa, grades and clades. *Journal of Anatomy 212*, 354–376.

Wood, B. A., & Strait, D. (2004). Patterns of resource use in early *Homo* and *Paranthropus, Journal of Human Evolution 46*, 119–162.

Wrangham, R. (2009). *Catching fire: How cooking made us human*. New York: Basic Books.

CHAPTER 9

The Rise of Modern Humans

This chapter addresses the following questions:

▲ Who and what were the hominins (whom we call archaic humans) who lived between about 500,000 and 30,000 years ago?

▲ How were the archaic humans similar to and different from us?

▲ When and where do anatomically modern humans appear?

▲ When and how does modern human behavior appear?

▲ What different models are proposed for the evolution of *Homo sapiens sapiens* from earlier forms of *Homo*?

For more than a century, people have been insulting others with the epithet, "You Neanderthal!" The name conjures up images of a large, hairy, semihuman being with thick brow ridges and limited brain power. We picture the Neanderthal as a brutish caveman, an apish "throwback," carrying a club on his shoulder and dragging a female by the hair into his cave.

As with so many popular interpretations of science, this picture is highly distorted. It arose out of misconceptions surrounding the early fossil finds of this hominin. Neanderthal bones were thick, their crania relatively massive, and their tools unimpressive. As with Piltdown Man (see chapter 7), many people had preconceived notions of how their ancestors should look and act, and the thick-boned Neanderthals were not it! Compounding the issue was the discovery of modern human bones dating to nearly the same time. The fossils of these humans, called Cro-Magnon, were found with more finely constructed tools and weapons and hints of complex symbolic expression. The popular literature of the 19th and 20th centuries is rife with contrasts between the intelligent and refined Cro-Magnon humans and the brutish and slovenly Neanderthals, much in the same way that modern human groups have been compared in racist literature (Figure 9.1).

In contrast to these stereotypes, Neanderthals actually represent one of the most fascinating and complex early human cultures. They were a rugged people with complex social and material lives who lived under diverse environmental conditions and displayed remarkable adaptiveness. They had complex tool cultures and burials, and

Two images of the Neanderthal. Previous ideas about
Neanderthals pictured them as
brutish creatures (a); current
ideas picture them as robust
archaic humans (b).

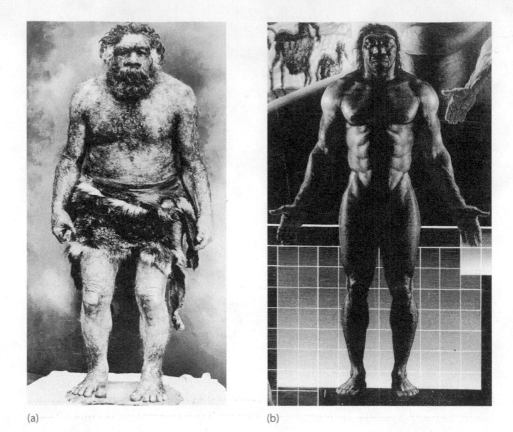

(a)   (b)

relatively complex social groups. Furthermore, they had the largest average brain size
of any hominin, ever! Since the mid-1800s, scientists and amateur fossil hunters in
Europe and other parts of western Eurasia have been recovering bones and tools left
behind by the enigmatic Neanderthals, and in our time, scientific investigations have
produced a more accurate picture of these people. The Neanderthals have even been
depicted in movies (such as *Quest for Fire*) and books (the *Clan of the Cave Bear* series)
as a people not quite like us but as an important piece in the puzzle of humanity.
Today, the Neanderthals are part of the ongoing debate about the evolutionary pathways leading to modern humans.

   We saw in the previous chapter that members of the genus *Homo* had spread
across Africa and Eurasia by at least 500,000 years ago. We also discussed the various
names assigned to the different forms. There may be as many as three species of *Homo*
between 2.0 and 0.5 million years ago: *Homo ergaster*, the early African form; *Homo
erectus*, a form that spread across Eurasia; and *Homo antecessor*, a form arising from
erectus-like ancestors in what is today Spain. It is also possible that all three are variations of one species, *H. erectus*, the variations resulting from the broad distances
between populations and the differing environments they inhabited. The debate over
the definition and number of species of the genus *Homo* in this period will continue
into the foreseeable future; in this book, we are concerned primarily with the morphological and behavioral changes that have occurred in our lineage over time. Over the
last half million years or so, a number of significant changes occurred in our lineage
that eventually left only one subspecies of one species remaining—us, *Homo sapiens
sapiens*.

   In chapter 8 we outlined the morphology of the early and middle Pleistocene members of the genus *Homo*. By the later Pleistocene (about 0.5 to
0.2 mya) changes in both morphology and material culture force us to
consider that one or more new species had emerged. The classic *H. erectus*
traits—a cranium characterized by a long and low shape with a fairly robust,
continuous projection at the front of the frontal bone (the supraorbital
torus) a sagittal keel, an occipital (or nuchal) torus, and robust mandibles

CONNECTIONS

See chapter 2, pages 50–51, for details
about the structure of the skull.

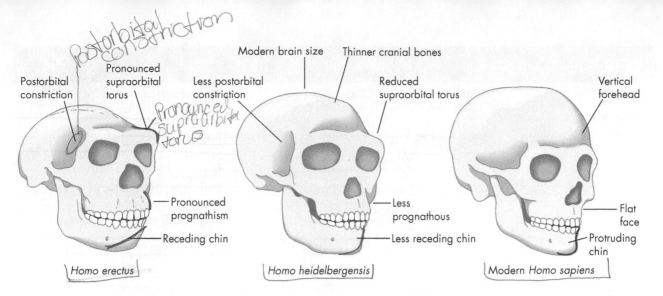

Postorbital constriction (handwritten)

Postorbital constriction

Pronounced supraorbital torus

Modern brain size

Thinner cranial bones

Less postorbital constriction

Reduced supraorbital torus

Vertical forehead

Pronounced supraorbital torus (handwritten)

Pronounced prognathism

Receding chin

Less prognathous

Less receding chin

Flat face

Protruding chin

Homo erectus

Homo heidelbergensis

Modern Homo sapiens

■ FIGURE 9.2
Cranial features of *Homo erectus*, *Homo heidelbergensis*, and *Homo sapiens*.

with receding chin—began to change as robustness decreased and cranial capacity increased. The forms that exhibited these changing morphologies, found throughout parts of Africa and Eurasia, are frequently called either archaic *Homo sapiens* or *Homo heidelbergensis* (Figure 9.2). Regardless of their name, they are almost—but not quite—us (Conroy, 1997).

Throughout the terminal Pleistocene (200,000–25,000 years ago), most fossils of the genus *Homo* displayed further changes in morphology, resulting in a high, rounded cranium, relatively gracile skeletal structure, and the appearance of a chin. These anatomical changes denote the appearance of modern humans and are accompanied by dramatic and substantial changes in the material culture and behavior of the genus *Homo*. As with all of human history, debate and contention continue over how many species are represented even in this very recent past. It remains possible that as recently as 28,000–12,000 years ago, there were at least two, if not more, species or subspecies of humans on the planet. There is no debate that today only one human species remains. In this chapter we review the fossil record of archaic and modern humans, and we discuss the differing interpretations of that record in an attempt to explain why, when, and where we became fully human.

Archaic *Homo sapiens* and the changing speed of innovation

Fossils of the genus *Homo* found in Africa and Eurasia dating from about 500,000 to 100,000 years ago exhibit morphological changes from the characteristic patterns of *Homo erectus*. These changes include slightly thinner cranial bones; reduced **postorbital constriction** (less indention of the parietal bones behind the orbits—see Figure 9.2); smaller and separated supraorbital tori; a larger and slightly higher cranial vault; a less prognathic face and reduced supraorbital torus; and increased size of the occipital relative to the nuchal plane at the back of the skull. Depending on the dates, their locations, and certain morphological characteristics, these fossils are called archaic *Homo sapiens*, *Homo heidelbergensis*, or *Homo neanderthalensis*. Here we refer to these fossils as **archaic humans** (see Table 9.1). Before looking at the naming quandaries, let's consider the temporal and geographic setting of the fossils.

The Oldest Archaic Human Fossils Are Found in Africa

The oldest probable archaic human specimen from Africa is the Bodo cranium discovered in 1976 in Ethiopia (Figure 9.3). This cranium has been dated to approximately 600,000 years ago and was found in association with a number

postorbital constriction
condition in which the width across the orbits is greater than the width of the area behind them (where the frontal, temporal, and parietal bones intersect)

archaic humans
those fossil hominins in the genus *Homo* found in Africa and Eurasia between about 600,000 and 30,000 years ago that reflect morphologies relatively distinct from both *Homo erectus* and modern humans; referred to as *Homo heidelbergensis* and *Homo neanderthalensis* by some

TABLE 9.1 Archaic and Modern *Homo sapiens*

Species	Location	Date	Characteristics
Archaic forms			
Homo heidelbergensis	Africa, Europe, Asia?	600,000–200,000 years ago	Robust, thick cranial walls, separated supraorbital tori Brain >1000 cc (>61 cubic in.)
Homo neanderthalensis	Europe, Middle East	300,000–27,000 years ago	Brain avg. 1400 cc (85.4 cubic in.) Midface prognathism Retromolar gap Very large incisors
Modern form			
Homo sapiens	Global	~95,000–present	Brain avg. 1350 cc (82.4 cubic in.) Canine fossa MQ 0.9 High, rounded cranium Chin, no retromolar gap

of Acheulean-style tools. The cranium is robust and the cranial walls are quite thick, but the supraorbital tori are well separated and the cranial capacity is large—1300 cc (79.3 cubic in.)—much larger than the norm for *Homo erectus*. Interestingly, there is evidence of intentional defleshing of the cranium after death (White, 1986), a topic we discuss later in this chapter.

Another well-known cranium is the Kabwe, or Broken Hill, cranium (see Figure 9.3). This skull has been dated to between 300,000 and 130,000 years ago (Conroy, 1997; Stringer; 2002) and was found with a few postcranial bones and a number of stone tools that are more advanced than the Acheulean types found with the Bodo cranium. The Kabwe fossil has a cranial capacity of about 1100 cc (67 cubic in.), large supraorbital tori, and frontal and parietal bones that are more similar to those of some *Homo erectus* than to those of later humans.

■ **FIGURE 9.3**
Two archaic human crania. Note the differences in robustness. The Bodo cranium dates to approximately 600,000 years ago; the Kabwe cranium dates to approximately 300,000–130,000 years ago.

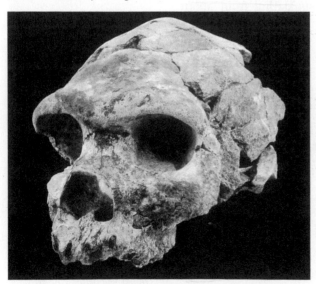

Bodo

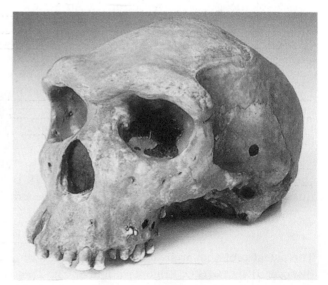

Kabwe

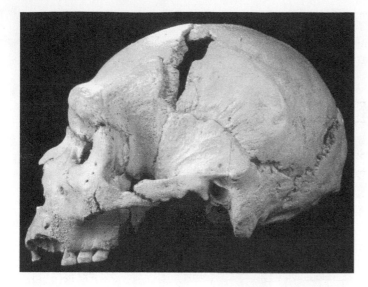

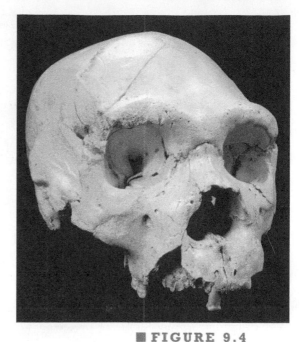

Specimen from Sima de los Huesos, Spain. This site dates to between 300,000 and 200,000 years ago. Crania found at this site show a mixture of traits characteristic of both *Homo erectus* and archaic humans.

A third specimen, the Lake Ndutu skull, dates from about 400,000 to 200,000 years ago and was found in Olduvai Gorge in Tanzania. Although this cranium has a number of typical *H. erectus*-like characteristics, it also has parietal bones shaped more like those of *Homo sapiens*, no sagittal keel, and a cranial capacity of 1100 cc. It was found with slightly more advanced stone tool types. These crania appear to affiliate more closely with *H. erectus* than later archaic humans, but many factors indicate their trajectory of change toward physical traits similar to those found in later *Homo* species (Rightmire, 2008).

There are several finds dating from about 110,000 years ago in north Africa and the Middle East that are frequently called Neanderthals. We discuss these finds in a later section because they appear to be a separate cluster from these earlier African archaic forms.

Archaic Human Fossils Are Found Across Eurasia

The oldest archaic human sites in Eurasia are found in southern and eastern Europe. At the well-known Spanish site of Atapuerca, in a location called Sima de los Huesos ("pit of bones"), one of the richest archaic human finds reveals a great deal about variation in early populations (Arsuaga, Bermudez de Castro, & Carbonell, 1997). At least 32 individuals are represented in a sample that includes more than 1000 fragments, with three crania all dated to approximately 300,000 to 200,000 years ago. The crania are characterized by substantial variation, with some characteristics typical of *H. erectus*, some typical of later archaic humans (Neanderthals, discussed later in the chapter), and others more typical of modern humans (Figure 9.4). The cranial capacities range from 1125 to 1390 cc (~69–85 cubic in.), the midfaces project forward, and the supraorbital tori are large, separated, and well rounded. It is argued that these Sima de los Huesos finds are humans descended from the earlier Atapuerca finds called *Homo antecessor* (described in chapter 8) and that they are ancestral either to later Neanderthals, to modern humans, or to both (Arsuaga et al., 1997; Bermudez de Castro et al., 1997).

Other early archaic humans have been found in modern-day Germany, Hungary, and Greece (Figure 9.5). For example, the Mauer mandible from Germany, dating to between 700,000 and 400,000 years ago, exhibits a mix

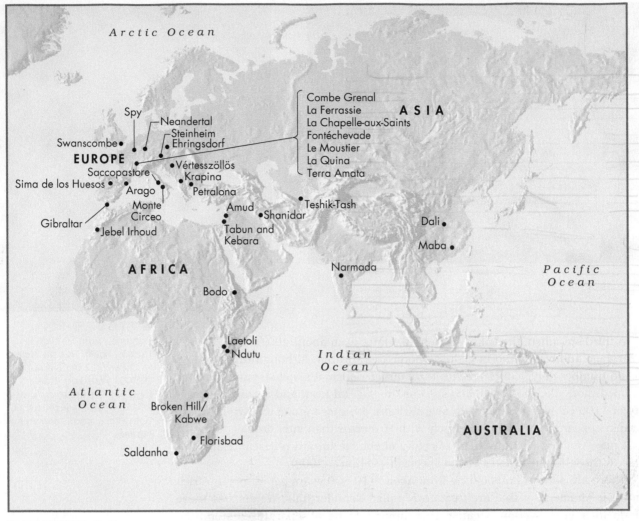

■ FIGURE 9.5
Archaic human sites. Fossils of archaic humans have been found throughout Africa, Europe, and Asia.

of *Homo erectus*- and *Homo sapiens*-like characteristics. The site of Vértesszöllös in Hungary has produced fossils representing at least two hominins dating to about 200,000 or more years ago. At least one of the two has a large cranial capacity (about 1300 cc, or 79.3 cubic in.) and relatively thin cranial bones, but other facets of the fossils have similarities with *H. erectus*, and the tools associated with the find reflect a very old and simple tool kit. The Greek site of Petralona yielded a complete cranium dating to between 400,000 and 200,000 years ago and also displaying a mix of *erectus*-like and *sapiens*-like characteristics (Figure 9.6). The cranial capacity is more than 1200 cc (~73 cubic in.), but the rear of the skull (the occiput) and the thickness of the skull are more *erectus*-like. However, the face is very pneumatized (it has large, air-filled sinuses) and thus may share a relationship with the later European and Middle Eastern archaic humans (Neanderthals). There are also fossils from England, France, and other parts of Germany, all dating to between 500,000 and 200,000 years ago, that follow these same trends of having a mix of characteristics and possible associations with Neanderthals or later human forms. Currently, many researchers assign these fossils to the species *Homo heidelbergensis* (Rightmire, 2008).

Archaic Humans Are Found in China but Not in Southeast Asia

Several fossil finds in China dating to between 300,000 and 150,000 years ago display the same kind of mixed trait assemblages that have been found

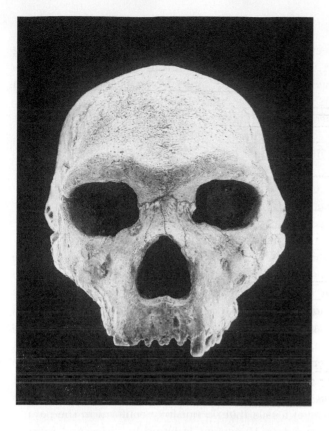

FIGURE 9.6
The Petralona cranium. Dating to 400,000 to 200,000 years ago, this cranium also displays a mixture of *H. erectus* and archaic human traits.

in Africa and western Eurasia. For example, the Dali cranium, dating to between 300,000 and 200,000 years ago, has a cranial capacity of 1120 cc (~68 cubic in.) and exhibits a mix of *erectus*-like and *sapiens*-like morphology (Conroy, 1997). The site of Jinniu Shan produced a large-brained fossil cranium with a capacity of more than 1300 cc that is dated to more than 200,000 years ago, suggesting that archaic humans and *Homo erectus* may have overlapped temporally in China (given the dates for some of the Zhoukoudian specimens, discussed in chapter 8).

The Maba cranium, dating to about 150,000 years ago, is especially interesting because it exhibits specific characteristics (the shape of the orbits and supraorbital tori) that appear to link it with the later archaic humans in western Eurasia (the Neanderthals). Finds in Siberia suggest that archaic humans may have made it into very northern areas of Asia earlier than previously thought; possible stone tools—but no fossils—have been found there and dated to about 300,000 years ago. If these are tools, it is assumed that they represent archaic humans because there is no evidence that *H. erectus* ever moved into extreme northern climates.

Although modern *Homo sapiens* fossils are found in Southeast Asia and Australia dating from at least 50,000 years ago, there are no currently accepted, clearly archaic human fossils from the region. In chapter 8 we noted the possible dating of *H. erectus*-like material found in Java to as late as 30,000 to 27,000 years ago and the existence of *H. floresiensis* until about 12,000 years ago in the same region. It is possible that archaic humans did not enter Southeast Asia and that *H. erectus* and *H. floresiensis* lingered as outliers in human evolution in that region until the appearance of modern humans. This is the subject of a contentious debate, one that we examine later in this chapter.

Archaic humans = Neanderthals

Is *Homo heidelbergensis* a True Species?

The number of named species in the genus *Homo* identified as existing during the Pleistocene (the last 1.8 million years) ranges from one to eight, depending on the researcher. However, fossils of the genus *Homo* dating from between about 0.5 and 0.2 million years ago are increasingly being called *Homo heidelbergensis*, as many researchers see this as a viable taxon representing most if not all of those archaic humans (Rightmire, 2008; Stringer, 2003). The name was first assigned to the Mauer mandible by its discoverer, a professor at the University of Heidelberg. Subsequent assignments of fossils to this taxon were based on the fact that they seem to link *H. erectus* and *H. sapiens* but are not easily placed in either one. They are seen as a transitional form that has a specific evolutionary pattern and thus is a valid species.

CONNECTIONS

See the "lumper-splitter" discussion in chapter 8, pages 239–240.

Some researchers (see Stringer, 2002 and Rightmire, 2008 for overviews) see *H. heidelbergensis* as ancestral to modern humans and to the Neanderthals. Others refer to it as archaic *Homo sapiens* (see Conroy, 1997) because it appears to be transitioning into a *sapiens*-like morphology with a relatively large cranial capacity (and therefore brain size). In this case, the definition of *H. sapiens* allows for substantial variation in form. Finally, other researchers suggest that the older Atapuerca material, called *H. antecessor*, is ancestral to modern humans and *H. heidelbergensis*, which then gave rise to the Neanderthals but not to modern *H. sapiens* (Bermudez de Castro et al., 1997). Regardless of classification, a clear cluster of fossils that do not fully conform to the parameters of either *H. erectus* or modern *H. sapiens* is found in Africa and Eurasia from at least 500,000 to less than 200,000 years ago. These fossils display an evolving morphology that includes increased brain size (entering modern ranges) and decreased cranial bone thickness and overall robustness over time.

A substantial part of this classification argument has to do with individual researchers' perspectives on the pattern of evolution leading to modern humans. Specifically, many classification questions rest on whether the Neanderthals are a separate species or simply another archaic human form in the modern human line. As we see later in this chapter, there is substantial debate about the way in which modern human anatomy evolved and what that implies about the human lineage during the Pleistocene.

■ FIGURE 9.7

Neanderthal fossils. Note the skeletal robustness, the heavy brow ridges, and the large brain cases.

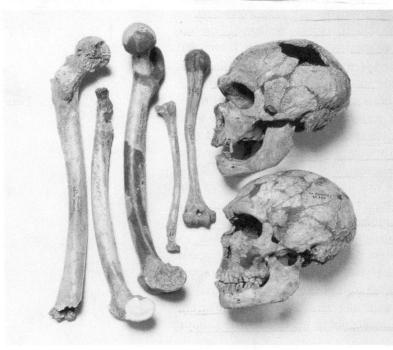

The Neanderthals Were Not as Different as First Thought, but They Were Different

Probably no other aspect of human evolution has generated as much public interest for so long a time as the fossils of the genus *Homo* that occur in many parts of Europe and the Middle East dating from about 300,000 to 27,000 years ago (Figure 9.7). These fossils are characterized by mean cranial capacities of greater than 1400 cc (85.4 cubic in.—larger than the average for modern humans), large midfaces

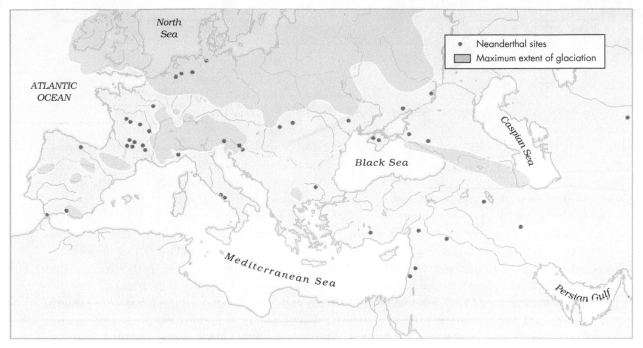

■ **FIGURE 9.8**
Distribution of Neanderthal
fossils and maximum extent of
glaciation. Neanderthals were
well adapted to live in the cold
climates of Europe at the end
of the Pleistocene.

and noses that project forward (midface prognathism), a large gap behind the
third molar (a **retromolar gap**), large protruding occipital bones, and marked
neck muscle attachments on the skull (called a suprainic fossa). The incisor
teeth are very large, and there is a weak or receding chin.

The Neanderthals were well within the range of modern human height and
weight, just a bit stockier (see Figure 9.1). Most researchers have hypothesized
that most of these morphological characteristics are adaptations to cold
weather and harsh climates. However, recently it was suggested that this body
type was the result of adaptation for high mobility and close-contact hunting
of large game (Finlayson, 2004). Some of these conjectures are supported by
the geographic range of these fossils and the pattern of glaciation at the end
of the Pleistocene (Figure 9.8). It is also clear that these archaic humans, or
near-humans, led harsh lives. Many of the fossils exhibit broken bones and
substantial wear and tear that did not result in immediate death.

As we saw at the opening of this chapter, amateur and professional
researchers have been uncovering Neanderthal fossils and interpreting them
in various ways for 150 years. We have more material remains and evidence
of behavioral patterns for these fossils than any temporal or geographic cluster before them. Today, researchers are divided on whether these fossils represent a separate species, *Homo neanderthalensis*, or a subspecies or population
of *Homo sapiens* (an archaic *Homo sapiens* form). These arguments rest on
one's view of the pattern of human evolution.

What evidence is there about relationships between the Neanderthals and
other *Homo sapiens* fossils? First, there is relatively strong evidence that fossils fitting into the Neanderthal morphology and fossils that fit into modern
human morphology overlapped in time, for 10,000 years or more, in the Middle East and Mediterranean Europe. Some sites in Europe and the Middle
East have yielded evidence of Neanderthals using modern humanlike tool kits
and modern humans using Neanderthal-like tool kits. There is also strong
evidence that as modern human forms began to show up in western Europe,
the Neanderthal-like groups disappeared.

retromolar gap
space behind the last molar
tooth and the mandibular
ramus

STOP & THINK

If the Neanderthals had,
on average, larger brains
than we do, what might
that say about absolute
brain size and brain
function?

I'm No Neanderthal!

The recent work comparing human, Neanderthal, and chimpanzee DNA tells us a lot and very little at the same time. Humans and chimpanzees share 98% of their DNA which tells us about our relative close placement as branches on the tree of life, but this does not necessarily mean we have the same behavior or appearance (no one has any trouble telling a chimpanzee and a human apart on either of those factors). The comparisons between human and fossil Neanderthal DNA might tell us a bit more about humans, past and present. Someone might have trouble telling apart a Neanderthal and a modern human if the two were strolling down the street and recent DNA suggests that Neanderthals were different enough from modern humans to possibly be a different subspecies. However, the sequencing of the Neanderthal genome also lets us know that humans and Neanderthals interbred, at least in a limited fashion, when they co-existed in Europe between 30–45,000 years ago. This is interesting and informative in two ways. First, it reemphasizes that all humans alive today are the same subspecies, and are extremely similar to one another (see chapter 10). And it also tells us that, up until recently in evolutionary time, different types of humans have shared the planet (remember *Homo floresiensis* and late *H. erectus* as well). But, we have to be careful with the Neanderthal DNA—it is very old and very limited, and the work with human and chimpanzee DNA tells us that we have to be careful about assuming what similarities and differences in DNA actually mean. As greater details emerge from the Neanderthal genome we may have an even better picture of how different types of humans co-existed.

Finally, two recent, contradictory pieces of information further confound the debate. One is the fossil of a young child, dated to about 25,000 years ago, that, according to some, displays characteristics of both Neanderthals and modern humans (Duarte et al., 1999). It is argued that this fossil is evidence of mating between Neanderthals and modern humans, suggesting that they are not two species but rather two distinct populations (or sub-species). On the other hand, reports indicate that the mitochondrial DNA (mtDNA) extracted from a Neanderthal is quite different from modern human mtDNA. One 379-base-pair mtDNA sequence was found to have 27 differences (substitutions) with modern humans. In the same mtDNA sequence, there are about 8 mtDNA differences among modern human groups and about 55 between humans and chimpanzees (Krings et al., 1997). Subsequent retesting from a second, larger sample, consisting of about 600 base pairs, supported the initial results (Krings et al., 2000), as did testing from another Neanderthal (Ovchinnikov et al., 2000). One conclusion is that humans and Neanderthals may have had a common ancestor about 700,000 or more years ago. Recent analyses of recovered Neanderthal genomic DNA and human and chimpanzee DNA suggest a human and Neanderthal ancestral population split around 370,000 years ago (Noonan et al., 2006). In 2010 Green et al., published a draft sequence of the Neanderthal genome. The preliminary results from this study suggest that humans and Neanderthals had some interbreeding and that humans appear to differ from Neanderthals in areas of the genome involved in metabolic, cognitive, and skeletal development (Green et al., 2010). Interestingly, the Neanderthal genome appears to share more alleles with Eurasion human populations than with sub-Saharan African ones. This suggests that the gene flow between humans and Neanderthals occurred in Europe/Central Asia prior to ~30,000 years ago.

Material culture of the archaic humans

Much of what we know about the material culture and behavior of members of the genus *Homo* between 500,000 and 200,000 years ago comes from a few finds in Africa and Europe. Some information comes from stone tool assemblages in Asia, but that information is limited. Actually, many of our assumptions about the material culture and behavior of these forms comes from Neanderthal sites from between 300,000 and about 25,000 years ago. In this section we discuss what we know about both the earlier archaic humans, *Homo heidelbergensis*, and the later archaic humans, *Homo neanderthalensis*, before turning to the dramatic changes that occur after modern humans show up on the scene.

Increased Complexity in Tool Use and Hunting

Acheulean and even more basic tool kits remained in use into relatively recent times, but by 400,000 to 250,000 years ago, some archaic populations were demonstrating new and more complex tool-making abilities. We know that as early as 400,000 years ago, archaic humans were using wood spears 2 meters long and hunting large game in an organized fashion at a site in present-day Germany (Dennell, 1997). There are also hints that wooden spears were used in eastern Africa at an even earlier date. It appears possible that archaic humans organized group hunts and ran large game animals over cliffs at Atapuerca, Spain. Almost certainly by this time, archaics were using and controlling fire, if not producing it themselves. There is also evidence from sites in western and eastern Europe, and in east Africa, that shelters of wood and possibly hide were built at some times of the year (Figure 9.9). *400,000 to 250,000*

Starting in Africa and spreading to parts of Eurasia by 200,000 years ago, a new tool-making technique supplanted the Acheulean and other, simpler tool kits. This new method, called the **Levallois technique**, involves more complex preparation of the stone to make the tool and provides a higher quality tool that can be refined for a wide variety of uses (Figure 9.10). In many Neanderthal

CONNECTIONS

See older tool types in chapter 8, page 236 for comparison

Levallois technique
type of stone tool production that supplanted the Acheulean tool kit and provided a higher quality tool that could be refined for a wide variety of uses

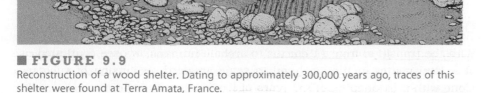

■ **FIGURE 9.9**
Reconstruction of a wood shelter. Dating to approximately 300,000 years ago, traces of this shelter were found at Terra Amata, France.

■ FIGURE 9.10

The Levallois technique. Produce a margin along the edge of the core (a); shape the surface of the core (b); prepare the striking platform (the surface to be struck) (c, d); remove the flake (e). The lower photo shows a replica of a Levallois core and tool.

Side views   **Top views**

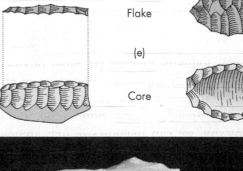

(a)   (b)

(c)

(d)

Flake

(e)

Core

many Neanderthal

sites, we see a further refinement of stone tool making, centered on a disk-core technique, called the **Mousterian industry** (Figure 9.11). This technique, an enhancement of previous patterns, allowed the tool makers to produce many good flakes with little effort and then turn those flakes into a wide variety of fine tools. There are at least 60 known types of Mousterian tools. This increase in the type of tools and in their size range meant that tools could be used for a broader array of activities, opening new opportunities for the Neanderthals.

Mousterian industry
stone tool technology centered on a disk-core technique that represented a refinement of the Levallois technique; it allowed tool makers to produce many good flakes and turn them into a wide variety of tools

Dietary and Behavior Changes Associated with New Tool Kits

With the transition from *H. erectus* to archaic humans, we see continued use of animal matter in the diet, and in some areas an expansion of such use, along with a broadening of the types of foods eaten and the methods used to

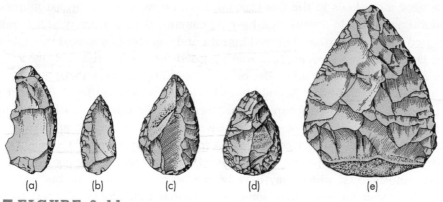

FIGURE 9.11
Mousterian tools. Scrapers (a, c); points (b, d); hand axe (e).

acquire them. The use of wooden spears by at least 400,000 years ago indicates that archaic humans were able to take fairly large game and hunt in coordinated groups. Although it is assumed that late *H. erectus* was capable of some large game hunting (maybe as *H. antecessor,* as described in chapter 8), archaic humans were doing so regularly by 500,000 to 400,000 years ago, as shown by spears associated with assemblages of bones from deer, bison, elephants, and other large mammals. The Levallois technique allowed for the production of a wide range of flake tools, and the Neanderthal-associated Mousterian industry allowed for rapid production of high-quality flakes and other tools, greatly expanding the usability of stone tools in general. Having more tools allowed archaic humans to apply them to more uses, such as enhanced scraping, piercing, puncturing, and gauging. As tool kits increased in complexity, we can hypothesize that archaic humans were able to exploit plant materials with increasing effectiveness and more readily manipulate animal hides and bones to serve a variety of ends.

Tool kits from different sites and geographic locations are different, even when the same general techniques were used. These differences hint at regional cultural variation, with different groups of archaic humans developing their own patterns of tool making, partly as a function of the types of materials available.

We know that Neanderthals exploited a wide range of diets, including shellfish, fish, and even dolphins, in coastal areas (Stringer et al., 2008).

Social Patterns: High Levels of Communal Cooperation

We know that the earliest archaic humans, *H. heidelbergensis,* lived in groups (possibly large groups, as evidenced by the Sima de los Huesos site), but we do not have much information about their communal lives. There is evidence for cooperative hunting and complex tool production, which require coordination and communication, but there are no clear signs of how they thought or whether they used spoken language to communicate.

For the later archaic humans, the Neanderthals, we also have evidence that they lived and worked together in communities. We have further evidence that they may have provided assistance for injured or aged individuals, that they buried some of their dead, and that they may have had items of personal or group adornment. The high number of healed injuries in the Neanderthal fossils has led some researchers to suggest that communal care for the injured was common. The appearance of relatively aged individuals in the fossil record has also been interpreted as suggesting care for the aged and infirm. However, some researchers argue against these interpretations, pointing out that there are only

STOP & THINK

Exploitation of marine animals and plants seems to show up with later Neanderthals and modern humans but not before. Why might that be?

STOP & **THINK**

Is it possible that advanced cooperation was more important to human evolution than stone tools?

a few aged individuals in the fossil record and that we also see healed injuries in nonhuman primate species that have no communal care. Currently, it is not contested that Neanderthals suffered injuries and sometimes survived them, but there is debate over whether care was provided for the injured and aged. As more sites are excavated, a broader data set may help address these issues.

There is little doubt that Neanderthals buried their dead, at least in western Eurasia and the Mediterranean region. More than 35 burial sites have been discovered, where evidence suggests that Neanderthals excavated an area and placed the body of a deceased individual in a hole. In some of these graves the dead are placed in specific positions, and some contain "grave goods," such as tools and flowers, which may have been placed on or near the bodies.

Evidence also suggests that some Neanderthal individuals adorned their bodies with shells or other nonfunctional items. However, it is far from certain how common this practice was, since there are only a few examples in the archaic human fossil record.

Postmortem Modification of Bodies

Some archaic human fossils, from the Bodo cranium in Africa, to more recent fossils in China and elsewhere across Eurasia, show evidence of defleshing, or removal of the flesh, especially from the skull, after death. Although initial interpretations usually focused on cannibalism, it is also possible that other forms of postmortem practices were at play (Walker, 2001). Some occurrences may be related to various forms of mortuary practice, which in turn suggest some kind of cognizance of death and the possibility of belief systems incorporating an "afterlife." Both the Neanderthal burials and the interesting cases of defleshing offer tantalizing suggestions of cultural patterns and beliefs, but there is far too little evidence for any viable hypotheses to be proposed about their belief systems and cultural patterns (Figure 9.12)

Why Did the Neanderthals Disappear?

We now know that the Neanderthals used both terrestrial and marine resources, engaged in some scheduling or seasonal shifting in resource use, overlapped in living areas, and occasionally interbred with modern humans. If the Neanderthals had complex tool use, advanced hunting skills, and complex material and social culture, then why did they disappear as modern humans spread around Europe and the Mediterranean? What separated "us" from "them" (Shipman 2008)?

It is possible that increased evolutionary success from extensive cooperation may have played a role in the differential success of *Homo sapiens* and Neanderthals as they co-existed between 50,000 and 28,000 years ago in Europe and Southwest Asia. Traditionally researchers have suggested that *Homo sapiens* and Neanderthals directly competed over food, water, raw materials, living areas, and passage routes and that humans won out, but there is little evidence for such direct competition. Recently a group of researchers (Horan et al., 2005) argued that the differences in overall success between *Homo sapiens* and Neanderthals was due to scramble competition (see chapter 5) where modern *Homo sapiens* outcompeted Neanderthals at "being human." They suggest that modern humans were less adapted to the cold north than were the Neanderthals, that both were adept at hunting large animals, that there is little evidence of direct conflict between the two species, and that Neanderthal tools might have been less expansive and innovative than those of *Homo sapiens* but were fully functional and quite suited for

■ FIGURE 9.12
Neanderthal burial. The act of burial might indicate increased social and intellectual complexity relative to earlier human forms.

their needs. If these assumptions all hold true, why did the Neanderthals go extinct? One suggestion is that trade, exchange, and long-distance social networks played an important role. Neanderthals might have exchanged goods, resources, and ideas across groups in local areas, but the potential volume of this exchange as shown in the archaeological record is miniscule as compared to that seen for modern humans (Horan et al., 2005). While some Neanderthal material culture might have traveled over 150 km, the bulk of it was confined to 20 km between its source and the place of its use (Milsauskas, 2002). Modern *Homo sapiens* groups at about the same time show exchange of commodities over 200 km. Shell and stone materials were exchanged over distances of 1,000 km in the Ukraine, Northern Europe, and Africa (Oka and Kusimba, in press; Sofer, 1985).

These trading networks could have been established and negotiated during seasonal events where disparate modern human groups got together, with the exchange of materials cementing social relationships or by individuals or small groups traveling between larger groups, facilitating exchange for economic reasons. This mobilization of resources from a wider area, a broader spectrum of resources, new technologies, and the exchange of peoples themselves may have benefitted to modern humans over the Neanderthals. The interchange of resources and social ideas would create an interdependency of peoples and have dramatic impacts on the surrounding ecologies or at least humans' abilities to deal with environmental challenges. The continual movement of ideas, genes, and materials across Africa and Eurasia between modern *Homo sapiens* groups would lead to increased success for humans even as Neanderthals and other hominins became increasingly isolated (Ofek, 2001) (remember *Homo floresiensis* and the *Homo erectus* fossil at 25,000 years ago in Southeast Asia, from chapter 8). Under this model, Neanderthals could have engaged in some successful local-level niche construction, but the more far-reaching and substantial biocultural patterns and niche construction by modern humans simply outcompeted them during tough environmental circumstances. This leads us into the discussion of when, where, and why modern humans came to be.

The appearance of "anatomically modern" *Homo sapiens*

As the Pleistocene epoch entered its terminal phase, humans became more and more modern in appearance. The trends that became evident in archaic humans nearly 500,000 years ago continued, including the changing shape of the skull, the thinning of the cranial walls, and the overall reduction in robustness relative to *H. erectus*. Brain size, as measured by cranial capacity, remained roughly the same as it had been from about 200,000 years ago, but the shape of the cranium changed significantly. The oldest fossil representatives of anatomically modern humans come from Africa and the Middle East, followed by similar fossils throughout Eurasia, Australia, and finally the Americas—the first appearance of any hominin in the Western Hemisphere. In this section we review the fossil record of our most recent ancestors and examine modern behavioral patterns, which lagged behind modern anatomy.

Anatomically Modern Humans Are Defined Morphologically, Not Behaviorally

The difficulty in pinpointing an exact dividing line between "anatomically modern" humans and archaic humans should not be surprising if you recall our discussion of evolutionary theory and patterns. Just as there is no missing link, there is no miraculous moment when modern humans suddenly appeared on the African savanna. There are, however, specific and marked changes in the cranium that arise relatively quickly in the fossil record and that serve to distinguish "moderns" from "archaics." These physical characteristics, rather than any particular behaviors, define this development in the human lineage.

Anatomically modern humans (*Homo sapiens sapiens*) have a high, rounded cranium, with the widest point on the sides of the parietals above the midpoint of the skull. The cranium has a tall, almost vertical frontal bone; small to minimal supraorbital tori; a highly flexed cranial base (with a small angle); and a face that is largely pulled in under the cranium, nearly flush with the frontal bone (see Figure 9.2). The mean cranial capacity is about 1350 cc (82.4 cubic in.) but ranges from 1000 to 2000 cc (and all within that range are fully normal in functioning).

The teeth are the smallest of any of the hominins relative to body size, with a megadontia quotient of only about 0.9, and there is a distinct **canine fossa** (the indentation in the maxilla where the root of the canine tooth causes a bulge). Unlike the late archaics or Neanderthals, anatomically modern humans

CONNECTIONS

See chapters 7, pages 202–206, and 8, pages 219–225, for cranial capacities in earlier hominins.

canine fossa
the indentation on the maxilla above the canine root

have no retromolar gap; rather, the third molar is almost running out of room at the back of the mandible.

Finally, there is a protruding chin. The bony protrusion at the **mandibular symphysis** (where the two halves of the mandible join) results from the collision between the changing shape of the cranium and face and the pressures and physical forces exerted by the chewing muscles. The chin is a uniquely modern human characteristic (see Figure 9.2). All of the features of anatomically modern humans described in this section are characteristics that human beings today—you and I—possess.

mandibular symphysis
the point where the two halves of the mandible contact one another

The Earliest Anatomically Modern Fossils Are Found in Africa

The oldest fossils classified as modern humans are found at the site of Herto Bouri in Ethiopia in eastern Africa (near the place where the much older hominin *Australopithecus garhi* was discovered) and at the site of Tu Kibish formation, also in Ethiopia. Three crania were uncovered at Herto Bouri, two adults and one juvenile, dating to between 160,000 and 154,000 years ago (Figure 9.13). Although they are slightly more robust than many modern

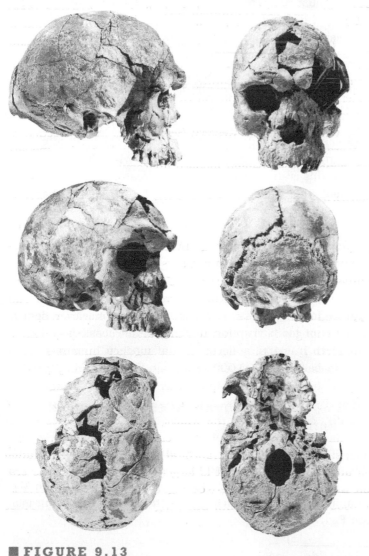

■ **FIGURE 9.13**
A Herto Bouri cranium. These are the oldest crania considered to belong to fully modern humans. They date to around 160,000 years ago and come from east Africa.

humans, they exhibit a number of anatomically modern features, such as maximum cranial width high on the skull, a relatively rounded cranium with a relatively flexed cranial base, and a clear canine fossa. However, these fossils also have relatively large teeth and pronounced supraorbital tori compared to most living humans (White et al., 2003). The discoverers of these fossils propose that they are modern humans but a distinct subspecies (*Homo sapiens idaltu*) that is directly ancestral to *Homo sapiens sapiens*. There is some debate about this classification, because most anthropologists have no problem classifying these fossils as some of the earliest modern humans. Fossils discovered in 1967 at the Kibish formation in Ethiopia have recently been redated to as much as 195,000 years ago (McDougall et al., 2005). These crania are similar to the Herto Bouri fossils but also show some overlap with aspects of archaic forms (such as the Kabwe cranium).

There are several other modern human finds in Africa, dating to between 130,000 and 100,000 years ago. A number of mandibular and postcranial fossils representing up to 10 individuals and dating from between about 118,000 and 60,000 years ago were found at the well-known Klasies River mouth site in South Africa. The mandibles show evidence of chins and no retromolar gap, but they are relatively robust compared with later humans. The sites of Border, Die Kelders, and Equus caves, all in South Africa, also contain fragmentary fossils dating to between 100,000 and 50,000 years ago that fit the criteria for modern humans. A partially complete cranium found at the Florisbad site, also in South Africa, dates to about 100,000 years ago and shares features with both the Herto Bouri fossils and a few of the late archaic forms (the Kabwe cranium, for example, discussed earlier in this chapter). These features suggest that it too reflects a transition between archaic and modern humans.

The famous fossil site of Laetoli (described in chapter 7) turned up at least one human fossil dating to about 120,000 years ago, While it retains some archaic characteristics, this cranium has two modern features; a canine fossa, and a maximum cranial width that occurs between the parietals rather than lower down (Conroy, 1997).

In north Africa, at the site of Jebel Irhoud, two crania (an adult and a juvenile) and a mandible dating to between 160,000 and 90,000 years old exhibit a variety of modern human features. The crania are long and wide (similar to the crania of archaics) but the frontal bone is more vertical and the face is nearly flush with the frontal. The one mandible shows a clear chin but also has relatively large molars. Interestingly, recent research demonstrates that the pattern of tooth eruption in the juvenile fossil here is very similar to that of modern humans, suggesting that modern human developmental patterns extend back to ~160,000 years ago (Smith et al., 2007).

The Eurasian Record Demonstrates the Spread of Modern Humans

CONNECTIONS

See chapter 4, page 100, to remind yourself about the core role of migration in evolution.

It is commonly agreed that the oldest anatomically modern human fossils currently known are found in Africa. Fossils defined as modern humans by most researchers show up slightly later in the Middle East and then begin appearing in western and eastern Eurasian sites (see Figure 9.14).

The Oldest Sites: The Middle East

Two sites in the Middle East, at Skhul and Qafzeh, have revealed the remains of early modern humans. At Skhul, crania dating to approximately 110,000

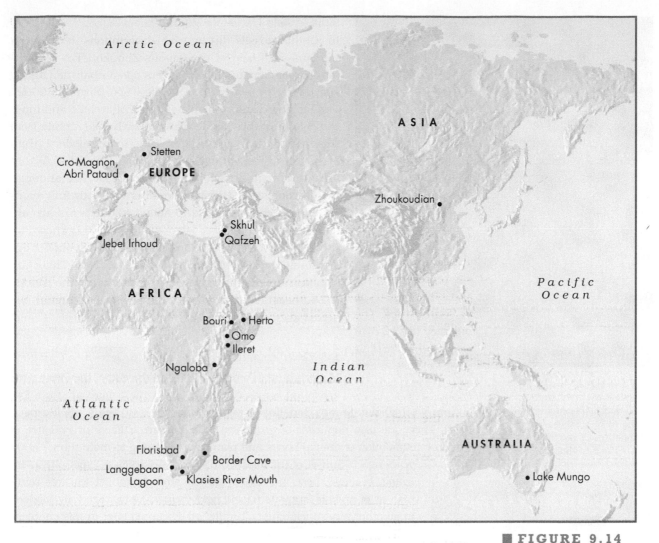

■ **FIGURE 9.14**
Early *Homo sapiens* sites. The earliest specimens of *Homo sapiens* come from east Africa. Soon after, fully modern humans appeared in the Middle East and Europe. Sites in east Asia have been dated to 70,000 years ago; in Australia, fully modern humans were present by 60,000 years ago.

to 80,000 years ago have features associated with late archaic humans (Neanderthals), as well as many modern features, such as high, rounded crania and a more vertical frontal bone. The site of Qafzeh, roughly the same age as Skhul (dating to about 100,000 to 90,000 years ago), has yielded fossils of several individuals. These fossils again show some transitional features, but they are more like moderns than archaics, especially in the shape of the skull, the thickness of cranial bones, and the presence of a chin (Figure 9.15).

Later Sites in Europe

As discussed earlier, the majority of European sites dating from the middle and later Pleistocene contain fossils of archaic humans. Nearly all of the modern human fossils discovered in Europe come from sites that date to less than 40,000 years go. At a few of these sites, such as Predmosti in central Europe, the crania display features of both late archaics (Neanderthals) and moderns. As in the Middle Eastern group, the principal archaic feature is robustness, and the modern features are the shape of the cranium, the presence of a chin, and the lack of a retromolar gap. Interestingly, by the time modern human skeletons begin showing up in the fossil record throughout western Eurasia (after 40,000 years ago), the majority of the finds are burials.

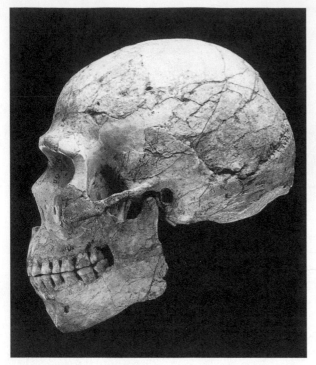

FIGURE 9.15
Homo sapiens cranium from Skhul, Israel. This cranium, dating to 110,000 years ago, has features of early modern humans and of Neanderthals.

CONNECTIONS

See chapter 8, page 242, for a discussion of *H. floresiensis* and *H. erectus* living concurrently in the same areas as modern humans.

STOP & THINK

Does this mean that there may have been three types of humans in Asia at the same time?

Sites in Asia Dating to 70,000 Years Ago

In China, fossils fitting the descriptions of modern humans are found at the famous Zhoukoudian site dating to approximately 30,000 years ago and at the Liujang site dating to nearly 70,000 years ago (Stringer, 2002). The Liujang cranium displays a mix of archaic and modern characteristics, as do many other human crania from this period, but again there are more modern than archaic features. As discussed earlier, it is possible that archaic humans are not found in Southeast Asia (although this is contested). However, fossil crania with fully modern characteristics dating to about 40,000 years ago are found on the Indonesian islands of Java and Borneo (Figure 9.16). Modern human fossils of a slightly younger age are found on the Philippine Islands as well. There are significant problems dating fossil material on the islands of Southeast Asia, so, as with the *H. erectus* material, the actual ages of these fossils remain tentative.

Arrival in Australia: 60,000 Years Ago

Modern human remains dating to the end of the Pleistocene are found across Australia. The earliest dates are for a fossil from a burial site, Mungo 3, dating to approximately 60,000 years ago (Stringer, 2002). There are also non-fossil-bearing sites with human artifacts or evidence of human manipulation of animal bones and plant matter dating to more than 50,000 years ago. A subset of the fossil crania from Australia is especially interesting, because these individuals exhibit strongly robust features reminiscent of archaic humans (*Homo heidelbergensis*) but are fully modern in all other ways (including culturally, as discussed later in this chapter).

The emergence of modern humans in Australia is even more interesting because at the time (and currently), Australia was separated from the nearest land masses (also islands) by at least 100 km (62 miles) of deep and dangerous ocean. These early modern humans must have used boats or rafts to cross the sea. No archaeological remains have yet been found that offer material support for this hypothesis (the oldest known boats are about 20,000–10,000 years old), but there are also no other plausible hypotheses for how humans arrived in Australia. Recall from chapter 8 that there have also been *H. erectus* finds on the island of Timor, just north of Australia, and *H. erectus*-like tools on Flores; so humans and prehumans may have been using some form of rafts or boats much earlier than the archaeological evidence currently shows.

Arrival in the Americas: 15,000 Years Ago?

There is an extremely contentious debate over when the first humans arrived in the Americas. There is no evidence whatsoever that any other hominin, including archaic humans, occurred in the Americas. The oldest agreed-upon human sites in the Western Hemisphere are in South America and date to nearly 14,000 years ago, and the oldest human remains in the Americas date to just over 12,000 years ago. However, there are several disputed sites purported to date to as early as 40,000 years ago.

Nearly all researchers agree that modern humans came into the Americas via the Bering Strait, probably when there was a land mass connecting northern

Asia to northern North America, about 15,000 years ago. Recent evidence indicates that archaic humans were in northern Asia, but there is no evidence that they ever crossed into the Americas. All fossil human remains found in the Americas are clearly and fully modern.

Material culture becomes very complex with the appearance of modern humans

Although fossils that we call anatomically modern humans are found as early as about 195,000–160,000 years ago, the material culture that we associate with the advent of modern humanity does not become common in the archaeo-logical record until approximately 50,000 to 40,000 years ago. Why did anatomically modern humans use tool kits similar to those of the Neanderthals and other archaic forms for nearly 100,000 years after their initial appearance in the fossil record? It may be that the size of the brain reached maximum size over 150,000 years ago but that certain physiological changes in the brain occurred later, around 50,000 years ago, just as changing climatic and demographic conditions favored increased behavioral complexity.

For the first time in hominin history, modern humans had the capacity to substantially alter and expand their behavior, and they developed this capacity in a very short time (relative to ancestral hominins). It should not be surprising that in this case changes in behavior evolved after changes in morphology, especially if the changes in morphology, such as brain structure, were required to lay the groundwork for the changes in behavior. Regardless of why these changes occurred, by the end of the Pleistocene we begin to see a new level of complexity in tools, in hunting and foraging behavior, and in symbolic and individual expression. It is also only with extremely recent *H. sapiens sapiens* that we see the social complexity, environmental modification, and niche construction on a massive scale that characterizes humanity today.

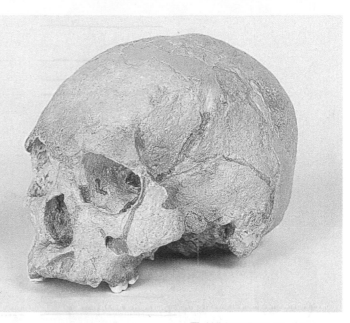

■ FIGURE 9.16
Homo sapiens cranium from Wadjak, Java. This cranium, with modern characteristics, is about 40,000 years old.

STOP & THINK

Why were the Americas the last major land masses colonized by humans?

Blades and Associated Industries Revolutionized the Human Tool Kit

A **blade tool** is a stone flake that is at least twice as long as it is wide. The advent of blade tools and smaller flakes substantially increased the capabilities of stone tools and gave humans an increased technical ability to modify nonstone items. Long points could now be made and efficiently hafted to wood or bone handles (Figure 9.17). Wood, ivory, and bone could be carved to produce very small tools, such as fishhooks and needles, that were both durable and of high quality. Blade tool kits varied from location to location, and not all modern human groups used them. Some retained older stone tool kits, and some used other, nonstone materials as their main tools.

Overall, between approximately 40,000 and 17,000 years ago, the tool kits became ever more complex and incorporated items that

blade tools
tools made from stone flakes that are at least twice as long as they are wide

CONNECTIONS

See pages 267–268 in this chapter, and chapter 8, pages 236–237 and 247–249, for previous tool types.

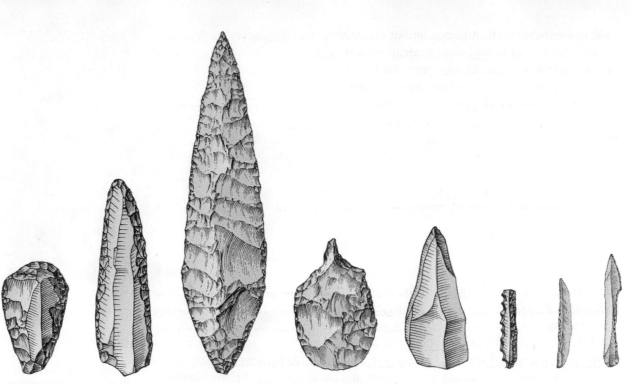

■ FIGURE 9.17
Blade tools. The long flakes were worked to have very sharp edges and used for a variety of purposes. Blade technologies mark a significant advance over earlier tool forms.

substantially enhanced the physical capabilities of humans. The *atlatl,* or spear thrower, and the barbed harpoons, for example, expanded the power of humans to exploit their own morphology and the surrounding environment in ways that no other animal on the planet can (Figure 9.18). Small bone tools like the needle also expand the ways in which humans interface with environmental challenges and mark themselves culturally (Figure 9.19). By at least 28,000 years ago, we have evidence from sites in Eurasia of clothing and shoes, which offer protection from the elements and increase the ability to move across harsh landscapes.

(a)

■ FIGURE 9.18
Atlatl, or spearthrower. The hunter inserts the hook of the spearthrower into the base of the spear and throws (a). A spearthrower from the site of Enlène, France (b). The handle is missing.

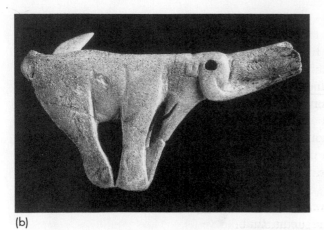

(b)

These new tool kits did not appear out of thin air. The Mousterian industry included some crude blades and a wide variety of smaller tools that were effective for working wood and bone. Remember that in both the Middle East and in other parts of western Eurasia, late archaic forms (Neanderthals) and modern humans overlapped (or at least were found with similar Mousterian tool kits). The blade tool industry of the upper Paleolithic emerged from the Mousterian industry of the middle Paleolithic, which in turn emerged from the Acheulean and even Olduwan industries of the lower Paleolithic. The upper Paleolithic industries were extensions and elaborations of prior patterns, not novel creations, much as the morphology of modern humans resulted from the series of modifications that occurred in the anatomy of earlier hominins.

Changing Technologies and Behavioral Patterns Affected Diet

The advent of new tool technologies and the movement of humans into new environments opened up a variety of possibilities for the expansion of dietary patterns. The ability to work fine points and create small tools enhanced the ability of humans to collect fish and other small, hard-to-capture organisms. At coastal sites across all continents there was intense exploitation of marine organisms, especially fish and shellfish, and occasionally marine mammals as well. Due to tool kit and material culture limitations, this high-quality diet may not have been broadly available to hominins before the appearance of modern humans.

The wider range of tools combined with continuous use of fire also allowed for substantial food processing. As a result, the mouth now had to do less work. The ability to crush, chop, cut, and cook food reduces the stress on the jaw and teeth and thus reduces the selection pressure for massive jaw muscles and large molar dentition. This ability to modify food before eating it also allowed for the exploitation of nutritious foods that may have been either extremely tough to eat or even poisonous before processing.

Strength-enhancing tools such as the atlatl and, later, the bow and arrow, allowed for hunting at a distance, reducing the danger to individual humans and increasing the damage that one human could do, thus increasing the effectiveness of each individual's hunting and the overall return on each hunt. Using their new technologies, humans became more efficient at foraging for a wider variety of foodstuffs. They began to use social, behavioral, and extrasomatic materials to deal with external pressures and challenges, resulting in the modern form of human niche construction: massive manipulation of local ecologies.

Modern Humans Used Art and Symbols

Probably the most unique ability of modern humans is our incredible use of imagination. By at least 50,000 years ago in Africa and Australia, and presumably everywhere else modern humans existed, fossil sites are increasingly associated with items of nonfunctional symbolism, or art. By 20,000 years ago, art and symbolism are ubiquitous in human fossil sites (Figures 9.20, 9.21, 9.22). The early art of modern humans ranges from simple etchings on cave walls and marks on the handles of tools to elaborate cave paintings and complex carved figurines. Regardless of the items themselves, this cultural pattern marks an enormous change in the way humans behave. Images include both abstract forms and clear and accurate representations of animals

■ **FIGURE 9.19**
Eyed needles. Needles with eyes, usually made of ivory or bone, were made at least 25,000 years ago.

STOP & THINK

How did it affect human hunting when we began throwing our tools rather than holding on to them?

■ FIGURE 9.20

A variety of Upper Paleolithic carved objects. Note the objects that have an obvious function as well as others that appear to represent symbolic elements. Top: a shaft straightener. Left: a carved harpoon made from antler. Bottom right: an example of the famous "Venus" figurines.

and humans. There are even hybrid figures with mixed human and animal features. Sometimes single colors are used, and other times a panoply of pigments are exploited.

Labeling these objects nonfunctional implies that they did not serve a clear, identifiable function, as a spear or a chopper does. Rather, they had a cultural meaning to the individuals who produced them, to the group, and perhaps to a wider local or regional population. How and why humans developed the ability to create pigments and then to apply them to surfaces in complex and aesthetically imaginative ways remains a fascinating, although difficult, question. A partial answer may lie in the changing structure of the brain and in the realm of culture. These patterns may mark the emergence of belief systems and attempts to understand the world and the place of human beings in it beyond the easily observable material surroundings. The symbols may have been related to beliefs about hunting or foraging, about the changes in the seasons, or about events that had occurred in the past.

Because of the variations in theme, in materials used, and in location, there are probably multiple explanations for the creation and use of art and symbols across both space and time.

This use of symbols is associated with another modern human characteristic: language. It is hard to image how a symbol can exist without some

■ FIGURE 9.21

Upper Paleolithic wall painting. A painting from the famous cave of Lascaux in southwest France, showing an aurochs (an extinct ox) and horses. This is actually a photo of Lascaux II, a modern replica created to protect the original cave from damage caused by visitors to the site.

■ FIGURE 9.22
Aboriginal wall painting from Queensland, Australia. Australian aboriginal people made both wall paintings and carvings, continuing a trend from Paleolithic times.

means of complex communication to explain it. Although it is highly likely that archaic humans and even older members of the genus *Homo* used some form of fairly complex communication, no concrete evidence supports such a hypothesis. With the explosion of symbolic expression associated with modern humans, we have the first indication that a system of communication had emerged that allowed humans to refer to objects and topics that were not immediately present. Language allows people to communicate about

CONNECTIONS

Art for Art's Sake?

Anthropologists get really excited when we find cave paintings, carved figurines, or even a few beads at ancient human sites. Most people today take the human creative minds for granted. Symbolic expression is the most important unique ability in humankind. Try to tell a story without any symbols or descriptions of non-visible things or basic objects. Think of your favorite story, fairy tale, movie, video game, or song and see if any of those things are not packed with symbolic elements. Something happened around the planet when our ancestors started going into caves or rock shelters and using the juices of fruits and other plants to smear colors and shapes on the walls. Think about what it means for these early modern humans to take a seashell and purposely carve it into a set of small beads that were strung on a vine and worn. Arts for art's sake, the creation and use of symbolic representation, is a core of daily human life today. When you wake up in the morning and choose your clothing, when you decide what color to paint your room, when you wear the colors of your sports team—these are all symbolic expression and an important part of being human. When and why did this start? When did humans start creative innovation with our imagination? We have some fossil evidence, but that likely underestimates the age and spread of the earliest art. What were the responses of the members of the group when they first saw the art on the wall? How is that different from today when we see new forms of art and symbolic expression? Who knew that art was an important topic for biological anthropology?

the present and the future, about what they saw yesterday and might see tomorrow, about what is around the bend and invisible to the eye. It enables symbolism, storytelling, and myth. The use of language is critical to the story of humanity and dramatically differentiates the way we transfer and inherit information among ourselves from the ways used by all other organisms on the planet.

Burial of the Dead Was Ubiquitous and Postmortem Modification Common

Many fossil sites dating to 40,000 years ago are in the form of burials. Modern humans buried their dead in a variety of patterns and with varying kinds and quantities of grave goods. Again, this behavior marks a substantial difference between early members of the genus *Homo* and modern humans, and it links late archaic humans to the modern humans. Although human burials are more complex and consistent in detail over the last 40,000 years, the practice of burying the dead emerged at least 80,000 to 100,000 years ago in at least some populations.

In addition to burials, many modern human groups practiced some form of postmortem modification. These practices ranged from dismemberment to defleshing to placement of the body in specific positions. Some of the defleshing and anatomical modification patterns may reflect nutritional cannibalism, but most modifications were probably ritualistic. Although there is evidence of postmortem modification in archaic humans, it is not always clear what these behaviors represented. It is clear, however, that modern humans were able to conceptualize death and that diverse modern human

CONNECTIONS

Why We Love Our Dogs (At Least Some of Us Do)

How many times have you sat with a dog, petting it, and felt some kind of connection? Have you played fetch or just run around in the park with a dog and enjoyed it? If so, you are taking part in a 10,000–20,000-year or older relationship between humans and canids. One of the most important and widespread domestication stories is that of humans and dogs. For thousands of years the two species have been living together mutually shaping our behavior and bodies. We know from recent research that humans and wild dogs (types of wolves) spent thousands of years watching each other and moving closer and closer together (Olmert 2009). We know that humans selectively bred dogs for generations for particular behavioral and morphological traits,

but what many people do not realize is that dogs have been shaping us as well. Dogs have changed the ways humans get food (hunting), the ways humans set up their households and protect their goods (guarding), and the way in which human young and old are socialized (pets). We now know that humans often seek out their dogs for comfort after stressful conflicts with their partners, that simply looking at your pet dog from across the room can have a calming effect on your physiology, and that physical contact and interactions with dogs can assist distressed humans' physiological and psychological well being. All of these are indications that while we were shaping dogs into everything from Great Danes to Chihuahuas, they were also shaping us. Humans and dogs share a social niche and have co-evolved for thousands of years—this is why we feel a connection to human's best friend.

groups had different beliefs and practices associated with the treatment of their dead.

Current Human Patterns Began to Emerge 20,000 Years Ago

Before approximately 20,000 years ago, humans did not live in very large groups, nor were they consistently sedentary. Between 20,000 and 10,000 years ago, those patterns began to change, and by 5000 years ago, large population centers had emerged, along with the beginning of the political, economic, and social structures we have today. The emergence of agriculture, socioeconomic class distinctions, and clear and materially demarcated gender distinctions are all aspects of our most recent past. We detail a few of these briefly in chapter 11 and use them to speculate about future changes in humanity.

The origin of modern humans is a matter of debate

The debate over the origin of modern humans is one of the most contentious in anthropology. Over the past three decades, two models have dominated the discussion. One model, the Recent African Origin (RAO) model, proposes that modern humans are the result of a speciation event in the late Pleistocene in Africa (Figure 9.23). The second model, the Multiregional Evolution (MRE) model, proposes that modern humans are the most recent morphological form in a species, *Homo sapiens,* that has been around for nearly 2 million years (Figure 9.24). This model assumes that we have an ancient rather than a recent African origin. Since they were initially proposed, both

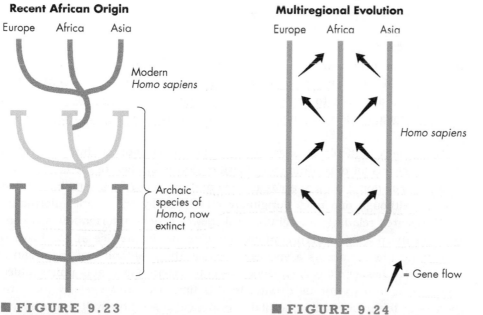

■ FIGURE 9.23
The Recent African Origin (RAO) model of human evolution. This model assumes that modern *Homo sapiens* evolved recently in Africa and that earlier species of *Homo* are now extinct.

■ FIGURE 9.24
The Multiregional Evolution (MRE) model of human evolution. This model proposes that the species *Homo sapiens* has been around for 2 million years but that numerous variants have existed over that time.

The Multiple Dispersal (MD) model of human evolution from Templeton, 2002. Diagonal lines represent gene flow. Red arrows represent major population expansions. This model takes into account physical evidence as well as recent genetic information.

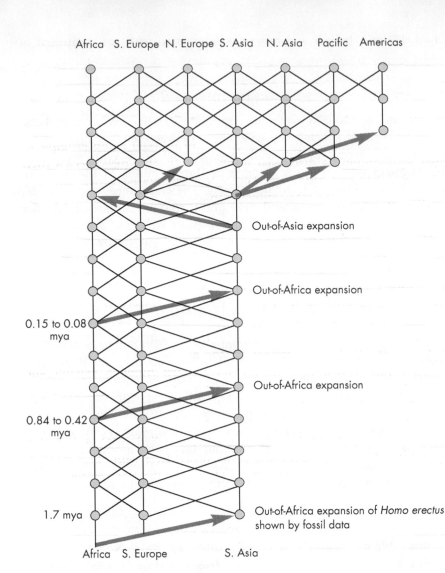

models have been modified to accommodate changing evidence. A third model, the Multiple Dispersal (MD) model, has been proposed recently. This third option attempts to incorporate seemingly contradictory aspects of the two traditional models and mesh them with emerging complexities in genetic data sets (Figure 9.25).

Three basic difficulties arise in the debate over modern human origins. First, there is a lot of contradictory fossil evidence for each of the models, and fossil information from key areas in Asia and parts of Africa remains limited. Second, although one model originally relied heavily on genetic information that appeared relatively straightforward, newer genetic information has complicated the possible interpretations. Finally, the debate lies at the heart of explaining who we are as a species: Because the positioning of the origin of our species has great consequence, in both evolutionary and philosophical contexts, it raises vigorous debate. In this final section we review the three models in terms of the best available evidence to see how well that evidence fits their basic predictions.

The Case for a Recent African Origin

The RAO model rests on the hypothesis that *Homo sapiens sapiens* is a relatively young species that arose from a population of archaic humans in

Africa approximately 150,000 to 200,000 years ago. According to this model, selective pressures acted on a regional population of archaic humans in either eastern or southern Africa, causing certain traits to become overrepresented. These traits included the morphological characteristics that are generally considered typical of modern humans. This constellation of traits is distinct enough from the traits of other archaic humans to constitute a new species. In a sense, this speciation event can be seen as an example of punctuated equilibrium (as discussed in chapter 4). This new species then expanded in number and range and began to move across Africa and into Eurasia, where groups came into contact with archaic humans already living there.

At this point there are two variants of the RAO model, differing in their hypotheses about the interactions between the new species (*Homo sapiens*) and the archaic forms (considered to be two species, *Homo heidelbergensis* and *Homo neanderthalensis*) (Stringer, 2002). The first and more traditional version is the replacement model, which scientists call *RAO-replace*. In this version, modern humans replace archaic humans with minimal or no inter-breeding: Modern humans outcompete archaic humans in the same environments, until the archaics eventually become extinct. In the second, or hybridization and replacement, model (called *RAO-hybrid*), as modern humans expand and encounter archaics, they sometimes (but not always) engage in interbreeding. The main difference between these two versions is that in RAO-replace, the archaic humans do not contribute to the modern human gene pool, and in RAO-hybrid, they do. (A third model, sometimes called *RAO-assimilation*, includes aspects of the RAO model and is discussed later with other multiple dispersal models.) Let's now consider the evidence for the RAO model.

The Earliest Modern Human Fossils Are Found in Africa

Nearly all researchers who consider only modern humans or only modern and archaic humans to be members of *Homo sapiens* (as opposed to those who consider all *Homo* specimens in the last 2 million years to be *Homo sapiens*) agree that the earliest fossils that can be called modern humans are found in Africa. The Herto Bouri, Umo, Jebal Irhoud, and Klassies River mouth fossils are the earliest known representatives of anatomically modern *Homo sapiens*. The next oldest fossils are the Skhul and Qafzeh material in the Middle East and subsequent finds throughout Eurasia, dating to approximately 50,000 to 40,000 years ago. This distribution of fossils, if the dates are correct, gives the impression that modern humans arose in Africa and then spread to Eurasia, Australia, and the Americas. By 25,000 years ago, modern humans are everywhere except possibly isolated areas in Southeast Asia (where we still find *H. erectus* and *H. floresiensis* isolated populations). The cluster of traits that defines archaics no longer appears in any human population. This seems to support the RAO-replacement model. However, fossils such as the small child in Portugal said to have both Neanderthal and modern human traits, and the presence of modern populations around the globe that exhibit some "archaic" traits, such as pronounced supraorbital tori and large teeth and mandibles, suggest that the RAO-hybrid model may be more likely.

Unfortunately, the fossil record is not precise. Significant contention remains over the dating of many of the Asian and south African fossils, partly because the dates are derived from correlation with animal bones found at the same sites and other relative techniques. There are also those who argue that morphological aspects of modern humans show up gradually across the range of archaic humans and that some modern populations retain similarities with

[Handwritten margin note: By 25,000 yrs H. erectus ? H. floresiensi are the only ones (in the genus Homo) to be in Southeast Asia. Also by 25000 yrs ago the cluster of traits that defines archaics no longer appears in any human population.]

the archaic populations that were geographically ancestral to them (see the discussion of the MRE model later in the chapter).

The Genetic Data Provide General but Not Explicit Support

Aside from the fossils, research in the 1980s and 1990s purported to discover genetic support for the RAO model. The initial results came from two areas: nuclear genetics and mitochondrial DNA (mtDNA). Assays of nuclear DNA demonstrated that Africa had higher levels of allelic diversity than all other areas of the planet combined. Because changes accumulate over time, this finding suggests that humans have been in Africa longer than anywhere else. The mtDNA studies, first released in 1987 (Cann, Stoneking, 8 Wilson, 1987), reported that all modern human mtDNA (which is inherited only maternally, as discussed in chapter 2) can be traced to a population in Africa that lived approximately 150,000 to 200,000 years ago. Because, unlike nuclear DNA, mtDNA does not recombine, and it also has a constant mutation rate, we can compare samples from different humans and see how many changes have occurred since the samples shared a common ancestor. If we know how many changes (mutations) have occurred, we can count backwards and see how much time has elapsed since the time of the common ancestor. This is the methodology used by the mtDNA researchers who claimed to have found "Eve."

As soon as these data were published, they were strongly challenged, and on closer look they did appear to be much less dramatic than originally thought. Recent revisions and retesting of similar and larger data sets suggest that rather than one female ancestor, all living humans can trace their mtDNA back to one or more populations that lived sometime between 150,000 and 200,000 years ago. In addition, as discussed earlier, the tests of extracted Neanderthal mtDNA indicate that those specific sequences are not present in modern humans, a finding suggesting that modern humans and Neanderthals had a common ancestor much earlier than 100,000 to 200,000 years ago (perhaps as much as 370,000 years ago). However, the recent Neanderthal genome data show more overlap in nuclear DNA, thus suggesting some interbreeding between modern humans and Neanderthals (Green et al., 2010).

Additional work on the Y chromosome of males (inherited paternally) has demonstrated that at least some sections of the DNA on the Y chromosome appear, in all living humans, to come from ancestral populations that lived in Africa about 90,000 years ago. Taken together, these two lines of genetic data strongly support the RAO-replacement model, because they seem to indicate that no archaic mtDNA or sections of Y chromosome DNA are present in modern humans and thus that there was no interbreeding with the archaics.

Again, reality is not so clear cut. Because mtDNA is inherited only from the mother, it is possible for entire lineages of mtDNA to disappear; in small populations, for example, genetic drift and other chance events could cause this. That means that if we sample all living mtDNA lineages, we might not actually be sampling all of the lineages that have existed in the last 100,000 years. Thus sampling could give a false picture of human mtDNA diversity and miss archaic contributions to the modern gene pool. More important, although the mtDNA and some Y chromosome DNA sequences tested appear to be uniquely modern and relatively recent, other genetic markers show both older and younger ancestral nodes. In other words, although the mtDNA and some Y-chromosome DNA in modern humans appear to be about 100,000 to

200,000 years old, other parts of our DNA have origins earlier and later than the period 100,000 to 200,000 years ago. We elaborate on the genetic tests that have yielded these results in a later section.

The Case for Multiregional Evolution

The original version of the MRE model proposed that all humans in the last 1.7 million years have been members of the same species, *Homo sapiens*, and that over time all populations have undergone similar patterns of change, resulting in modern human morphology by 100,000 to 40,000 years ago. This gradual evolutionary pattern was a result of gene flow and common modes of adaptation. The MRE model assumes that modern human populations have some morphological and genetic continuity with the archaic humans who inhabited the same geographic areas (Thorne & Wolpoff, 1992). In other words, humans currently living in Asia would have some continuity with the archaic humans who lived there, and so on in every part of the world.

Current versions of this model incorporate a larger African influence than the original version. They suggest that because population sizes were larger in Africa than in most parts of Eurasia, gene flow from populations on the African continent had a stronger impact than gene flow from other regions (Hawkes, Hunley, Lee, & Wolpoff, 2000). In other words, morphological traits of African origin spread more broadly than did other traits from smaller populations. This model explicitly states that there was no speciation event in Africa between 100,000 and 200,000 years ago; rather, the speciation event took place approximately 1.7 million years ago, and we have seen a gradual accumulation of genetic and morphological differences in the human species since that time (an example of Darwinian gradualism, as discussed in chapter 4). What is the evidence for this model?

There Is Some Continuity in the Fossil Record

The main contention of the MRE model is that humans have been the same species for a long time and that modern humans are the current representatives of a species with a long and varied history. Accordingly, there should be regional continuity in morphology between humans today and archaic humans. Continuity is measured by morphological similarity, so continuity is supported if populations of modern humans share more specific traits with the archaic humans who lived in the same geographic region than with archaics from other regions. Some researchers have reported finding continuity between archaic and modern humans, especially in cranial traits, in Southeast Asia and Australia (Thorne & Wolpoff, 1992). Others challenge those assertions (Stringer, 2002). The mixture of archaic and modern traits seen in many early modern humans also suggests some gradual transitions in form rather than an abrupt speciation event. The possible hybrid found in Portugal is also potential evidence that archaic and modern forms are not actually distinct species. The presence of *H. erectus* and *H. floresiensis* fossils at 25,000 and ~12,000 years ago respectively in Southeast Asia also causes some problems for this hypothesis.

A group of proponents of the MRE model recently analyzed a broad collection of modern and archaic crania from Africa and Eurasia. They reported wide variation in the crania; regional continuity was strongly present in some cases, weakly present in others, and in yet others (such as Qafzeh), the crania were more like recent African crania (Wolpoff, Hawkes, Frayer, & Hunley, 2001). These results support the notion that there was widespread mixing between archaic and modern humans and that because of greater population sizes, African populations and populations near Africa may have had a greater impact on the human gene pool than more peripheral populations.

There is still substantial disagreement over what constitutes regional continuity and why it shows up in some areas and not in others (Stringer, 2002). Traits considered continuous may simply be primitive for both archaics and moderns and therefore not a measure of continuity; they may simply indicate that two species shared a common morphological ancestry. However, as noted above, the find of miniature *Homo erectus*-like *Homo floresiensis* on the island of Flores (see chapter 8) and the late dates on some *H. erectus* finds in Java do appear to make a strong case *against* continuity for parts of Southeast Asia. The *H. floresiensis* find also demonstrates that at least two forms of hominins coexisted in Southeast Asia until very recently.

Some Genetic Markers Are Older Than 100,000 to 200,000 Years

Although the mtDNA and some of the Y-chromosome DNA data clearly suggest a recent African origin for modern humans, other genetic systems do not. At least three modern human autosomal genes show points of common ancestry dating to more than 200,000 years ago (Templeton, 2002). These three date to 630,000, 640,000, and 820,000 years ago, respectively. If these data are correct, as is suggested by the recent Neanderthal genome data, genetic contributions from populations existing well before any anatomically modern humans occurred are present in modern human populations. This genetic evidence supports the MRE model, but it could also be seen as supporting the RAO-hybrid model, since that model allows for some interbreeding between modern and archaic populations.

The Case for Multiple Dispersals

Clearly, neither the RAO model nor the MRE model fully explains the available evidence. A third model, the Multiple Dispersal (MD) model has been proposed, dubbed the "Out of Africa, Again and Again" model (Templeton, 2002) to resolve this dilemma. The MD model takes into account the complex nature of the genetic evidence. In this model, African populations continue to play an important role in human evolution, as in the RAO and the current MRE models, but the way in which this occurs differs from either of the earlier models.

In the MD model, the initial dispersal out of Africa is by members of the genus *Homo* (*Homo erectus/ergaster*) at approximately 1.7 million years ago. *Homo* spreads around western, central, and southern Eurasia (see Figure 9.25). After this point, there is recurrent gene flow across Africa and Eurasia, via either movement of populations or movement of alleles (through breeding), possibly with some isolation of peripheral populations like those that became the late *H. erectus* and *H. floresiensis* isolates in Southeast Asia. Another African dispersal event occurs between about 800,000 and 400,000 years ago, affecting Eurasian populations through interbreeding and changing the genetic patterns of the genus *Homo*. A third major African dispersal event occurs between about 150,000 and 80,000 years ago, again causing changes in allele frequencies and genetic shifts throughout the genus *Homo*. Both of these later dispersal events are followed by extensive gene flow throughout the range of *Homo*, again with the possibility that some populations become highly isolated.

A fourth dispersal event, this time out of Asia, occurs about 60,000 years ago, affecting both central Eurasian and African population genetic patterns. This event is also followed by recurrent gene flow and isolation by distance. Finally, by about 50,000 years ago, there are dispersals into northern Eurasia, Australia, the Pacific Islands, and eventually the Americas via migration.

This model predicts a strong, repeated impact by African populations on the genetic (and therefore on some aspects of the morphological) characteristics of humans over the last 1.7 million years. It also predicts recurrent gene flow between populations, with those closer to each other geographically sharing more genes than those more distant. Aspects of the RAO model can be seen in this model, in the inclusion of a highly influential dispersal event at 150,000 to 80,000 years ago, although this is not seen as a speciation event. Aspects of the MRE model are also present, in that populations are seen as evolving over time via gene flow, although there is not as strong an emphasis on continuity.

The Fossil Record Shows Support for the MD Model

Because of the hypothesized multiple dispersals, the fossil evidence does fit reasonably well with the MD model. The initial dispersal would account for the fossil evidence of *H. erectus* (or *H. ergaster*) around Africa and Eurasia. The second dispersal coincides with the changes in morphology associated with archaic humans (*H. heidelbergensis*), and the third dispersal reflects the emergence of modern humans (*H. sapiens*). Regional variation would be expected in such a model, as would clusters of similar morphologies, especially when gene flow is reduced, such as is possible for the late archaics (Neanderthals) in western Eurasia.

The Genetic Evidence Supports This Model

The available genetic evidence—from modern human mtDNA, Y-chromosome DNA, X-chromosome DNA, and six autosomal DNA regions—support this model (Templeton, 2002). By looking at the extant genetic variation in modern humans and calculating back to common ancestor sequences, we can calculate the times of divergence and time since divergence. Studies of X-chromosome DNA and four autosomal DNA regions have found evidence of gene flow between 1.7 and 0.4 million years ago. Three autosomal DNA regions show dispersal out of Africa between 800,000 and 400,000 years ago. Multiple genes suggest gene flow across Africa and Eurasia between 400,000 and 150,000 years ago, and the mtDNA and some Y-chromosome DNA evidence clearly show a significant dispersal from Africa between 150,000 and 80,000 years ago. Some Y-chromosome DNA evidence supports an Asian dispersal at about 60,000 years ago, and many genes support the dispersal of modern humans into northern Eurasia and the Pacific by 50,000 years ago, a finding that is also in line with the fossil evidence.

CONNECTIONS

See chapter 3, pages 72–90, for details about DNA, chromosomes, and genes.

As Usual, Reality Is Not This Clear

Although scientists increasingly agree on most dates and patterns in the fossil record, the meaning and implications of those dates and patterns are still matters of debate. The fact that there appear to be morphological dispersal events that roughly coincide with the genetic data and genetic time frame does not mean that the number of species has been determined. In fact, this issue remains contentious. If all humans have belonged to one species for the past 1.7 million years, the MRE and MD models are the best representatives of human history. However, if multiple species have been present over this time period (and this is what a slight majority of researchers believe), we have to explain species relationships with at least some genetic mixing. That is, if *H. heidelbergensis* and *H. sapiens* are truly two species, but modern humans have some genetic history that goes back more than 200,000 years, there must have been some interbreeding. Alternatively, perhaps the transition from archaic to modern humans occurred in at least a few populations that retained strong genetic similarities with archaics. If this is the case, a version of the RAO-assimilation model and the MD model best represent human history. The MD model can be seen as a kind of compromise between the extremes of the RAO and MRE models; it accords with the RAO-assimilation model and the current MRE model that includes strong African influence.

A major dilemma in solving this riddle is the lack of agreement about what constitutes "modern." What criteria determine the appearance of fully modern

STOP & THINK

Does it make any difference which of these three scenarios is correct?

What We Know
Questions That Remain

What We Know
Changing morphologies in the human fossil record show substantial changes in human form throughout the last 500,000 years.

What We Know
Members of the species *Homo sapiens* that have what we define as modern form show up in the fossil record approximately 195,000 years ago.

What We Know
The Neanderthals are identifiable as distinct in many ways from other humans that lived roughly at the same time and subsequently.

What We Know
Evidence for the appearance of modern humans does not unequivocally point to one of the theories as being "correct" over the others.

What We Know
The pace and complexity of human material culture and niche construction increases dramatically in the last 50,000 years and explodes in the last 20,000.

Questions That Remain
If a speciation event did occur between archaic and modern forms (or *erectus* and *sapiens*), what selective and other evolutionary forces caused it?

Questions That Remain
Why is there such a long time lag between anatomically modern humans and the material evidence of modern human behavior (symbolic representation)? Is it related to changes in the structure and function of the brain?

Questions That Remain
What do these differences mean in an evolutionary sense? Were the Neanderthals different enough to be a separate species? a subspecies? a highly differentiated population(s)? Could they interbreed with other humans, and if so, did they? How did the various groups of humans think of one another when they encountered each other?

Questions That Remain
What does this imply in terms of understanding our "roots"? Will we ever be able to reconcile the disparate arenas of information (genetic, morphological, and archaeological) into one complete model? In an evolutionary context can we really expect to?

Questions That Remain
How was this increased rate and pattern of change facilitated? Is the biocultural nature of human evolution in the last 20,000 years different from the biocultural evolution previous to that time?

human beings? Should these criteria involve morphology, genetics, or behavior? All three elements are extremely important, and all three follow slightly different time lines. In this text we are attempting to approach this question, and all others, from an evolutionary and anthropological perspective. Therefore, we should not be surprised that there is both a continuity and change, with different aspects changing at different rates and patterns: This is the way evolution seems to work. We have seen this throughout our investigations of the primate fossils, the hominin fossils, and now the human fossils. We cannot expect to find a clear and definitive line demarcating us from our ancestors any more than we expect to find a clear and definitive line demarcating the earliest hominins from the other hominids. Evolutionary change and the emergence of species are not creation events; they occur gradually as morphological, genetic, and behavioral shifts over time. Finally, at a certain point, enough changes have occurred that we can say, in retrospect, that a new species or form has emerged.

These Models Influence the Way We Think About Human Differences

Does it make a difference which model is "correct" or how we understand the evolution of our species? The answer is yes. The pace and patterns of our evolution say much about modern human diversity. How old or how recent are the morphological differences between human populations? Why have those differences evolved? What does it mean to belong to a species whose members are morphologically more variable today than the members of many other mammalian species but who are almost identical genetically? How do the models of evolutionary history described in this chapter fit with our current understanding of human morphology and genetics? And what about behavior? Are human behavioral patterns young, old, or both? All of these questions are affected by the study of our past and how we interpret the findings. In chapter 10 we look at the morphological and molecular variation found in living human populations and try to understand how this variation—and sometimes, lack of variation—fits with our knowledge of past and present evolutionary patterns.

SUMMARY

▲ Fossils showing specific characteristics deemed to be transitional between *Homo erectus* and *Homo sapiens* are grouped in the category of archaic humans and referred to as archaic *Homo sapiens*, or as *Homo heidelbergensis* and *Homo neanderthalensis*.

▲ The earliest fossils displaying the morphological characteristics associated with early archaic humans, or *Homo heidelbergensis*, are found in eastern Africa and date to about 600,000 years ago. Similar fossils are found in Eurasia at Mauer, Germany, by about 500,000 years ago; at Atapuerca, Spain, by 300,000 years ago; and at Dali, China, by 200,000 to 300,000 years ago. It is unclear whether archaic humans occurred in Southeast Asia.

▲ Fossils found in western Eurasia, dating to between about 200,000 and 28,000 years ago, and characterized by specific morphological characteristics, are referred to as late archaic humans (*Homo sapiens*) or Neanderthals (*Homo neanderthalensis*).

▲ Archaic human sites in the late Pleistocene reveal evidence of increased tool complexity, increased hunting efficiency, social cooperation, burials, and possibly the practice of postmortem modification of bodies.

▲ The earliest fossils characterized as anatomically modern humans (*Homo sapiens sapiens* or *Home sapiens idaltu*) are found in eastern Africa and date to about 195,000 years ago. Subsequent finds of similar fossils occur in southern and northern Africa dating to 160,000 years ago and in the Middle East dating to 110,000 years ago. Thereafter the fossils defined as modern humans show up at sites in China by 70,000 years ago, Australia by 60,000 years ago, western Europe by 40,000 years ago, and the Americas by at least 15,000 years ago.

▲ Recent analysis of the Neanderthal genome draft suggests that there was some interbreeding between Neanderthals and modern humans ~30–45,000 years ago.

▲ Material culture associated with modern human sites is increasingly complex relative to archaic forms. These complexities include blade tools, dramatic increases in the types of tools, ubiquitous burials, some postmortem modification of bodies, and use of symbols and art. By 20,000 years ago the first hints of modern human sedentariness and population patterns begin to appear. Over the past 200,000 years modern humans have taken niche construction to levels not previously seen in other hominins.

▲ Scientists disagree over the way in which modern humans arose. Three main models have been proposed.

▲ The Recent African Origin (RAO) model assumes that modern humans appeared as the result of a recent speciation event in Africa and subsequently dispersed throughout the rest of the world, replacing or assimilating all archaic human populations.

▲ The Multiregional Evolution (MRE) model assumes that *Homo sapiens* is an old species (originating about 1.7 million years ago) and all populations of archaic humans transitioned to modern forms due to consistent gene flow and similar adaptive trajectories.

▲ The Multiple Dispersal (MD) model assumes three major dispersals of human populations from Africa in the last 1.7 million years, the first coinciding with the movement of *H. erectus* out of Africa, the second with the appearance of early archaics (or *H. heidelbergensis*), and the third with the appearance of anatomically modern humans. This model also predicts recurrent gene flow across all time periods.

▲ Fossil and genetic evidence offer some support for both the RAO and MRE models. The MD model may be the best fit for current genetic data sets.

CRITICAL THINKING

1. Some researchers label the fossils representing archaic humans *Homo heidelbergensis* and/or *Homo neanderthalensis,* while other researchers label them *Homo sapiens.* How can different groups of researchers look at the same fossils and call them different things? What does this disagreement have to do with concepts of species and the way evolutionary change proceeds?

2. Many researchers suggest that there were no archaic humans in Southeast Asia. Why would archaic forms not get there when *H. erectus* did? What about the modern humans that occurred in Australia by 60,000 years ago? Where did they come from, and why are there no similar fossils just before that time in the Indonesian islands?

3. Why are anthropologists so excited about finding evidence of burials or personal adornment in the fossil record? Why is there a time lag between the appearance of modern human morphology and the appearance of the complex symbolic behavior we associate with modern humans? Is there an evolutionary explanation for this?

4. How can there be partial support for different hypotheses of human origins (RAO, MRE, MD)? Shouldn't one be right? How can the genetic and fossil evidence not always match up? In what ways are population genetics and evolutionary theory so important to the debate on modern human origins?

5. Which model of modern human origins do you think is most accurate? What specific evidence would we need to further refine these models and achieve a clear picture of our origins?

RESOURCES

UNDERSTANDING WHAT IS A "MODERN" HUMAN

Balter, M. (2002). What made humans modern? *Science, 295,* 1219–1225.
Balter reviews ideas about why modern humans developed as they did.

Gibbons, A. (2003). Oldest members of *Homo sapiens* discovered in Africa. *Science, 300,* 1641.
This brief overview summarizes current views on modern human evolution.

Stringer, C. (2003). Out of Ethiopia. *Nature, 423,* 692–695.
This is another excellent overview of current views on modern human evolution.

BONES AND GUIDED TOURS OF THE *HOMO SAPIENS* FOSSILS

www.modernhumanorigins.com Visit this site for a good look at human origins.

FOSSIL *HOMO SAPIENS* ART AND MATERIAL CULTURE

www.originsnet.org This site includes some arguable assertions about archaic human symbolic expression, but it also provides some excellent images of archaic and modern human tools and symbolic art.

REFERENCES

Arsuaga, J. L., Bermudez de Castro, J. M., 8 Carbonell, E. (Eds.). (1997). The Sima de los Huesos hominid site. *Journal of Human Evolution, 33,* 105–421.

Bermudez de Castro, J. M., Arsuaga, J. L., Carbonell, E., Rosas, A., Martinez, I., & Mosquera, M. (1997). A hominid from the lower Pleistocene of Atapuerca, Spain: Possible ancestor to Neanderthals and modern humans. *Science, 276,* 1392–1395.

Cann, R. L., Stoneking, M., & Wilson, A. C. (1987). Mitochondrial DNA and human evolution. *Nature, 325,* 31–36.

Conroy, G. C. (1997). *Reconstructing human origins: A modern synthesis.* New York: Norton.

Dennell, R. (1997). The world's oldest spears. *Nature, 385,* 767–769.

Duarte, C., Mauricio, J., Pettitt, P. B., Souto, P., Trnkhaus, E., van der Plicht, H., et al. (1999). The early upper Paleolithic human skeleton from the Abrigo do Lagar

Velho (Portugal) and modern human emergence in Iberia. *Proceedings of the National Academy of Sciences USA, 96,* 7604–7609.

Finlaysen, C. (2004). *Neanderthals and modern humans: an ecological and evolutionary perspective.* Cambridge: Cambridge University Press.

Green, R. E., et. al. (2010). A draft sequence of the Neanderthal genome. *Science 328,* 710–722.

Hawkes, J., Hunley, K., Lee, S., & Wolpoff, M. (2000). Population bottlenecks and Pleistocene human evolution. *Molecular Biological Evolution, 17(1),* 2–22.

Horan, R. D., Bulte, E., and Shogren, J. F. (2005). How trade saved humanity from biological exclusion: An economic theory of Neanderthal extinction. *Journal of Economic Behavior and Organization 58,* 1–29.

Krings, M., Capelli, C., Tschentscher, F., Geisert, H., Meyer, S., von Haeseler, A., et al. (2000). A view of Neanderthal genetic diversity. *Nature Genetics, 26,* 144–146.

Krings, M., Stone, A., Schmitz, R. W., Krainitzki, H., Stoneking, M., & Paabo, S. (1997). Neanderthal DNA sequences and the origin of modern humans. *Cell, 90(1),* 19–30.

McDougall, I., Brown, F. H., and Fleagle, J. G. (2005). Stratigraphic placement and age of modern humans from Kibish, Ethiopia, *Nature, 433,* 733–736.

Milisauskas, S. (2002). *European prehistory: A survey.* New York: Academic Press.

Noonan, J. P., et al. (2006). Sequencing and analysis of Neanderthal genomic DNA. *Science 314(17),* 1113–1118.

Ofek, H. (2001). *Second nature: Economic origins of human evolution.* Cambridge: Cambridge University Press.

Oka, R. C., and Kusimba, C. M. (In Press). Archaeology of Trading systems—Part 2: The Development and evolution of local, regional and global trading patterns. *Journal of Archaeological Research.*

Olmert, M. D. (2009). *Made for each other: The biology of the human animal bond.* Philadelphia: Da Capo Press.

Ovchinnikov, I., Anders, G., Gotherstrom, A., Romanova, G., Kharitonov, V., Liden, K., et al. (2000). Molecular analysis of Neanderthal DNA from the northern Caucasus. *Nature, 404,* 490–493.

Rightmire, G. P. (2008). *Homo* in the middle Pleistocene: hypodigms, variation, and species recognition. *Evolutionary Anthropology, 17,* 8–21.

Shipman, P. (2008). Separating "us" from "them": Neanderthal and modern human behavior. *PNAS 105(38),* 14241–14242.

Smith, T. M., et al. (2007). Earliest evidence of modern human life history in North African early *Homo sapiens. PNAS 104(15),* 6128–6133.

Soffer, O. (1985). *The Upper Paleolithic of the Central Russian Plain.* Orlando: Academic Press.

Stringer, C. B., et al. (2008). Neanderthal exploitation of marine mammals in Gibraltar. *PNAS 105(38),* 14319–14324.

Stringer, C. (2002). Modern human origins: Progress and prospects. *Philosophial Transmissions of the Royal Society of London, 357,* 563–579.

Templeton, A. R. (2002). Out of Africa again and again. *Nature, 416,* 45–51.

Thorne, A. G., & Wolpoff, M. (1992). The multiregional evolution of humans. *Scientific American, 266*(4), 76–83.

Walker, P. (2001). A bioarchaeological perspective on the history of violence. *Annual Reviews in Anthropology, 30,* 573–596.

White, T. (1986). Cutmarks on the Bodo cranium: A case of prehistoric defleshing. *American Journal of Physical Anthropology, 69,* 503–509.

White, T., Asfaw, B., DeGusta, D., Gilbert, H., Richards, G. D., Suwa, G., et al. (2003). Pleistocene *Homo sapiens* from Middle Awash, Ethiopia. *Nature, 423,* 742–747.

Wolpoff, M., Hawkes, J., Frayer, D. W., & Hunley, K. (2001). Modern human ancestry at the peripheries: A test of the replacement theory. *Science, 291,* 293–297.

CHAPTER 10

Human Biological Diversity in Context

This chapter addresses the following questions:

▲ How do humans vary in external morphology (size, shape, and color)?

▲ How do humans vary genetically?

▲ How can the biocultural approach explain these patterns of variation?

▲ How do we know that there are no races, or biological subspecies, in modern humans?

▲ Why do we continue to use simplistic racial categories for humanity when we know they are not accurate?

What does skin color mean in our society? What does "race" mean? Why should we care? All of us encounter issues of race in our lives, but many Americans are loathe to talk about it. This is a problem in many areas. However, one issue that is common in the media is the impact of race on health. If you look at U.S. medical records, you find that rates of hypertension (high blood pressure) are higher, on average, in Americans of primarily African descent (called "Black") than in those of primarily western European descent (called "White"). Many doctors, and the public in general, frequently associate this biological difference with what we call race; the truth is much more interesting and not what most think. Work by anthropologists such as Clarence Gravlee and Lorena Madrigal demonstrates that our assumptions about genetic explanations based on underlying biological differences between Blacks and Whites are wrong. Madrigal's work shows us that unlike in the United States, African descendant populations in the Caribbean do not have this same hypertension issue. Gravlee's work shows us that hypertension risk is correlated with an individual's perceptions of their skin color, with Blacks with darker skin (or who perceive their skin to be darker) having higher risks of hypertension. How can this be? It is because our perceptions of race can affect our bodies, and the social history of what race means in the United States creates a series of difficult and negative relationships that can have real impacts on our individual health as well as our ability to function as a nation. This chapter will discuss what we actually know about human biological variation, how it challenges simple ideas about race,

■ FIGURE 10.1

Choosing your race. Note the numerous choices for "race."

→ **NOTE: Please answer BOTH Questions 7 and 8.**

7. Is Person 1 Spanish/Hispanic/Latino? *Mark* ☒ *the* **"No"** box if **not** *Spanish/Hispanic/Latino.*

☐ **No,** not Spanish/Hispanic/Latino   ☐ Yes, Puerto Rican

☒ Yes, Mexican, Mexican American, Chicano   ☐ Yes, Cuban

☐ Yes, other Spanish/Hispanic/Latino—*Print group.* ⤵

8. What is Person 1's race? *Mark* ☒ **one or more races** *to indicate what this person considers himself/herself to be.*

☐ White   ☐ Yes, Puerto Rican

☐ Black, African American, or Negro   ☐ Yes, Cuban

☐ American Indian or Alaska Native—*Print name of enrolled or principal tribe.* ⤵

☐ Asian Indian   ☐ Japanese   ☐ Native Hawaiian

☐ Chinese   ☐ Korean   ☐ Guamanian or Chamorro

☐ Filipino   ☐ Vietnamese   ☐ Samoan

☐ Other Asian—*Print race.* ⤵   ☐ Other Pacific Islander—*Print race.* ⤵

☒ Some other race—*Print race.* ⤵

M	E	X		I	C	A	N		A	M	E	R	I	C	A	N		

STOP & THINK

Why is it important for the U.S. government to know if someone is Spanish/Hispanic/Latino separately from the person's official race?

■ FIGURE 10.2

Variation in the human population. To which "race" would you assign each person in this photo? On what would you base your decision?

and finally why the United States has such difficulty talking about and dealing with issues of racial equality and interactions.

In the United States, we classify people into a cluster of races. These categories (Figure 10.1 shows the official census categories for race) reflect commonly held assumptions about the meaning of human biological variation, ethnicity, and our genetic and morphological diversity. In particular, we tend to think that groups of humans can be categorized as different races, usually about 3–5: Asian, Black, White, and sometimes Hispanic and American Indian.

What racial categories do reflect are some commonly held assumptions about how human variation, our biological diversity, is arranged. Many people assume that clear differences exist between cultural groups based on biological/genetic realities. These assumptions of patterned differences give us such stereotypes as "Black people are good athletes" or "Asians do well in academic settings."

The fact is that "race" in the sense that we normally use it is not a biological reality. As it is used in the United States today, "race" is a socially constructed notion, a social and cultural category arising from our history, demography, and sociopolitical circumstances. As we will see in this chapter, our commonly used racial categories do not reflect the patterned distribution of biological diversity in the human species (Figure 10.2).

With nearly 7 billion members, *Homo sapiens* is the most numerous and widespread of all the primates. In previous chapters we focused on the patterns and processes that have shaped humanity from our most distant ancestors to our current form. One striking outcome of these processes is that modern humans have very high levels of morphological variation but extremely low levels of interpopulational genetic diversity. In other words, humans come in many shapes, sizes, and skin colors, but our genetic variation across populations is relatively low for a primate or any mammal. In this chapter we review how and why modern humans vary biologically, and we explore the implications of these variations.

A Basic Summary of Human Evolution: the origin of behavioral and biological diversity

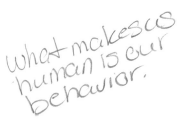

By reading chapters 1–9, you have learned a great deal about evolution, human biology, and human evolutionary history from primate studies and the fossil record. But we need to keep in mind that humans are much more than the form of our bodies and the artifacts we make. What truly makes us human is our behavior. We know that our earliest human ancestors lived in multi-adult groups that were at least as socially complex as contemporary ape and monkey societies. We also know that our ancestors used basic tools and showed sexual dimorphism, with males and females varying in size. Moreover, between ~2 million to 500,000 years ago early humans co-existed with other hominins, namely members of the genus *Paranthropus* (remember chapter 8). Our ancestors had to have interacted with these other hominins, and these interactions might even have affected our eventual success and the eventual extinction of the other hominins. Could it have been our abilities to exhibit more complex behavior than *Paranthropus* that helped us succeed? And as ancestral humans moved around and out of Africa, they encountered diverse ecologies and novel landscapes, leading to an expansion of the kind and complexity of behavior they required and the ways in which their bodies responded to ecological pressures. Our ancestors probably also began to show different ways of interacting with other groups as humanity spread across a broader and broader swath of the planet.

From the previous chapters we know that with the transition from early *Homo* through *Homo erectus* and *Homo ergaster* came increased energetic and child-rearing costs, and changes in their bodies. At the same time our ancestors began to engage in cooperative food collection, such as scavenging, hunting, and exploitation of tubers and roots; substantial food sharing; and cooperative caretaking of the young. Also during this time (~1.5–.5 million years ago), innovation in tool creation and use and an overall increased manipulation of the environment occurred, resulting in real and dramatic changes in the landscape and substantial niche construction by humans.

By 500,000–45,000 years ago (give or take 10,000 years) the human brain stopped growing in size, but it probably continued to increase in neurological complexity, maybe as a by-product of the increasingly complex tool kits, social behaviors, and challenges exerted by moving into new areas. Human groups exploited a wide variety of resources (on land, in coastal areas, rivers, swamps, mountains, etc.), and they increased both their geographic range (into higher-stress ecologies with more seasonal variation) and their energy acquisition (expanding the types and intensity of hunting and gathering of foods). In this later period, they expanded their use and control of fire. Also in this period, humans engaged more frequently in hunting very large animals and in cooperative care of the ill and elderly within groups. The human tool kit expanded into more fine-tuned tools of diverse types and uses, resulting in the emergence of traditions or styles of making items in some groups. These styles were not related to specific functions, but rather to an emerging human sense of beauty and group identity.

Language emerged at some point in this history, as did role differentiation along age and gender lines. Language enabled individuals to share histories within their groups, along with ideas about life, myths, histories, and futures across regions. Symbolic representation (like paintings of horses and people and figurines of men and women and mythical beasts) also became common, indicating that symbols and arts were becoming part of everyday life. And toward the end of this period, we see burial of the dead, sometimes with artifacts such as flowers, tools, or beads, suggesting the beginnings of belief systems involving an afterlife. These patterns all tell us that human societies were getting more complicated, that group and regional identities were becoming important, and that religious beliefs and practices were becoming ubiquitous in human groups.

Moving forward in history, from 45,000 years ago through today, human language and material culture became what we now take for granted as typical human behavior. The beginnings of settlements, early agriculture, and the domestication of animals may have led to the large-scale societies, groups that saw themselves as a distinct "people" with claims to the land and to mythological pasts and futures. Conflict between such populations became more common, as such groups invested more and more in a sense of local ethnicity, ownership of lands and shared (or different) religious belief systems. Along with this comes the division of labor (people doing different tasks in the community—farmers, warriors, chiefs, and so on), gender stratification (differences in social roles between men and women), wealth stratification (some unequal distribution of resources), and social restrictions on mating (who you can and cannot have children with). At this point the creation of socioeconomic unions of marriage also became standard in human societies.

Humans have long exhibited biological diversity

Morphological variation is well documented in our genus. The debate over the taxonomies of archaic humans, from *Homo erectus/ergaster* through archaic *Homo sapiens* and the Neanderthals, is strong evidence that variation in size and shape has long characterized our genus and perhaps our species. Along with this morphological variation, we can assume that genetic variation existed in the past, as we know it does in the present. However, genetic and morphological variation do not always follow the same patterns. Some characteristics, such as nuclear DNA and skin color variants, follow opposite patterns of distribution, while others, such as blood types and cranial measures, follow similar patterns.

To discuss these patterns of variation in humans effectively, we need to establish a framework for comparison. This framework has to take into account the basic evolutionary processes that we have been discussing throughout this text. Based on these processes, we can describe variation at several different levels (Figure 10.3). The first level is the variation that exists in our species as a whole. The second is the variation across major geographic regions in which members of our species exist. The third is the variation between populations within regions, and the fourth is the variation within single populations. This approach allows us to ask questions about similarities

CONNECTIONS

See chapters 8, page 219–245, and 9, pages 259–291, for the details of morphological evolution.

and differences across the entire species, between regions, and between and within specific populations of humans; it helps to give us the most effective overview of how our species varies biologically (Relethford, 2002).

A Visible but Misunderstood Variation: Skin "Color"

The most overemphasized and misunderstood aspect of human variation is skin color. The differences in the color or tone of human skin are not really color at all. Human skin has one main pigment (called **melanin**), and it comes in the colors black and brown. In addition to melanin, skin "color" is influenced by the thickness of the skin, the blood vessels (and the blood in them), and a minor pigment called *carotene*. In terms of color, there is very little variation in human skin. What makes a difference in appearance is the differential distribution of melanin and the other related biological components in the skin (or stratified epithelium, as it is called in chapter 2), which results in different intensities of light absorption and reflectance. Let's take a closer look at this process.

The skin consists of several layers, broadly divided into the dermis and the epidermis (Figure 10.4). The inner layers (the dermis) contain the blood vessels, hair follicles, and glands (such as sweat glands). The outer layers (the epidermis) consist of cells that continuously divide and replace themselves, moving toward the outermost layers (these are what we generally think of as "skin"). In the boundary between the dermis and epidermis is a type of cell called a **melanocyte**. Melanocytes produce melanin and distribute it into the cells of the epidermis. As the epidermal cells divide and move into the outer layers, they bring the melanin with them and distribute it across the epidermis. It is the density and distribution of melanin that causes different levels of reflection and absorption of light in the skin and thus the different skin "colors."

The number of melanocytes does not vary significantly from one human to another, but their relative clumping or dispersal and the

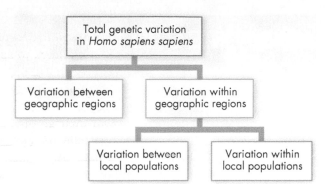

■ FIGURE 10.3
Levels of human variation. Variation exists within our species as a whole, as well as at the levels of geographic regions and local populations (derived from Relethford, 2002).

melanin
the main pigment in human skin, occurring in two forms: black and brown

melanocytes
cells that produce melanin

CONNECTIONS

See chapter 2, pages 49–50, for details about tissues, including skin.

■ FIGURE 10.4
Cross-section of human skin. Melanocytes lie between the dermis and the epidermis.

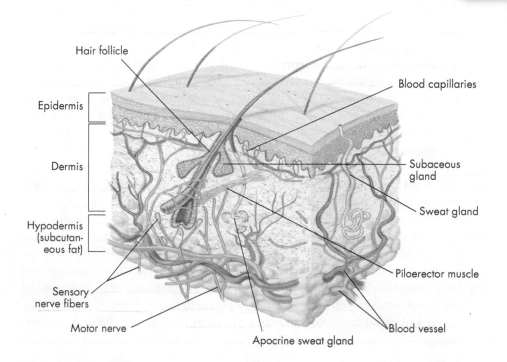

Hair follicle
Blood capillaries
Epidermis
Dermis
Subaceous gland
Sweat gland
Hypodermis (subcutaneous fat)
Piloerector muscle
Sensory nerve fibers
Blood vessel
Motor nerve
Apocrine sweat gland

Everyone Tans! But Skin Color is Still Culturally Defined

Knowing how melanin works also tells us that everyone tans. That is, all humans have a response to direct sunlight, a temporary increase in melanin production. Now, if your skin is already fairly dark, the tanning response is not that visible, but it does happen. However, if you have light skin, then the tan and the freckles that can accompany it are very prominent. Tanning response brings up a very interesting biocultural situation: in many parts of North America and Europe people with darker skins are discriminated against, but at the same time many people with lighter skins expose themselves to dangerous overdoses of UV light (sunshine) in order to initiate the tanning response and make their skins darker, but are not discriminated against when they achieve it. Some people even pay money to specialized stores to enclose them in UV radiation chambers to cause tanning or even to spray their bodies with chemicals that mimic the look of melanin production. In other parts of the planet (many parts of East and Southeast Asia), darker skinned individuals apply chemicals to their skins to lighten them and lessen the effects of melanin production. Aside from demonstrating that humans are sometimes weird, this also shows us how cultural perceptions interact with our biology to create some really interesting behavioral patterns. Here we can see that in some cultures "dark" skin can be considered negative if you have it, but positive if you obtain it chemically or by exposure to possible cancer-causing radiation. Alternatively, in other places it is considered positive to chemically block the actions of your own melanin, and appear lighter. Skin color, tanning, and cultural perceptions show us that humans are complicated biocultural beings and that even our biology can act as cultural symbol more than physiological trait.

density of melanin does. The more melanin produced and distributed to the epidermis, the less one type of light (white light) is reflected and the more another type of light (ultraviolet, or UV, light) is blocked from entering the dermis. If melanocytes are evenly distributed throughout the skin, melanin is widespread, but if melanocytes are relatively clumped, then melanin is not evenly dispersed. Thus, if a human's melanocytes are actively producing large amounts of melanin that is being effectively distributed throughout the epidermis, that individual will look darker (reflect less light) than an individual with less active melanin production and distribution. Because individuals with less reflection have more melanin in the epidermis, their skin can prevent more UV light from reaching the dermis.

Ultraviolet light in high doses can cause severe damage to the layers of the dermis and even plays a role in initiating melanomas (skin cancer) and possibly disrupting other aspects of skin and physiological functioning (Jablonski, 2004; Jablonski & Chaplin, 2000). Until recently, when a hole formed in the ozone layer near the South Pole, much of the planet was moderately protected from UV light by ozone in the atmosphere. However, the intensity of UV light has always been greater at lower latitudes (closer to the equator) and less at higher latitudes (nearer the poles). Therefore, increased rates of melanin production and distribution through the epidermis would be favored by natural selection in areas of higher UV stress. In fact, this is exactly what we see on average in human populations that have lived in different geographic areas for long periods of time (Figure 10.5). It is hypothesized, with substantial research support, that this relationship between melanin density and UV light is the basis of variation in human skin reflectance (Jablonski, 2004; Jablonski & Chaplin, 2000; Relethford, 1997).

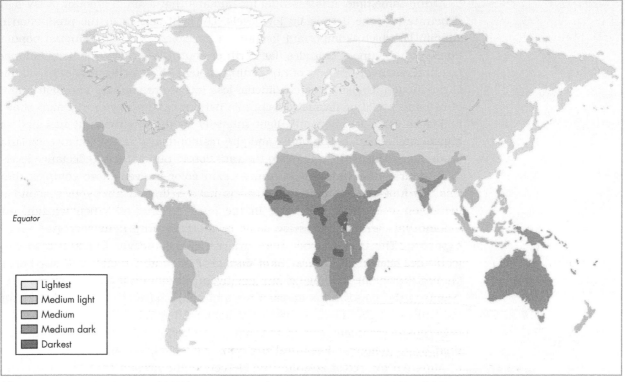

(a)

Lightest
Medium light
Medium
Medium dark
Darkest

Equator

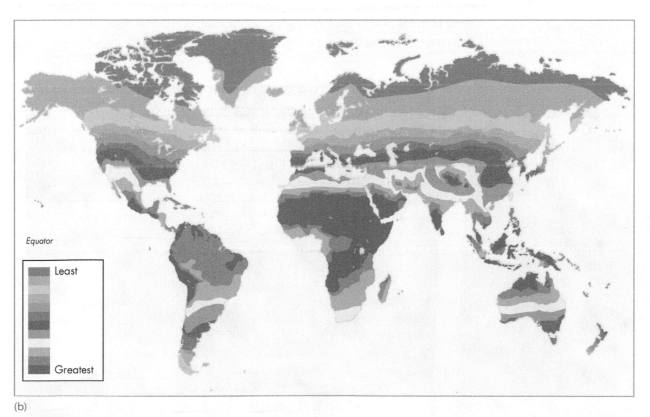

(b)

Equator

Least

Greatest

■ FIGURE 10.5

Skin "color" (a) and ultraviolet light intensity (b). Map a shows distribution of human skin "color," based on five arbitrary categories. In general, ultraviolet light intensity is greatest close to the equator. Note the similarities between the two maps. What factors might account for the differences?

At the same time, it is essential for humans that a small amount of UV light penetrate into the dermis. In low levels, UV light assists in the production of vitamin D, which is important for human physiological health. Human populations near the upper latitudes (far north or south), where UV intensity is lower, face the potential problem of not getting enough UV light for sufficient vitamin D production. Under these conditions, less intense production and distribution of melanin would be favored. Again, this pattern can be seen in the map shown in Figure 10.5. In short, UV light intensity in the environment has had an impact on human populations, and the resultant adaptation (relative melanin production/density) helps explain the variation in human skin reflectance levels.

Of course, the variation in human skin color is even more complex than this. As just one example, all humans have a limited ability to respond to increased stress from UV light, in the form of tanning. When we tan, our melanocytes temporarily increase their melanin output in response to UV exposure. The effectiveness and patterns of melanocyte function also vary with age, health, and a variety of diseases, as in all functions of our bodies (Jablonski, 2004). Finally, movement by humans across latitudes and gene flow between populations across time and space have resulted in a substantial mixing of the adaptations to UV light with other factors. Thus, current skin "color" parameters are set by natural selection but modified and distributed by gene flow and cultural patterns (Jablonski, 2004).

Although skin color is quite variable across the human species, most of the variation is accounted for by regions (latitudes); very little variation occurs among regional populations or within a population. We can find darker skinned populations in areas of sub-Saharan Africa, south Asia, Southeast Asia, and Melanesia/Polynesia (See Figure 10.6). We can find lighter skinned populations in the

■ **FIGURE 10.6**
The individuals in this picture represent populations from northern and southern areas of the planet, but not necessarily from where you think. The guy in red is from Eastern and Southern European descent but the three kids are not from Africa, they are from Melanesia (Indonesian Papua in western New Guinea)!

Americas, northeast Asia, and northern Eurasia (Europe). The main exception to this pattern is found in populations that have experienced large, recent migrations from various locations around the planet (such as in the United States). In sum, skin color cannot be used as a characteristic to lump specific populations together aside from general assignment to regions of lower or higher latitudes. These patterns of pigment distribution, and the resultant variation in reflectance levels (that we mistakenly call color), are due in large part to human adaptation and gene flow.

Another Visible Difference: Body Shape and Size

Another characteristic in which modern humans vary quite a lot is the size and shape of our bodies. Such variations can be quantified with a series of measurements that assess the relative contributions of different parts of the body to the overall shape. Some of these measurements are in the form of indices, such as the **cormic index,** the ratio of sitting height to standing height, and the **intermembral index,** the ratio of arm length to leg length. These sorts of measures demonstrate that two humans of the same stature may in fact have very different body types. We also measure the pattern and density of adipose tissue on the body (body fat) to get further information about shape and composition. Finally, the Body Mass Index (BMI, a measurement of weight over squared height) is often used to assess patterned variations in human size and shape.

How variable are modern humans? Average body mass (measured as weight within each sex) varies by as much as 50%, meaning that the largest humans are half again as heavy as the smallest (or more in some extreme cases). The width of the human body at the pelvis (measured as the length between the iliac blades) varies by about 25% across our species (Ruff, 2002), and average heights range from about 150 to 185 cm (just under 5 feet to about 6 feet). Aside from the extreme ends of the height spectrum, the human species exhibits about a 10% variation in height overall (Figure 10.7). Sexual dimorphism between males and females in human populations is about 15%.

cormic index
standing height divided by sitting height

intermembral index
ratio of arm length to leg length

■ **FIGURE 10.7**
Human body builds. The body builds of an Inuit (a) of northern North America and Nilotics of the eastern African savanna (b) show the extremes of human variation.

(a)

(b)

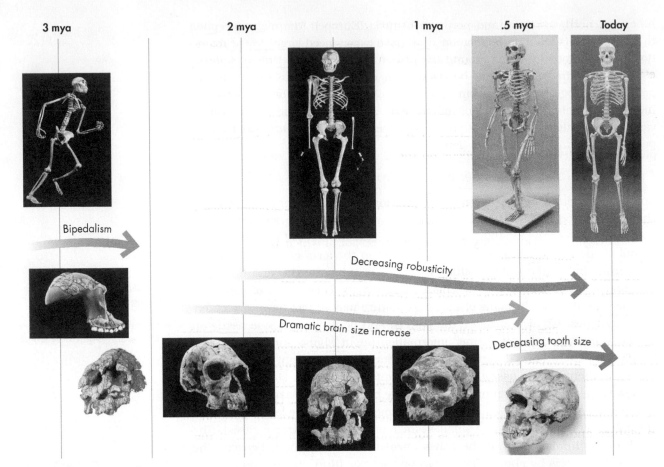

3 mya 2 mya 1 mya .5 mya Today

Bipedalism

Decreasing robusticity

Dramatic brain size increase

Decreasing tooth size

■ **FIGURE 10.8**

Trends in body shape and structure in *Homo* species. In the past 2 million years, the human lineage has shown decreasing robustness, important changes in the size and shape of the cranium (resulting from dramatic increases in brain size), and decreasing tooth size. All of these changes have occurred since the early hominins became bipedal more than 3 million years ago.

Although this amount of variation may seem significant, it is small compared to the variation seen in the early hominins and the earlier members of the genus *Homo*. Since the first appearance of *Homo erectus* (or *ergaster*) in Africa approximately 1.8 million years ago, a series of trends in body size and shape have influenced how modern humans look today, including changes in cranial structure, tooth size, and robustness (Figure 10.8). Modern levels of height and sexual dimorphism had been reached by about half a million years ago. Body mass increased in late archaic humans (Neanderthals) and then started to decrease again about 50,000 years ago (Ruff, 2002). The patterns of change that have occurred over the last 50,000 years probably result from increasingly efficient food processing technologies and other biocultural means of reducing the environmental stresses on the human body, such as more protective shelter and clothing. As humans made the transition from foraging to food growing, and as global climates warmed up in the last 10,000 years or so, human bodies continued to become slightly smaller in terms of body mass (except for a small increase in body mass in some northern populations) (Ruff, 2002). There also appear to be some very recent pronounced increases in stature (height) and body mass in many developed nations, as health care and nutritional patterns change dramatically.

If we think about this variation at the level of the species, regions, and populations, we see that, in general, there are correlations with region (again measured as latitude) for body mass and width. Peoples closer to the extreme northern and southern regions of the planet (such as Alaska or southern Chile) are larger. These correlations do not hold for height, however (Ruff, 2002). For height, there tends to be less variation within populations and more differences between populations. As discussed later in this chapter, however, the size and shape of modern human bodies are greatly affected by our behaviors, migrations, dietary patterns, activity patterns, diseases, and of course, the parameters established by natural selection.

STOP & THINK

Where does most variation in size and shape of people come from today?

A Cornerstone of Variation Research: Skull Morphology

As is evident from our discussions of the fossil hominins and humans in previous chapters, we tend to focus on the size and shape of the skull when we talk about the morphology of humans and human ancestors. Because of its role in housing the brain, arguably our primary adaptive organ, the skull has special significance in the study of human evolution. Researchers have a long history of trying to use proxy measures on the skull to assess everything from intelligence to personality to biological race (all of which have met with failure to varying degrees).

We have seen that the size of the brain, and thus the cranium, increased over human history, until the brain reached its current size about 200,000 to 300,000 years ago. With the first modern humans, the shape of the cranium also changed, from the long, low shape of the archaic humans to the high, rounded form we have today. Although simple measures of cranial shape, such as the cephalic index, have been used to categorize human skulls, modern techniques involve multiple measures, with the best using as many as 57 different measurements per skull (Figure 10.9). Because of variation in stature and body shape, there is substantial variation in the size of the

CONNECTIONS

See chapter 2, pages 50–51, for details on the structure of the skull.

CONNECTIONS

Skulls Are Us?

Anyone watching forensics shows on TV knows that any DNA or a skull can tell you everything you need to know about a mystery murder victim. In reality, that is only partially true. In the United States, we do have DNA databases, but they are still very limited in providing positive identification—the victim's DNA has to be in the database already—but having a skull can tell you a great deal about the victim. A talented forensic scientist can get a good idea of gender, age, lifestyle, and even social race by examining a mystery skull. Gender, age, and diet make sense, but if races are socially constructed and don't exist biologically, why can you indentify it from a skull? Although there is only one biological race in modern humans, the reality of social races can affect our biology. Racial divisions not only reflect relative degrees of ancestry from different parts of the planet (which affects skull shape), but also strongly affect marriage customs, settlement patterns, work patterns, and nutrition. These all create social race clusters in skull shape. On average (but not always) one can assign a mystery skull from today in the United States to one of the general racial categories (Black, White, Asian). But, these are not fixed clusters (biological races); they are more reflective of social structures. For example, White skulls from the 1840s are as easy to tell apart from White skulls from the 1970s as current Black, White, and Asian skulls are to tell apart. Are 1840s Whites and 1970s Whites two races? No, but they are affected by different social, dietary, and living patterns, so their skulls look like different clusters. None of this is to say that telling skulls apart is always accurate (it is not), or that the measures of differentiation for American skulls will work in Brazil, France, or India. What this tells us is that social divisions can affect our bodies in real ways.

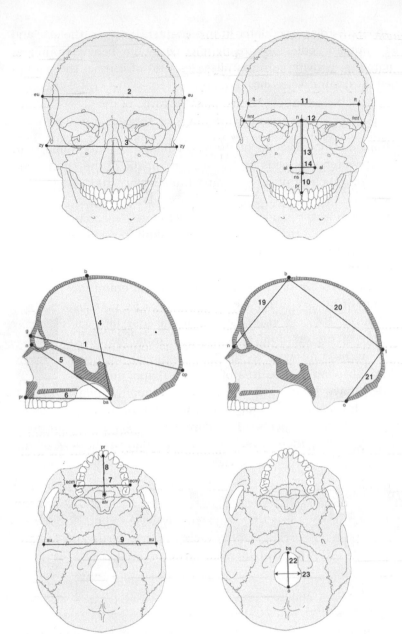

■ FIGURE 10.9
Basic measurements of skulls. Skull shape has varied greatly over time, and it varies today both within and between populations. In this figure we see some of the more common cranial measurements used in biological anthropology, such as the width of the cranium, the width and breadth of the nasal opening, the shape of the foramen magnum, the shape of the dental arcade on the maxilla, and the overall shape of the skull.

CONNECTIONS

See chapter 9, pages 272–274, for an overview of what brain size actually means in modern humans.

cranium in humans, with normal size for a fully functional brain ranging from about 1000 to about 2000 cc (61–110 cubic in.). This means that some human brains are nearly twice the size of other human brains, but all function equally well.

Because of the very broad distribution of humans across the planet, different climates and differential rates of gene flow have had an impact on the shape of the skull. If we look closely at how this variation is distributed, we see that the vast majority of the variation in skull morphology is within populations, not between populations or regions, as for skin reflectance. However, there is slightly more variation between regions than between populations within a region (Relethford, 2002). In other words, within any population, you will have a variety of cranial morphologies, and across nearby populations, there will be little difference; but comparing disparate regions will demonstrate noticeable skull differences (Relethford, 2009). Since most features of the skull (including size) are fully functional within a wide range of shapes, there does not appear to be tight selection pressure on the details of skull structure. This may be partly why we see so much variation within human populations. Some aspects of skull morphology appear to be responsive to changes in nutrition, climate, and other aspects of development, and they are also highly correlated with gene flow (Jantz & Meadows Jantz, 2000; Sparks & Jantz, 2002).

Sex Differences Are Seen in the Skeletal and Soft Tissue of Humans

In addition to the basic pattern of sexual dimorphism in body size in modern humans, there are also specific differences in aspects of skeletal and soft tissue. A pronounced difference is found in the width and shape of the pelvis. In females, the ilia are more broadly flared outward, the subpubic angle is greater, and the size of the space created by the pelvic girdle (birth canal) is larger than in males. The cranium in females has a more vertical forehead, less pronounced brow ridges, smaller mastoids, and fewer overall muscle markings. The angle of the jaw (ramus of the mandible) is also greater, on average, in females than males (Figure 10.10).

In the soft tissues, the reproductive organs and external genitalia also differ between males and females. These differences are more of degree than of kind, since the same embryonic tissue masses give rise to both the female and male genitalia (Fausto-Sterling, 2002). Females give birth and lactate, necessitating specific differences in internal structures (such as the presence of a uterus and mammary glands) and resulting in some external differences as well (development of breasts). Again, because the tissue masses are the same during embryonic development, structural similarities remain in spite of developmental differences (for example, males have nipples but not the ability to lactate, because they do not have developed mammary glands). The male reproductive tract engages in spermatogenesis for the majority of the life span, whereas females cease reproductive activity at some point between 45 and 60 years of age (menopause). The cycling hormones in males and females are the same, but there are differences between the sexes in the levels and patterns of some of those hormones (such as estrogen, testosterone, progesterone, and follicle stimulating hormone). In addition to these basic differences, there are also muscular differences, with males having on average higher muscle density per unit area than females.

Human females and males follow the general pattern of adipose tissue deposition (subcutaneous fat) for mammals (Figure 10.11). This pattern is similar for both sexes in overall location of fat deposition, but males and females exhibit slightly different rates of deposition by location and rates of fat utilization (Pond, 1997). Because of our unique locomotary adaptation (bipedality), humans have a different relationship with gravity than do other mammals. So, although we lay down fat around the body in similar ways, the pull of gravity on that fat and the structure of our bipedal bodies create

CONNECTIONS

See chapter 2, pages 49–50, for discussions of the muscles and tissues.

STOP & THINK

The sex differences in fat distribution of pelvic girdles help us better understand some culturally important differences in the way men and women look when they walk.

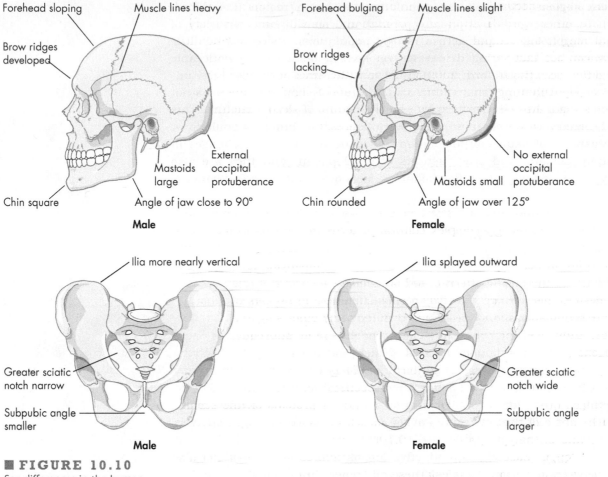

Male

Forehead sloping
Brow ridges developed
Muscle lines heavy
Mastoids large
External occipital protuberance
Chin square
Angle of jaw close to 90°

Female

Forehead bulging
Brow ridges lacking
Muscle lines slight
No external occipital protuberance
Mastoids small
Chin rounded
Angle of jaw over 125°

Male

Ilia more nearly vertical
Greater sciatic notch narrow
Subpubic angle smaller

Female

Ilia splayed outward
Greater sciatic notch wide
Subpubic angle larger

■ **FIGURE 10.10**
Sex differences in the human cranium and pelvis. These differences allow biological anthropologists to identify skeletal remains as belonging to either males or females.

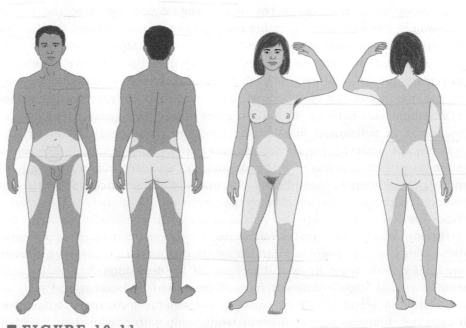

■ **FIGURE 10.11**
Subcutaneous fat distribution in males and females. Note the slightly different areas of fat deposition in men and women.

different adipose accumulations than in other mammals. This also creates the differences in the general appearance of male and female human bodies.

Returning to our comparisons at the species, regional, and population levels, we can see that variation between the sexes exists at the species level, but specific patterns of differentiation between the sexes may also be found between populations, given patterns of height and weight variations. These differences can also be enhanced by specific cultural patterns, including the gender-based division of labor in different cultures.

The Impact of Disease Environments: Variation in the Human Immune System

The forces of evolution (natural selection, gene flow, genetic drift, and mutation) combine with increasingly complex cultural patterns in humans to make diseases a major factor in creating and influencing human diversity. When humans began to live in permanent settlements, with an accompanying focus on agriculture and animal domestication, and subsequent increased human population densities, disease began to play a substantial role in human evolution.

Modern humans are more widely spread than any other single mammalian species; thus, we encounter more environments and subsequently more pathogens (infectious diseases) as well. Clearly, the immune system's ability to respond to a diverse array of pathogen challenges is important in human evolution. One vital part of our immune response is the **Human Leukocyte Antigen (HLA) System**, which consists of a series of proteins on the surface of white blood cells that recognize foreign particles or infectious agents. These proteins (the phenotypic products of the HLA system) differentiate between "self" and "other" based on specific chemical structures and help signal the immune system that foreign substances are present in the body.

The HLA system is one of the most variable genetic systems in humans. There are multiple loci (genes) involved, each having a few to more than 100 alleles. Thus, an enormous array of possible genetic combinations is involved in the HLA system, so that very few humans, even within the same family, share a genotype and subsequent phenotype that are exactly alike. This means that within any human population there can be substantial variation in immune system response. The rate and pattern of human movements around the globe in the last 50,000 years suggest that this variability has been favored by natural selection, since it may result in increased chances of individual survival and reproduction. In modern times, this variation has an interesting by-product: It makes organ transplants very difficult. Because our immune systems are so variable, transferring tissue from one human to another, even from one family member to another, can still result in rejection of the transplanted tissue by the host body due to its different HLA phenotype.

Several diseases have specific origins in the allele frequencies found in different populations. For example, albinism, the lack of melanin production or distribution, is a disorder that appears to reside in some rare alleles at specific loci on chromosomes 9, 11, and 15, which are involved in the production and distribution of melanin (Molnar, 2002). Albinism comes in two types. One type is found in a set of alleles whose presence and products result in lack of production of the compound tyrosinase, which is required for melanin production. This form of albinism is rare and found primarily in some populations from parts of western Eurasia. In the second type of albinism, tyrosinase is

Human Leukocyte Antigen (HLA) System
part of the human immune system that helps signal the presence of foreign substances in the body

CONNECTIONS

See details on genetics in chapter 3, pages 82–87.

STOP & THINK

How does the HLA system affect operations and modern medicine?

produced, but the melanin pathway fails and ultimately no melanin production occurs, resulting in depigmentation. This second type is more common and is found in a variety of populations across the globe, especially in Africa and the Americas. Interestingly, because each of the types has a functioning melanin system except for one component, two individuals with the two different types of albinism can mate and produce a non-albino child, because their allele patterns complement one another.

Many other diseases and genetic disorders are more common in some human populations than in others due to factors such as mutation, gene flow (or lack thereof), genetic drift, and cultural and ecological/environmental factors. Because people carry different alleles and mutations in their immune systems and have been exposed to different pathogens, there is tremendous diversity in humans in reactions and susceptibilities to disease.

Again, with genetically variable systems such as the HLA system, we see the majority of the variation within populations and some variation at the level of the species, but not necessarily by regions. With specific allelic disorders, we see substantial variation within populations and between populations within a region, but not so much between regions. The exceptions to this pattern are found in the genetic disorders that arise in response to specific environmental challenges (such as sickle cell disease, discussed later in this chapter). In these cases most variation occurs between regions (or environmental zones) or between populations within those regions.

Blood Groups Vary Within and Across Populations

Among the most studied areas of human variation are the sets of proteins that coat the red blood cells and serve a variety of functions in the human body. We call these different protein sets *blood types*. The best-known blood type classification is the ABO system, which is often coupled with another system, the Rhesus blood type (expressed as Rh+ or Rh−). Overall, we know of more than 15 different blood type systems whose alleles appear in variable frequencies across the human species.

In chapter 3 we briefly introduced the ABO system, which is characterized by four alleles, A1, A2, B, and O. A1 and A2 are very similar, so they are usually considered to be a single phenotype. The three main alleles, A, B, and O, have a specific set of dominance relationships with one another, in which A and B are dominant to O and codominant to one another. In other words, the phenotype of the genotypes AA and AO is A, that of BB and BO is B, that of OO is O, and that of AB is AB. In this system there are six possible genotypes and four possible phenotypes. Overall, the specieswide distribution of these alleles is approximately 62.5% O, 21.5% A, and 16% B (Molnar, 2002). However, as discussed in chapter 2, in each human population we see very different distributions (Figure 10.12).

How do we explain this variable distribution of the allele frequencies across human populations? First, O is probably the most common because it is the original allele and A and B are more recent variants (mutations of the original allele). This relationship is suggested by the chemical structure of O, A, and B, with the latter two being the same as the O molecule with the addition of a terminal sugar. Second, it appears that differential disease resistance may be conferred by the different ABO phenotypes. This suggests that in some environments, specific blood types may increase or decrease one's chance of surviving a pathogen attack. Finally, because of the patterns of movements of humans over the last 50,000 years or so, it appears that certain founder

STOP & THINK

Why do so many human groups use "blood" as a defining characteristic, and think their blood is different from other groups' blood?

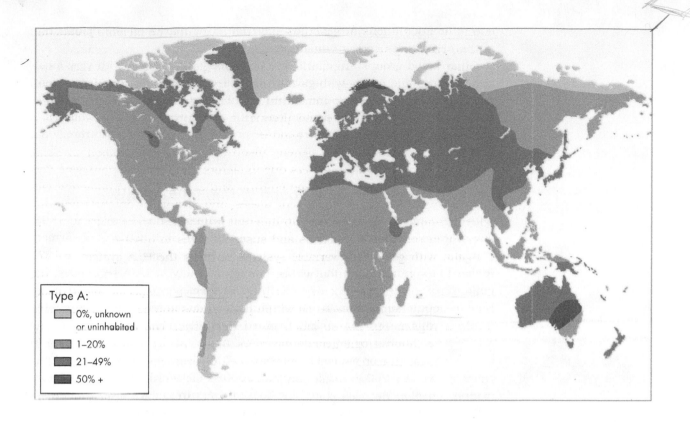

Type A:

▢ 0%, unknown
  or uninhabited

▢ 1–20%

▢ 21–49%

▢ 50% +

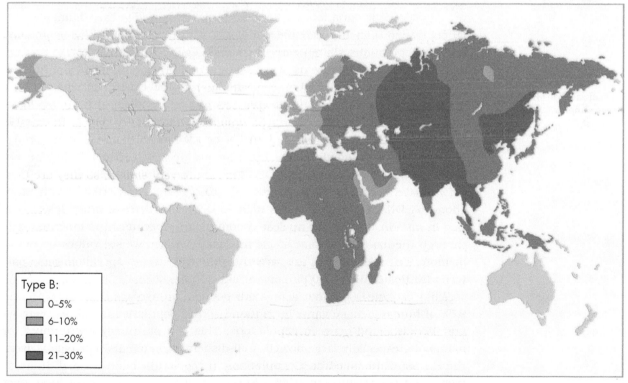

Type B:

▢ 0–5%

▢ 6–10%

▢ 11–20%

▢ 21–30%

■ FIGURE 10.12

Distribution of A and B phenotypes. These maps show the distribution of blood types A and B. Note that no obvious pattern appears.

effects or fluctuations in gene flow have left their marks on the distribution of the ABO alleles across human populations.

Other blood groups are distributed in various ways, some with very localized patterns and others with globally dispersed patterns. In the ABO system, much of the variation is found within populations, but in some cases, especially in those regions and populations with substantial founder effects (as is proposed for the Americas), there can be pronounced regional or intraregional variation.

Most Genetic Variation Is Found Within Populations

With the completion of the first draft of the human genome project in 1998, one of the most startling propositions about human variation was confirmed: Humans demonstrate little genetic variation between populations. In 1972 Richard Lewontin argued that despite wide variability in DNA sequences, the majority of genetic variation in the human species can be found in every human population (Lewontin, 1972). Multiple research teams have supported this assertion and demonstrated its reality, whether they are looking at nuclear or mitochondrial DNA, amino acid sequence variation in proteins, or noncoding regions of DNA (Kittles & Weiss, 2003; Long et al., 2009; Hunley et al., 2009; Relethford, 2002; Templeton, 1999). But this statement doesn't seem to make sense. It suggests that, despite the wide dispersal of our species across the planet and observed variations in morphology, the vast majority of human genetic variation lies between individuals *within* each human population rather than between the populations themselves. In other words, all human populations share nearly the same genetic variation.

The statistical measure used to assess genetic variation is Fst, the fraction of variation that is found between samples. In the case of genetic Fst, the variations we refer to are the frequencies of a given allele at a known locus (genes), and the samples used are human populations. An Fst of 0.0 means no genetic differences at all, and an Fst of 1.0 means the compared populations are 100% different for that locus (or multiple loci). When we look at Fst across multiple human nuclear DNA loci, we see values ranging from 0.03 to 0.17 (Kittles & Weiss, 2003; Relethford, 2002; Templeton, 1999). With mitochondrial DNA, we see values as high as 0.24, but there is much less variation in mtDNA than in the nuclear genome, partly because it is inherited only through the mother. At some single nuclear DNA loci, we see values up to 0.4 or more, but these values are rare and primarily due to specific disease patterns (Kittles & Weiss, 2003; Long et al., 2009).

What this means is that across our genome an average between 83% and 97% of human genetic variation is found within populations, and between 3% and 17% is found between populations. This is a startlingly low number for mammals, especially large-bodied, well-dispersed mammals. For comparison, the Fst for white-tailed deer populations in the southeastern United States is more than 0.7 (Templeton, 1999). In other words, a population of these deer from northern North Carolina and a population from Florida have more genetic differences than do human populations from Central America, central Asia, and central Africa. Along similar lines, if you compare any two humans from anywhere on the entire planet, you will find, on average, one fourth the amount of genetic diversity between them than you would if you compared any two chimpanzees, which are found in only a limited distribution in Africa (Kittles & Weiss, 2003).

CONNECTIONS

See chapter 3, pages 72–82, for details on DNA.

Fst
statistical measurement of the fraction of variation found between samples

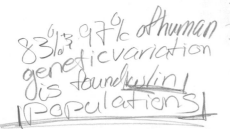

83% to 97% of human genetic variation is found within populations

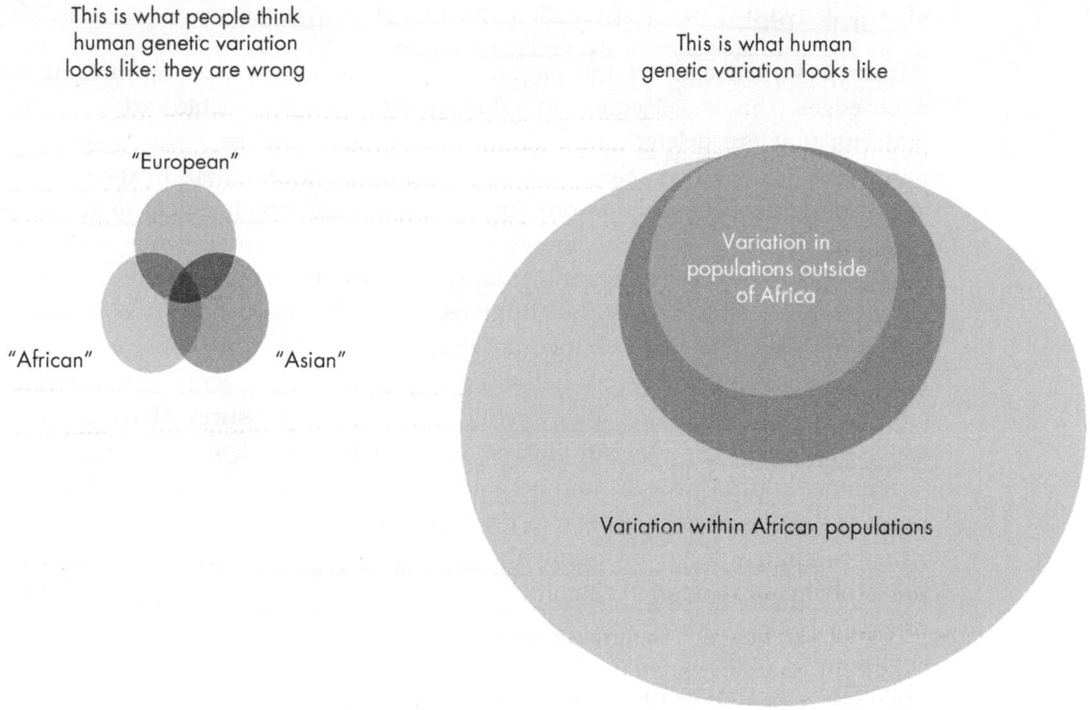

This is what people think
human genetic variation
looks like: they are wrong

This is what human
genetic variation looks like

"European"

"African"   "Asian"

Variation in
populations outside
of Africa

Variation within African populations

■ FIGURE 10.13
What the distribution of human
genetic variation looks like.

A final and very important aspect of the distribution of genetic diversity in humans is its pattern relative to the African continent. There is nearly twice as much genetic divergence (higher Fst values) among African populations than among non-African populations (Kittles & Weiss, 2003). In fact, if you take all the genetic variation in African populations and compared it to all the genetic variation in populations outside of Africa, you would find that all outside-Africa variation is found within Africa as well. See Figure 10.13. This pattern, coupled with the fact that there appears to be more DNA sequence variation within Africa than outside of Africa, suggests that modern humans have been in Africa longer than anywhere else on the planet. This finding could support either the Recent African Origin model, which proposes a single movement out of Africa between 150,000 and 200,000 years ago, or a Multiple Dispersal model, which proposes many movements in and out of Africa (see chapter 9), with African populations contributing prominently to modern gene pools.

Human biological diversity is best explained using a biocultural approach

Humans are highly variable in morphology, but we do not vary in random or simple ways. In fact, given the patterns of variation just reviewed and everything covered in the preceding chapters, it should be apparent that human variation can best be explained when viewed from a biocultural perspective. By viewing human biology as fully integrated and intertwined with human cultural behavior patterns, we can better understand why humans vary the way they do. The basic evolutionary patterns of natural selection, gene flow, and genetic drift, coupled with genetic mutation, can tell us a great deal about human variation. However, these patterns are interconnected with human cultural behavior, such as mating patterns, subsistence patterns, and the human tendency to use extrasomatic means to alter their environment.

Natural Selection and Human Cultural Behavior

Natural selection can set the parameters of human variation by molding its outer edges. That is, selection can influence the range of possible variants, since patterns that are deleterious in given environments will be reduced or eliminated over time. When selection pressures are strong, we would expect to see less variation; when selection pressures are weak, we would expect to see more variation. However, cultural factors also play a role: Humans use tools and other items to deal with environmental challenges and even to modify the environment itself. This means that humans can influence the kinds of selection pressures they face. For example, the dramatic reduction in robustness in our lineage over time can be explained in part by our ability to acquire and process foodstuffs with tools. This ability reduces the direct pressures of selection for traits such as large, powerful molars, stout bodies, and dense muscles.

Human cultural patterns and behaviors also allow us to exploit extreme environments that we could not live in if we had to rely solely on our morphologies. Humans change their environments by altering patterns of food availability, predator threats, and even climate, such that the types and patterns of selection pressures change as we change our niche (the way in which we relate to our environment and the other organisms within it). For example, today when we build cities we change the actual climate by paving much open area and increasing ozone (smog) and carbon dioxide emissions, which raises the ambient temperature. The changes in temperature and atmosphere alter the soil chemistry and increase the environmental challenges for plants. This in turn affects what types of animals can live in and on the plants, which changes the faunal makeup and the potential disease host reservoir. As the number of specific animals goes up or down, so do the populations of disease parasites carried by these animals (such as rats, for example). So as we modify our environment culturally to benefit us (shelter, transportation, industry), we alter its structure such that the potential selective pressures (types and patterns of diseases) also change: humans "do" niche construction more than any other organism.

Gene Flow: Population Movement and Mating

Gene flow clearly plays a prominent role in any explanation of modern human variation. Movement by populations and mating between individuals from different populations must have been common throughout the history of our species, as it continues to be today. The sheer lack of dramatic genetic differences between populations suggests that, on average, gene flow across the human species is quite extensive. The role of gene flow is also demonstrated by the isolation-through-distance model, which shows that human populations with some of the highest Fst differences are those that are most widely dispersed geographically or have been isolated geographically for a substantial period of time (Hunley et al., 2009; Long et al., 2009; Templeton, 1999).

In modern humans, cultural and economic patterns influence how we associate with one another. This in turn affects the distribution of allele frequencies and morphological patterns, affecting how populations look, at both the phenotypic and the genotypic levels. Mating within and between populations is decidedly social. The movement of alleles (mating) in the human species is very much influenced by cultural facets such as language, religion, socioeconomic class, nationality, kin group, and so on. This is abundantly seen when we examine marriage and mating patterns and how they are influenced by religion, social class, ethnicity, language, and other

CONNECTIONS

See chapter 4, pages 99–101, to review the definitions of these processes of evolution.

cultural factors in any given society. Thus, our biological diversity is inextricable from our cultural patterns of marriage, sex, and exchange; they are integrated as a single complex system.

Genetic Drift: Founder Effects

Genetic drift also has a role in causing genetic differences (increasing Fst measures), especially in small, isolated, or founder effect populations. For humans, founder effects can occur for cultural reasons. In chapter 4 we described the Tristan da Cunha islanders as an example of the founder effect. Their allele frequencies, especially for the disease retinitis pigmentosa, were dramatically different from those in their population of origin or in the human species as a whole. Although the founder effect is a biological or genetic phenomenon, the decision of the initial settlers to leave South Africa for the island of Tristan da Cunha was cultural—a cultural decision with evolutionary (biological) consequences.

Mutation: Allele Variation in an Exploding Population

Finally, mutation is ongoing in all human populations and occurs within a cultural context. Mutation keeps adding to the allelic variation in humans, and the more humans there are, the more variants we can expect. The recent rapid and dramatic changes in human culture, such as agriculture, medical technologies, and so on, have resulted in a population explosion of mind-boggling proportions and an increase in our genetic variation. There are now more than 6.8 billion humans on the planet; whereas just a century ago there were fewer than 1 billion, and 20,000 years ago, there were probably fewer than 150 million. This rapid population increase is a result of the way we change our surroundings and ourselves and thus is truly and inextricably biocultural and niche constructive.

STOP & THINK

In the four years between editions of this textbook, the world's population grew by about 8%!

Examples of Selection and Adaptation in Human Variation

If human variation is best explained in a biocultural context, and if natural selection is one of the principal driving forces in biological change, then human culture and natural selection must have a complex and fascinating relationship. Unlike the simplistic assertions of the social Darwinists (as described in chapter 1), the real relationship between humanity and natural selection is complex and provides us with excellent examples of the biocultural context of human variation.

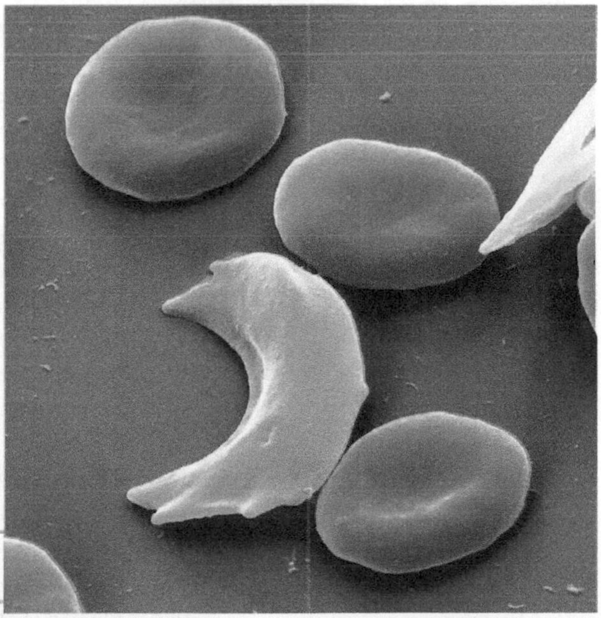

FIGURE 10.14
A sickle-shaped red blood cell. Compare the sickled cell to the normal, healthy red blood cells that surround it.

Sickle Cell Disease, Malaria, and Human Habitat Alteration

One of the best-known examples of the interrelationship between natural selection and culture is the case of sickle cell disease, malaria, and human habitat alteration. Sickle cell disease is a blood disorder that can occur in individuals who carry two copies of a recessive allele for a protein that is part of hemoglobin (an oxygen-transporting component of red blood cells). In times of physiological stress, the protein causes some red blood cells to become sickle shaped, which prevents them from effectively transporting oxygen (Figure 10.14). The resulting

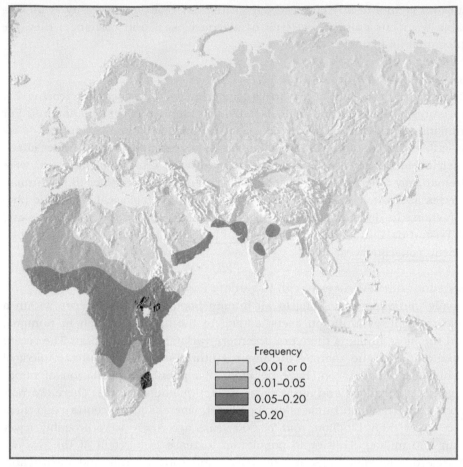

Frequency

	<0.01 or 0
	0.01–0.05
	0.05–0.20
	≥0.20

■ FIGURE 10.15
Distribution of the sickle cell allele. Compare with Figure 10.16.

CONNECTIONS

See chapter 3, pages 82–85, for mendelian genetics and the ideas of dominant and recessive alleles.

illness can be lethal, especially if there are other diseases in the environment that can attack the weakened individual.

The mutation that causes the malfunctioning allele shows up in all human populations (at least five separate forms of the mutation are known) but tends to disappear rather quickly, since it has a negative impact on fitness and would be readily selected out of the population over time. However, in some populations in Africa, the Arabian Peninsula, and the Indian subcontinent, we see relatively high, sustained frequencies of one or more forms of the sickle-cell-inducing allele (Figure 10.15). The survival of the allele is due, in large part, to its relationship with malaria.

Malaria is a disease caused by a family of microorganisms that are parasites in human (and some other mammalian) bodies. During part of its life cycle, the parasite lives in mosquitoes, and if an infected mosquito bites another organism, the parasite can be transferred. Within the new host, the parasite can cause problems in the circulatory and respiratory systems that can result in death. In most cases, malaria is a problem for humans only if there are very high densities of mosquitoes in the area.

In areas where malaria is endemic, we often see high frequencies of the sickle cell mutant allele (Figure 10.16). Interestingly, individuals with sickle cell disease (who are homozygous for the gene, meaning they have two copies of the recessive sickling allele) usually do not contract malaria. It seems that the malarial parasite cannot effectively reproduce in an environment

■ FIGURE 10.16
Regions where malaria is endemic. What does this suggest about the relationship between the sickle cell allele and malaria?

with even slightly sickled red blood cells. Individuals who are heterozygous for the gene (they have one recessive and one dominant allele) may experience mild sickling but do not have sickle cell disease; these individuals have relative immunity to malaria. It is hypothesized that in areas where there is a high risk of malaria, the heterozygotic condition has a higher relative fitness than the homozygous dominant state (the individual gets malaria) or the homozygous recessive state (the individual gets sickle cell disease). Because the heterozygotic state is favored, the deleterious recessive allele remains in the population at relatively high frequencies. This is called a **balanced polymorphism.**

It is further hypothesized that this balanced polymorphism has arisen in these regions because of human behavior—the alteration of habitat for settlement and agriculture. When humans clear forested areas, they create open areas and many places for stagnant water to accumulate, which in turn increases breeding opportunities for mosquitoes. If malaria is present, these conditions also increase the likelihood that humans will contract the malarial parasite. In short, human alteration of the environment changed selection pressures such that a deleterious recessive allele in a heterozygous state was favored, and over time, frequencies of the alleles in humans were altered. In other words, human cultural patterns influenced natural selection, which in turn influenced evolution. The result is higher-than-expected frequencies of the sickle cell allele in certain populations.

balanced polymorphism
a situation in which selection favors a heterozygotic state for a given locus and thus maintains both the recessive and the dominant alleles in a population, even if one or both are deleterious in the homozygous state

It is interesting that this process has not happened everywhere that malaria occurs. One reason might be the time depth of habitat alteration in these regions; that is, humans have changed the environment in some areas too recently for evolutionary changes to have occurred. Another reason is chance. Remember, mutation is fairly random; the effective mutation has to co-occur with the appropriate conditions in order for allele frequencies to change significantly.

In modern times we can add another biocultural facet to this story. As humans move across regions of the planet, they change allele frequencies. For example, culturally based migrations from both Southwestern Asia and western Africa have caused higher frequencies of the recessive sickle cell alleles to become present in North American populations. Again, we see that human cultural patterns have had an impact on evolution, this time via gene flow.

Human Morphological Variations as Heat and Cold Stress Adaptations

Another area in which we see a good deal of variation is body shape and size (see Figure 10.7). Zoologists John Allen and Carl Bergmann made a series of observations (independently of each other) that enlighten us about mammalian body form. In environments where organisms are stressed by cold (the arctic, for example), mammals tend to have increased body mass relative to body surface area (Figure 10.17). In environments where they are stressed by heat (deserts and tropical savannas, for example), the opposite is true: Mammals have a decreased body mass and increased body surface area (refer back to Figure 10.6). The reasons for these patterns in mammals involve thermoregulation (recall from chapter 5 that internal thermoregulation is one of the defining characteristics of mammals). Because mammals can live only within a relatively small range of body temperatures, they must constantly retain or lose heat when they are in environments that are above or below those temperatures. Over time, body size and shape are influenced by natural selection as those variants that more effectively negotiate thermal stresses become most common in a population.

As mammals, humans display this same pattern of morphological variation. Human populations that have spent long periods of time in cold stress environments have larger torsos and shorter, stockier arms relative to many other human populations. Examples of populations with these characteristics are some groups of Alaskan natives and the Lapp peoples of northwestern Eurasia.

■ **FIGURE 10.17**

The relationship between temperature and body size. Both shapes have the same volume, but the short, squat shape has a smaller surface area. In a cold climate, a larger surface area is less efficient at retaining body heat. Therefore, short stature is an adaptation to cold climates. Compare Figure 10.7.

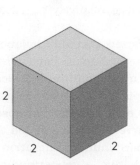

Volume = 2 × 2 × 2 = 8 cc
Surface area = (2 × 2)(6 sides)
= 24 cm^2

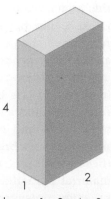

Volume = 1 × 2 × 4 = 8 cc
Surface area = (1 × 2) (2)
+ (1 × 4) (2)
+ (2 × 4) (2)
= 28 cm^2

These body proportions effectively maximize mass and minimize surface area, resulting in more efficient heat retention. (Note that humans also adapt to cold environments with cultural adaptations, such as clothing and fire.) The reverse is true of some populations that have lived for long periods in heat stress environments. Here we can see either very large or tall bodies with long arms and legs or very small but proportional bodies. In either of these cases, surface area is effectively maximized and mass minimized, increasing the effectiveness of heat loss.

Although natural selection has clearly influenced human body form in climatically stressful environments, the majority of humans do not live in such environments, and thus most populations are not under these kinds of selection pressures. What then accounts for all of the variation in body size and shape we see in humans? If we envision selection as setting the range of possible morphologies for humans, we can then see this variation being moved around via gene flow throughout the species. Because most populations are not under strong climatic stress, the selection pressures on body size and shape are relaxed, and a wide array of variation can be expressed. This variation is then shaped by gene flow, mating patterns, and nutrition. In a population with little gene flow and fairly equally distributed nutrition, individuals tend to converge at a similar body shape and size, whereas in populations with high rates of gene flow and variable nutrition, individuals are more variable.

As a result of this flexibility in response to environmental stresses, each human population has a good deal of variation in body size and shape. As in the case of sickle cell disease, processes of evolution (natural selection, gene flow) are integrated with cultural patterns (migration, mating, material culture) to influence a biological characteristic of human beings.

Race is a very poor way to describe variation in *Homo sapiens sapiens*

One of the most misused and misunderstood words in the English language is *race*. All human cultures divide and categorize humans into clusters, usually based on ethnic, linguistic, or other cultural characteristics. However, many assume, incorrectly, that race, a biological concept, is reflected in these cultural categories.

There are two distinct concepts of race. The **scientific concept of race is** defined as a population, or group of populations, within a species that has measurable, defining biological characteristics and an Fst of at least 0.25 relative to other populations in the species (Kittles & Weiss, 2003; Templeton, 1999). Biologists also call this a **subspecies**. In essence, a subspecies, or race, is a unit within a species that is taking an evolutionary trajectory different from the trajectory of other populations within the species and thus is becoming increasingly differentiated from them at the genetic level.

The other concept is a **socially constructed concept of race**, in which a set of cultural or ethnic factors is linked with easily perceived morphological traits (like skin reflectance, body shape, or cranial structure) to create an artificial, "biologized" category (Marks, 1995). Over the last 300 years there have been many proposals for ways of classifying humans into races, but nearly all of them use a form of the general categories erroneously constructed and promulgated by Linnaeus (the "father of taxonomy," as described in chapter 1). Linnaeus suggested that there were five races, or subspecies, of humans:

scientific concept of race
a population or group of populations within a species that has measurable, defining biological characteristics and an Fst of at least 0.25 relative to other populations in the species

subspecies
a population that meets the criteria defined within the scientific concept of race

socially constructed concept of race
set of cultural or ethnic factors combined with easily perceived morphological traits (such as skin reflectance, body shape, cranial structure) in an artificial "biologized" category

Homo sapiens afer, Homo sapiens americanus, Homo sapiens asiaticus, Homo sapiens europeaus, and *Homo sapiens ferus.* The first four of these categories correspond to today's categories of Black, Native American, Asian, and White. The last category was a catchall for "wild-men" or true "savages," which Linnaeus mistakenly thought existed. Linnaeus used absurd elements like clothing patterns, "character," and behavior to classify humans into these biological races or subspecies.

Although Linnaeus's categories are scientifically incorrect, the "big few" race categories of Asian, Black, and White are still with us today (Harrison, 1999; Kittles & Weiss, 2003; Marks, 1995; Relethford, 2009). Many people, including some scientists, argue that there are identifiable biological races in humans, but they are wrong. There is substantial and unequivocal evidence that there is currently only one race, or subspecies, of human on the planet: *Homo sapiens sapiens.* As we saw earlier in this chapter, humans do not show enough genetic variability *between populations* for any given population to be categorized as a subspecies. However, human variation does exist, and it can be examined across and within populations and regions, but a three-to-five race concept hinders rather than assists research in this area.

This is not to say that there are no sociocultural distinctions among different groups in the United States, such as African American, White, Hispanic/Latino, Native American, Asian Pacific Islander, and so on. However, these categories are not biological. In the next section we consider the evidence regarding biological race and then briefly discuss why the evidence is so frequently ignored.

What is the Evidence Regarding Biological Races in Humans?

Testing the hypothesis that there are races in modern humans is a fairly simple matter. All we need do is identify the biological characteristics that define a subspecies within the human species and then assess that group to see if its Fst is sufficiently high relative to other populations in our species. Obvious places to look for these defining differences are in the DNA, in the morphology of our bodies, and in disease patterns.

Genetic Evidence

As discussed earlier in the chapter, the level of genetic differentiation required to classify a population or group of populations as a subspecies is an Fst greater than 0.25. Multiple studies of a variety of segments of DNA in humans clearly demonstrate that this level is not reached with any consistency or any between-region measures in humans, even in mtDNA (Kittles & Weiss, 2003; Relethford, 2002; Weiss, 1998; Long et al., 2009; Hunley et al., 2009). Human Fst scores average about 0.17, well under the subspecies mark. It is also extremely important to note that there is not a single unique genetic marker that can be used to differentiate the "big few" races; that is, there are no Asian, Black, or White genes or alleles, and that all extant genetic variation is subsumed within the variation found in African populations.

Craniometrics

What about differences in morphology? A long-term mainstay in forensic analyses has been the use of **craniometrics** (cranial measurements) to differentiate populations. In the United States today, forensic experts are frequently able to classify a skull as Asian, Black, or White with about 80% accuracy.

craniometrics
the measuring and study of cranial morphology

Some argue that the fact that crania can be placed in cultural categories means the categories are biologically based. However, this is not the case. As we have seen, cranial variation is strongly influenced by nutrition, health, and gene flow, and the pattern of cranial variation in our species matches the pattern of variation in our DNA (as reflected by an Fst statistic using cranial measures). About 80% of the variation in cranial shape occurs within each human population, and about 20% occurs between populations across geographic regions (Relethford, 2002).

How then can forensic scientists classify skulls into socially constructed race categories here in the United States with relatively high levels of accuracy? Classification depends on the definitions used and the ways the crania are classified. If we have 3 categories in which to place crania, we can cluster them into those 3. If we had 6 or 8 or 10 categories, we could do that as well. For example (recall the earlier Connection box on skull sizes), we can differentiate the crania of White American males dating from 1979 from the crania of White American males dating from 1840 just as easily as we can differentiate the crania of modern White and Black males from each other (Jantz & Meadows Jantz, 2000). Does that mean that White American males living in 1979 belong to a different race than White American males living in 1840? No, of course not. What is being measured is changes in cranial form, and numerous studies have shown that cranial form changes measurably across time within a population. If there are differences in health and nutrition in subgroups within populations or regions and there are variable patterns of gene flow between those subgroups, some measurable cranial differences will emerge, especially if these subgroups or segments of populations derive some ancestry from diverse geographical regions on the planet.

Furthermore, the measurements used to differentiate skulls in the United States would not be exactly like the measurements taken in other parts of the world, given the differences in populations and morphologies. In other words, measurements indicating "Black" in the United States would not allow us to classify all the crania found on the African continent, nor would measurements indicating "Asian" in the United States encompass the diversity of skull morphology found in Asia. Additionally, none of the cranial measurements used to identify groups is unique to any of the socially constructed race categories. The divisions are based on averages and ranges, so any specific cranium may or may not fit within the "correct" range. This is why there is a certain amount of error when experts attempt to place crania in categories. The differences between crania, and between groups, are those of degree, not of kind (Ousley et al., 2009).

Patterns of Skin Reflectance

Another aspect of morphology frequently used as a marker of race is skin "color," or reflectance. As explained earlier, the distribution of skin reflectance patterns in our species cannot be used to differentiate humans into subspecies. That is, "darker" skinned people are found around the planet, as are "lighter" skinned people. The distribution is related to ancestry from different latitudes and the relative intensity of UV light in those regions. Gene flow has produced a wide distribution of the myriad skin tones that we see in modern humans.

There is a very broad range of skin reflectance among Americans because of the diverse ancestry represented in the United States. If we used skin

Is High Blood Pressure a Black Thing?

One of the most prevalent myths in racial thinking is that races are biological units. This is a mistake as a basic idea, but the more complicated reality is that social races can have biological effects. Obvious instances come from genetic diseases that are more common in certain parts of the planet. That is, genetic disorders that are most commonly found in parts of Western Europe might be more common in United States Whites than in United States Asians due to patterns of geographic ancestry. But more complicated are the actual results of racist structures on human populations. Recent work shows that hypertension (high blood pressure) in Blacks in the United States is, in part, a biological effect of cultural racial structures. It turns out, that there is a connection between the relative darkness of one's skin, the socioeconomic positions one occupies,

and hypertension. In the United States there is a correlation between skin color darkness and the frequency and intensity of racist encounters (even within dark-skinned groups). There is also a correlation between one's own perception of their skin color as dark (whether it is relatively dark or not) and the frequency of hypertension. That is, individuals who see themselves as darker tend to have higher rates of hypertension, as do individuals in areas of reduced access to high-quality and regular health care and individuals with lower-income-based poor-quality diets. In this case greater rates of hypertension in Black communities in the United States can be attributed to many factors that come from a history of racial social structures, not because of some inherent biological facet of being "Black." So as the anthropologist Lance Gravlee states: race is not biology, but race can become biology. Racist structures can affect our bodies in real physiological and important ways.

reflectance to classify people, we would have to lump together people from south Asia, southeastern Asia, Australia, and central Africa in a "dark" category and people from western and northern Europe and northern Asia in a "light" category. In sum, skin reflectance patterns are of no use in classifying humans into specific subspecies.

Patterns of Disease

Another place that people look for "racial" differences is in disease susceptibility. For example, sickle cell disease is associated with Blacks in the United States. Many, but not all, African Americans have ancestors from western Africa, where the balanced polymorphism selection has resulted in fairly high frequencies of the recessive sickling allele. Therefore, it is accurate to state that some African Americans have an increased risk for sickle cell disease. However, people from the Arabian Peninsula and the southern portion of the Indian subcontinent also have an increased risk of sickle cell disease. A higher risk for sickle cell disease is related not to a race but to genetic ancestry in a particular geographic region.

Many other genetic disorders occur at increased frequencies in particular populations. For example, Tay Sachs disease, a fatal development disorder, has a relatively high frequency in the Ashkenazi Jewish ethnic group (primarily from eastern Europe). Cystic fibrosis, a disease of the epithelial tissue, has a relatively high frequency in populations from parts of northern and western Europe. Thus, both of these diseases show up more often in people who are placed in the socially constructed racial category White.

These diseases have nothing to do with belonging to that category, however; rather, they are associated with some populations that are placed in that category.

Social and economic conditions affect health and nutrition differently for individuals placed in different "racial" categories, and this in turn affects health and disease. As a result, we see some differences in the rates of various diseases (such as diabetes, high blood pressure, or heart disease) among different culturally defined groups, but these differences result from social and economic conditions, not from biological characteristics. For example, rates of cardiovascular diseases and diabetes in the United States correlate with elements of socioeconomic status, skin color, and ethnicity. People with restricted access to education, medical care, and healthy diets are more likely to suffer from these disorders. This correlation does not result from biological distinctions between wealthy and poor people but rather from social factors, such as access to medical care, environmental and social stress, education, and nutrition (Sapolsky, 2004). For example, a study of cardiovascular risks among southern rural women found that the only significant health risks were body mass index (a measure of obesity) and education. Race was not a significant risk factor (Appel, Harrell, & Deng, 2002). We also know that social inequality can lead to health inequalities so that socially constructed race impacts biology (Gravlee, 2009).

At this point it should be clear that although humans vary, that variation does not sort itself out into clusters with marked differentiation and potentially divergent evolutionary trajectories. Although the use of racial categories in the United States remains a deeply ingrained cultural pattern, it has no biological validity.

There is a Scientific Study of Human Biological Variation

Currently there is a widespread agreement among biological anthropologists when it comes to describing and interpreting variation in the human species. This can be summarized in the following five points that represent our core understanding of biological variation in humanity (Edgar & Hunley, 2009):

1. There is substantial variation among individuals within populations.

2. Some biological variation is divided up between individuals in different populations and also among larger population groupings.

3. Patterns of within- and between-group variation have been substantially shaped by culture, language, ecology, and geography.

4. Race is not an accurate or productive way to describe human biological variation.

5. Human variation research has important social, biomedical, and forensic implications.

Even though many common assumptions about biological differences among humans are incorrect, it is nevertheless very important to study the ways in which humans vary, at the level of both the individual and the population, and to try to understand the patterns and processes of that variation. The basal unit for the study of human biological variation is the population, since that is the basal unit for examining evolutionary change. In chapter 4 we defined *population* as a cluster of individuals of the same species who share a common geographical area and find their mates more often in their own cluster than in others. Modern human populations can be described based on geography and biology, but other cultural considerations, such as language, nationality, and ethnicity, also bind people together, even when they are not a biological population.

When we study population biology, we must be careful to look at actual populations rather than imagined ones (such as the socially constructed races). We also need to assess patterns across human populations, such as **clines** (biological traits that vary in a specific pattern across geography). Skin reflectance is a clinal trait in that it varies across space relative to UV light incidence. This pattern of variation can tell us that what we are seeing (varying skin tone) is probably related to some environmental factor. The distribution of traits across populations, coupled with the study of the variation of traits within populations, can produce robust and effective assessments of how and why humans vary.

Why Does the Notion of Biological Race Persist?

If we have a solid understanding of how humans vary biologically, and if we also have clear evidence that there is currently only one race in the human species, why do we continue to associate the "big few" socially constructed races (Asian, Black, White) with biological reality? Why does the U.S. Census Bureau ask citizens which "race" they belong to? The practice results from several broad factors: the history of global expansion and colonialism, the particular history of the United States, the inability of scientists to convey correct information effectively outside of academia, and the refusal by the general public to discard a refuted hypothesis even when they have correct information. Because of these factors, most people rely on popular misconceptions and stereotypes when thinking about race and human variation.

A Very Brief History of Racism

Many of our currently held misconceptions about race probably originated during the 15th, 16th, and 17th centuries, when global maritime travel became commonplace and humans from disparate places began to come into contact with one another on a regular basis. These contacts frequently occurred at the end of transoceanic journeys, when travelers disembarked in places thousands of miles from their homelands and so did not have the opportunity to see the patterned distribution of humanity across space. Those on the boat and those on shore would be from populations that were separated by great distances (and thus would have experienced little reciprocal gene flow), that were from different climates and environments (and thus would have experienced potentially different selection for some traits), and that had developed very different languages and material cultures. In other words, they looked extremely different from one another, and this made it easy for each to classify the other as somewhat less than human (or different from "normal" humans).

Because these encounters frequently resulted from conflict over resources, disputes emerged, and one group often defeated the other in battle and gained control over their resources (and possibly the people as well). As differential power relationships emerged between different cultural groups and populations, the groundwork was laid for classifications such as those of Linnaeus and many who followed him. Cultural differences and differences in easily perceived morphological traits (such as body shape, skin reflectance, cranial form, and so on) led many people to believe that there were distinct, deep-seated

Columbus's first contact with Native Americans. This is a 17th-century version of a 1594 engraving. Notice the pronounced differences between the Spaniards and the native people. Whose point of view does this engraving present?

biological differences between these groups of humans. The erroneous applications of Darwin's and Wallace's ideas of natural selection to human cultural relations contributed to the growth of a common misconception that certain humans (generally some European groups, in this case) were more "fit" than other types of humans, since they were able to exert control through military actions (Figure 10.18).

For much of the early history of physical anthropology, the goal was to use cranial and skeletal measurements to discover the biological basis for classifying humans into different types or subspecies. Although some anthropologists used the same techniques to demonstrate that one could *not* classify humans into different subspecies based on morphological traits (Marks, 1995), the basic notion of race in humans became thoroughly entrenched in mainstream scientific studies as well as in popular thinking. Note that the current popular view of race is not the same as it was a century or two ago. For example, during their early colonial period, many English considered the Irish a separate race, and in the United States at the turn of the 20th century, the growing presence of immigrants from southern and eastern Europe was considered biologically damaging to the predominantly western European population. However, it was the emergence of eugenics as a field of study, especially in the United States, that cemented popular ideas about systems for classifying humanity.

Eugenics is the study of human beings with the idea of improving human biology and biological potential. In the early 1900s, Mendel's work on simple genetic systems was just becoming widely known. The idea of a simple dominant/recessive system, which is actually rare in humans and in most organisms, dominated the early understanding of genetics and was easily grafted onto existing notions of human heredity. The early geneticists were frequently interested in eugenics, especially the improvement of the human species via careful and selective mating, and the establishment of human pedigrees. There was a widespread, erroneous pattern of associating stereotypical ethnic traits with simple

eugenics
study of genetics with the notion of improving human biology and biological potential; often associated with erroneous and/or simplistic assumptions about the relationship of behavior or cultural traits with simple genetic systems

genetic systems. For example, "feeblemindedness" (low intelligence) was considered a simple dominant/recessive trait that occurred in high frequencies among immigrants to the United States from southern Europe.

Many in the eugenics movement sought to use genetics to explain the social and cultural differences among groups in the United States and across the planet. They used simplistic ideas about taxonomy and racial categories based on cranial measurement to support their notions of biological reality. Their ideas were incorrect, and over time eugenics fell out of favor, especially after World War II, when the Nazis used aspects of the eugenicist paradigm to bolster their attempts to exterminate several ethnicities and "behavioral categories," including Jews, Slavs, Gypsies, and homosexuals.

Even though eugenics studies have fallen out of favor, their assumptions about the association of "biobehavioral traits" (that is, genetically based traits) with socially constructed racial categories remains a powerful under-current in American culture. Because the historical and current patterns of discrimination, especially against African Americans, are at odds with the political and moral principles on which our nation was founded, people have often fallen back on biological explanations to rationalize injustice. Unfortunately, many citizens, scientists among them, still cling to the nonscientific and erroneous classification of the human species into races—in large part because they do not understand natural selection, population genetics, and human variation (Gould, 1996; Harrison, 1999; Marks, 1995; Peregrine, Ember, & Ember, 2003).

STOP & THINK

Why do people use the concept of natural selection to justify oppression?

Modern Notions Are Also Due to a Lack of Context

Despite the points made throughout this chapter, many Americans assume that because they seem to be able to determine a person's race just by looking at the person, the concept of race must have some biological validity. This is wrong because very few people have the background knowledge to make accurate statements regarding the extent and patterns of human biological variation. Let's consider an analogy. The notion that the earth is round is currently accepted as a fact by nearly all human beings. We accept it despite the fact that the earth appears to us in our daily experience to be flat. Only a few humans (for example, astronauts or people who sail around the world and arrive back at the same place) have personally experienced the earth as round. The rest of us accept the evidence as scientifically valid even though our personal experience contradicts it. We simply do not have the context or experience to verify it ourselves.

A similar situation holds with the concept of race. Most people do not have the opportunity to see the patterned distribution of humanity across the globe. Although most of us in the United States can generally classify the people we see on a daily basis into three to five groups (not always as easily or reliably as one might think), these groups might not be valid in other locations. Further, these "groups" reflect only a small percentage of the global biological variation in humanity (Figure 10.19). Thus, as with the shape of the earth, the broader situation is not necessarily obvious from our limited perspectives. In sum, if we have the context (broad exposure, scientific data, or the understandings reviewed here), we can realize that although our personal experience and cultural context might seem to show us one thing, the overall pattern of human biological diversity demonstrates something else: that *Homo sapiens sapiens* is one species, undivided into races or subspecies.

What We Know

Humans vary in external morphology (size, shape, and color), and this variation is based on both biological and cultural factors.

Questions That Remain

Will expanded medical technologies (and access to these technologies) continue to change what humans look like over time? What repercussions will the complex culturally based eating patterns have on human populations in the future?

What We Know

Humans vary genetically more within populations than between them.

Questions That Remain

How will our increasing knowledge of the human genome enhance our abilities to discuss the differences at the level of DNA and thus to better understand which of these differences are functional and what their functions might be?

What We Know

Because of our intensive reliance on extrasomatic materials as well as on culturally defined ways of living (eating, activities, clothing, body alteration, etc.), we must use the biocultural approach to truly understand patterns of human biological variation.

Questions That Remain

What are the aspects of humanity (if any) that remain relatively unaffected by cultural impacts, and how might understanding these biological patterns allow us to better understand humanity? While there have been many suggestions as to what these might be, very few solid data sets remain to support the assertions. This arena is a difficult but important avenue of investigation in a collaborative manner by researchers interested in understanding evolutionary patterns in humans.

What We Know

All living humans are part of the same biological subspecies, *Homo sapiens sapiens*. There are not multiple races in humans today.

Questions That Remain

Were there multiple subspecies in the past? In previous chapters we discussed the debates over human ancestors and archaic forms. Is it possible that the Neanderthals and the modern humans living at the same time were two separate races? If so, would this make it more important to understand the relationships between them?

What We Know

Simplistic, socially constructed race categories are not biologically sound, but nevertheless remain culturally salient.

Questions That Remain

Will human cultures eventually move beyond such categories? Will the United States cope with increasing diversity and gene flow in its population by adding or changing the socially constructed categories to match new stereotypes, or will the system itself begin to change as it becomes increasingly outmoded?

Efe, Zaire

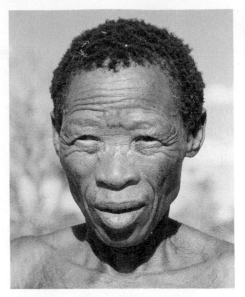
San, Bafswana

Aborigine, Australia

Bagish, China

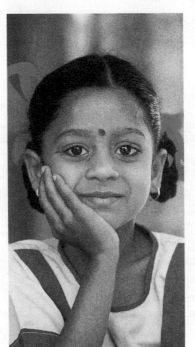
Bangalore, India

Mendi, New Guinea

■ **FIGURE 10.19**
Human diversity. Could you categorize the people in these photographs according to common ideas of race? Would this be a meaningful exercise?

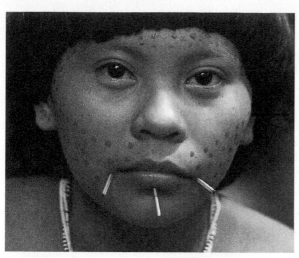

Yanomama, Brazil

Hamadan, Iran

Lapplander, Northern Europe

Western European

Taos Pueblo, USA

Southeast Asian

SUMMARY

▲ Humans vary more than most similar-sized mammals in size and body shape but less in genetic patterns.

▲ Human variation in skin color is due to differential density of melanin in the epidermal layers. All humans have the same number of melanocytes, but the activity of these cells is related to adaptations to UV light stress. More melanin production leads to darker skin color.

▲ Human body size and shape are determined in large part by natural selection, gene flow, and nutrition. Allen's and Bergmann's rules demonstrate the mammalian-wide patterns of heat/cold stress on body form. Combined with gene flow and cultural patterns, these stresses impact the distribution of body size and shape in human populations.

▲ Human males and females have about a 10%–15% difference in body size, as well as specific morphological differences in skeletal and muscle morphology.

▲ Human cranial form is quite flexible, but nearly 80% of cranial variation is found within populations, and only about 20% is found between populations. Forensic scientists can identify clusters of cranial variation within populations and between populations; however, these clusters generally reflect gene flow and other evolutionary processes.

▲ Disease may play an important role in human evolution. Some populations have higher allele frequencies for certain genetic disorders and so may be more susceptible to those disorders. Human cultural modification of the environment can alter the patterns and contexts of natural selection through disease patterns.

▲ Blood group allele frequencies vary across human populations due to both natural selection and gene flow.

▲ Human genetic variation is surprisingly distributed. Nearly 85% of the genetic variation in the species *Homo sapiens sapiens* is found in each *H.s.s* population. The overall genetic Fst for our species is approximately 0.17, well below the level for subspecies distinction.

▲ There is no evidence from any morphological or genetic measures that supports the division of modern humans into biological races or subspecies. No morphologically or genetically unique or even substantially divergent populations of humans can currently be divided into specific geographic clusters. Despite this, there is a continued use of Linnaean-like taxonomies for humanity that place humans into the "big few" categories of Asian, Black, and White.

▲ In the United States we use socially constructed race categories rather than biological ones. Comparing differences in socially constructed race categories cannot involve biological comparisons or causes, only socio-cultural ones. The history of colonial expansion, Linnaean classification, the eugenics movement, and specific aspects of U.S. history all contribute to the use of these categories.

CRITICAL THINKING

1. There are no biological races in humans today, but could there have been in the past? What conditions would have facilitated subspecies distinctions in humans in the past? Think about the debates over the number of species in

the genus *Homo*. Could these also be seen as debates about subspecies? What about the potential overlap of modern *Homo sapiens* and *Homo erectus* or other archaic forms (such as Neanderthals) in Eurasia? Does this overlap reflect the presence of races?

2. How can there be more genetic variation in African populations if there are more people outside of Africa? How do the fossil record and the debate over the Recent African Origin model versus the Multiple Dispersal model (described in chapter 9) help resolve this quandary?

3. How could modern, human-induced changes in the environment (such as the hole in the ozone layer) be affecting human variation? How do modern medical technology and the reduction in infant mortality rates worldwide affect human variation? Would you predict more or less biological variation in our species over the next few centuries? Why?

4. Is there something about our biology and our primate heritage that predisposes us to use easily perceived traits in order to classify other humans? What role do popular misunderstandings about biology and genetics play in modern, everyday conceptualizations of human differences and "race"? What could one do to dispel these misunderstandings?

5. Will the ways in which race is used as a biological classifier in the United States change as more people gain accurate information about the subject? Why or why not? Has your perspective on race changed in your own lifetime? Can socially constructed race ever be truly detached from notions of biological distinction?

RESOURCES

ANTHROPOLOGICAL ASSOCIATIONS' STATEMENTS ON RACE

www.understandingrace.org The best interactive site for understanding what race is and what it is not. Sponsored by the American Anthropological Association.

www.aaanet.org/stmts/racepp.htm You can read the American Anthropological Association's statement on race at this site.

www.aaanet.org/gvt/ombdraft.htm This site contains the American Anthropological Association's comments on the U.S. government's *OMB Directive 15: Race and Ethnic Standards for Federal Statistics and Administrative Reporting*.

www.physanth.org You can read the American Association of Physical Anthropologists' statement on race at this site.

WHAT DATA ARE COLLECTED ON HUMAN REMAINS?

www.cleber.com.br/standard.html This site includes a copy of the standards for data collection from human remains in the *Proceedings of a Seminar at the Field Museum of Natural History*, organized by Jonathan Haas. Volume editors: Jane E. Buikstra and Douglas H. Ubelaker. Arkansas Archeological Survey Research Series No. 44, 1994.

HISTORY OF RACIST "SCIENCE" AND SOME REAL DATA ABOUT HUMAN VARIATION

Jablonksi, N. (2008). *Skin: a natural history*. Berkeley, CA: University of California Press.
This is an excellent overview of the biology, and culture contexts of human skin.

Kevles, D. J. (1995). *In the name of eugenics: Genetics and the uses of human heredity.* Cambridge, MA: Harvard University Press.
This is an excellent overview of the eugenics movement and its impact on American science and culture.

Marks, J. (1995). *Human biodiversity: Genes, race, and history.* New York: Aldine de Gruyter.
This book combines anthropological, biological, and historical perspectives on the patterns and cultural interpretations of human variation.

Molnar, S. (2002). *Human variation: Races, types and ethnic groups.* Upper Saddle River, NJ: Prentice-Hall.
This is a comprehensive review and evaluation of human biological variation.

REFERENCES

Appel, S. J., Harrell, J. S., & Deng, S. (2002). Racial and socioeconomic differences in risk factors for cardiovascular disease among Southern rural women. *Nursing Research, 51*(3), 140–147.

Edgar, H. J. H., & Hunley, K. L. (2009). Race reconciled? How biological anthropologists view human variation. *American Journal of Physical Anthropology 139*(1), 1–4.

Fausto-Sterling, A. (2002). *Sexing the body: Gender politics and the construction of sexuality.* New York: Basic Books.

Gould, S. J. (1996). *The mismeasure of man.* New York: Norton.

Gravlee, C. (2009). How race becomes biology: Embodiment of social inequality. *American Journal of Physical Anthropology 139*(1), 47–57.

Harrison, F. (1999). Expanding the discourse on "race." *American Anthropologist, 100,* 609–631.

Hunley, K., Heuly, M. E., & Long, J. L. (2009). The global pattern of gene identity variation reveals a history of long-range migrations, bottlenecks, and local mate exchange: Implications for biological race. *American Journal of Physical Anthropology 139*(1), 35–46.

Jablonski, N. G. (2004). The evolution of human skin and skin color. *Annual Reviews in Anthropology, 33,* 585–623.

Jablonski, N., & Chaplin, M. (2000). The evolution of human skin color. *Journal of Human Evolution, 39,* 57–106.

Jantz, R. L., & Meadows Jantz, L. (2000). Secular change in craniofacial morphology. *American Journal of Human Biology, 12,* 327–338.

Kittles, R. A., & Weiss, K. M. (2003). Race, genes and ancestry: Implications for defining disease risk. *Annual Reviews in Human Genetics, 4,* 33–67.

Lewontin, R. C. (1972). The apportionment of human diversity. *Evolutionary Biology, 6,* 381–398.

Long, J. C., Li, J., & Heuly, M. E. (2009). Human DNA sequences. More variation less race. *American Journal of Physical Anthropology 139*(1), 23–34.

Marks, J. (1995). *Human biodiversity: Genes, race, and history.* New York: Aldine de Gruyter.

Molnar, S. (2002). *Human variation: Races, types and ethnic groups.* Upper Saddle River, NJ: Prentice-Hall.

Ousley, S., Jantz, R., & Fred, D. (2009). Understanding race and human variation: why forensic anthropologists are good at identifying race. *American Journal of Physical Anthropology 139*(1), 68–76.

Peregrine, P. N., Ember, C. R., & Ember, M. (2003). Cross-cultural evaluation of predicted associations between race and behavior. *Evolution & Human Behavior, 24,* 357–364.

Pond, C. M. (1997). The biological origins of adipose tissue in humans. In M. E. Morbeck, A. Galloway, & A. L. Zihlman (Eds.), *The evolving female* (pp. 147–162). Princeton, NJ: Princeton University Press.

Relethford, J. H. (1997). Hemispheric differences in human skin color. *American Journal of Physical Anthropology, 104,* 449–457.

Relethford, J. H. (2002). Apportionment of global human genetic diversity based on craniometrics and skin color. *American Journal of Physical Anthropology, 118,* 393–398.

Relethford, J. H. (2009). Race and global patterns of phenotypic variation. *American Journal of Physical Anthropology 139*(1), 16–22.

Ruff, C. (2002). Variation in human body size and shape. *Annual Reviews in Anthropology, 31,* 211–232.

Sapolsky, R. M. (2004). Social status and stress in humans and other animals. *Annual Reviews in Anthropology, 33,* 393–418.

Sparks, C. S., & Jantz, R. L. (2002). A reassessment of human cranial plasticity: Boas revisited. *Proceedings of the National Academy of Sciences, 99(23),* 14636–14639.

Templeton, A. (1999). Human races: A genetic and evolutionary perspective. *American Anthropologist, 100,* 632–650.

Weiss, K. M. (1998). Coming to terms with human variation. *Annual Reviews in Anthropology, 27,* 273–300.

CHAPTER 11

The Present and Future of Human Evolution

In this final chapter we will briefly address the following questions:

▲ How do we study the evolution of human behavior?

▲ How are evolutionary processes affecting humans today?

▲ Given our understanding of our evolutionary history, what predictions might we make about our future?

▲ Why is biological anthropology critical for understanding human nature(s) and human biology?

What will the humans of the future look like? Will they have the giant crania and brains of the superintelligent aliens illustrated in *Star Trek, The X-Files,* and countless grocery store tabloids? Will our vast technological might render our physical bodies useless? Will our ability to genetically engineer humans and other organisms result in a society of clones? Will the pollution in our cities and the chemicals in our environment alter our morphology and physiology? Will we eventually look like the being pictured in Figure 11.1? No, none of these outcomes are likely. Our cranial capacity is limited by the size of the birth canal and the physics of bipedality (see chapter 7); most current technologies still require substantial manual labor; and our ability to genetically engineer humans remains in its infancy. Our ability to create extrasomatic means (chapters 8 and 9) to deal with environmental pressures probably works against the evolution of significant changes in body structure in modern humans. Over the last 100,000 years, the explosion in symbolic culture and the increasing complexity of our tool kits have allowed us to do remarkable things, especially in the 200 or so years since the Industrial Revolution. Nevertheless, our basic morphology and physiology have changed very little.

Throughout this book we have taken a broad view of human evolution. We began with background on evolutionary theory, genetics, and the human body. Moving on to the living nonhuman primates and their behavioral ecology, we set the stage for a review of the fossil evidence for the evolution of the primates, the hominins, and finally, the human species. In chapter 10 we reviewed modern human diversity in both its

■ FIGURE 11.1
The human of the future?
Probably not. Why might
someone think this scenario is
probable? What evolutionary
factors are working against
these changes?

biological contexts and cultural interpretation. Our goal was to look at our past and our present to understand our current condition. In this final chapter we focus on human behavior and biology today and in the future.

How do we study human behavioral evolution?

Having reviewed basic behavioral ecology, some examples from the nonhuman primate world, and the hominin and human fossil record, along with modern human biological variation (chapters 5–10), we now briefly look at various perspectives on the evolution of human behavior; that is, frameworks within which current researchers consider evolutionary questions about humanity. Among these perspectives are sociobiology, human behavioral ecology, evolutionary psychology, dual-inheritance theory, and biocultural anthropology.

Sociobiology

Established in 1975 with the publication of E. O. Wilson's *Sociobiology,* this perspective makes three basic assumptions: (1) understanding behavior can be done in basically the same way as understanding a simple genetic system, (2) natural selection is the main force behind the evolution of behavior, and (3) genes promoting a variety of human social behaviors have been favored over time.

The core of this approach is called the autocatalysis (or self-generating) model of human evolution. Wilson summarizes it as follows:

> When the earliest hominids became bipedal as part of their terrestrial adaptation, their hands were freed, the manufacture and handling of artifacts was made easier, and intelligence grew as part of the improvement of the tool-using habit. With mental capacity and the tendency to use artifacts increasing through mutual reinforcement, the entire materials-based culture expanded. Cooperation during hunting was perfected, providing a new impetus for the evolution of intelligence, which in turn

permitted still more sophistication in tool using, and so on through cycles of causation. At some point, probably during the late Australopithecus period or the transition from Australopithecus to Homo, this autocatalysis carried the evolving populations to a certain threshold of competence, at which time the hominids were able to exploit the antelopes, elephants, and other large herbivorous mammals teeming around them on the African plains. Quite possibly the process began when the hominids learned to drive big cats, hyenas, and other carnivores from their kills. In time they became the primary hunters themselves and were forced to protect their prey from other predators and scavengers. (Wilson 1975 pp. 567–568)

In this view the shift to big-game hunting sped up the process of mental evolution, and the sexual division of labor became standard for modern humanity. That is, as males and females formed special bonds, males became specialized in hunting, while females remained at home bases or households to care for children and forage for vegetable foods.

Over the past 30 years, researchers in the biological and social sciences, and even some philosophers, have incorporated Wilson's perspectives. As a result, most major approaches to the study of human behavioral evolution today owe at least part of their origin to sociobiology. However, most anthropologists (including the author of this book) see many problems in Wilson's assumptions about humans, especially his overly simplistic treatment of human cultures.

Human Behavioral Ecology (HBE)

Human behavioral ecology (HBE) focuses on how ecological and social factors affect behavior. HBE combines natural selection with a focus on specific types of ecological pressures: those that affect an individual's energy expenditure and gain (see chapter 5 on basic ecological challenges) and those affecting fitness (number of offspring produced over one's lifetime; see chapter 4). HBE asks, "What ecological forces select for, or favor, a specific behavior?"

HBE assumes that organisms strive for optimal—the best possible—adaptive responses to environmental problems. Those responses with lower success (fewer offspring produced and/or more energy lost) will eventually disappear from the population, leaving only the most successful variants. In other words, this model applies basic principles of natural selection to behavior patterns. However, HBE recognizes that most behavior in the real world does not reflect optimal responses, so HBE models serve as yardsticks to identify constraints that interfere with optimal responses. Because behavior is a collection of adaptive responses, HBE sees flexibility in individual behavior as itself adaptive—a result of individuals striving to optimize lifetime reproductive success in diverse ecological circumstances. For example, it is unlikely that at any time in our evolution any group of humans has been able to optimize their hunting strategy to get the largest possible amount of food for the energy expended during the hunt. But HBE assumes that the group does try to achieve this end. Thus, HBE sees humans as possessing a strong evolved ability to weigh costs and benefits. Living involves a series of trade-offs, and HBE analysis explores the way these trade-offs work in humans.

Evolutionary Psychology (EP)

The basic goal of evolutionary psychology (EP) is to understand the evolution of the psychological mechanisms that have resulted in human behavior throughout history. This approach emerged after the publication of Wilson's treatise on sociobiology. Thus, EP fuses basic natural selection with the concepts of psychological modules (areas of the mind specifically targeted toward certain functions).

The main idea behind EP is that culture in the human mind evolves to resolve the challenges of natural selection (Barkow et al., 1992).

EP is based on the following three premises:

1. All individuals possess the same basic set of evolved psychological mechanisms.

2. These psychological mechanisms are adaptations resulting from natural selection.

3. The human mind is adapted not to modern circumstances but to the lifeways of our hunter-gatherer ancestors. We spent 99% of our evolutionary history as hunter-gatherers and less than 1% in modern contexts.

EP focuses on the "environment of evolutionary adaptiveness" (EEA), or the period of time in which humans underwent the majority of their adaptation (that is, the time from the appearance of the first early humans to the modern time, probably between 1.5 million and 10,000 years ago). Because the genus *Homo* spent the majority of its evolutionary history in the Pleistocene (1.8 million years ago until ~10,000 years ago) existing in forager groups with limited technology, EP considers this the EEA for humans. If this is true, our adaptations should reflect the pressures of the generalized Pleistocene forager lifeways rather than the pressures of modern industrial and agricultural environments and would, thus, be out of step with modern environments.

Dual-Inheritance Theory (DIT)

Focusing on culture, dual-inheritance theory (DIT) (sometimes called "gene-culture coevolution") is more rooted in anthropology than are HBE or EP. We can define DIT by looking at its five basic assumptions (Boyd and Richerson 2005):

1. Culture is information that people acquire from others by teaching, imitation, and other forms of social learning.

2. Culture change should be modeled as a Darwinian evolutionary process.

3. Culture is part of human biology.

4. Culture distinguishes human evolution from the evolution of other organisms.

5. Genes and culture co-evolve.

Dual-inheritance theorists see culture as a set of information just as geneticists see the genetic code as a set of information. In this perspective, culture is an evolving pool of ideas, beliefs, values, and knowledge transmitted between individuals, very much like the gene pool concept in population genetics. This view of culture differs significantly from that held by the majority of anthropologists in that it is both highly simplified and it is particulate. Central to this comparison of culture to the gene pool is the idea that culture variants and genetic variants (genes) interact to shape the evolution of human behavior. Cultural variants, such as beliefs, behaviors, or any other cultural elements, are seen as acting in somewhat the same way as genes and alleles do. As such the process of natural selection can result in varying frequencies of genetic variants and culture variants across time.

Biocultural Approaches to Studying Modern Humans

Emerging as a synthesis of human biology and biological anthropology perspectives, the earliest biocultural approaches began with researchers initiating studies of human populations with the assumption that "environment" is more than the external physical conditions surrounding a human population (Dafour, 2006). However, this perspective did not become a common component in human biology studies until the last quarter of the twentieth century. While many anthropologists were looking at human ecology as a complex symbolic and biotic system, most human biology studies lagged behind in infusing cultural patterns and behavior into their concepts of integrated environments. In general, "biocultural" studies remained heavily focused on the biology of systems but also attempted to correlate the biological variation with variation in the "cultural" environment (Dafour 2006). However, many current long-term projects have developed substantial databases of human physiological traits (especially health disorders) correlated with different cultural contexts and patterns.

Anthropology and allied disciplines have demonstrated substantial advances in the understanding of the relationship and interfaces between social structures, cultural behavioral contexts, and human physiology and health. Within this arena of research, there is a focus on comparative approaches to examine health experiences across space and time, ideally linking evolutionary approaches and sociocultural fields with medical anthropology (Dafour, 2006; Panter-Brick and Fuentes, 2009).

In general those with a focus biased toward biology see health across populations as shaped by the expression of genetic inheritance and the relative fitness of individuals confronting environmental challenges over evolutionary time. For researchers biased toward the social, health experiences are individually and socially constructed, often embedded in a hierarchical society that controls and filters the construction of knowledge (i.e. Krieger, 2001). The common ground of biocultural studies is the promoting of systematic ways of understanding the relationship of biology with culture, primarily in the evaluation of health disparities within and between populations (Goodman and Leatherman, 1998; Dressler, 2005; Dufour, 2006). This echoes the symbolic dimension of inheritance from Jablonka and Lamb, the first three premises of DST, and perspectives in niche construction (covered in chapter 4).

This biocultural approach can provide a powerful complement to studies of human behavior and to our efforts to model the evolution of human behavior. The explicit recognition of mutual engagement between human biology and behavior and the major role of culture is central to most of the emerging themes in evolutionary theory as applied to humans; however the biocultural approach adds a set of methodologies for this integration that is missing from most traditional approaches. It is worth noting that both human behavioral ecology (HBE) and gene-culture coevolution/dual inheritance theory (DIT) do overlap somewhat, almost by definition, with this biocultural approach. Also, the basic ideas of niche-construction theory fit well within the set of assumptions and practices of the biocultural approach.

A Modern Approach to Studying the Evolution (Past and Future) of Human Behavior

Having considered the many theoretical perspectives presented at the start of this chapter, combined with what we have covered in the preceding chapters

Read over

(1–10), we can frame our approach to human behavioral evolution using the following seven assumptions (modified from Fuentes, 2009):

1. Human behavioral evolution must be primarily seen as a system evolving rather than as a set of independent or moderately connected traits evolving. While we might offer hypotheses to explain specific behaviors, these behaviors also need to be seen in broader contexts. Human behavior and human culture are not a set of individual actions but rather a consortium of action, experience, and innovation.

2. Niche construction is a core factor in human behavioral evolution. The ability of humans to modify their surroundings is central to any explanation of human behavior. Natural selection pressures can be modified as they are occurring, and human response to challenges can be non-genetic, behavioral, and niche-constructing.

3. Ecological and social inheritance are central to human behavior and its change. For at least the past 20,000 years—and much longer in areas of Africa and Eurasia—humans have been born into places where humans already lived. Everything about our lives is affected by the previous generations; thus we inherit huge amounts of information as well as local ecologies. Even when moving into new territories, humans carry some portion of the knowledge of past members of their group with them.

4. Enhanced communication and information transfer are central to understanding human behavior. Humans are the only species with language. Thus, we cannot ignore this critical factor in our questions about human evolution and behavior.

5. Feedback models are central in human behavioral evolution. Rather than humans adapting directly to a local environmental challenge over time, they may alter small parts of the environment, which then reduces or changes the ecological pressures. The group then shifts to new types of interaction with their environment. For example, a change in a group's tool kits (cultural) might change hunting success; this then changes the local populations of the animals hunted. Changes in animal populations in turn alter the presence of predators, which might allow the humans to expand their range, possibly encountering new kinds of ecologies and pressures. This interactive feedback occurs within lifetimes, not just across generations. Thus, humans occasionally construct responses to selection during their lives, altering ecological pressures and in turn, potentially changing the way in which selection works on human bodies.

6. Researchers should consider the potential impacts of a diverse set of biological and social or cultural processes that shuffle variation in evolutionary change. Most hypotheses for the evolution of human behavior rely on natural selection as the only significant force. However, it should be clear from the first ten chapters in this book that gene flow and genetic drift as well as the cultural, social and symbolic practices that alter human demography, residence, movement, and interaction patterns have roles in genetic, phenotypic and behavioral changes. In short, selection need not always be the only process invoked to explain the innovation and spread of behavior in humanity.

7. Models must include a role for flexibility and plasticity in behavioral response. It is unlikely that the majority of human behavioral changes over time are optimal, that they are the best possible ways to deal with an

ecological challenge, even if they do result in adaptation. Further, any particular behavioral adaptation is unlikely to have come in response to a single selective pressure. Instead, the majority of successful human responses likely reflect a pattern of behavioral plasticity and flexibility.

Trying to incorporate as many of these perspectives as possible expands the potential validity of any hypothesis/model we might propose for our evolution, for our current behavior, and for where we are going as a species. Having covered these theoretical perspectives, let's end the book with a brief set of overviews of some of the patterns and pressures that might be affecting human evolution today.

Humans are still evolving

There is a common misconception that evolutionary processes are linear, that evolution has a goal or endpoint. This is simply not the case (see chapters 1 and 4). Change over time, or more specifically change in allele frequencies over time, results from biological processes of mutation, gene flow, genetic drift, and natural selection in combination with niche construction, multiple modes of inheritance, and cultural/historical variables. These processes of evolution are driven by organisms'-interactions with the environments and with the social context in which they live. Evolution has no goal. All organisms still extant on this planet are continuing to evolve and change over time, humans included. However, as we showed in chapters 8–10, modern humans are not limited to responding to environmental pressures via morphological or simple behavioral means. We can do much more: When it is cold we can put on warm clothes, go indoors, turn on a heater, and heat water to make ourselves a cup of tea. This ability to address challenges in a biocultural manner makes the discussion of current human evolutionary patterns complex. In this section we will briefly examine this complexity by surveying two factors, disease and cultural context, as they influence our evolution today.

Diseases and Modern Humans

Most readers of this book have suffered from what is commonly referred to as a "cold." This common viral infection (caused by a **pathogen**, or disease-producing agent) stimulates irritation in the mucous membranes of the head and an associated set of nonlethal discomforts, such as sniffles and sneezes. Colds are widespread in our species, and we have no truly effective means to eradicate them. However, the group of rhinoviruses that cause colds pose no great threat, or do they? The recent outbreaks of the disease referred to as SARS (severe acute respiratory syndrome) may be a newly emerging variant species from the family of common cold viruses (Peiris, Kwok, Osterhaus, & Stöhr, 2003) (Figure 11.2). Two factors—evolutionary change in another organism (a coronavirus in this case) and a human cultural behavior (butchering and dietary practices combined with travel patterns)—may have created an environment wherein this new virus emerged as a threat to our species and thus changed the evolutionary pressures on humans.

On June 11, 2009, the World Health Organization announced that a new strain of flu virus (called novel influenza A, or H1N1) had reached true pandemic status. Reported in over 140 countries by October 2009, this appears to be a new version of more common flu varieties that spreads especially quickly but does not seem to be very severe. We do not yet know why this particular

pathogen
a disease-producing agent

STOP & THINK

Are we in for more or fewer viral outbreaks in the future? Why?

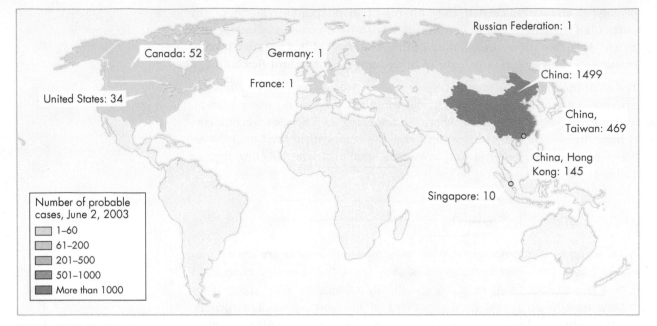

FIGURE 11.2

The SARS epidemic. SARS represents a new disease that arose because of evolutionary change and cultural change.

virus gets around more quickly and effectively than other flu viruses, but modern transportation and human behavior probably have a lot to do with it.

As we/humans modify our environments, we change such variables as forest cover, land use patterns, population density, birth rates (see chapter 10 and the sickle cell/malaria examples), and access to medical care. When we alter environments, other species that live in those environments may be forced to face new challenges. For example, large mammals, which require large continuous tracts of land, or amphibians, which require very specific, relatively stable environments, often cannot survive rapid and dramatic environmental change. Today countless species are going extinct or suffering substantial reductions in their numbers because of human modification of environments (Figure 11.3).

Conversely, viruses and other pathogens, which rely on high densities and frequent movement by their hosts, may be finding our modification of the environment very favorable. How might this affect human evolution? Nearly 1000 years ago, bacterial diseases (such as the bubonic plague) swept through much of the world, decimating human populations. In recent history we have been relatively successful in using our biocultural patterns, such as medicine, to eradicate or substantially diminish the threat of many common bacterial pathogens. Our current ability to fight viral pathogens with antiviral medications is less successful. Even some bacterial pathogens are making a comeback via evolutionary pathways (adaptation) and are having a renewed impact on humanity (remember chapter 4 and the use of antibiotics and antibacterial soaps).

For the majority of human history the basic challenges that most organisms face, such as avoiding predators, getting food and water, and finding or constructing shelter, were the driving environmental forces (selection pressures) that challenged humans. Since the time of *Homo erectus* humans and human ancestors have been modifying the environment to meet these challenges. During the last few centuries, avoiding predators and obtaining sufficient food to stay alive and reproduce have not been the main environmental pressures for most of humanity. While famine (an environmental context resulting in the lack of adequate food) remains a major problem in parts of the world, only a small percentage of the nearly 7 billion humans now alive are in such dire environments.

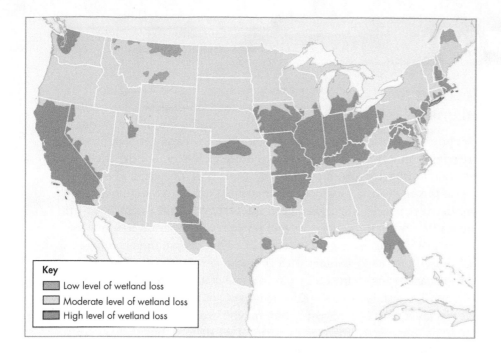

FIGURE 11.3
Wetlands loss, 1780s to 1990s.
Wetlands conversion is just
one way that people alter environments. When an environment changes, the selection
pressures on the organisms
living in that environment
change as well. Species that
cannot adapt may go extinct,
especially if individuals have
no other place to live.

Key
Low level of wetland loss
Moderate level of wetland loss
High level of wetland loss

Can Evolutionary Perspectives Be Applied to Modern Medicine?

The rapid increase in human populations, the move into cities by more and more people, and the increases in the uses of antibiotics and antibacterials around the world are changing the environmental pressures facing humans, especially diseases. Can we use what we know about human evolution and evolutionary patterns to help deal with these new challenges? The increased population density means higher risk for disease transmission, so more antibiotics and antibacterials are used to combat this risk. That is a good use of medicine, right? From an evolutionary perspective, in addition to eradicating some diseases, we are creating strains of diseases capable of dealing with our attacks on them (remember how natural selection works, chapter 4). By taking such extreme measures against all diseases, even minor germs, we might be creating fewer, but stronger, challenges. In addition, humans get sick often as they grow up. Getting sick is one of the ways our bodies learn how to fend off disease and other attacks on our immune system. If we take away all of those experiences (colds and such) from our bodies, we end up with weaker adult immune systems. These weaker systems are then coming into contact with the stronger diseases we are selecting for by our overuse of antibacterials and antibiotics. Knowledge of our evolutionary history suggests that maybe we should take a middle road, not get rid of all disease but instead try to focus our attacks on only the very serious ones. Let kids get dirty and get the sniffles now and then!

STOP & THINK

What changes will we see as transportation via air and mass transit becomes more and more accessible to all people?

Today, few predatory animals are responsible for any human deaths or reductions in individuals' fitness, and while wars and homicide do result in many humans' deaths, those deaths are a tiny minority of all human deaths on the planet. This suggests that given our species' ability to alter our environments and ameliorate the challenges organisms face, certain aspects of disease may have become extremely important selective pressures on humanity.

In the distant past, human population densities were low and the rate of long-distance travel limited. Therefore, infectious diseases could have substantial impact on local populations or groups but seldom significantly impacted large regions or areas. In our very recent past, diseases such as smallpox have had dramatic effects on large regional human populations. For example, many millions of Native Americans perished from the disease almost immediately after their first European contact. Smallpox remained a major killer of humans across vast areas in both the Old and New World until the last quarter of the 20th century. Other diseases, such as cholera and influenza, have also reduced numerous human populations in the last few centuries. The impact of epidemic disease on human populations is similar to that of a predator. Each time a killer disease strikes, different genetic complexes (individual humans) are eliminated from the population, in some cases due simply to chance, in others, to immune system resistance to the specific disorder. After the epidemic is over, the population that remains is genetically different from before (in terms of allele frequencies). Evolution has occurred.

Today, in the early part of the 21st century, our species is feeling the effects of virulent pathogens, such as HIV, the virus that causes AIDS. HIV is widespread, but its impact is highly variable across populations. Unlike the epidemics of the recent past, rapid advances in medical technologies mean that even without "cures," afflicted individuals can remain alive. This in turn increases the infected individual's chance of reproducing and reduces the

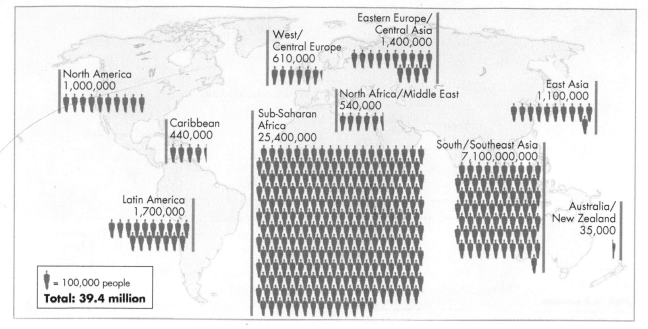

North America
1,000,000

Caribbean
440,000

Latin America
1,700,000

West/
Central Europe
610,000

Eastern Europe/
Central Asia
1,400,000

North Africa/Middle East
540,000

Sub-Saharan
Africa
25,400,000

South/Southeast Asia
7,100,000,000

East Asia
1,100,000

Australia/
New Zealand
35,000

= 100,000 people
Total: 39.4 million

■ **FIGURE 11.4**

Global distribution of HIV infection. This map shows the number of adults and children estimated to be living with HIV infection in each region as of December 2004.

selective impact of the disease. Because of modern cultural variables, however, not all humans have access to medical technologies; thus pathogens, especially viruses, are having different evolutionary impacts on different human populations. In Africa and other less-developed regions and nations of the world, AIDS remains a largely fatal disease, whereas in the developed world, it has become a chronic condition—for people with access to effective health care (Figure 11.4). In Africa in particular, AIDS is a disease of young adults, killing people in their most productive years.

In the case of HIV infection, global disparities in health infrastructure and access to health care, combined with economic and social variables, mean that the virus has different effects in different populations. Currently, due to variations in societal and economic patterns, HIV infection is increasing in women at a faster rate than in men, and this in turn has a direct impact on reproduction, as the virus can be passed directly to the fetus during pregnancy. These differences in infection patterns are related to a number of social factors: Average age of infection is lower in females than in males; females have a 40% higher chance of infection than males during unprotected copulation; females are economically disadvantaged in relative earning potential; some cultures emphasize male sexuality and restrict female sex education and access to health care. Because of higher infection rates among women in Africa, the rate of infection in children is also higher there, resulting in dramatic lowering of life expectancy (Figure 11.5). For example, life expectancy in many countries in sub-Saharan Africa is around 45 years. In many North American and European countries it is over 70 years.

Differential survivorship and reproduction in different human populations results in different selection pressures from the same diseases. Our cultural patterns affect the strength and impact of the environmental (pathogen) pressures. Therefore they have a potential impact on the ways in which allele frequencies change in response to them. This suggests that different populations on the planet are under distinct pressures from disease, not because of any underlying genetic composition or other biological factor, but rather because of socioeconomic and geopolitical realities. So our culture is truly acting to structure the ways in which natural selection acts on human populations.

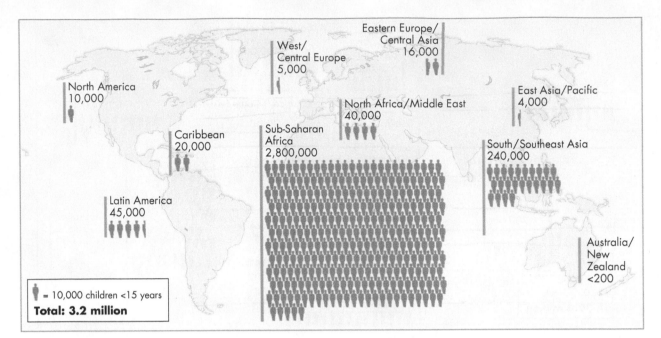

North America
10,000

Caribbean
20,000

Latin America
45,000

West/
Central Europe
5,000

Eastern Europe/
Central Asia
16,000

North Africa/Middle East
40,000

Sub-Saharan
Africa
2,800,000

East Asia/Pacific
4,000

South/Southeast Asia
240,000

Australia/
New
Zealand
<200

= 10,000 children <15 years
Total: 3.2 million

■ **FIGURE 11.5**
Children infected with HIV.
This map shows the estimated
number of children infected
with HIV as of 2002, by region.

Cultural Patterns Influence Morphology

Diet

Modern human diets are complex and strongly influenced by culture. All humans require similar nutrients to survive, grow, and reproduce, but there is enormous variation in how humans obtain and prepare food, as well as in what they eat. Social and economic differences, both among and within populations, lead to dramatic differences in dietary patterns (Figure 11.6).

From chapters 2 and 10 we know that growth and development are greatly influenced by nutrition and dietary patterns. Therefore, we can expect to see differences in shape and form between and within human populations arising from the differences in diets. These differences, however, are primarily developmental responses, not evolutionary changes. Inherited genetic parameters determine the potential height and weight an individual can attain. That person's dietary practices then interact with the physiology and morphology to determine the body form. For example, *Supersize Me,* a documentary film, followed an adult male human for one month while he ate only at McDonald's (resulting in an extremely high-fat/high-carbohydrate diet). Over the course of the month, he gained 25 pounds (~13% of his initial body weight) and suffered from severe physiological changes (including a 40% increase in his cholesterol level). In this case the change in dietary practice had a deleterious impact on his physiology and caused substantial change to his morphology. A reverse example can be found in the many people who have gone on low-carbohydrate/glycemic index diets. These dietary practices popular in the United States and United Kingdom have adults reduce their intake of high glycemic index foods (a ranking of carbohydrate levels in food based on their immediate effect on blood glucose [blood sugar] levels). The dramatic reduction in carbohydrates with sugars that break down easily (high glycemic index) combined with restrictions on prepared foods and other high-sugar items frequently result in a rapid loss of weight (1–5% of body weight in the first weeks, depending on original weight). This also changes the shape and appearance of an individual. However, to date there are no scientific long-term studies of these dietary practices, so their overall effects are poorly known.

CONNECTIONS

See chapters 2, pages 48–56, and 10, pages 299–321, to remind yourself of the details of human morphology.

(a)

(b)

■ **FIGURE 11.6**
Cultural differences in diet and food preparation. A San woman from southern Africa (a) teaches her daughter how to obtain and prepare gongo nuts, an important part of their people's diet. College students share pizza (b). What cultural differences are apparent in the way these two groups obtain and share food? How do their diets differ?

Most examples are less extreme, and across human culture the relative caloric, dietary fat, and carbohydrate contents of diets affect body shape and aspects of physiology. Differences across and within populations in morphology and behavior result in part from dietary differences. So a portion of the variation in the way humans' bodies look is not due to selective differences in dietary patterns, or even gene flow, but to the diet's impact on the existing physiology of the individual within a population. In recent times, at least in the United States, this is clearly borne out in the rapidly changing body shapes and dietary patterns brought on by cultural dietary practices resulting in widespread obesity (Figure 11.7) and also the variety of dieting and "slimming" practices resulting in rapid weight loss. Remember that all of this variation in dietary patterns and the resultant impact on physiology and morphology is not evolutionarily relevant unless it in some way impacts reproduction. So much of the variation in modern human size and shape today is based on genetic ranges already existing in our gene pool (see chapter 10) being variably expressed due to dietary patterns and practice. It is not clear whether any of the dietary variation in modern humans has evolutionary significance, especially as dietary patterns become increasingly globalized. If such patterns result in widespread reductions in specific nutrients, it is possible that some adaptive shifts (changes in allele frequencies), over long periods of time, could occur.

Body Modification

Diet alone does not account for human morphology. From chapter 9 we know that for thousands of years humans have been clothing themselves and otherwise adorning their bodies to change their appearance. It is highly likely that many forms of body modification, from tattooing to hair cutting to genital modification, have a long history. Today we can add medical modifications and activity patterns to this list of biocultural factors that change the human form. Again, as with diet, each person inherits basal physiological and morphological patterns, which he or she then modifies through cultural practices. For example, in many populations, human males grow facial hair. In many cultures, men remove that hair daily by shaving. In other populations, men have minimal facial hair growth. Past patterns of gene flow and possibly other

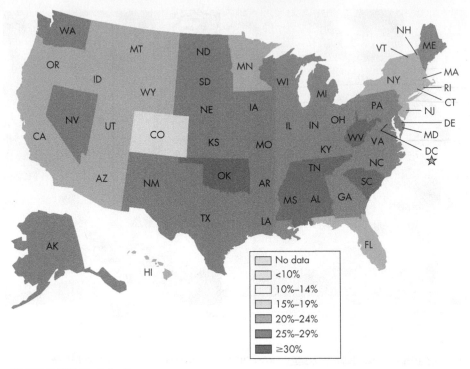

■ FIGURE 11.7

U.S. obesity rates, by state, 2008. This map shows the percentage of the population in each state that is obese, defined as having a body mass index (BMI) greater than 30. What factors might account for the differences? How do obesity rates here compare with those in other developed countries? In developing countries?

evolutionary processes have led to differences in appearance of males in different populations. These genetically based differences are then altered via cultural behavior.

Other alterations to modern human bodies are tied to cultural beliefs about attractiveness. These include scarification, tattooing, genital modification, breast augmentation, and other surgical modifications (Figure 11.8). Perhaps a motive behind many of these modifications is sexual attractiveness (which can be related to reproductive success). If body modification results in sterility or otherwise reduces or enhances reproductive potential, that individual

■ FIGURE 11.8

Body modification. Tattooing, piercing, and other types of body modification occur in almost all human cultures. Is there a likely reproductive impact of these practices?

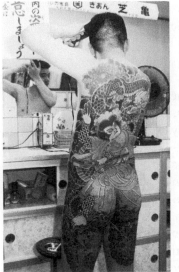

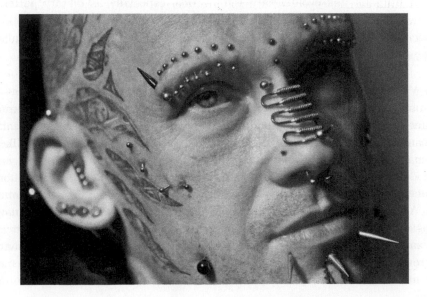

(a)

(b)

■ **FIGURE 11.9**
Changes in activity patterns. In some societies, people are physically active as part of daily life (a), whereas in other societies, many people are sedentary much of the time (b).

is impacting evolutionary patterns by altering the rate of contribution of his or her representation in the gene pool. Body modification does increase the amount of variation in form in our species, and this increased variation may result in some reproductive impact.

Activity Patterns

More so than diet or body modification, activity patterns may have a more direct impact on reproductive physiology; therefore, they have potential evolutionary consequences (Figure 11.9). Activity patterns of modern humans in some populations today differ dramatically from those of humans of even a few millennia earlier, especially in what are referred to as the high-**HDI** nations (such as Canada, Japan, the United States, and many European nations). Lower rates of daily activity, prolonged sitting, and little physical activity, combined with extended periods of social stress and poor dietary patterns, can have pronounced physiological consequences. These range from reduced fertility to hypertension and other potentially serious circulatory disorders.

Causes of death tend to differ widely between nations and populations of humans due to differing activity and lifestyle patterns, levels of access to health care, and disease environment (Molnar, 2002). In low-HDI countries, the three leading causes of death in 2001 were HIV/AIDS, respiratory infections, and heart disease. In high-HDI countries, the top three killers were heart disease, stroke, and chronic obstructive pulmonary disease (World Health Organization, 2002). A major question in assessing current evolutionary trends in humans relates to the patterns of mortality and birth across different human populations and how, if at all, allelic frequencies are changing as a result. Remember that physiological changes only become relevant to evolution if they change the age of death so much that they affect reproductive fitness.

HDI
Human development index, created by the United Nations, combining economic, life expectancy, education, and standard-of-living variables

The most easily observed evolutionary process in modern humans is gene flow. Dramatic changes in population allelic frequencies are going on across the planet because of high rates of migration. One might even argue that gene flow is the predominant evolutionary process in modern humanity. Two types of cultural change—improvement in travel technology and social changes promoting mobility—are having a significant impact on the distribution of alleles across the species (see chapter 10). In a truly biocultural fashion, populational gene pools are changing in response to the behavior and technology of modern humankind. Humans from differing populations are coming into more frequent contact. This has two potential results: reduction in differences in allele frequencies between populations; and increase in overall genetic variation as specific alleles are added to populations where they were previously absent. Evolution is occurring in modern humans as we move across the globe and continue to shift our cultural, linguistic, and commercial borders.

Culture, evolution, and the future: where are we headed?

The future evolutionary patterns in our species will not be the ones predicted in science fiction films and comic books. Giant brains, telepathic scientists, and super-mutants are probably not in our future. As noted in chapters 7 through 10, the hominin lineage ancestral to modern humans is characterized by specific evolutionary patterns: decreasing body and dental robustness, decreasing sexual dimorphism, increasing brain size (until ~300,000–200,000 years ago) and the increasing reliance on extrasomatic means to overcome environmental challenges. Given these patterns and the morphological constraints on human form, it is highly unlikely that our heads will grow larger, that our bodies will shrivel into useless appendages ruled by our cerebral powers, or that we will develop mutant superpowers due to radiation exposure. Rather, our form has been remarkably stable (within quite variable boundaries—see chapter 10) for at least the last 50,000–40,000 years. In that time, most changes have come at the genetic level (for example, gene flow); the physiological level (for example, changing immunities in response to changing disease environments); and the behavioral level (for example, changes in cultural patterns). Recently, changes related to technology have led to a dramatic increase in human populations around the planet, and this population explosion will most likely affect our evolutionary future.

Human Densities and Global Population are Dramatically Different Today

Ten thousand years ago there were under 150 million humans on the planet. Today there are nearly 8 billion (Figure 11.10). In 1970 there were approximately 3.6 billion. We nearly doubled our species population in less than four decades, not quite two human generations. In the context of evolutionary time, our population explosion is extremely recent, and its evolutionary implications are complex. Because of agricultural technologies, we have not yet reached the limit of our ability to feed ourselves (although food availability varies widely because of social and political factors). Because of medical technologies, infant mortality rates, on average, are going down and life expectancy rates continue to increase (as high as the mid-80s in some nations). However, these are mean

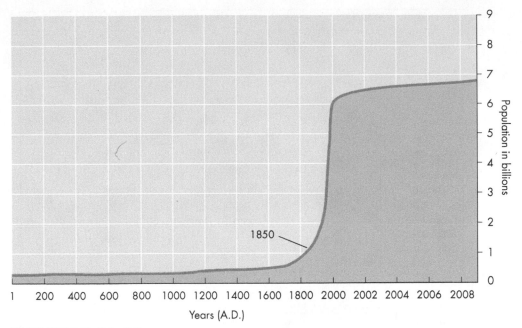

■ FIGURE 11.10

Population growth. What caused the dramatic increase in the population growth rate that occurred about 150 years ago?

patterns, and the actual distribution of medical technology also varies widely. Life expectancies and infant mortality rates can be dramatically different between nations, for different ethnic groups within nations, across socioeconomic groups within nations (Figures 11.11 and 11.12). Because of these differences, we can envision potential differences in reproductive patterns in such populations and groups, such as longer lives leading to increased possibilities for reproduction and higher infant mortality resulting in reduced reproductive success. However, cultural factors that influence reproductive choices and patterns complicate the picture. Many populations (such as in northern Europe) with the highest life expectancies have the lowest birthrates, and many countries with very low life expectancies have very high birthrates due to complex cultural and historical factors. This suggests, as noted earlier, that disease environments and other challenges to humanity have very different impacts, not necessarily due to differing genetic populational complexes, but rather due to cultural distribution of technology, wealth, and access to health care.

What are the potential effects of dramatic increases in population size? Increased genetic diversity is one likely outcome. As more individuals are born, the rate of novel genetic combinations increases. If these individuals survive into adulthood and reproduce, the species' overall gene pool increases in diversity. In general this is beneficial, as increased diversity generally increases adaptive ability.

A less benign consequence is the increase in highly industrialized farming techniques. With a large and increasing population, we can no longer rely on "wild-type" foodstuffs (unmodified by human intervention). Already we rely heavily on factory farming of livestock bred for specific characteristics and massive cropping of plants engineered, either through breeding or direct genetic modification, for high returns. These systems require substantial labor and technology and frequently conflict with other forms of land use by other

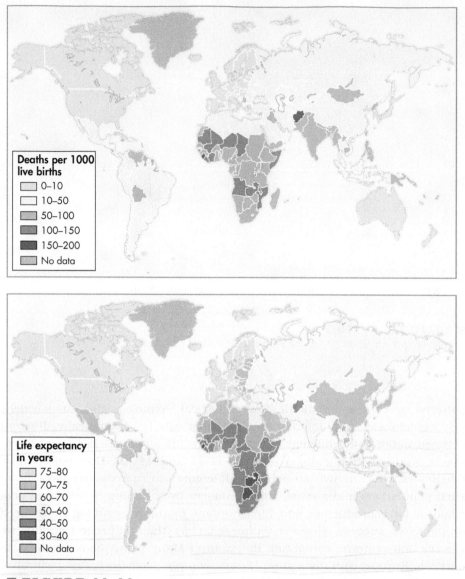

Deaths per 1000 live births
- 0–10
- 10–50
- 50–100
- 100–150
- 150–200
- No data

Life expectancy in years
- 75–80
- 70–75
- 60–70
- 50–60
- 40–50
- 30–40
- No data

■ FIGURE 11.11

Global infant mortality and life expectancy. Infant mortality rates and life expectancy are two key indicators of the general health of people in a society. What accounts for the large differences in these indicators across different societies?

organisms. This type of food production seriously affects both the environment and the specific types of nutrients we consume (Figure 11.13).

Yet another consequence of massive population numbers is a nearly complete reliance on manufactured goods. Many manufacturing processes have significantly negative effects on air, water, and soil qualities, potentially introducing novel environmental challenges to humans. However, the Industrial Revolution, and its massive niche-constructing impacts, is still in its infancy in evolutionary terms (2–3 centuries), so predicting its long-term impact (over the next few millennia) is difficult.

One clear result of the increase in the human population is increased population density in inhabited areas. Densities throughout our evolutionary history were quite low (few people per square mile and small settlements). Today, urban environments such as New York, Hong Kong, Mexico City, or Jakarta include millions of humans in close contact on a daily basis. These densities and urban contexts are totally new in an evolutionary sense, so it is difficult

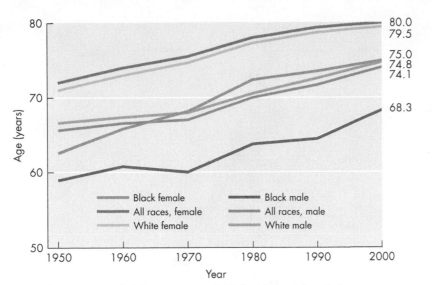

Note: Life expectancy calculations are not available for other racial or ethnic groups.

■ FIGURE 11.12
Life expectancy by "race" and sex in the United States. Although life expectancy has gone up across the board over the past half century, White Americans still live longer than Black Americans. If race has no biological basis, what factors could account for these disparities?

■ FIGURE 11.13
Two types of agriculture. Traditional small-scale agriculture grows a variety of crops and results in minimal environmental damage. Large-scale monoculture (single-crop fields) requires heavy applications of herbicides, pesticides, and fertilizers and has major environmental effects.

to predict their effects. One hint may be the changing patterns of noninfectious diseases in these areas. Increased rates of hypertension, cardiac disorders, cancers, and neurological disorders seem to be correlated with urbanization and development (Molnar, 2002). Correlation is not causation, however, and other factors such as increased longevity, increased pollution, and improved technologies for combating infectious diseases probably also play roles.

Another characteristic of the population explosion in our species is a change in the demographic structure of different populations. Throughout human history young individuals have always outnumbered the old, as natural mortality rates increase with age. This results in a population pyramid that is wide at the bottom and narrow on top (see Figure 11.14). Today, many populations, especially in high-density areas such as Europe and Japan, have inverted population pyramids that indicate large numbers of elderly people. This has potential repercussions for lifetime reproductive success (the longer a person lives, the greater his or her potential to reproduce), and for the distribution of energy and labor within a population. The long-term evolutionary impacts of such changing demographics are not clear, but it is clear that the

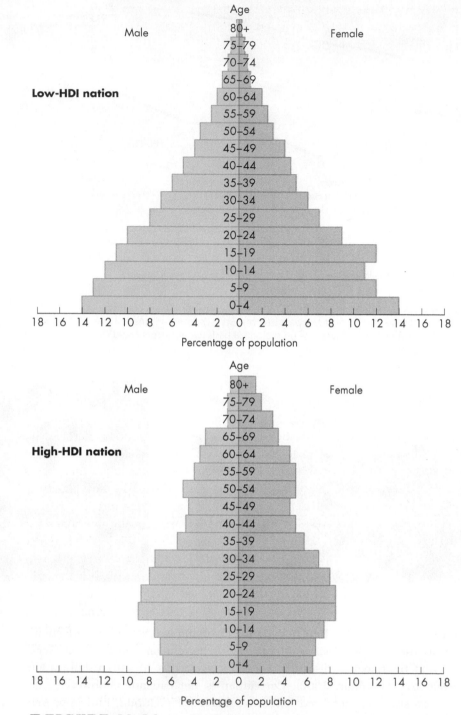

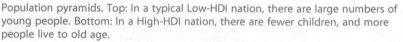

■ FIGURE 11.14

Population pyramids. Top: In a typical Low-HDI nation, there are large numbers of young people. Bottom: In a High-HDI nation, there are fewer children, and more people live to old age.

age structure of many human societies is changing and that those changes do have social and economic implications.

Genetic Manipulation can Influence Our Evolution

Throughout this book we have focused on the forces of evolution and how they may result in change in allele frequencies across time. Our review of hominin evolution focused on the changing morphologies and behaviors that

Where Is that Banana From?

Most of us love to have a banana or kiwifruit any time of year, but few of us think what it means to have either of those fruits in the United States during December. Up until recently (the last century or so) people had to make do with whatever food they had locally. Long-range transportation of frozen or refrigerated foods was not possible. Being the incredible niche-constructing organism we are, we did not settle for that. We developed technologies for long distance transport, we genetically engineered plants and animals to grow in ways and places they never could before, and we developed chemical treatments that allow us to harvest plants and animals long before they ever reach a dinner table. Should this concern us? Does it matter that the meat in the hamburger you might eat in Chicago is from cows that grew up quickly in Costa Rica, Brazil, and North Dakota (and that these are mixed together)? Does it matter that in order to satisfy the year-round desire for bananas in North America, most of the rain forest of Central America has been replanted as banana plantations? Well, the answers depend on whether you think we want sustainable food production on the planet or not. If we need to have any food anywhere at any time, then we will need to keep developing genetically altered, expensive, expansive land-using foods. However, if we agree that we can confine ourselves, largely, to what is available regionally (as for most of our evolutionary history), we might more effectively use the planet we occupy. In short, we need to actively decide what kind of food niche we are constructing.

emerged alongside changes in the genome over great periods of time. We looked to mutation, gene flow, genetic drift, and natural selection to explain these changes at the genetic level. Today humans are able to add a fifth, rapid force of evolution: direct genetic/genomic alteration. We can now alter the frequencies of alleles and create and introduce new alleles into organisms. Genetically modified foodstuffs, cloned animals, and genetic therapies for humans are all becoming components of human culture. While the majority of this work has been carried out with nonhuman organisms, some experimental gene therapy and modification is already going on with human subjects, and this pattern is likely to increase in the future. In **gene therapy**, humans alter sequences of DNA by inserting a normative sequence into a noncoding region of DNA to replace a nonfunctional gene. This may be done by replacing one sequence (an allele) with another at the same locus via recombination or induced mutation, or by altering the regulatory portions of a locus such that the alleles at the locus are turned on or off differentially (see chapter 3). As of 2010 gene therapy trials have shown only mixed success, but many potential avenues of exploration remain. As with most medical technologies, access to such therapies will be limited to the higher reaches of socioeconomic classes and not equally distributed across human populations and nations. It will be a minimum of tens, or more likely hundreds, of generations before we see any large-scale changes in human populations from genetic manipulation, but human biocultural behavior has crossed the boundary into direct influence of the genetic material.

gene therapy
when humans alter sequences of DNA via technological means in order to repair or alter the function of the given sequence of DNA

Some of Our Behavior Reflects Adaptations

In chapters 3 and 5 we discussed how behavior is related to the genome. We saw that some behavior can be seen as adaptive, because it became common in a species or population due to the reproductive benefits it conferred. At present, researchers disagree about how much of our current behavior reflects specific adaptations to our past environments and how much consists of expressions of our broad behavioral potential, as elicited by specific environments (Fuentes, 2009; Simpson & Kenrick, 1997; Sussman, 1999). Some argue that behavior in modern humans, such as sexual attraction, jealousy, male aggression and competition, and marriage patterns, reflect adaptations that arose during our past forager lifestyle and are now just being expressed in a new environment (the evolutionary psychology or sociobiology perspectives). Others argue that much of the specifics of modern human behavior are bioculturally mediated and that few details of modern human behavior reflect specific adaptations; rather they reflect our ability to exhibit a wide range of social behavior—some adaptive, some nonadaptive, and much irrelevant to reproductive success (a biocultural anthropology perspective, for example).

What does this tell us about our future? Few if any researchers, regardless of their theoretical perspective, believe that much of human behavior is "hardwired" and inflexible. However, many do see the expressions of human behavior as reflecting adaptations and thus having significant biological correlates. If much of our behavior reflects specific adaptations to past environments, it may not change much over the next millennia regardless of technological advances/changes. Details of technologies and cultures will change, but most human behavior will stay the same. If much of our behavior does not result from past focused acts of selection (specific adaptations), we may see continued and increased variation in the patterns and forms of what humans do.

Today and for the near future it is going to be increasingly difficult to ask the question "what specifically is adaptive behavior" in humans. As the changes in technologies, densities, cultures, and environments combine with massive globalization and information exchange across the planet, making calculations and scientific tests about the relationships of specific behaviors to both genomic elements and reproductive success will become increasingly complex. In a sense our biocultural nature has become so complex that it is now extremely difficult to divide biology and culture from one another in any assessment of human behavior. This does not mean that we will cease our inquiries into the origins and future of human behavioral evolution, just that our success in unraveling these complexities will be small and slow on average.

Understanding biological anthropology and understanding ourselves

The goal of this book has been to familiarize you with the basics of evolutionary theory, how our bodies work, the history of our order (the Primates) and our specific lineage (the hominins), and the variations and complexity of modern human biocultural reality. We began by focusing on three themes: the scientific method, concepts and connections, and critical thinking. These themes have been inherent in our discussion throughout the book. The hypotheses and theories presented have been generated via the scientific method, and our discussions have focused on presenting both core information and critical assessment of that information. All of the data presented result from collaborative ventures among researchers who represent diverse backgrounds and scientific disciplines. The holistic, comparative approach inherent in anthropology, combined with the focus on the biological aspects of humanity and the evolutionary processes influencing them, provides a powerful perspective for investigating humanity and connecting the details and data reviewed here to

What We Know
Questions That Remain

What We Know
Humans are not exempt from the processes of evolution; we are still evolving, as is all life on earth.

Questions That Remain
What substantive changes in our form, if any, will occur over the next centuries? How will genetic technologies affect human populational allele frequencies in the long run? How will increased human population densities affect our bodies and behavior?

What We Know
Many human cultural habits alter our morphologies and physiologies.

Questions That Remain
Will any of these patterns have lasting evolutionary impacts?

What We Know
Disease has played a significant role in recent human evolution, and viral diseases may be important environmental pressures for modern humans.

Questions That Remain
Will our medical technologies ameliorate the threat of viral diseases such as HIV/AIDS and H1N1? Can our technologies move fast enough to outpace the rates of evolutionary change in these pathogens?

aspects and patterns in our daily lives. Humans are complex biocultural organisms, and the field of anthropology, specifically biological anthropology, provides a powerful lens through which to view our past, present, and future. We have seen how interconnected are our everyday lives and behavior to our biological selves. When we study humanity, we cannot always separate what is biologically based from what is culturally constructed. We are the last remaining hominin, the most successful of the hominoids (arguably of all the mammals), and the vertebrate that has made the largest impact in the current history of the planet. To understand ourselves and our place in nature, we must integrate evolutionary, biological, and anthropological knowledge. Remember the power of the scientific method, remain a critical thinker and a collaborative investigator, and use your amazing human mind to arrive at a more profound understanding of yourself and your fellow humans.

SUMMARY

▲ There are five main approaches to the study of human behavioral evolution: sociobiology, human behavioral ecology, evolutionary psychology, dual-inheritance theory, and biocultural anthropology.

▲ Humans are still evolving. The processes of natural selection, gene flow, genetic drift, and mutation continue to affect human populational allele frequencies. However, human biocultural adaptations and behavior are changing the ways in which we deal with the challenges of the environments we face.

▲ While disease may still play an important role in human evolution, technology is altering the patterns of how diseases impact populations. Because not all populations or all segments of populations have equal access to technologies, the same disease can have very different effects on different groups of humans.

▲ Cultural behavior ranging from eating habits to body modification to gene flow is changing the morphologies of modern humans. It is not clear what long-term evolutionary impacts this will have.

▲ Enormous increases in human populations may be changing the types of local environments and their associated stresses for many human populations. These increases in survivorship are also potentially increasing the genetic diversity within populations.

▲ Human technological genomic modification may have the effect of accelerating allele frequency change (evolution) in some human populations.

▲ There is substantial debate as to how much of our current behavior reflects specific adaptations to past environments and how much is expressions of a broad potential for behavior inherent in our species.

▲ Biological anthropology and the themes of the scientific method, collaborative investigation, and critical thinking are core to understanding humanity.

CRITICAL THINKING

1. Will robotics and increased mechanization of manufacturing processes reduce the need for physical activity and thus initiate changes in our body form?

2. In an evolutionary sense, is there a difference between a cure for HIV/AIDS and drug therapies that allow infected humans to remain alive for 20+ years postinfection? What behavioral and reproductive impacts might each of these prospects have?

3. If the same diseases are having very different effects in different human populations, can that be driving the frequencies of alleles in these populations further apart? Think about this in the context of globalization of economies and migration.

4. If humans are so successful at using technologies to deal with environmental challenges, does it mean that natural selection is not truly impacting us any more? Attempt to identify a few arenas where selection can still be actively impacting human allele frequencies.

5. How do your own dietary habits and body modification impact your morphology? What, if any, long-term implications might these patterns have for you? For the population you live in?

RESOURCES

GENE THERAPY

www.ornl.gov/sci/techresources/Human_Genome/medicine/genetherapy. shtml This Web site has a brief overview of gene therapy with definitions and examples. It also contains a series of links to provide further information about the potentials and pitfalls of these endeavors.

UNITED NATIONS GLOBAL POPULATION

http://unstats.un.org/unsd/demographic/products/socind/socind2.htm
This Web site is part of the United Nations and has statistical information on world population figures and many other aspects related to density and growth.

GLOBAL DISPARITIES IN HEALTH

http://ucatlas.ucsc.edu/health.php This Web site offers graphic illustrations of the global disparities in health and related issues.

REFERENCES

Barkow, J. H., Cosmides, L., & John Tooby, J., Eds. (1992). *The adapted mind: Evolutionary psychology and the generation of culture.* Oxford University Press, New York.

Boyd, R., & Richerson, P. J. (2005). *The origin and evolution of cultures.* New York: Oxford University Press.

Dufour, D. L. (2006). The 23rd annual Raymond Pearl Memorial Lecture. Biocultural approaches in Human Biology. *American Journal of Human Biology 18*(1):1–9.

Fuentes, A. (2004). *Evolution of human behavior,* New York: Oxford University Press.

MacKinnon, K., & Fuentes, A. (2005). Assessing bio-reductionist views of human behavior based on non-human primate studies: Sex, violence, and sometimes science. In S. McKinnon & S. Silverman (Eds.), *Complexities: Beyond nature and nurture* (pp. 83–105). Chicago: University of Chicago Press.

Molnar, S. (2002). *Human variation: Races, types and ethnic groups.* Upper Saddle River, NJ: Prentice-Hall.

Panter-Brick, C. & Fuentes, A. (Eds.) (2008). *Health, risk and Adversity.* Berghahn Books: New York.

Peiris, J. S. M., Kwok, Y., Osterhaus, A., & Stöhr, K. (2003). The severe acute respiratory syndrome. *New England Journal of Medicine, 349,* 2431–2441.

Simpson, J. A., & Kenrick, D. T. (1997). *Evolutionary social psychology.* Mahwah, NJ: Lawrence Erlbaum Associates.

Sussman, R. W. (1999). *The biological basis of human behavior: A critical review* (2nd ed.). Upper Saddle River, NJ: Prentice-Hall.

Wilson, E. O. (1975). *Sociobiology: the new synthesis.* Belknap Press: Harvard.

World Health Organization. (2002). *World Health Report.*

Credits

Photo Credits

Chapter 8

Opener © Philippe Plailly/Photo Researchers, Inc.; **8.1** © Clive Bromhall/Photolibrary/Getty Images; **8.2** © Roderick Edwards/Animals Animals; **8.4** © Alan Walker/National Geographic Society Image Collection; **8.5** left Photo © Bone Clones®; **8.5** right National Museum and House of Culture, Tanzania; **8.6** left Photo © Bone Clones®; **8.6** right © National Museums of Kenya; **8.7** © Transvaal Museum; **8.8** Micrographs courtesy of Dr. Frederick E. Grine, SUNY, Stony Brook. Photographed by Chester Tarka; **8.9** © 1985 David L. Brill; **8.10, 8.11, 8.14** © David L. Brill/Brill Atlanta; **8.15** © The National Museums of Kenya; **8.16** © Eric Delson; **8.18** top © National Museum of Natural History, Leiden; **8.18** bottom Neg. #319781. Courtesy Department of Library Services, American Museum of Natural History; **8.22, 8.23** © David L. Brill/Brill Atlanta; **8.24** The Human Origins Program, Smithsonian Institution; **8.26** left © Boltin Picture Library/Bridgeman Art Library; **8.26** middle, **8.26** right Courtesy K. L. Feder

Chapter 9

Opener © Photo Researchers, Inc.; **9.1** left © The Field Museum, Neg. #A66700; **9.1** right © John Gurche; **9.3** left © David L. Brill; **9.3** right © The Natural History Museum, London; **9.4** © Javier Trueba/Madrid Scientific Films; **9.6** Courtesy Dr. Dennis A. Etler; **9.7** Image #327423. Courtesy Department of Library Services. American Museum of Natural History; **9.10** Courtesy Dr. Ian Tattersall, From The Human Odyssey; **9.12** Courtesy Phototheque du Musée de l'Homme, Paris. M. Lucas, photographer; **9.13** © Tim D. White/Brill Atlanta; **9.15** © John Reader/Science Photo Library/Photo Researchers, Inc.; **9.16** © The Natural History Museum, London; **9.18** © The British Museum; **9.19** © The Natural History Museum, London; **9.20** Neg. #39686. Photo by Kirschner. Courtesy Department of Library Services, American Museum of Natural History; **9.21** Courtesy Comité Départemental du Tourisme de la Dordogne; **9.22** © Ernest Manewal/SuperStock

Chapter 10

Opener © Gary Caskey/Reuters/Corbis; **10.2** © Getty Images/Digital Vision; **10.6** Courtesy of the author; **10.7** left Neg. #231604, Photo by D. B. MacMillan. Courtesy Department of Library Services. American Museum of Natural History; **10.7** right © Kazuyoshi Nomachi/Photo Researchers, Inc.; **10.8** top right Photo © Bone Clones®; **10.8** top middle left © 1985 David L. Brill/Brill Atlanta; **10.8** top middle right Photo © Bone Clones®; **10.8** top left © David L. Brill; **10.8** bottom left © National Museums of Kenya; **10.8** bottom middle left © David L. Brill; **10.8** bottom middle © The National Museums of Kenya; **10.8** bottom middle right © David L. Brill; **10.8** bottom right Image #327423. Courtesy Department of Library Services. American Museum of Natural History; **10.14** © Meckes/Ottawa/Photo Researchers, Inc.; **10.18** © The Granger Collection, New York; **10.19** top left, Efe man: © Tronick/Anthro-Photo; **10.19** top right, San man: © Irven DeVore/Anthro-Photo; **10.19** bottom left, Aborigine man: © George Holton/Photo Researchers, Inc.; **10.19** middle right, Bagish woman: © Bagish/Anthro-Photo; **10.19** bottom middle, Bangalore girl: © Mike Yamashita/Woodfin Camp & Associates; **10.19** bottom right, Mendi man: © Michael McCoy/Photo Researchers, Inc.; **10.19** top left, Yanomamo man: © C. Anderson/Rapho Division/Photo Researchers, Inc.; **10.19** top right, Hamadan man: © Paolo Koch/Photo Researchers, Inc.; **10.19** middle left, Lapplander man: © Ch. et J. Lenars/Explorer, Science Source/Photo Researchers, Inc.; **10.19** middle right, Western European man: © Owen Franken/Corbis; **10.19** bottom left, Taos Pueblo man: © Emil Muench/Aspa/Photo Researchers, Inc.; **10.19** bottom right, Southeast Asian woman: © Paul A. Souders/Corbis

Chapter 11

Opener © AP Photo/Lo Sai Hung; **11.1** © Alphonse Telymonde/SuperStock; **11.3** top © Michael Gadomski/Animals Animals; **11.3** bottom © Scott W. Smith/Animals Animals; **11.6** left © Anthony Bannister/Animals Animals/Earth Scenes; **11.6** right James Darell/Getty Images; **11.8** left © Gideon Mendel/Corbis; **11.8** right © AP Photo/Lefteris Pitarakis; **11.9** top © Abbas/Magnum Photos; **11.9** bottom © Royalty-Free/Corbis; **11.13** left © Wolfgang Kaehler/Corbis; **11.13** right © PhotoLink/Photodisc/Getty Images

Text and Line Art Credits

Introduction
Figure I.1 From John H. Postlethwait and J. L. Hopson, *The Nature of Life*. Copyright © John H. Postlethwait and J. L. Hopson. Reprinted with the permission of John H. Postlethwait. **I.4** From Kenneth L. Feder and Michael A. Park, *Human Antiquity: An Introduction to Physical Anthropology and Archaeology, Fourth Edition*. Copyright © 2001 Mayfield Publishing Co. Reprinted with the permission of The McGraw-Hill Companies. **I.6** From John L. Allen, *Student Atlas of World Politics, Third Edition*. Copyright © 2008 by The McGraw-Hill Companies. Reproduced by permission of McGraw-Hill Contemporary Learning Series.

Chapter 1
Figure 1.17 From John H. Postlethwait and J. L. Hopson, *The Nature of Life*. Copyright © John H. Postlethwait and J. L. Hopson. Reprinted with the permission of John H. Postlethwait. **1.18** From Michael A. Park, *Introducing Anthropology: An Integrated Approach, Third Edition*. Copyright © 2006 by The McGraw-Hill Companies. Reprinted with the permission of The McGraw-Hill Companies.

Chapter 2
Table 2.1 From P. Raven and G. Johnson, *Biology, Sixth Edition*. Copyright © 2002 by The McGraw-Hill Companies. Reprinted with the permission of The McGraw-Hill Companies. **Figure 2.4** From Kenneth Saladin, *Human Anatomy, First Edition*. Copyright © 2005 by The McGraw-Hill Companies. Reprinted with the permission of The McGraw-Hill Companies. **2.5** From D. R. Swindler, *Dentition of Living Primates* (London, New York: Academic Press, 1976). Reprinted with the permission of the Kathryn Rantala Swindler. **2.6** From Kenneth Saladin, *Human Anatomy, First Edition*. Copyright © 2005 by The McGraw-Hill Companies. Reprinted with the permission of The McGraw-Hill Companies. **2.11** Adapted from Stuart Fox, *A Lab Guide to Human Physiology: Concepts and Clinical Applications, Tenth Edition*. Copyright © 2004 by The McGraw-Hill Companies. Reprinted with the permission of The McGraw-Hill Companies. **2.12** From Kenneth Saladin, *Human Anatomy, First Edition*. Copyright © 2005 by The McGraw-Hill Companies. Reprinted with the permission of The McGraw-Hill Companies. **2.13** From Michael A. Park, *Biological Anthropology, Fourth Edition*. Copyright © 2005 by The McGraw-Hill Companies. Reprinted with the permission of The McGraw-Hill Companies. **2.15** From Paul M. Insel and Walton T. Roth, *Core Concepts in Health, Tenth Edition*. Copyright © 2006 by The McGraw-Hill Companies. Reprinted with the permission of The McGraw-Hill Companies. **2.16** From Paul M. Insel and Walton T. Roth, **Core Concepts in Health, Tenth Edition.** Copyright © 2006 by The McGraw-Hill Companies. Reprinted with the permission of The McGraw-Hill Companies.

Chapter 3
Figure 3.2 From John H. Relethford, *The Human Species: An Introduction to Biological Anthropology, Sixth Edition*. Copyright © 2005 by The McGraw-Hill Companies. Reprinted with the permission of The McGraw-Hill Companies. **3.3** From John H. Postlethwait and J. L. Hopson, *The Nature of Life*. Copyright © John H. Postlethwait and J. L. Hopson. Reprinted with the permission of John H. Postlethwait. **3.6** From John H. Postlethwait and J. L. Hopson, *The Nature of Life*. Copyright © John H. Postlethwait and J. L. Hopson. Reprinted with the permission of John H. Postlethwait.

Glossary

Acheulean relating to the type of stone tool that follows the Olduwan in the archaeological record, dating to about 1.5 million years ago and consisting of bifaced tools (flaked on both sides) that are more complex to make and allow more kinds of manipulation than the earlier types

Adapoids fossil primates; members of the infraorder Adapiformes, potentially related to both strepsirrhine and haplorrhine lineages

adaptation change in response to environmental challenges

adaptive radiation expansion by a single group of organisms into a diverse array of forms

affiliative bond enhancing or prosocial ("friendly")

agonistic aggressive or combative ("unfriendly")

allele a variant sequence of nucleotides in a gene; a form of a gene

allopatric speciation mode of speciation that involves a separation and isolation of populations of the parent species

altruism acting in a way that has a net loss of energy to the actor and a net benefit in energy to the receiver

amino acids building blocks of proteins

ancestral trait characteristic found in an ancestor and all (or most) of its descendants

Animalia a class of living things that includes all organisms that are heterotrophs (they eat other organisms to obtain energy)

anthropoids all monkeys, apes, and humans

anthropology the study of all aspects of the human experience

anticodon three-nucleotide sequence on a tRNA molecule that helps match the appropriate amino acid with a specific mRNA codon

archaeology the study of the patterns of behavior and the material record of humans who lived in the past

archaic humans those fossil hominins in the genus *Homo* found in Africa and Eurasia between about 600,000 and 30,000 years ago that reflect morphologies relatively distinct from both *Homo erectus* and modern humans; referred to as *Homo heidelbergensis* and *Homo neanderthalensis* by some

Archonta superorder of mammals made up of the extinct Pleseadapiformes and the living orders Primates, Scandentia (the tree shrews), Chiroptera (the bats), and Dermoptera (colugos)

assortative mating mate selection based on similarity (positive assortative) or differences (negative assortative) in traits

balanced polymorphism a situation in which selection favors a heterozygotic state for a given locus and thus maintains both the recessive and the dominant alleles in a population, even if one or both are deleterious in the homozygous state

behavioral ecology the study of behavior from ecological and evolutionary perspectives

behavioral inheritance system the system of imitation and learning by which behavior passes from generation to generation

biocultural evolution evolutionary change and adaptation through both somatic (biological) and extrasomatic (material/cultural) means

biological anthropology the study of the biological and biocultural facets of humans and their relatives

biological species population of individuals that interbreed

bipedal anatomy a set of anatomical adaptations that make it possible for an animal to use two legs for locomotion

bipedality use of two legs rather than four for locomotion

blade tools tools made from stone flakes that are at least twice as long as they are wide

bottleneck dramatic reduction in the size of a population such that the genetic diversity in the population is substantially curtailed

brachiator anatomy the balls-and-socket shoulder joint and the positioning of the scapula on the back allowing for 360° rotation of the arms

canine dimorphism difference between the sexes of a species in the size of the canine teeth

canine fossa the indentation on the maxilla above the canine root

catastrophism the belief that great catastrophes regularly wipe out much of life on earth

Ceboidea primate superfamily that includes all monkeys found in the Americas

Cercopithecoidea primate superfamily that includes all monkeys found in Africa and Asia

chromosomes complex structures that house the supercoiled DNA in the nucleus

chronometric dating techniques methods of dating that provide a specific age of a fossil based either on analysis of a piece of the fossil itself or analysis of the rocks surrounding the fossil

cline a distribution wherein biological traits vary in a specific pattern across geography

codon a three-nucleotide sequence in which the DNA's triplet code is written onto the mRNA

comparative approach the practice of comparing features across entities/cultures/organisms to elucidate similarities and differences

comparative primatology the study of our closest living relatives, the primates, for the purpose of understanding aspects of our own behavior

connective tissue tissues responsible for the internal cohesion of the body

continental drift theory that the present configuration of continents results from the movement of the earth's crust

convergent evolution type of evolutionary process whereby species come to share phenotypic characteristics due to similar environmental pressures

cormic index standing height divided by sitting height

craniometrics the measuring and study of cranial morphology

cranium set of bones encircling the brain and making up the skull, exclusive of the jaw

critical thinking taking control of information presented to you and examining it

crossing over homologous, or sister, chromosomes exchange segments

cultural anthropology the study of human culture in all of its complexity

culture patterns of behavior human societies exhibit in their families, relationships, religions, laws, moral codes, songs, art, business, and everyday interactions

dental formula one quarter of the full complement of teeth, counted from the centerline of the mouth back toward the throat

deoxyribonucleic acid (DNA) the chemical compound, found in most living organisms, that contains basic information for the structure of life

derived trait characteristic found only in one descendant branch and not in the ancestral form

Developmental System Theory (DST) an approach that includes the development of biological and behavioral systems as a core part of evolutionary processes

diploid having 46 chromosomes, arranged in 23 pairs

dominance set of relationships that results in different relative abilities to acquire desired resources

ecology interrelationships between living organisms and their environments

encephalization quotient (EQ) ratio of brain to body size; an EQ of 1 indicates a brain size expected for that mammalian body size

endocrine glands tissues that secrete hormones

epigenetic system the factors in the body that work in combination with the genes and proteins to affect phenotypes

epithelial tissue tissues that cover the surfaces of our bodies

estrus behavioral and physiological sexual receptivity

ethnography the focused study of a specific culture or aspects of a culture

ethnology the comparative study of many cultures

eugenics study of genetics with the notion of improving human biology and biological potential; often associated with erroneous and/or simplistic assumptions about the relationship of behavior or cultural traits with simple genetic systems

evolvability the notion that much DNA may act as reserve variation for future selective pressures

exaptation trait that is currently serving a function other than that for which it originally arose

fact a verifiable, observable truth

fit having the set of heritable traits that are best suited to existing and reproducing in a given environment

foraging the act of seeking and processing food

foramen magnum opening on the bottom of the skull through which the spinal cord passes

fossil material evidence of past life on this planet

founder effect evolutionary process in which a small group of individuals account for all of the genetic variation in a large population

Fst statistical measurement of the fraction of variation found between samples

gene segment of DNA that contains the sequence for a protein

gene flow movement of alleles within and between populations

gene pool all the alleles within a population

gene therapy when humans alter sequences of DNA via technological means in order to repair or alter the function of the given sequence of DNA

genetic drift random changes in allele frequencies across generations

genetics study of the basic structure and processes of DNA

genomics study of DNA including all associated molecules, chemicals, and evolutionary patterns

genotype the genetic representation; the alleles in an organism's DNA

haploid having 23 single chromosomes, half the genetic complement; found in gametes

Haplorrhini primate suborder that includes the tarsiers, monkeys, apes, and humans

HDI human development index, created by the United Nations, combining economic, life expectancy, education, and standard of living variables

heredity the passing of biological information from generation to generation

heritable capable of being passed to offspring biologically (through reproduction)

heterodontism having different types of teeth

heterozygous the state of having different alleles at both loci for the same gene

holistic approach the practice of drawing on all subdisciplines of anthropology, as well as other disciplines, to attempt to answer questions about humans

home range area used by a primate group or community

hominid member of the family Hominidae

hominin the division (called a tribe) in the superfamily Hominoidea that includes humans and our recent ancestors

hominine member of the subfamily Homininae, which includes the African apes and humans

hominoid member of the superfamily Hominoidea

homiothermy ability to generate and regulate internal body temperature

Homo the hominin genus to which humans belong; characterized by bipedal locomotion, large brains, and biocultural evolution

Homo sapiens the genus and species names for modern humans

homozygous the state of having the same allele at both loci for the same gene

hormones chemical agents produced in the endocrine glands that cause specific effects on target cells

human genome all the DNA in the human species

Human Leukocyte Antigen (HLA) System part of the human immune system that helps signal the presence of foreign substances in the body

hypothesis a testable explanation for the observed facts

inbreeding mating among close genetic relatives

independent assortment the observation that each locus sorts independently (in general)

infant dependency period period during which the infant is wholly reliant on others for nutrition, movement, thermoregulation, and protection

intermembral index ratio of arm length to leg length

internal gestation retention of the fetus inside the body of the female through the course of its prenatal development

kin selection behavioral favoring of one's close genetic relatives

lactation internal production of a nutrient-rich milk by the female to feed young offspring

Levallois technique type of stone tool production that supplanted the Acheulean tool kit and provided a higher quality tool that could be refined for a wide variety of uses

linguistic anthropology the study of language, its structure, function, and evolution

locus the place on a chromosome where a specific gene occurs

Mammalia an order of animals characterized by traits that include, among others, effective internal temperature generation and regulation (including the presence of hair for warmth) and mammary glands (which provide milk to suckle young)

mammary glands glands in female mammals that produce a high-fat nutrient, milk, for the offspring

mandibular symphysis the point where the two halves of the mandible contact one another

megadontia the characteristic of having larger postcanine teeth than would be expected for body size, measured as megadontia quotient (MQ)

megadontia quotient (MQ) measure of premolar/molar tooth area relative to body size

meiosis the production of gametes (haploid cells)

melanin the main pigment in human skin, occurring in two forms: black and brown

melanocytes cells that produce melanin

messenger RNA (mRNA) the form of RNA that takes the transcribed DNA message to the ribosome

migration movement of alleles in and out of populations

mitosis the process of cell division and replication

morphology the internal and external form and structure of an organism

mosaic habitat area that consists of two or more habitat types

Mousterian industry stone tool technology centered on a disk-core technique that represented a refinement of the Levallois technique; it allowed tool makers to produce many good flakes and turn them into a wide variety of tools

mutation changes to the nucleotide sequence in the DNA

natural selection process by which the better fit variants in a population become overrepresented over time

neurons nerve cells

niche habitat or ecological role filled by an organism; the way in which an organism "makes a living"

Niche Construction Theory the modification of niches by organisms and the mutual interactions between organisms and environments

nonrandom mating pattern of mating in which individuals mate preferentially with certain others

nucleotide bases the four chemical bases that make up the core portion of DNA (adenine, cytosine, guanine, and thymine)

occipital (or nuchal) torus pronounced ridge at the rearmost point on the occipital bone

Olduwan relating to the first stone tools in the archaeological record, dating to about 2.5 million years ago and consisting of relatively simple flakes and choppers

Omomyoids fossil primates; members of the infraorder Omomyiformes, suborder Haplorrhini

os coxae two sets of three bones each that are fused to the sacrum and make up the pelvic girdle

paleoanthropology the study of fossil humans and human relatives

paleospecies species defined on the basis of fossil evidence

paradigm predominant ways of thinking about ideas

parallel evolution type of evolutionary process whereby species come to share phenotypic characteristics due to recent common ancestry

parsimony economy in explanation; the least complex path

pathogen a disease-producing agent

performance the actual expression of a trait or behavior

phenotype an organism's observable, measurable traits

philopatric staying in one's natal group

phyletic gradualism slow accumulation of small changes in populations such that over time enough change has occurred to result in a speciation event

phylogenetic constraints limits on current behavior or traits due to patterns and trends in an organism's evolutionary past

phylogeny the evolutionary history of a group of organisms

Piltdown Man fossil find considered an important link in human evolution until it was shown to be a fake in 1953

placentals mammals that have a placenta (the organ that links the circulatory systems of the fetus and mother in the uterus during gestation)

plate tectonics process by which the earth's crustal plates move independently of one another, resulting in continental drift

pleiotropic the situation wherein one gene has many effects

Pleistocene epoch dating from 1.8 million to 10,000 years ago

Pleseadapiformes a group of early mammals thought to be peripherally related to primates

Pliocene epoch that occurred between 5.0 and 1.8 mya

Plio-Pleistocene boundary between the Pliocene and Pleistocene epochs, about 1.8 mya

polygenic the situation wherein many genes combine to have one effect

polypeptide a string of amino acids that folds in on itself and becomes a protein

pongid member of the family Pongidae (not used by the author of this book)

population cluster of individuals of the same species who share a common geographical area and find their mates more often in their own cluster than in others

population genetics the study of the distribution of the genetic variation within and between populations

postorbital constriction condition in which the width across the orbits is greater than the width of the area behind them (where the frontal, temporal, and parietal bones intersect)

potential the spectrum of possible expression created by morphology, evolutionary history, and other aspects of a genotype

precision grip ability to grip objects forcefully with the phalanges of the hand and yet exert fine-tuned control of the movement of the objects; includes the ability to grip items between the thumb and any of the fingers

Primates mammalian order to which humans belong

primatologist researcher who studies primates

Proconsulidae the earliest family of hominoids (apes), dating to the Miocene

prognathism condition in which the jaw projects beyond the upper parts of the face

proteins building blocks of organic life

protein synthesis the process by which the nucleotide "message" is taken from a gene, transcribed, and translated into a protein

punctuated equilibrium rapid biological changes in organisms followed by long, relatively static periods during which little biological change occurs

recombination shuffling of maternal and paternal chromosomes during meiosis

red blood cells (erythrocytes) a major component of blood, functioning primarily to transport oxygen

relative dating techniques methods of dating that provide us with assessments of a fossil's age relative to other fossils

replication the process by which DNA copies itself

reproductive success a measure of the number of surviving offspring an organism has

retromolar gap space behind the last molar tooth and the mandibular ramus

ribonucleic acid (RNA) a molecule similar to DNA that is responsible for taking the message from the DNA in the nucleus of a cell to the ribosome in the cytoplasm and facilitating translation into a protein

ribosome site of protein synthesis

sagittal crest a ridge running between the parietal bones along the top of the cranium, usually representing increased bone area for the attachment of chewing muscles

sagittal keel (ridge) raised area, much less pronounced than a sagittal crest, where the parietals meet on top of the cranium

scientific concept of race a population or group of populations within a species that has measurable, defining biological characteristics and an Fst of at least 0.25 relative to other populations in the species

sectorial premolar lower premolar that exhibits lateral (side-to-side) compression due to its role as a shearing surface for the upper canine tooth; related to the shearing complex

sexual dimorphism difference between the sexes of a species in body size or shape

shared derived trait characteristic found in more than one, but not all, descendant forms and not in the common ancestor

shearing complex condition in which the lower first premolar is somewhat sharpened or flattened from rubbing against the upper canine as the mouth closes

shovel-shaped incisors incisor teeth with a shovel-like grooved inner surface

Similiformes the infraorder of primates to which humans belong (also called anthropoid primates)

socially constructed concept of race set of cultural or ethnic factors combined with easily perceived morphological traits (such as skin reflectance, body shape, cranial structure) in an artificial "biologized" category

sociosexual behavior nonreproductive sexual behavior that serves to resolve conflicts and/or reinforce alliances and coalitions

spandrels by-products of structural change

speciation the process by which new species arise

strata layers of the earth

strategy set of behavior patterns that has become prominent in a population as a result of natural selection

stratigraphy the study of the layering of the earth's sediments

Strepsirrhini primate suborder that includes the Lemurs, Lorises, and Galagos (the prosimians)

subspecies a population that meets the criteria defined within the scientific concept of race

supraorbital torus a robust projection at the front of the frontal bone on the cranium

symbolic inheritance the passing down of knowledge via symbols and language

taxonomy naming and classification of organisms based on morphological similarities and differences

theory a set of supported hypotheses

transcription copying the DNA message to RNA

transfer RNA (tRNA) form of RNA that brings amino acids to the ribosome

translation converting the mRNA message into a protein

tribe taxonomic classification placed below subfamily and above genus

triplet three-nucleotide sequence in which the DNA's code is written

uniformitarianism the doctrine that geological processes operating in the present have also operated in the same way in the past and will do so in the future

vertebral column bony protection for the spinal cord consisting of vertebrae

white blood cells (leukocytes) a major component of blood, functioning primarily as part of the immune system

zygomatic arches cheekbones; arches created by the meeting of extensions of the temporal and zygomatic bones in the cranium

Index